CAPTAIN AMERICA

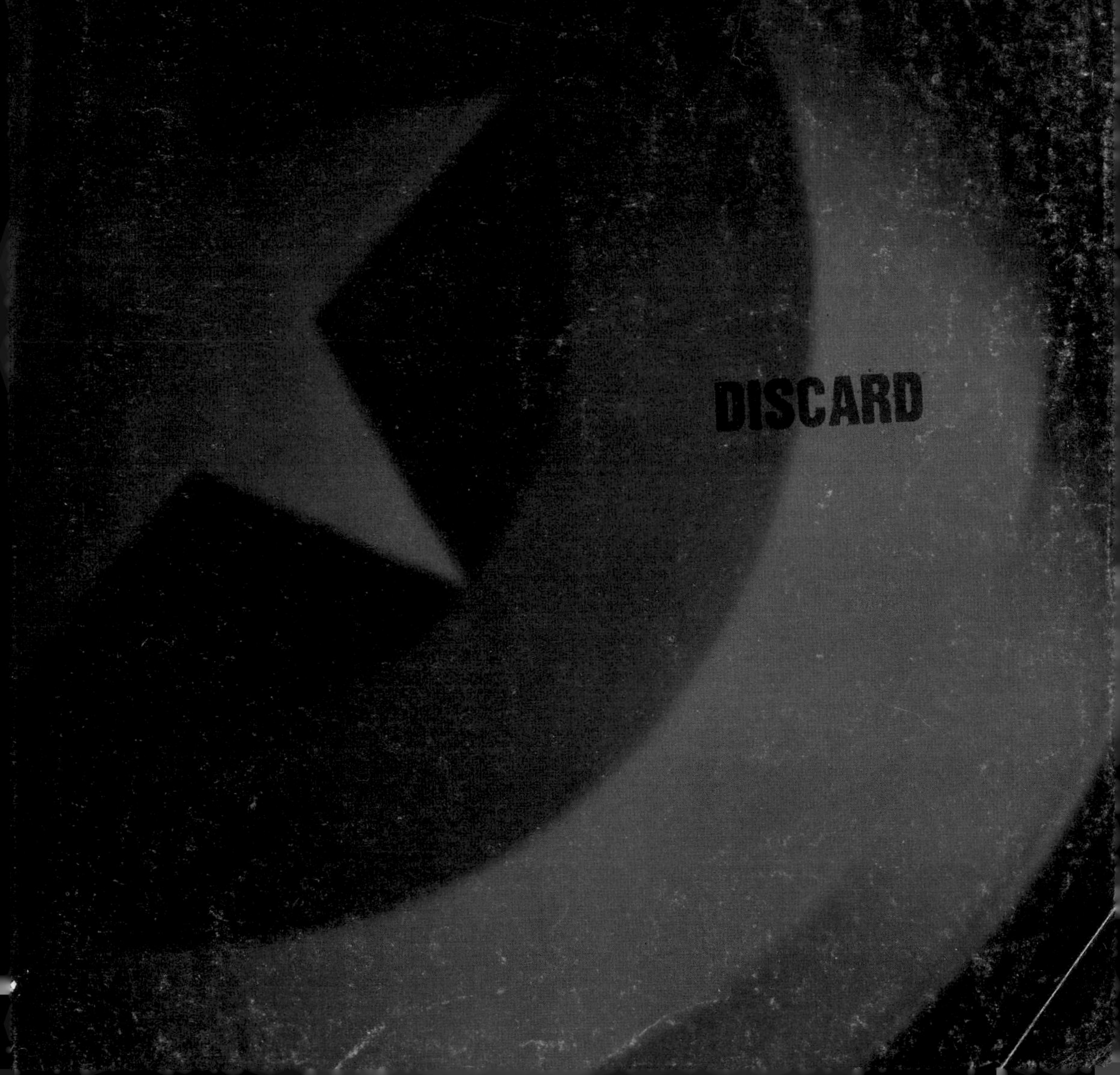

THE DEATH OF CAPTAIN AMERICA
THE BURDEN OF DREAMS

WRITER: Ed Brubaker

ART, ISSUE #31:
Steve Epting

ART, ISSUES #32-34:
PENCILER: Steve Epting
INKER: Butch Guice

ART, ISSUE #35:
PENCILER: Butch Guice
INKERS: Butch Guice &
Mike Perkins

ART, ISSUE #36:
ARTIST, P. 1-12: Butch Guice
ARTIST, P. 13-22: Mike Perkins

COLORIST: Frank D'Armata
LETTERER: Virtual Calligraphy's
Joe Caramagna
COVER ART: Steve Epting
VARIANT COVER ART: Alex Ross
ASSOCIATE EDITOR: Molly Lazer
EDITOR: Tom Brevoort

New Captain America costume
design by Alex Ross

Captain America created
by Joe Simon & Jack Kirby

COLLECTION EDITOR: Jennifer Grünwald
EDITORIAL ASSISTANT: Alex Starbuck
ASSISTANT EDITORS: Cory Levine & John Denning
EDITOR, SPECIAL PROJECTS: Mark D. Beazley
SENIOR EDITOR, SPECIAL PROJECTS: Jeff Youngquist
SENIOR VICE PRESIDENT OF SALES: David Gabriel
PRODUCTION: Jerron Quality Color & Jerry Kalinowski
VICE PRESIDENT OF CREATIVE: Tom Marvelli

EDITOR IN CHIEF: Joe Quesada
PUBLISHER: Dan Buckley

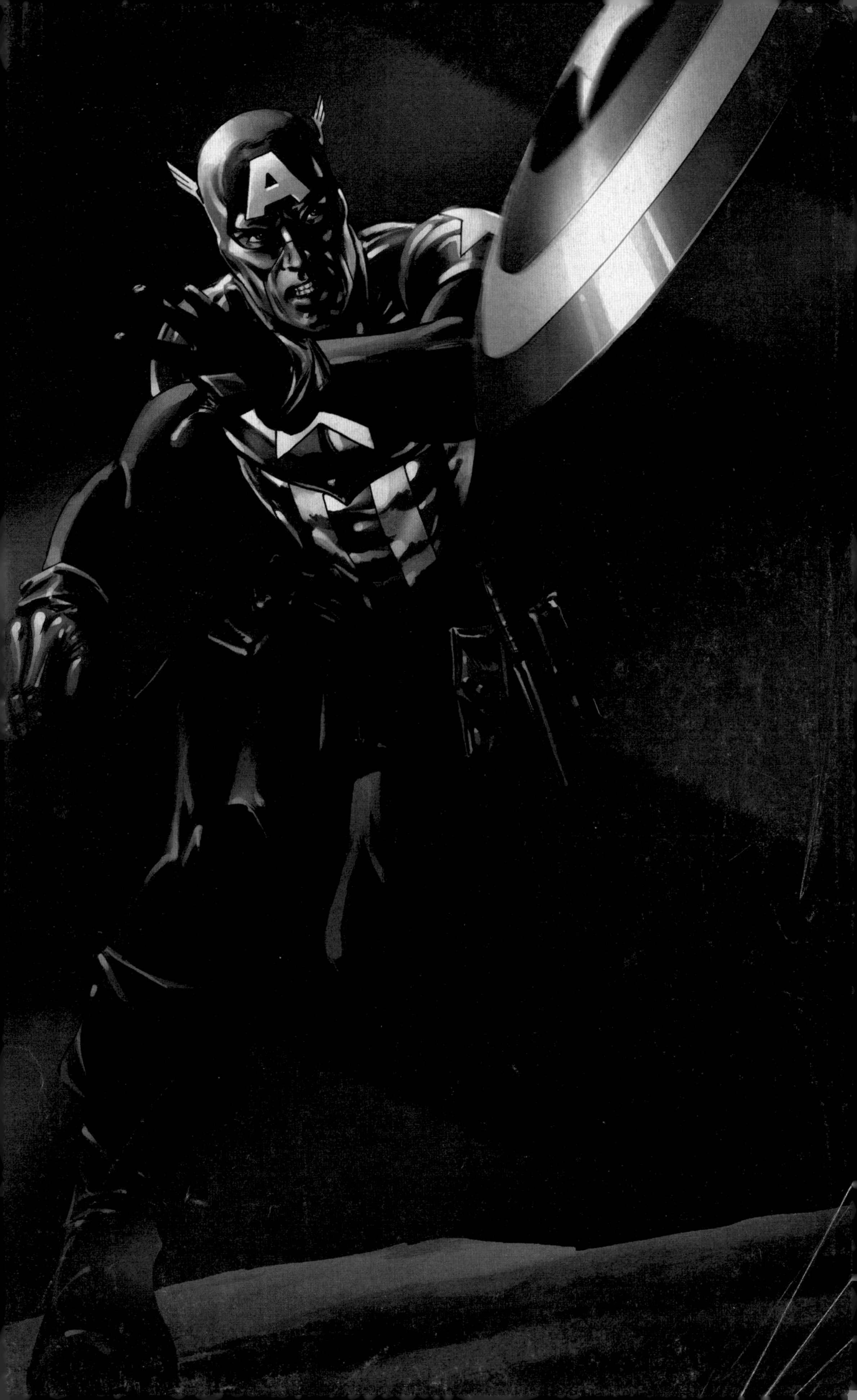

PREVIOUSLY:

Captain America is dead. The Red Skull, with the help of megalomaniacal psychiatrist Dr. Faustus, manipulated Sharon Carter, former Agent 13 of S.H.I.E.L.D., into taking the life of the man she loved. Mentally blocked from telling anyone what she's done, Sharon is spiraling downward, fighting to hold onto her sanity. But when she finds out she's pregnant, she loses control of her mind again, shoots her allies, the Falcon and Black Widow...and flees.

Meanwhile, Bucky has been seeking vengeance on the men he feels are responsible for the death of Steve Rogers. But on his hunt, he's fallen into the hands of the Red Skull, who has secretly been sharing the mind of Bucky's former master from his Winter Soldier days, ex-Soviet General Aleksander Lukin. And now Bucky must face Dr. Faustus's mind-manipulation...

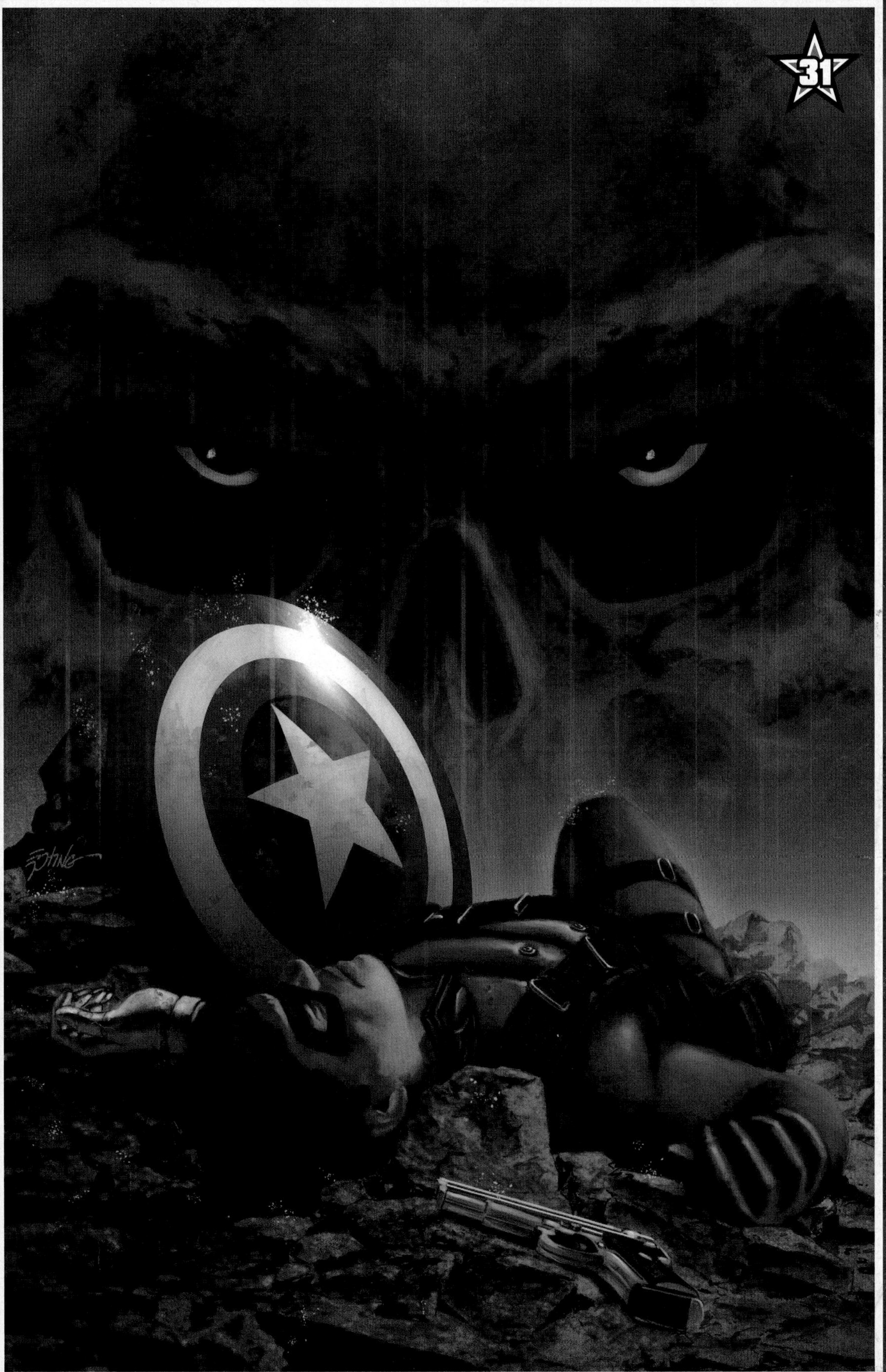
31

PART ONE

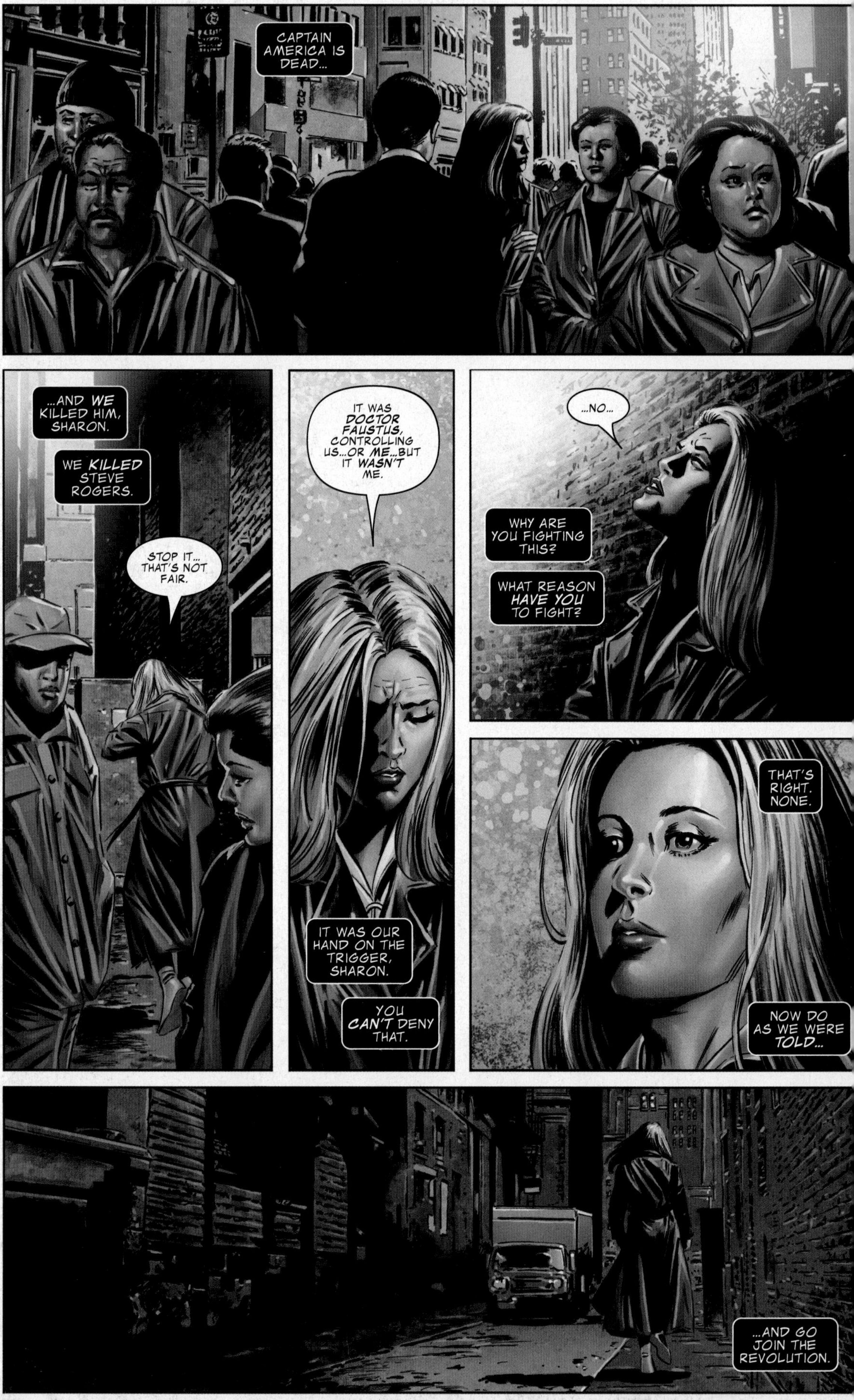
CAPTAIN AMERICA IS DEAD...
...AND WE KILLED HIM, SHARON.
WE KILLED STEVE ROGERS.
STOP IT... THAT'S NOT FAIR.
IT WAS DOCTOR FAUSTUS, CONTROLLING US...OR ME...BUT IT WASN'T ME.
IT WAS OUR HAND ON THE TRIGGER, SHARON.
YOU CAN'T DENY THAT.
...NO...
WHY ARE YOU FIGHTING THIS?
WHAT REASON HAVE YOU TO FIGHT?
THAT'S RIGHT. NONE.
NOW DO AS WE WERE TOLD...
...AND GO JOIN THE REVOLUTION.

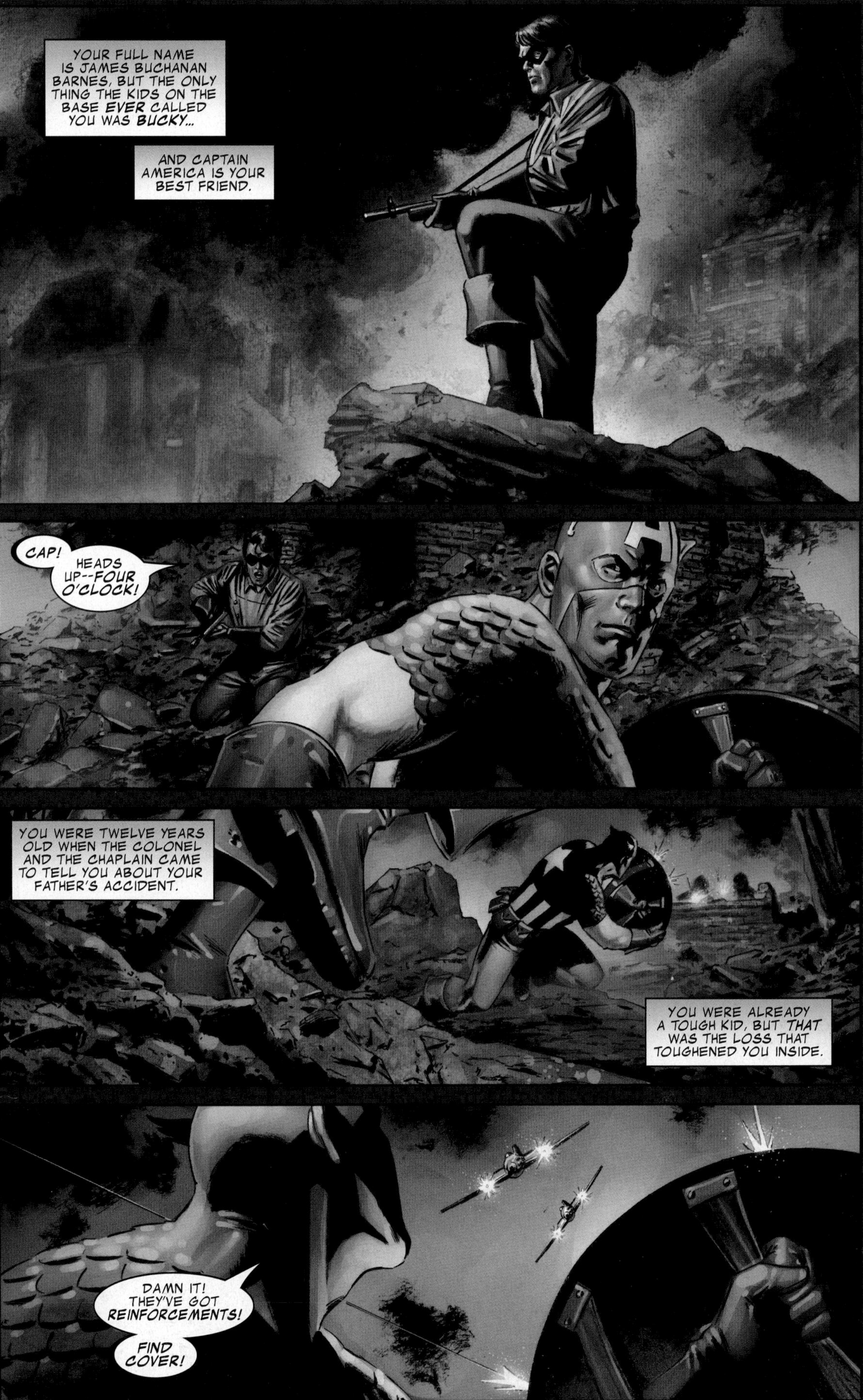
YOUR FULL NAME IS JAMES BUCHANAN BARNES, BUT THE ONLY THING THE KIDS ON THE BASE EVER CALLED YOU WAS BUCKY...
AND CAPTAIN AMERICA IS YOUR BEST FRIEND.
CAP!
HEADS UP--FOUR O'CLOCK!
YOU WERE TWELVE YEARS OLD WHEN THE COLONEL AND THE CHAPLAIN CAME TO TELL YOU ABOUT YOUR FATHER'S ACCIDENT.
YOU WERE ALREADY A TOUGH KID, BUT THAT WAS THE LOSS THAT TOUGHENED YOU INSIDE.
DAMN IT! THEY'VE GOT REINFORCEMENTS!
FIND COVER!

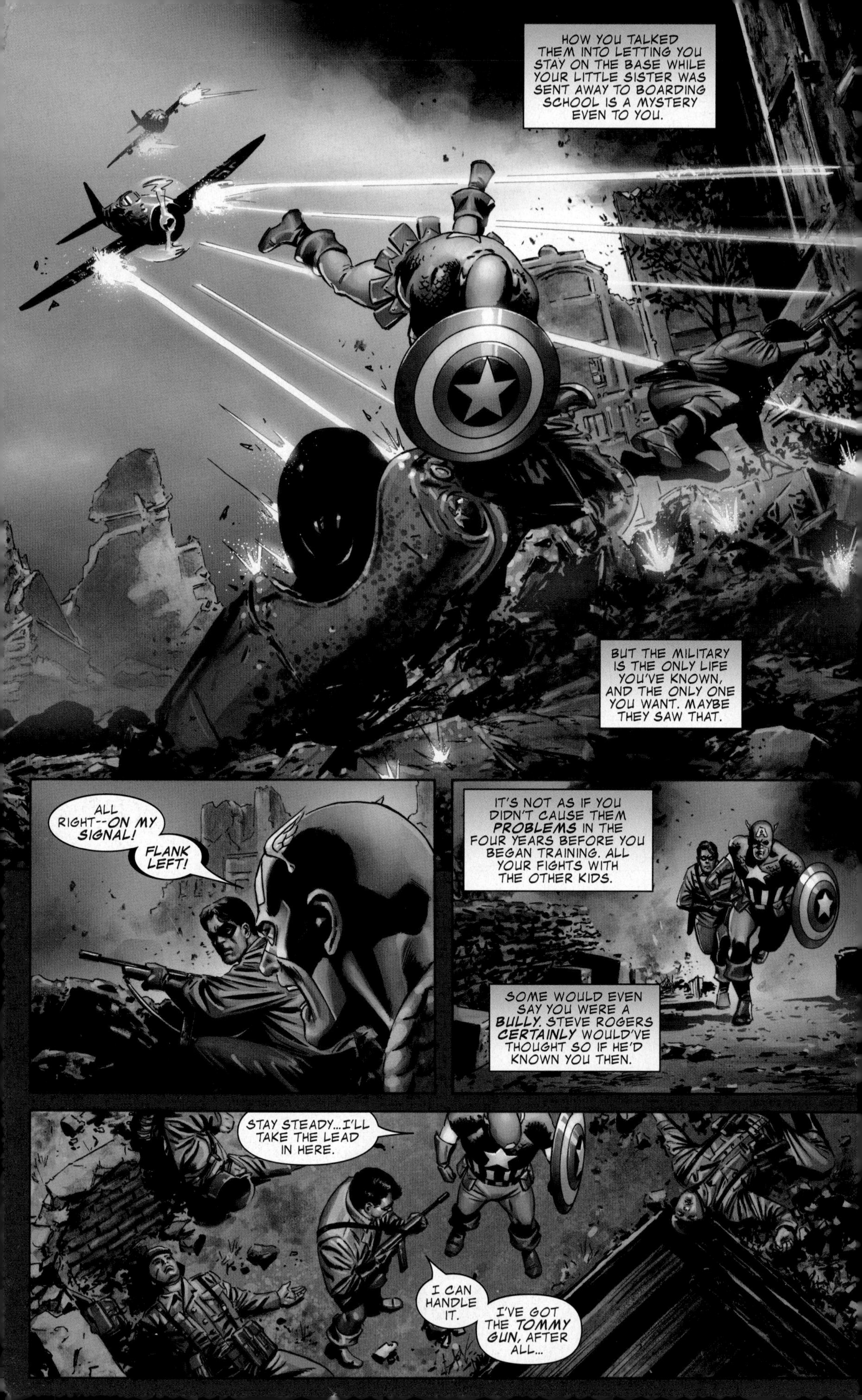
HOW YOU TALKED THEM INTO LETTING YOU STAY ON THE BASE WHILE YOUR LITTLE SISTER WAS SENT AWAY TO BOARDING SCHOOL IS A MYSTERY EVEN TO YOU.
BUT THE MILITARY IS THE ONLY LIFE YOU'VE KNOWN, AND THE ONLY ONE YOU WANT. MAYBE THEY SAW THAT.
ALL RIGHT--ON MY SIGNAL!
FLANK LEFT!
IT'S NOT AS IF YOU DIDN'T CAUSE THEM PROBLEMS IN THE FOUR YEARS BEFORE YOU BEGAN TRAINING. ALL YOUR FIGHTS WITH THE OTHER KIDS.
SOME WOULD EVEN SAY YOU WERE A BULLY. STEVE ROGERS CERTAINLY WOULD'VE THOUGHT SO IF HE'D KNOWN YOU THEN.
STAY STEADY...I'LL TAKE THE LEAD IN HERE.
I CAN HANDLE IT.
I'VE GOT THE TOMMY GUN, AFTER ALL...

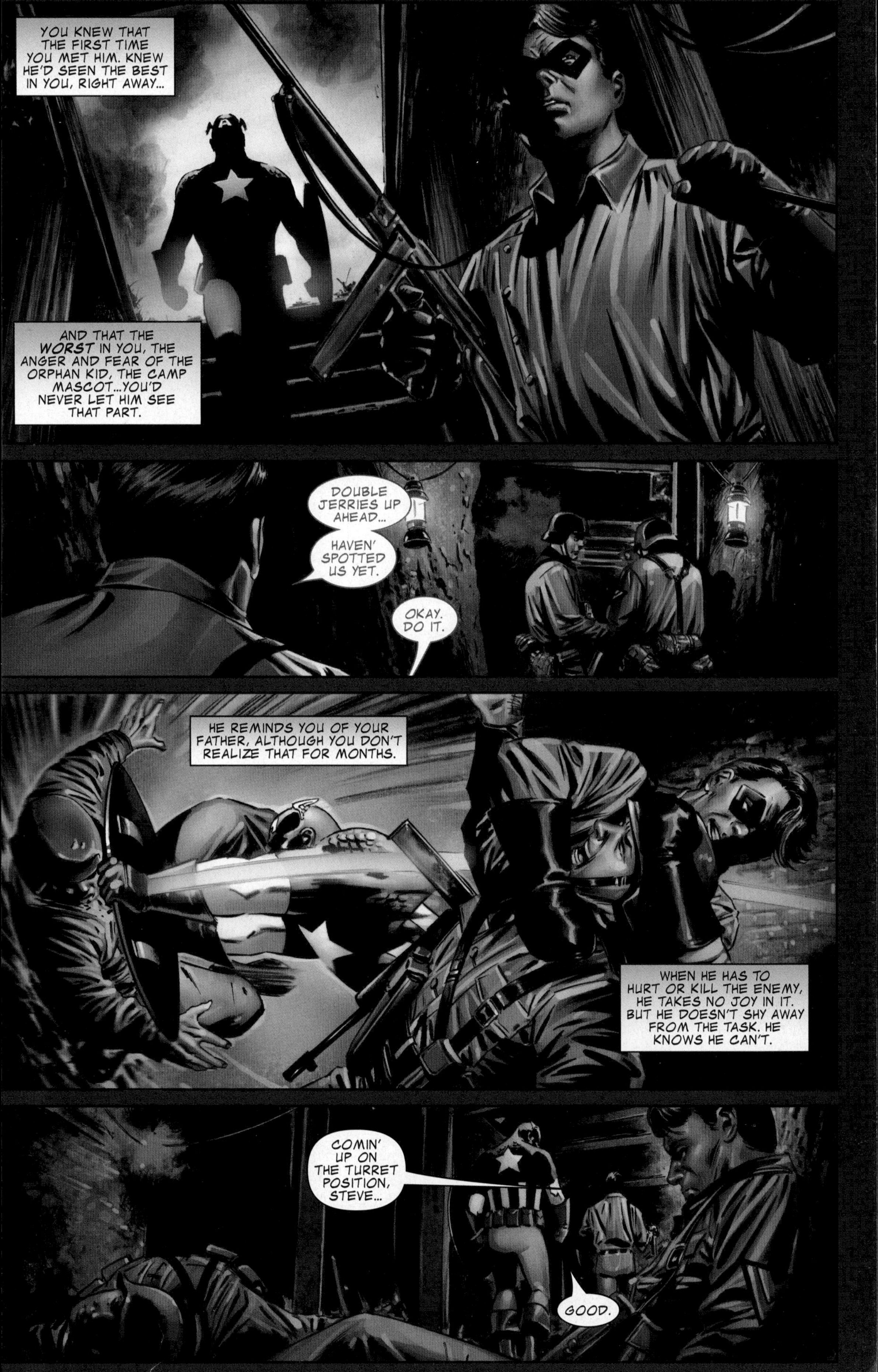
YOU KNEW THAT THE FIRST TIME YOU MET HIM. KNEW HE'D SEEN THE BEST IN YOU, RIGHT AWAY...
AND THAT THE WORST IN YOU, THE ANGER AND FEAR OF THE ORPHAN KID, THE CAMP MASCOT...YOU'D NEVER LET HIM SEE THAT PART.
DOUBLE JERRIES UP AHEAD...
HAVEN' SPOTTED US YET.
OKAY. DO IT.
HE REMINDS YOU OF YOUR FATHER, ALTHOUGH YOU DON'T REALIZE THAT FOR MONTHS.
WHEN HE HAS TO HURT OR KILL THE ENEMY, HE TAKES NO JOY IN IT. BUT HE DOESN'T SHY AWAY FROM THE TASK. HE KNOWS HE CAN'T.
COMIN' UP ON THE TURRET POSITION, STEVE...
GOOD.

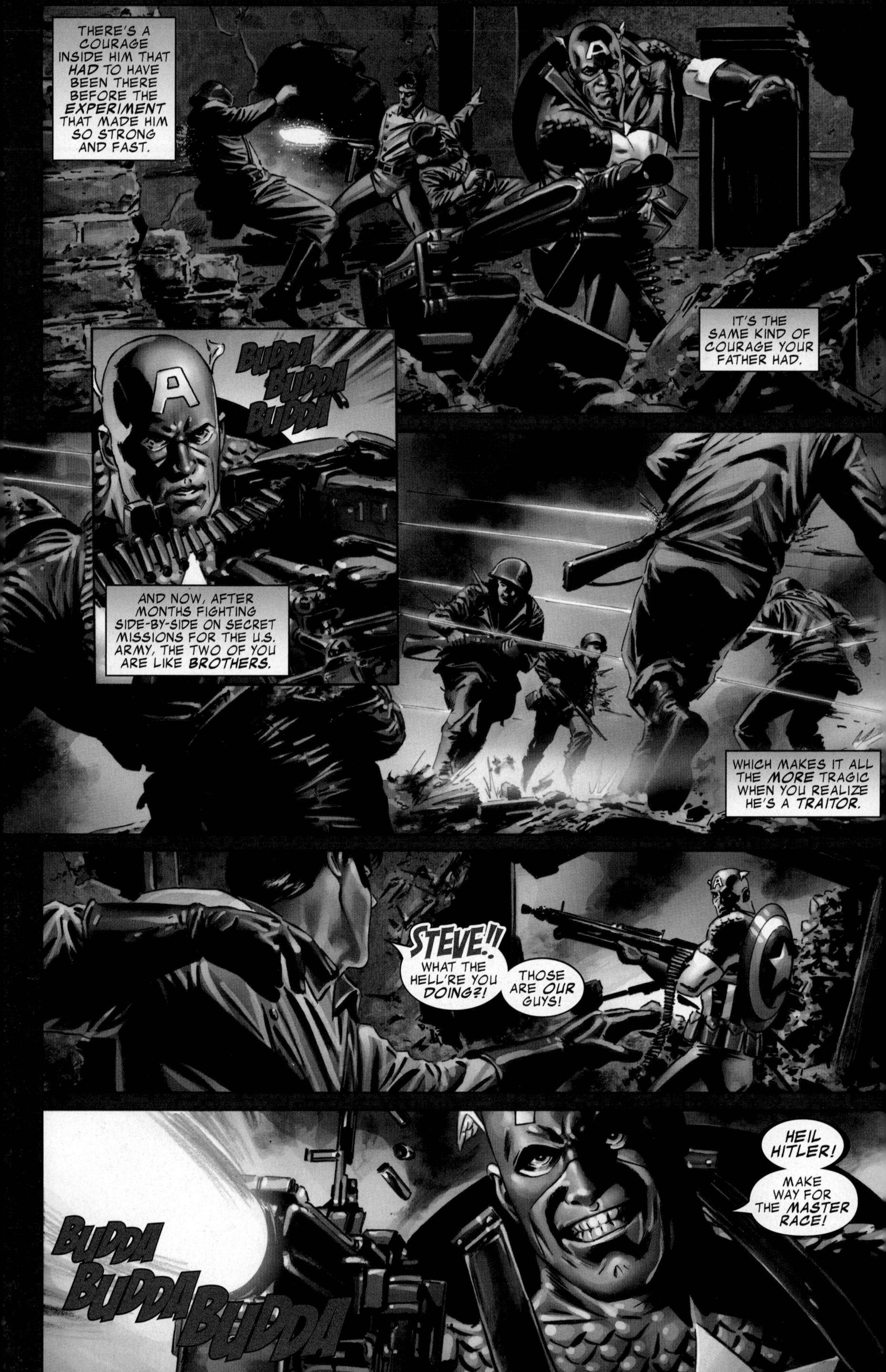
THERE'S A COURAGE INSIDE HIM THAT HAD TO HAVE BEEN THERE BEFORE THE EXPERIMENT THAT MADE HIM SO STRONG AND FAST.
IT'S THE SAME KIND OF COURAGE YOUR FATHER HAD.
BUDDA BUDDA BUDDA
AND NOW, AFTER MONTHS FIGHTING SIDE-BY-SIDE ON SECRET MISSIONS FOR THE U.S. ARMY, THE TWO OF YOU ARE LIKE BROTHERS.
WHICH MAKES IT ALL THE MORE TRAGIC WHEN YOU REALIZE HE'S A TRAITOR.
STEVE!! WHAT THE HELL'RE YOU DOING?!
THOSE ARE OUR GUYS!
HEIL HITLER!
MAKE WAY FOR THE MASTER RACE!
BUDDA BUDDA BUDDA

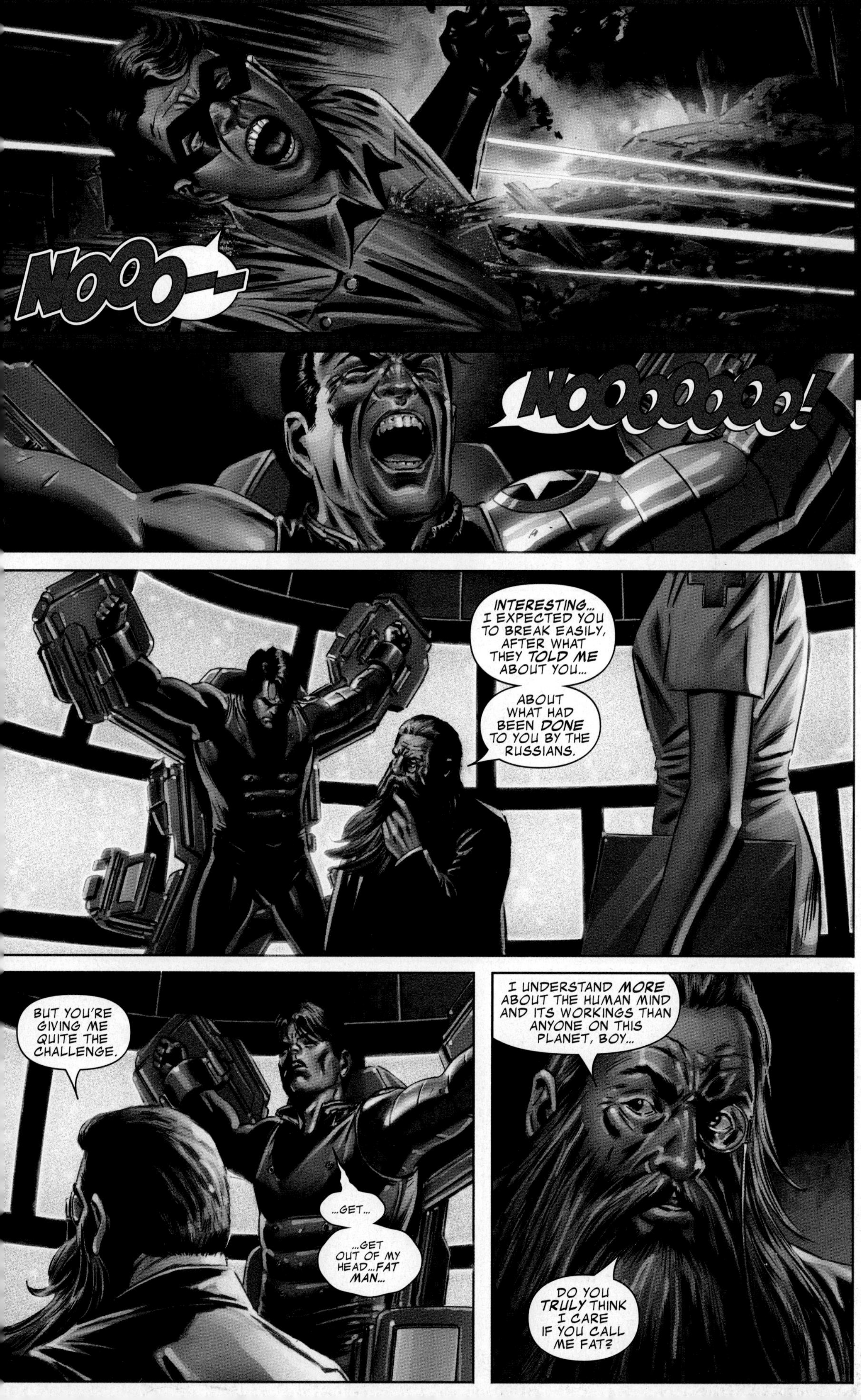

NOOO--
NOOOOOOO!
INTERESTING... I EXPECTED YOU TO BREAK EASILY, AFTER WHAT THEY TOLD ME ABOUT YOU...
ABOUT WHAT HAD BEEN DONE TO YOU BY THE RUSSIANS.
BUT YOU'RE GIVING ME QUITE THE CHALLENGE.
...GET...
...GET OUT OF MY HEAD...FAT MAN...
I UNDERSTAND MORE ABOUT THE HUMAN MIND AND ITS WORKINGS THAN ANYONE ON THIS PLANET, BOY...
DO YOU TRULY THINK I CARE IF YOU CALL ME FAT?

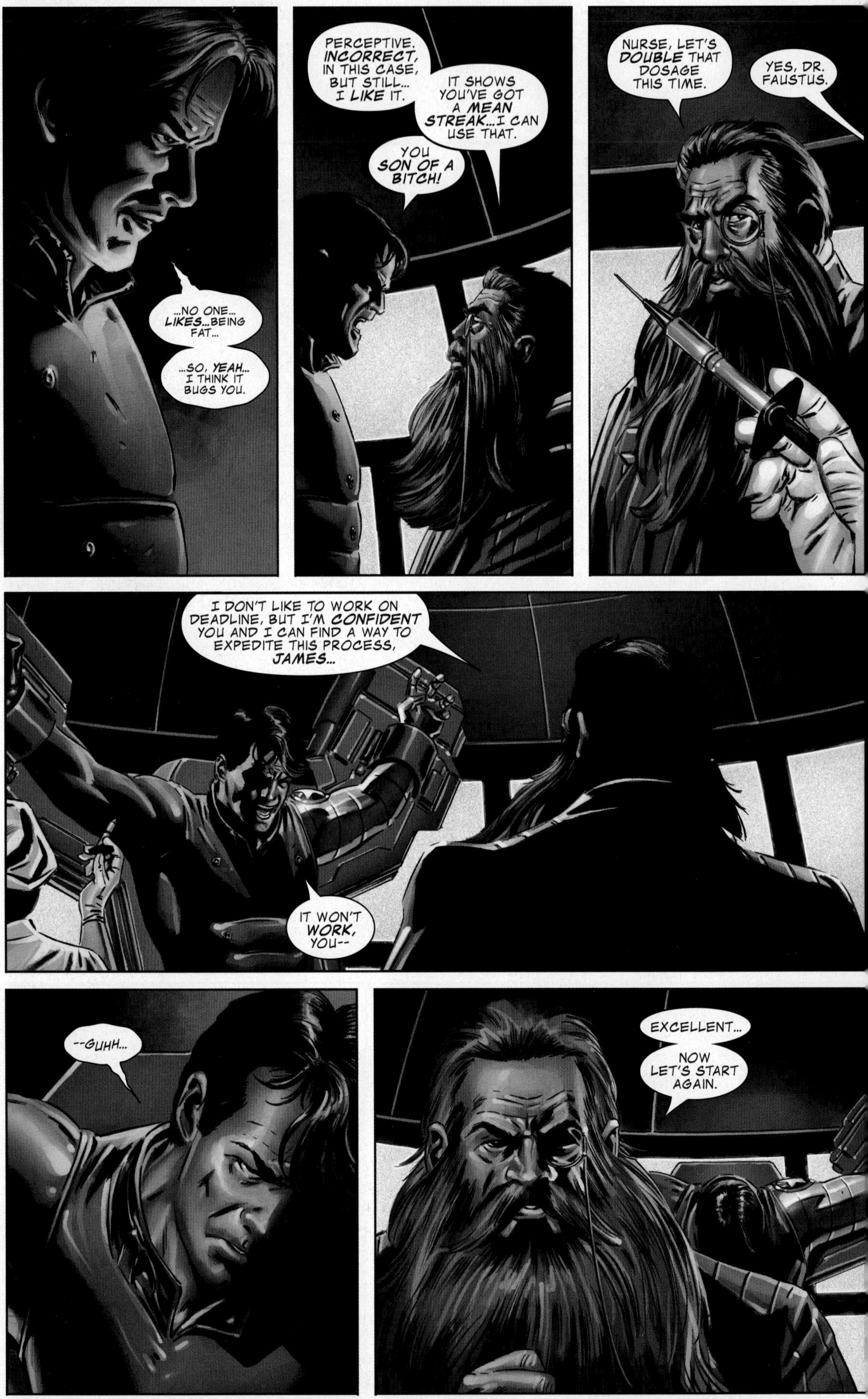
...NO ONE... LIKES...BEING FAT...
...SO, YEAH... I THINK IT BUGS YOU.
PERCEPTIVE. INCORRECT, IN THIS CASE, BUT STILL... I LIKE IT.
IT SHOWS YOU'VE GOT A MEAN STREAK...I CAN USE THAT.
YOU SON OF A BITCH!
NURSE, LET'S DOUBLE THAT DOSAGE THIS TIME.
YES, DR. FAUSTUS.
I DON'T LIKE TO WORK ON DEADLINE, BUT I'M CONFIDENT YOU AND I CAN FIND A WAY TO EXPEDITE THIS PROCESS, JAMES...
IT WON'T WORK, YOU--
--GUHH...
EXCELLENT...
NOW LET'S START AGAIN.

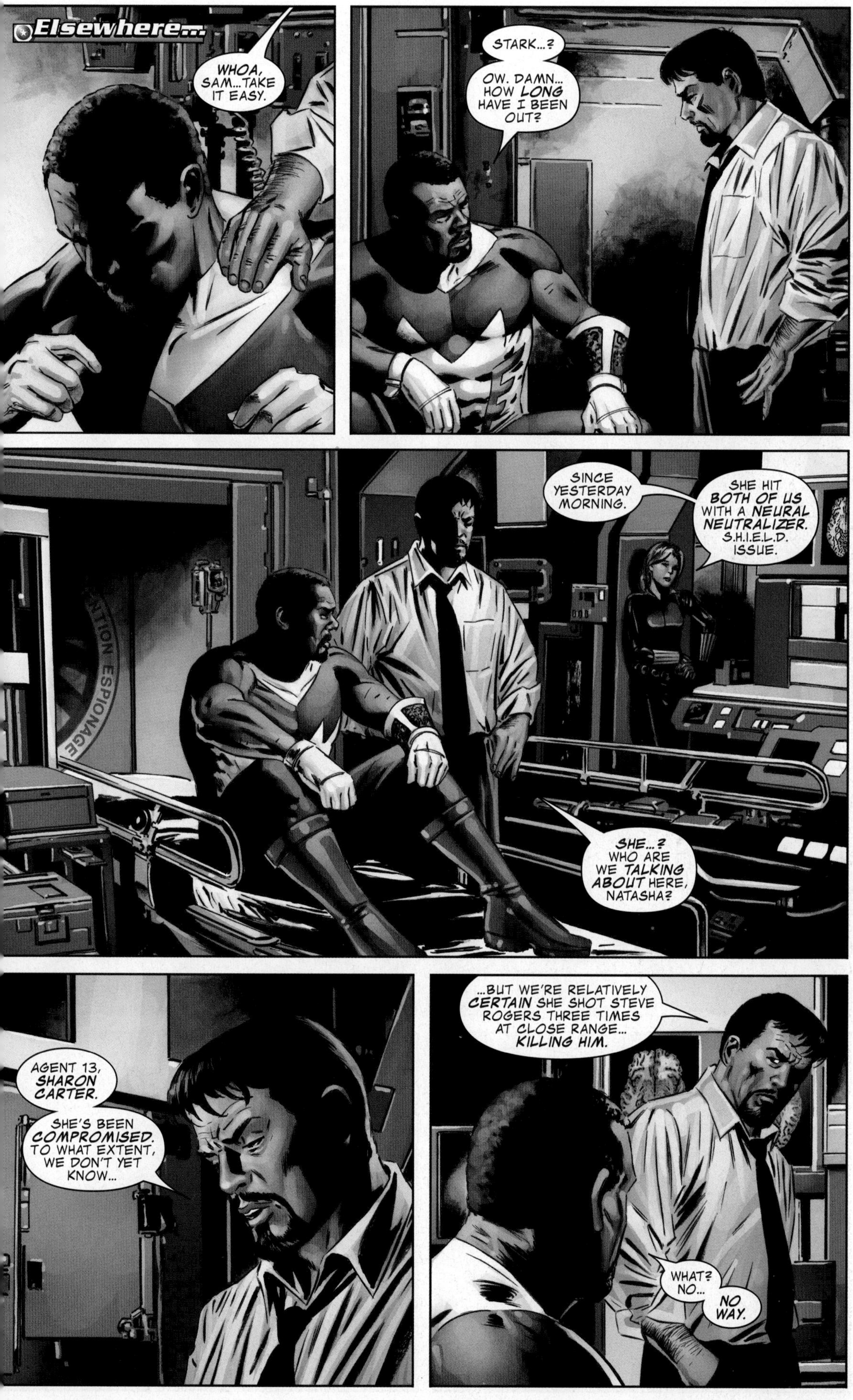
Elsewhere...
WHOA, SAM...TAKE IT EASY.
STARK...?
OW. DAMN... HOW LONG HAVE I BEEN OUT?
SINCE YESTERDAY MORNING.
SHE HIT BOTH OF US WITH A NEURAL NEUTRALIZER. S.H.I.E.L.D. ISSUE.
SHE...? WHO ARE WE TALKING ABOUT HERE, NATASHA?
AGENT 13, SHARON CARTER.
SHE'S BEEN COMPROMISED. TO WHAT EXTENT, WE DON'T YET KNOW...
...BUT WE'RE RELATIVELY CERTAIN SHE SHOT STEVE ROGERS THREE TIMES AT CLOSE RANGE... KILLING HIM.
WHAT? NO... NO WAY.

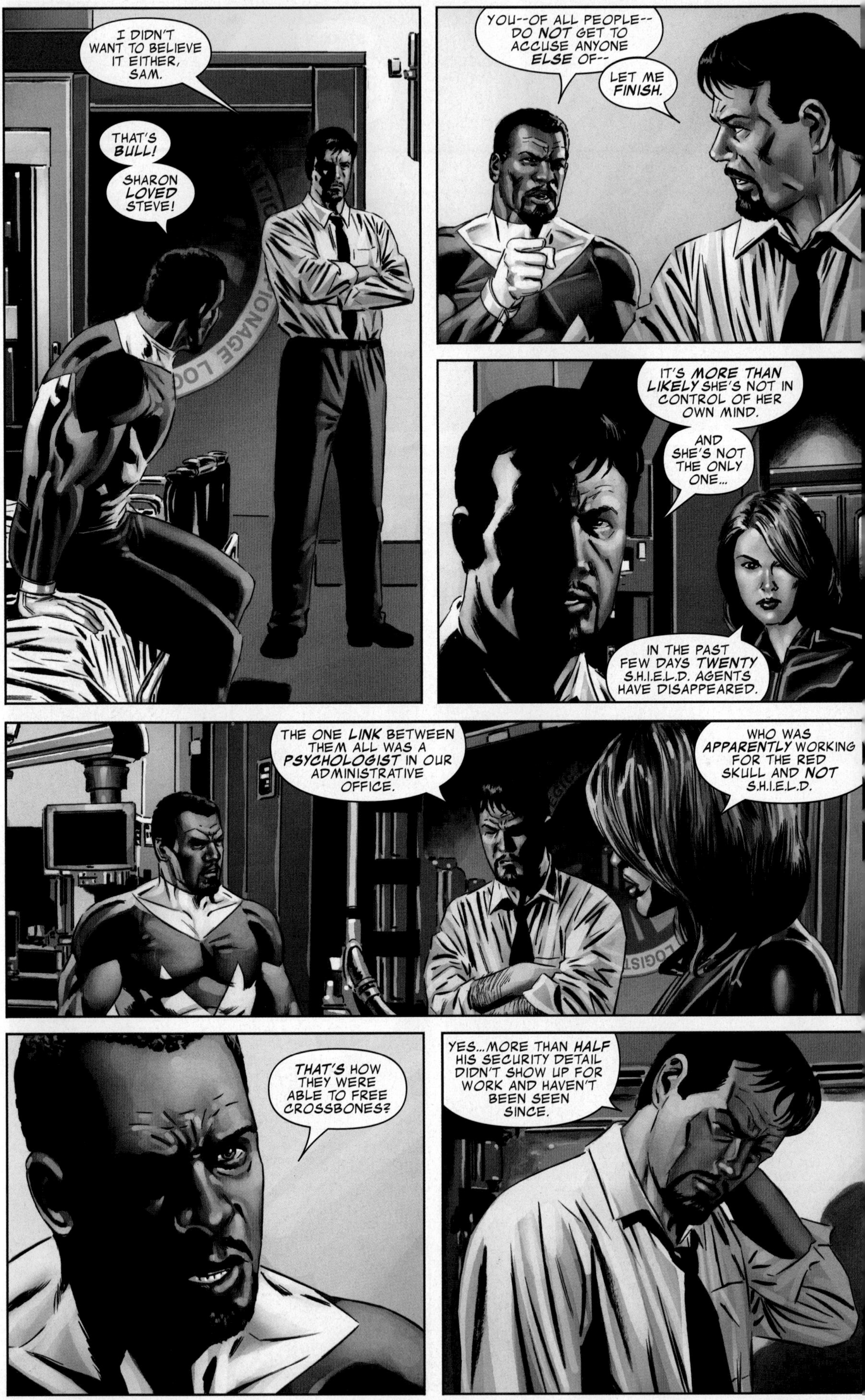
I DIDN'T WANT TO BELIEVE IT EITHER, SAM.
THAT'S BULL!
SHARON LOVED STEVE!
YOU--OF ALL PEOPLE--DO NOT GET TO ACCUSE ANYONE ELSE OF--
LET ME FINISH.
IT'S MORE THAN LIKELY SHE'S NOT IN CONTROL OF HER OWN MIND.
AND SHE'S NOT THE ONLY ONE...
IN THE PAST FEW DAYS TWENTY S.H.I.E.L.D. AGENTS HAVE DISAPPEARED.
THE ONE LINK BETWEEN THEM ALL WAS A PSYCHOLOGIST IN OUR ADMINISTRATIVE OFFICE.
WHO WAS APPARENTLY WORKING FOR THE RED SKULL AND NOT S.H.I.E.L.D.
THAT'S HOW THEY WERE ABLE TO FREE CROSSBONES?
YES...MORE THAN HALF HIS SECURITY DETAIL DIDN'T SHOW UP FOR WORK AND HAVEN'T BEEN SEEN SINCE.

SO, YOU'RE SAYING THIS...SHRINK...THAT HE BRAINWASHED SHARON?

AND A LOT OF OTHER AGENTS.

WE'RE STILL ASSESSING THE FULL EXTENT OF THE DAMAGE.

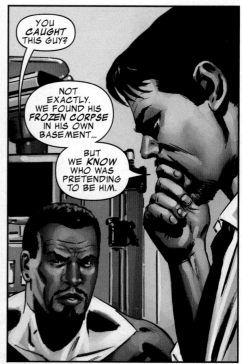

YOU CAUGHT THIS GUY?

NOT EXACTLY. WE FOUND HIS FROZEN CORPSE IN HIS OWN BASEMENT...

BUT WE KNOW WHO WAS PRETENDING TO BE HIM.

DOCTOR FAUSTUS'S GRAVE WAS EXHUMED EARLIER TODAY...

THERE WAS NO BODY IN IT.

FAUSTUS AND THE RED SKULL ARE WORKING TOGETHER... AND SHARON'S UNDER THEIR CONTROL...

THAT IS NOT GOOD NEWS, PEOPLE.

NO, IT'S NOT... BUT I HAVE ANOTHER QUESTION.

SHARON ONLY STUNNED YOU TWO, WHEN SHE COULD HAVE KILLED YOU...WHY?

I DON'T KNOW, TONY... DOES IT MATTER?

IT MIGHT.

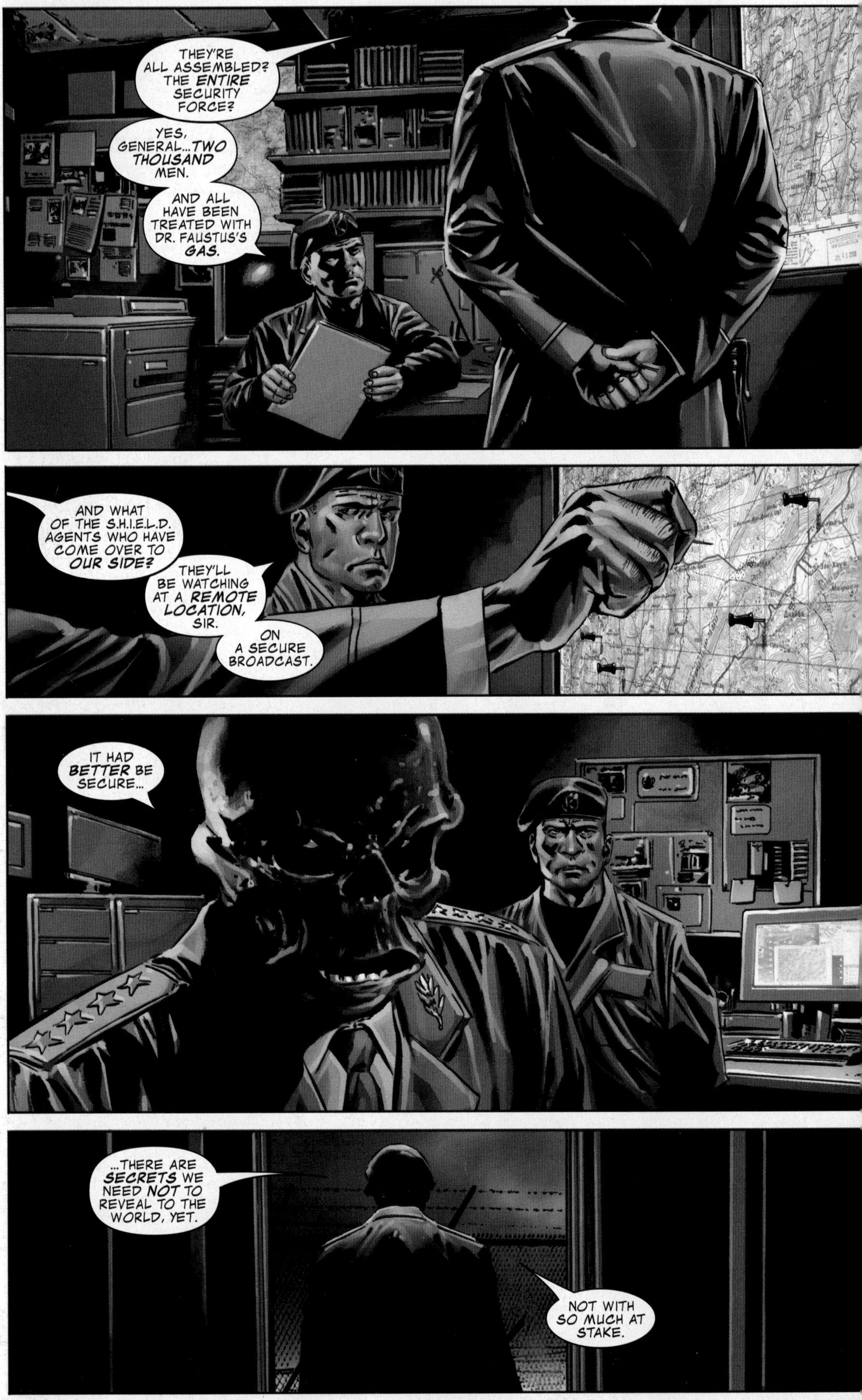
THEY'RE ALL ASSEMBLED? THE ENTIRE SECURITY FORCE?
YES, GENERAL...TWO THOUSAND MEN.
AND ALL HAVE BEEN TREATED WITH DR. FAUSTUS'S GAS.
AND WHAT OF THE S.H.I.E.L.D. AGENTS WHO HAVE COME OVER TO OUR SIDE?
THEY'LL BE WATCHING AT A REMOTE LOCATION, SIR.
ON A SECURE BROADCAST.
IT HAD BETTER BE SECURE...
...THERE ARE SECRETS WE NEED NOT TO REVEAL TO THE WORLD, YET.
NOT WITH SO MUCH AT STAKE.

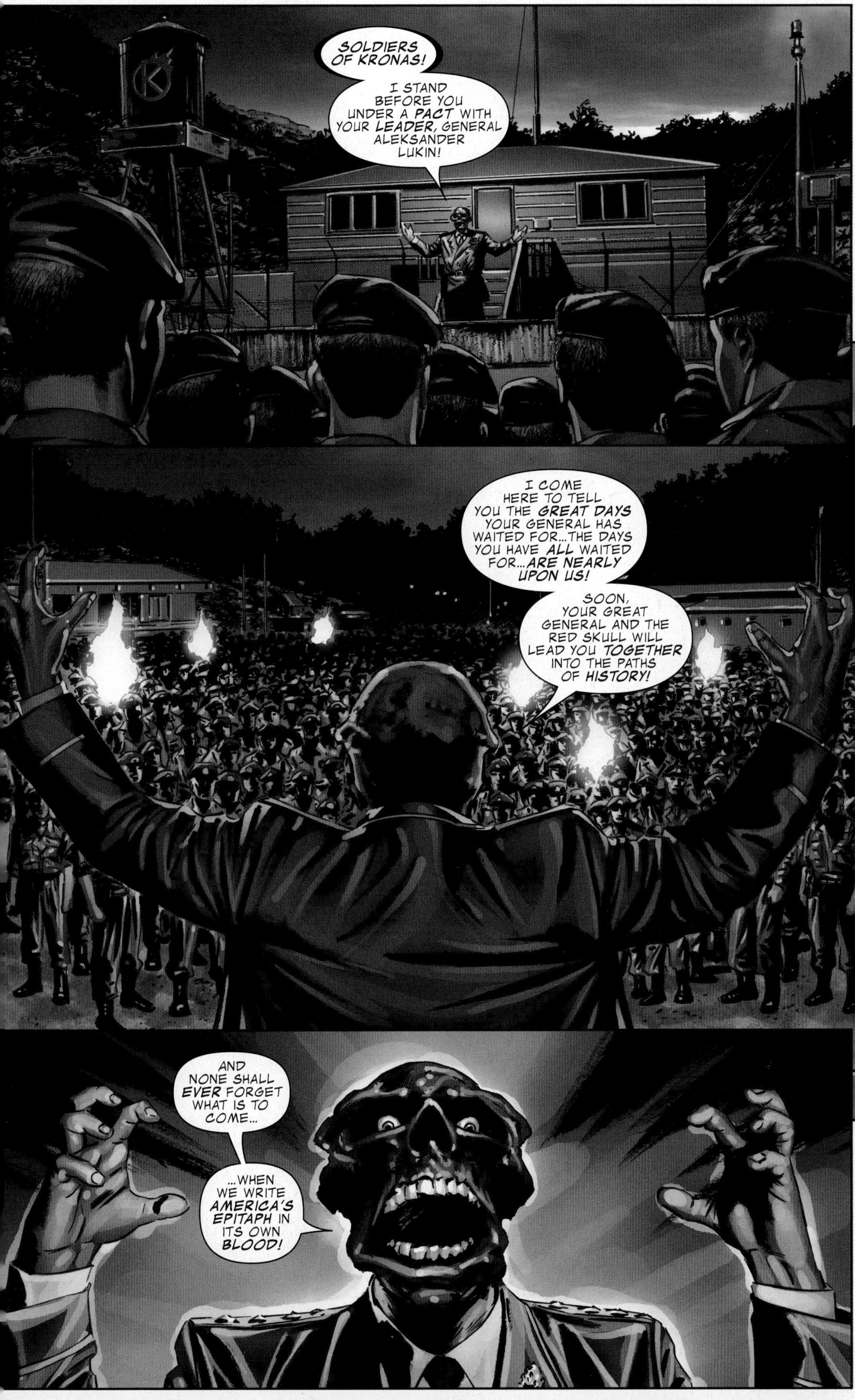
SOLDIERS OF KRONAS!
I STAND BEFORE YOU UNDER A PACT WITH YOUR LEADER, GENERAL ALEKSANDER LUKIN!
I COME HERE TO TELL YOU THE GREAT DAYS YOUR GENERAL HAS WAITED FOR...THE DAYS YOU HAVE ALL WAITED FOR...ARE NEARLY UPON US!
SOON, YOUR GREAT GENERAL AND THE RED SKULL WILL LEAD YOU TOGETHER INTO THE PATHS OF HISTORY!
AND NONE SHALL EVER FORGET WHAT IS TO COME...
...WHEN WE WRITE AMERICA'S EPITAPH IN ITS OWN BLOOD!

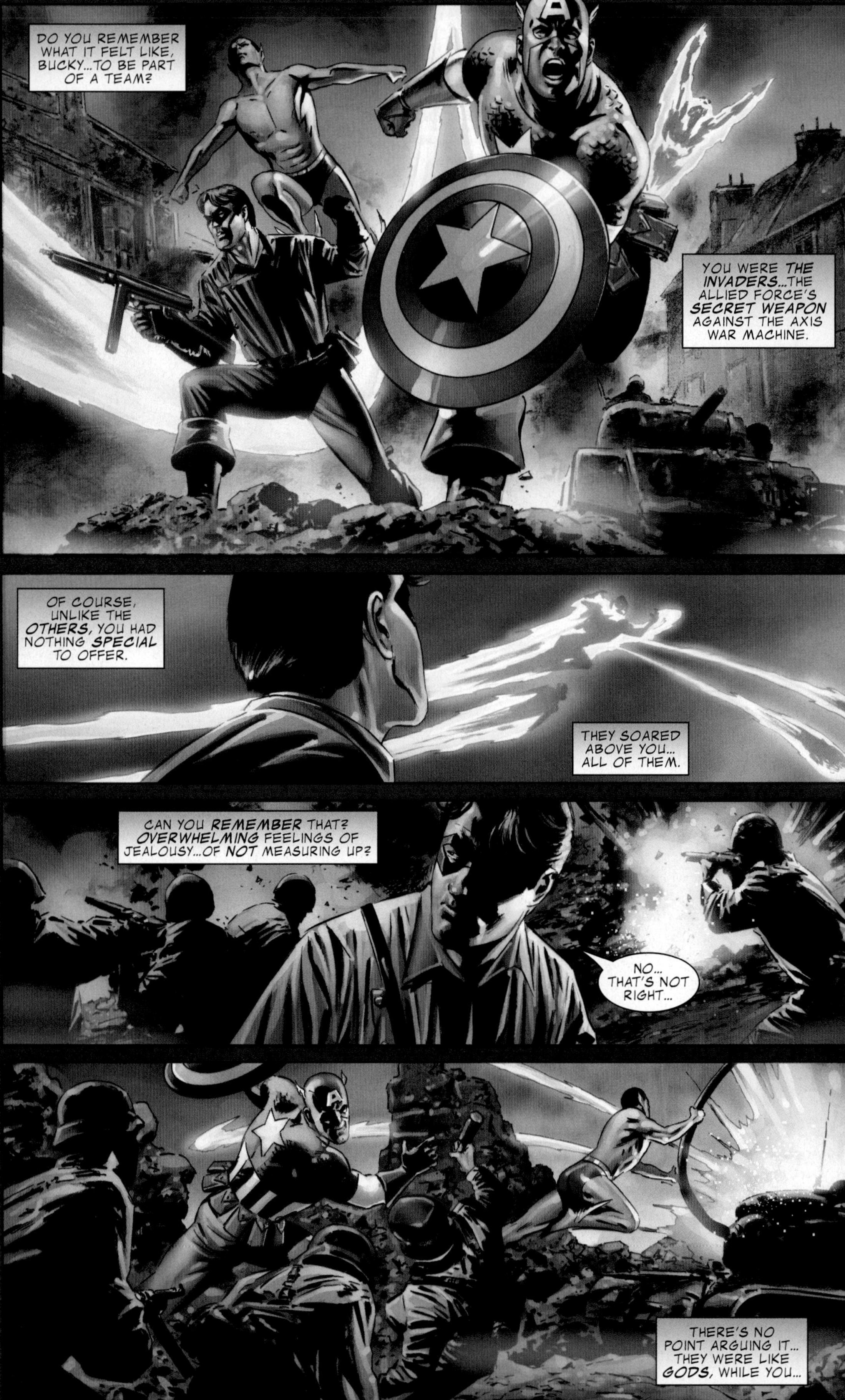
DO YOU REMEMBER WHAT IT FELT LIKE, BUCKY...TO BE PART OF A TEAM?
YOU WERE THE INVADERS...THE ALLIED FORCE'S SECRET WEAPON AGAINST THE AXIS WAR MACHINE.
OF COURSE, UNLIKE THE OTHERS, YOU HAD NOTHING SPECIAL TO OFFER.
THEY SOARED ABOVE YOU... ALL OF THEM.
CAN YOU REMEMBER THAT? OVERWHELMING FEELINGS OF JEALOUSY...OF NOT MEASURING UP?
NO... THAT'S NOT RIGHT...
THERE'S NO POINT ARGUING IT... THEY WERE LIKE GODS, WHILE YOU...

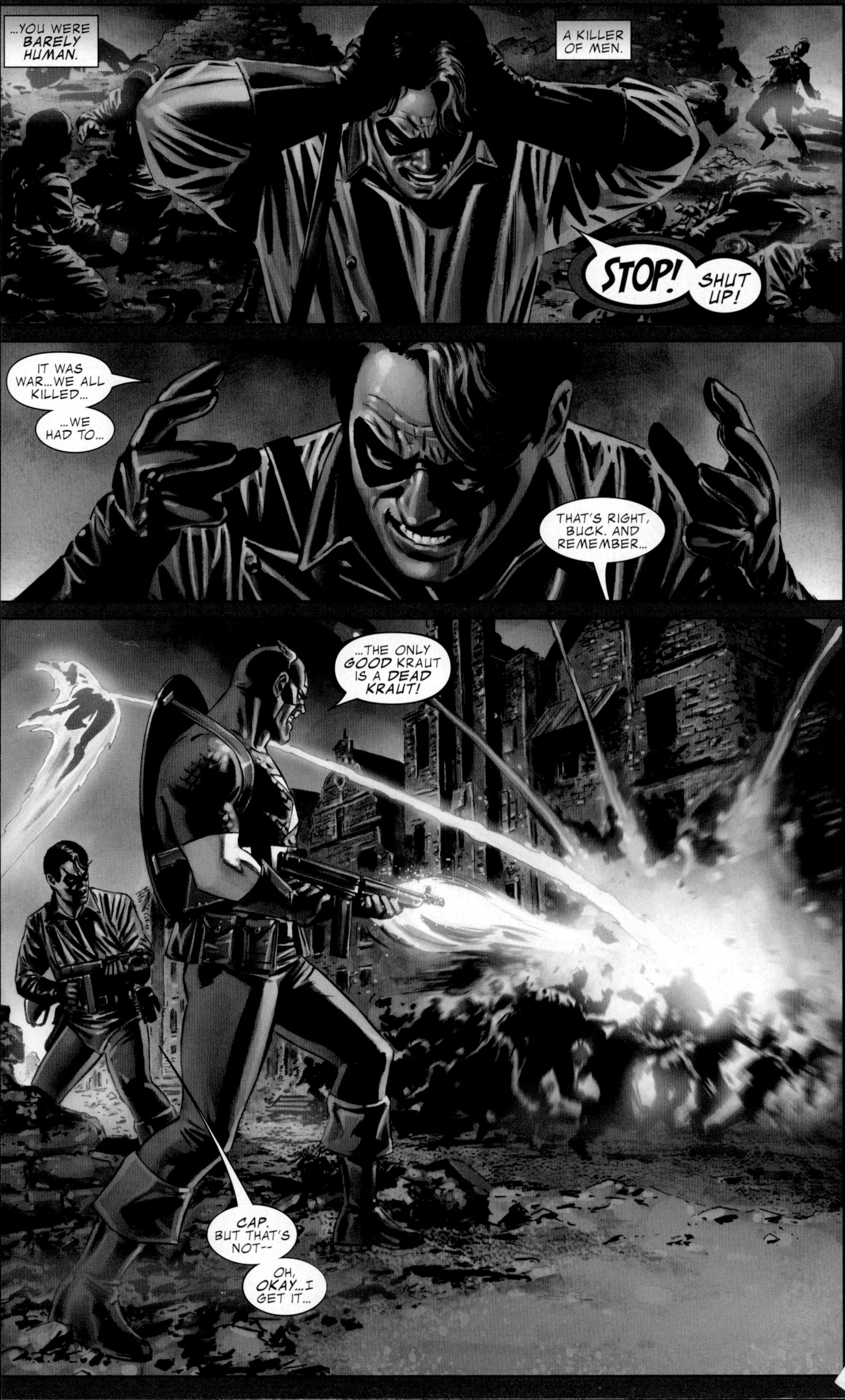

...YOU WERE BARELY HUMAN.
A KILLER OF MEN.
STOP!
SHUT UP!
IT WAS WAR...WE ALL KILLED...
...WE HAD TO...
THAT'S RIGHT, BUCK. AND REMEMBER...
...THE ONLY GOOD KRAUT IS A DEAD KRAUT!
CAP. BUT THAT'S NOT--
OH, OKAY...I GET IT...

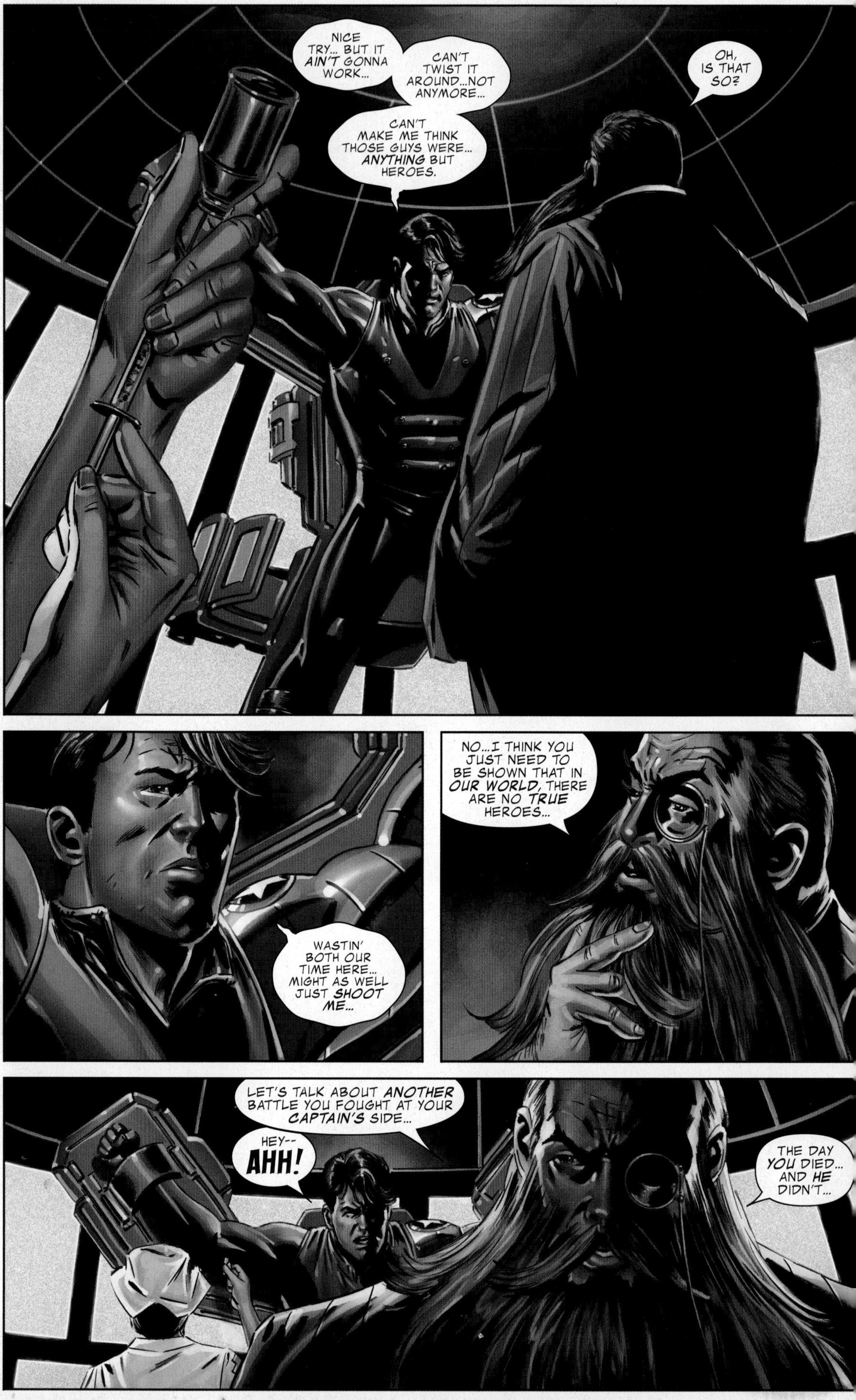
NICE TRY... BUT IT AIN'T GONNA WORK...
CAN'T TWIST IT AROUND...NOT ANYMORE...
CAN'T MAKE ME THINK THOSE GUYS WERE... ANYTHING BUT HEROES.
OH, IS THAT SO?
WASTIN' BOTH OUR TIME HERE... MIGHT AS WELL JUST SHOOT ME...
NO...I THINK YOU JUST NEED TO BE SHOWN THAT IN OUR WORLD, THERE ARE NO TRUE HEROES...
LET'S TALK ABOUT ANOTHER BATTLE YOU FOUGHT AT YOUR CAPTAIN'S SIDE...
HEY-- AHH!
THE DAY YOU DIED... AND HE DIDN'T...

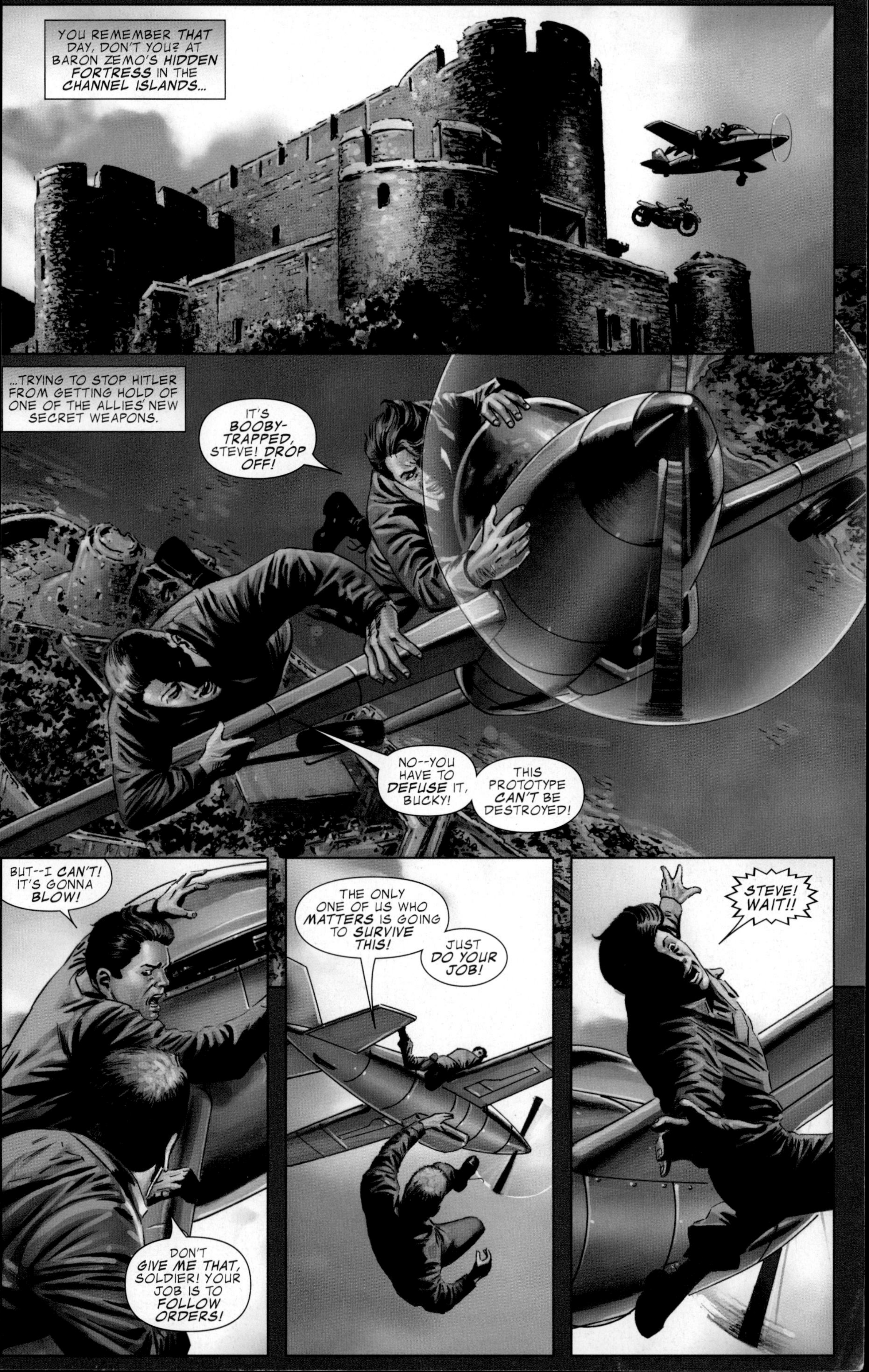
YOU REMEMBER THAT DAY, DON'T YOU? AT BARON ZEMO'S HIDDEN FORTRESS IN THE CHANNEL ISLANDS...
...TRYING TO STOP HITLER FROM GETTING HOLD OF ONE OF THE ALLIES' NEW SECRET WEAPONS.
IT'S BOOBY-TRAPPED, STEVE! DROP OFF!
NO--YOU HAVE TO DEFUSE IT, BUCKY!
THIS PROTOTYPE CAN'T BE DESTROYED!
BUT--I CAN'T! IT'S GONNA BLOW!
DON'T GIVE ME THAT, SOLDIER! YOUR JOB IS TO FOLLOW ORDERS!
THE ONLY ONE OF US WHO MATTERS IS GOING TO SURVIVE THIS!
JUST DO YOUR JOB!
STEVE! WAIT!!

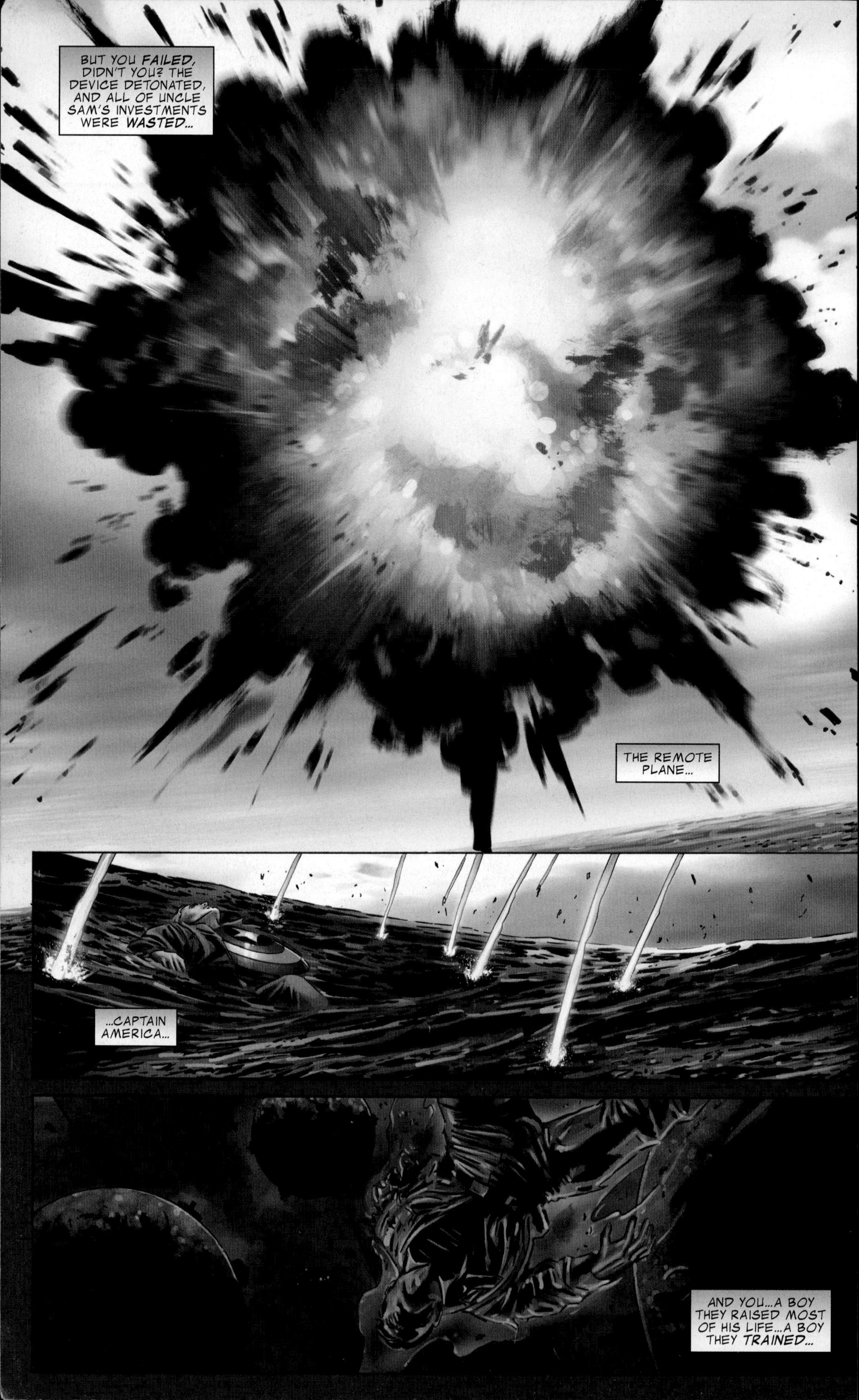
BUT YOU FAILED, DIDN'T YOU? THE DEVICE DETONATED, AND ALL OF UNCLE SAM'S INVESTMENTS WERE WASTED...
THE REMOTE PLANE...
...CAPTAIN AMERICA...
AND YOU...A BOY THEY RAISED MOST OF HIS LIFE...A BOY THEY TRAINED...

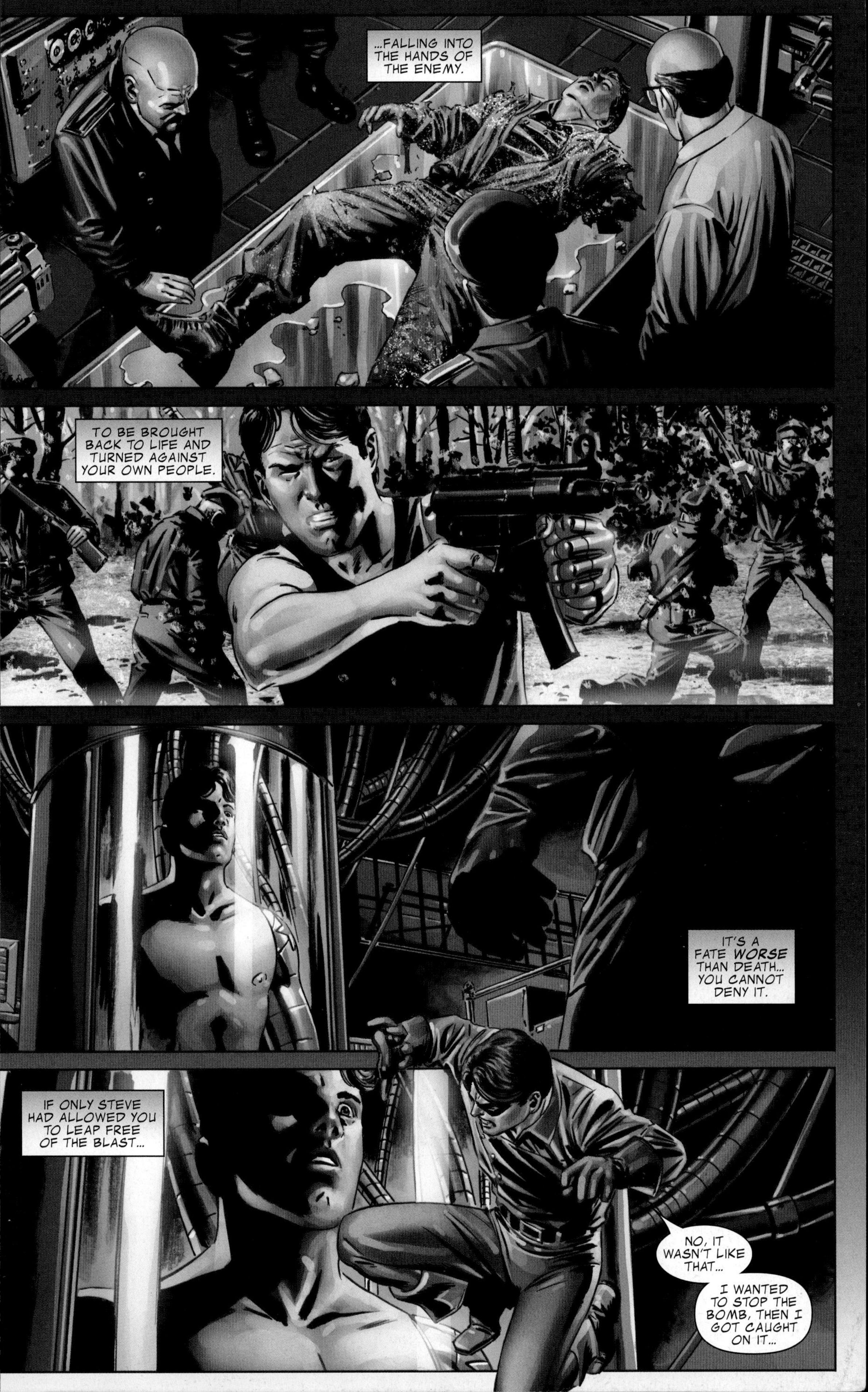
...FALLING INTO THE HANDS OF THE ENEMY.
TO BE BROUGHT BACK TO LIFE AND TURNED AGAINST YOUR OWN PEOPLE.
IT'S A FATE WORSE THAN DEATH... YOU CANNOT DENY IT.
IF ONLY STEVE HAD ALLOWED YOU TO LEAP FREE OF THE BLAST...
NO, IT WASN'T LIKE THAT...
I WANTED TO STOP THE BOMB, THEN I GOT CAUGHT ON IT...

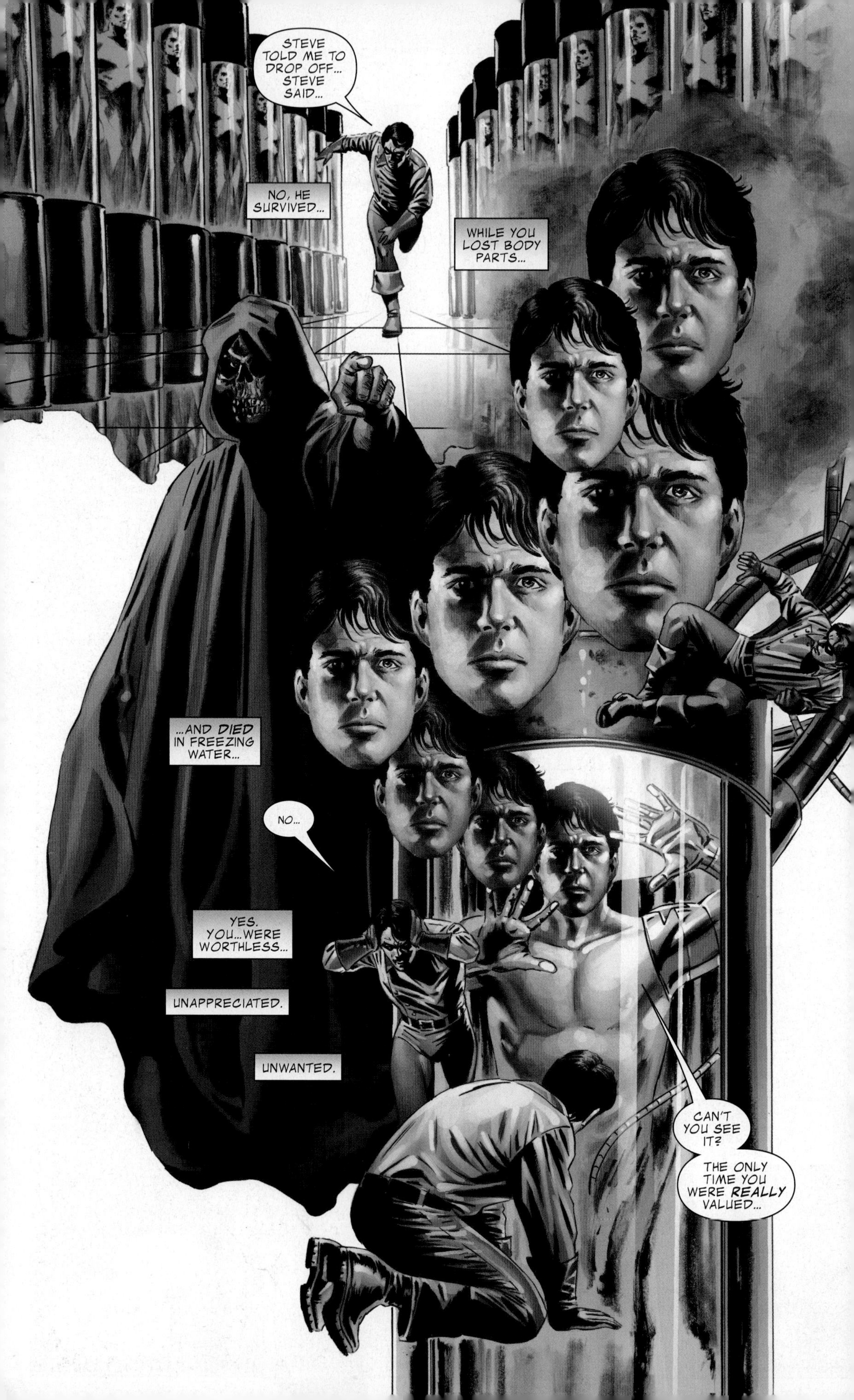
STEVE TOLD ME TO DROP OFF... STEVE SAID...
NO, HE SURVIVED...
WHILE YOU LOST BODY PARTS...
...AND DIED IN FREEZING WATER...
NO...
YES. YOU...WERE WORTHLESS...
UNAPPRECIATED.
UNWANTED.
CAN'T YOU SEE IT?
THE ONLY TIME YOU WERE REALLY VALUED...

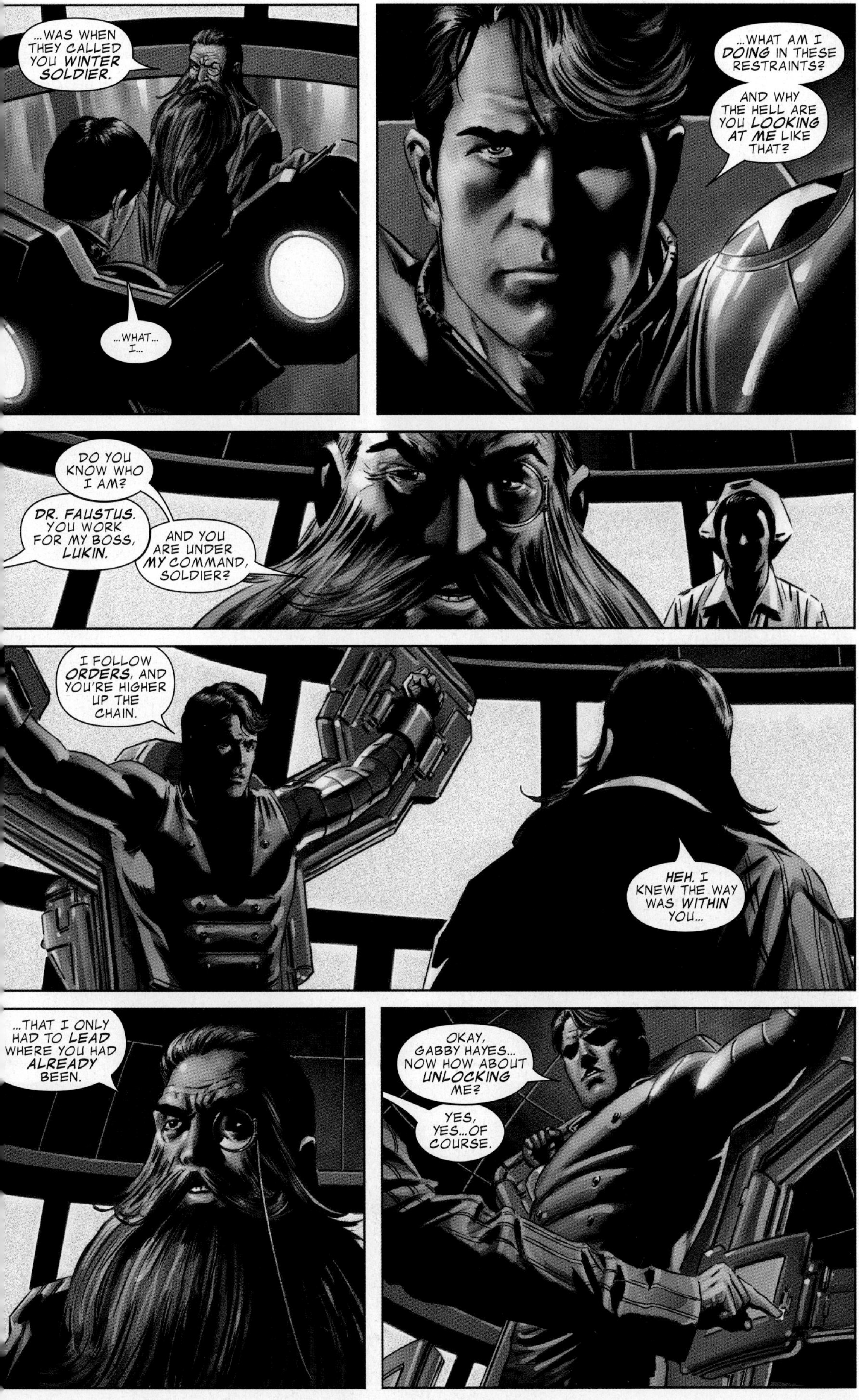
...WAS WHEN THEY CALLED YOU WINTER SOLDIER.
...WHAT... I...
...WHAT AM I DOING IN THESE RESTRAINTS?
AND WHY THE HELL ARE YOU LOOKING AT ME LIKE THAT?
DO YOU KNOW WHO I AM?
DR. FAUSTUS. YOU WORK FOR MY BOSS, LUKIN.
AND YOU ARE UNDER MY COMMAND, SOLDIER?
I FOLLOW ORDERS, AND YOU'RE HIGHER UP THE CHAIN.
HEH. I KNEW THE WAY WAS WITHIN YOU...
...THAT I ONLY HAD TO LEAD WHERE YOU HAD ALREADY BEEN.
OKAY, GABBY HAYES... NOW HOW ABOUT UNLOCKING ME?
YES, YES...OF COURSE.

THAT'S MORE LIKE IT. NOW WHERE ARE MY--

ONE MOMENT, SOLDIER...

...EVEN I CAN BECOME OVERCONFIDENT.

WHAT DO YOU MEAN?

THAT I DON'T TAKE ANYTHING AT FACE VALUE.

YOU WILL FOLLOW MY ORDERS, JUST AS YOU WOULD THOSE OF GENERAL LUKIN?

OF COURSE, SIR. I THOUGHT WE'D ALREADY ESTABLISHED THAT.

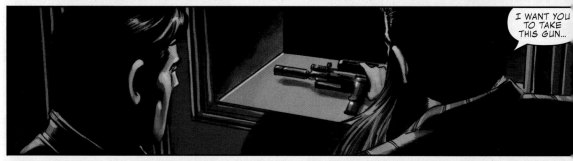

I WANT YOU TO TAKE THIS GUN...

...AND KILL YOUR NURSE.

WHAT? WHAT DID YOU JUST SAY?!

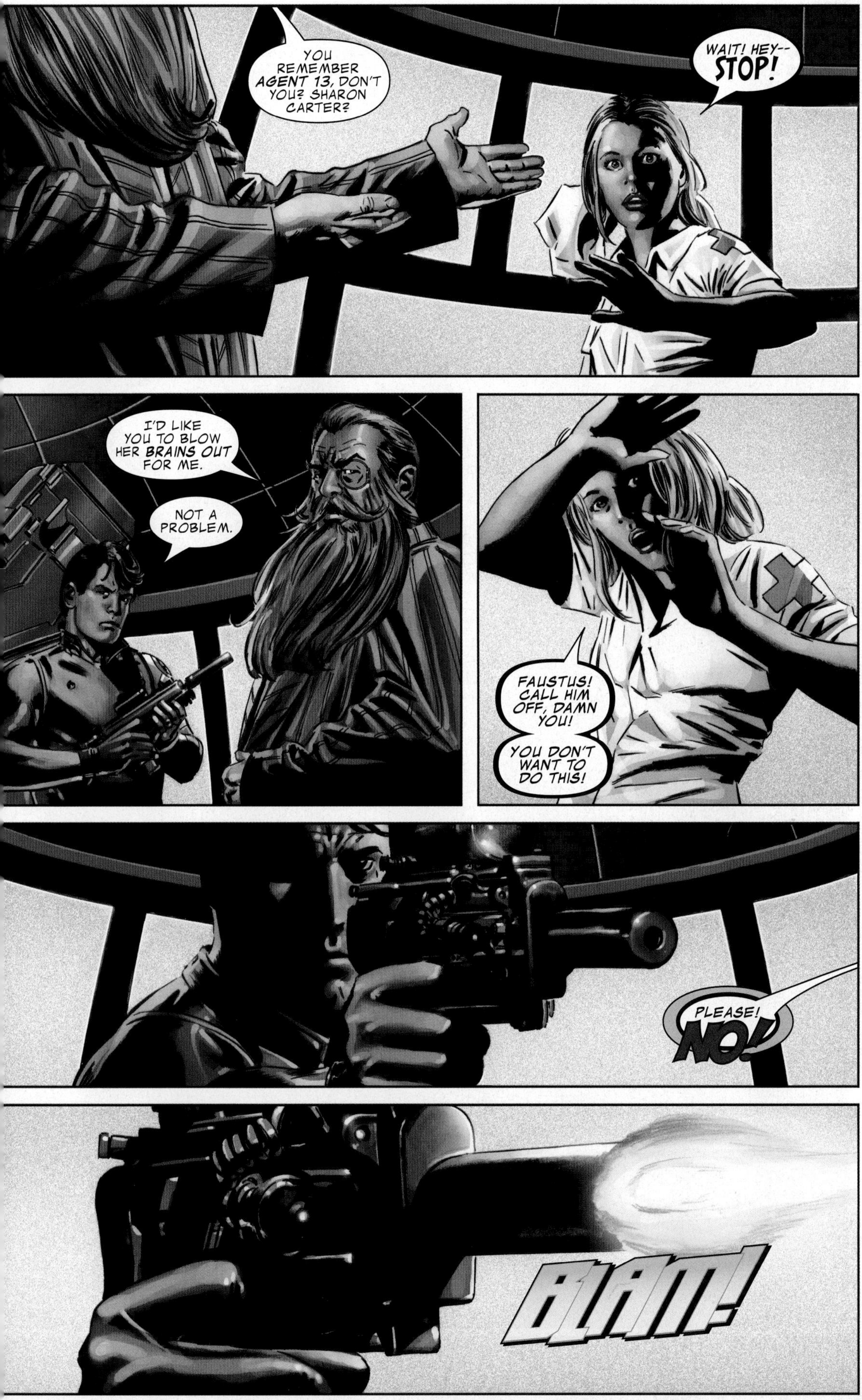
YOU REMEMBER AGENT 13, DON'T YOU? SHARON CARTER?
WAIT! HEY-- STOP!
I'D LIKE YOU TO BLOW HER BRAINS OUT FOR ME.
NOT A PROBLEM.
FAUSTUS! CALL HIM OFF, DAMN YOU!
YOU DON'T WANT TO DO THIS!
PLEASE! NO!
BLAM!

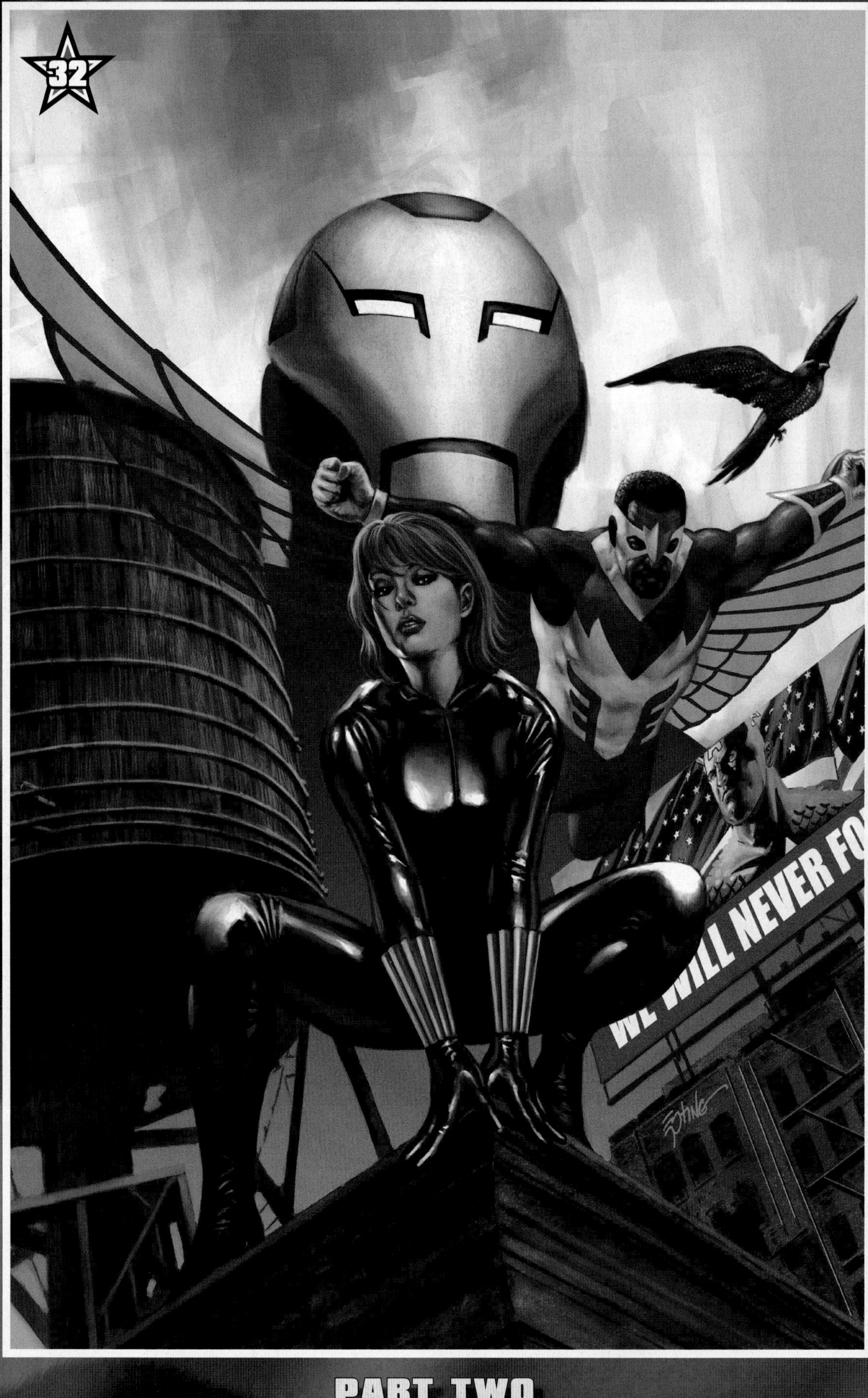
32
WE WILL NEVER

PART TWO

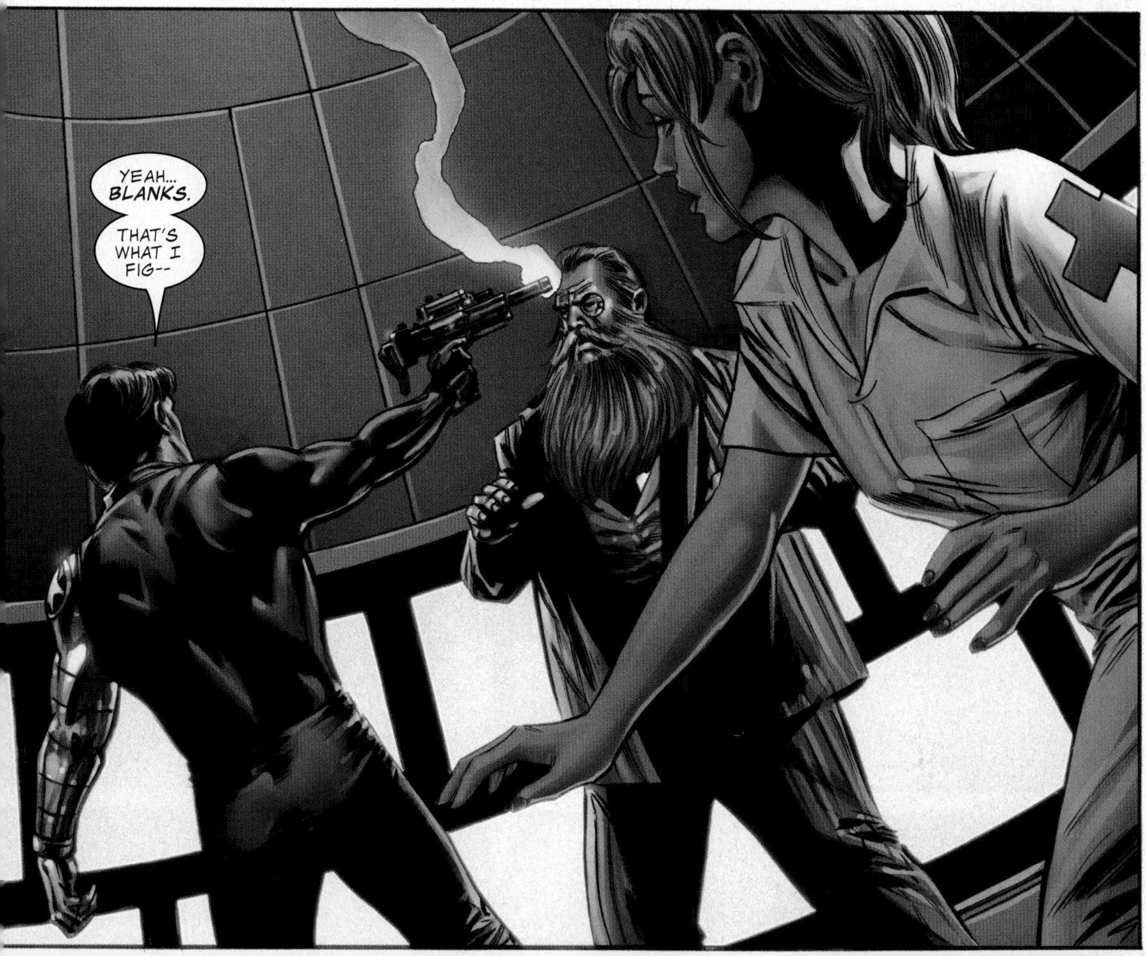
YEAH... BLANKS.
THAT'S WHAT I FIG--

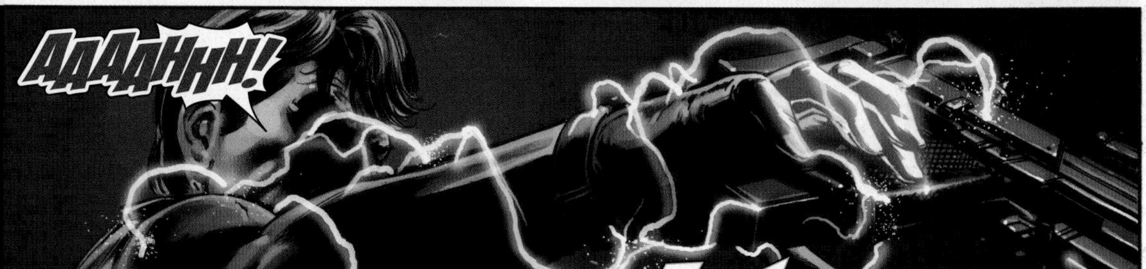
AAAAHHH!
FRAAAZZTT

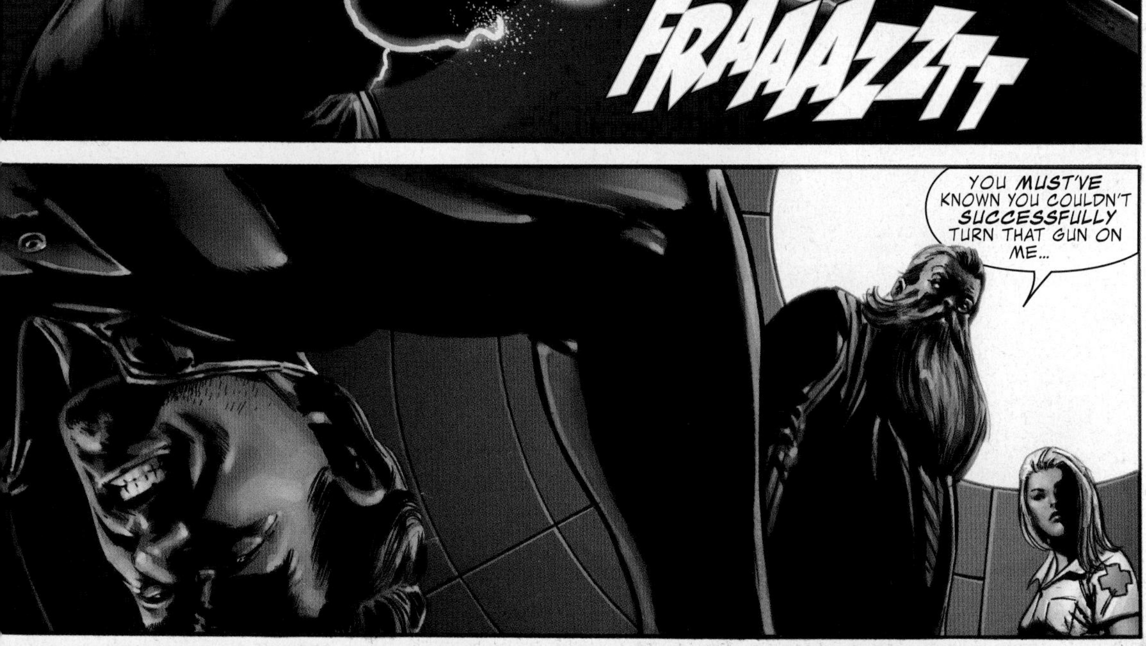
YOU MUST'VE KNOWN YOU COULDN'T SUCCESSFULLY TURN THAT GUN ON ME...

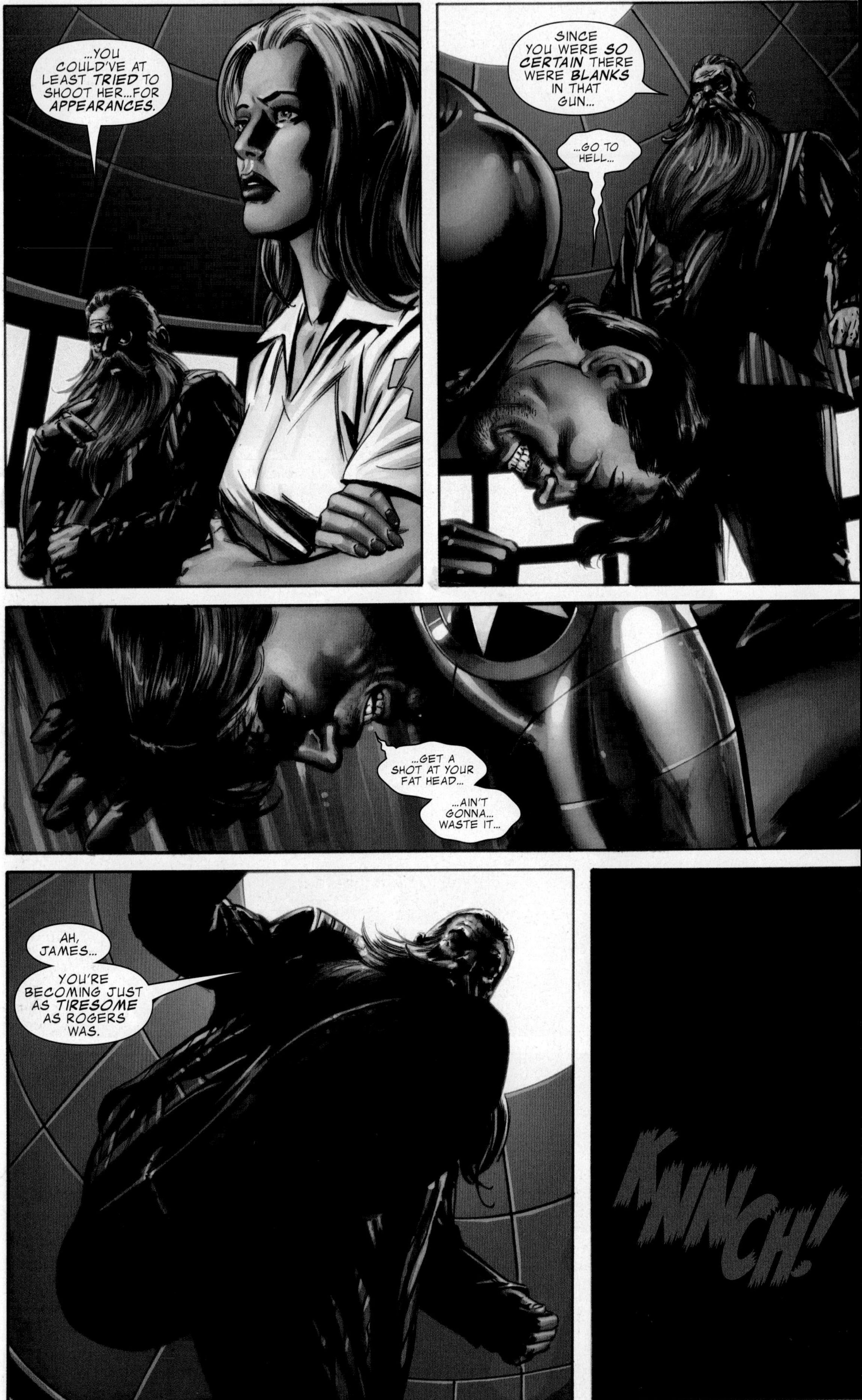
...YOU COULD'VE AT LEAST TRIED TO SHOOT HER...FOR APPEARANCES.
SINCE YOU WERE SO CERTAIN THERE WERE BLANKS IN THAT GUN...
...GO TO HELL...
...GET A SHOT AT YOUR FAT HEAD...
...AIN'T GONNA... WASTE IT...
AH, JAMES...
YOU'RE BECOMING JUST AS TIRESOME AS ROGERS WAS.
KNNCH!

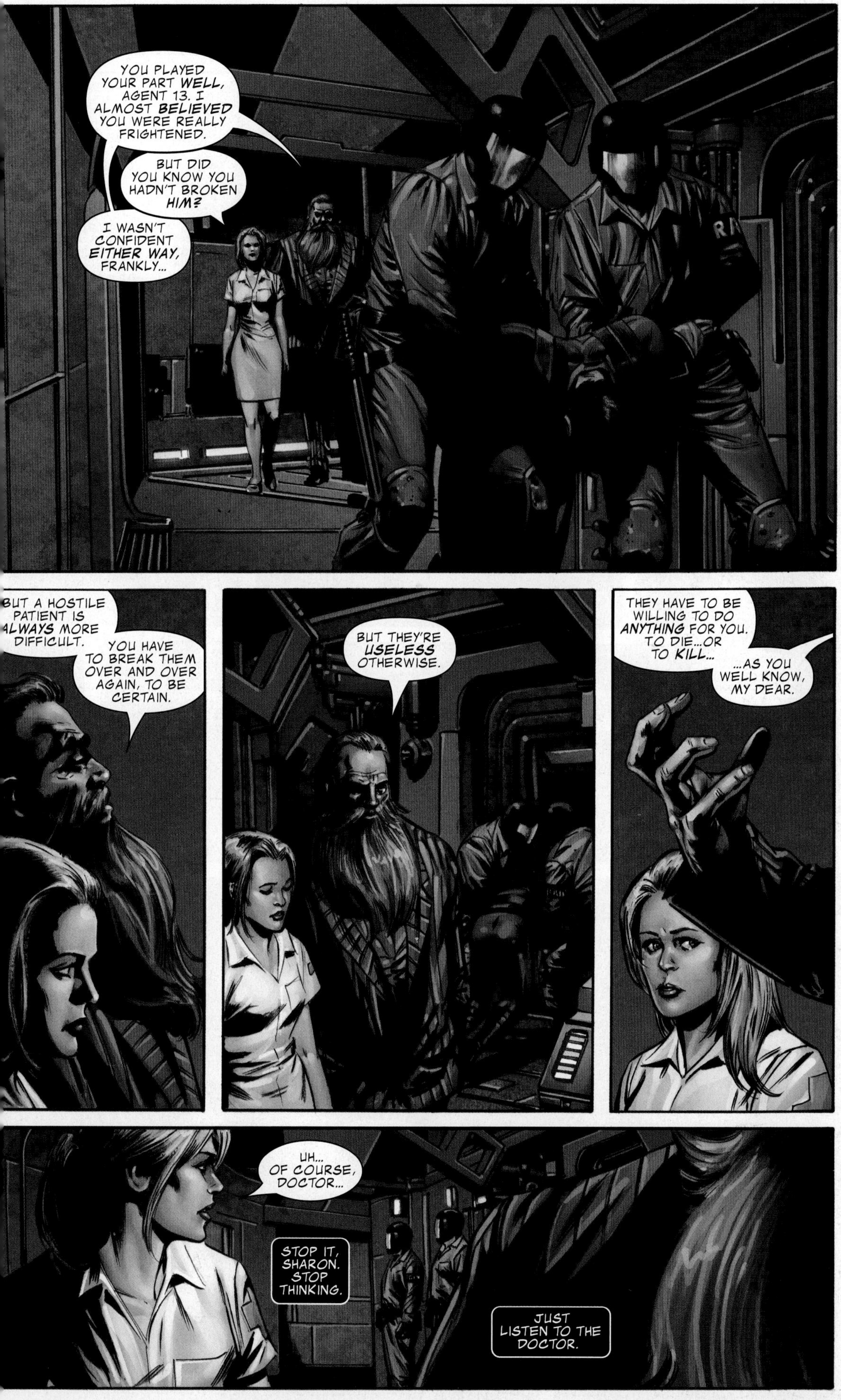
YOU PLAYED YOUR PART WELL, AGENT 13. I ALMOST BELIEVED YOU WERE REALLY FRIGHTENED.
BUT DID YOU KNOW YOU HADN'T BROKEN HIM?
I WASN'T CONFIDENT EITHER WAY, FRANKLY...
BUT A HOSTILE PATIENT IS ALWAYS MORE DIFFICULT.
YOU HAVE TO BREAK THEM OVER AND OVER AGAIN, TO BE CERTAIN.
BUT THEY'RE USELESS OTHERWISE.
THEY HAVE TO BE WILLING TO DO ANYTHING FOR YOU. TO DIE...OR TO KILL...
...AS YOU WELL KNOW, MY DEAR.
UH... OF COURSE, DOCTOR...
STOP IT, SHARON. STOP THINKING.
JUST LISTEN TO THE DOCTOR.

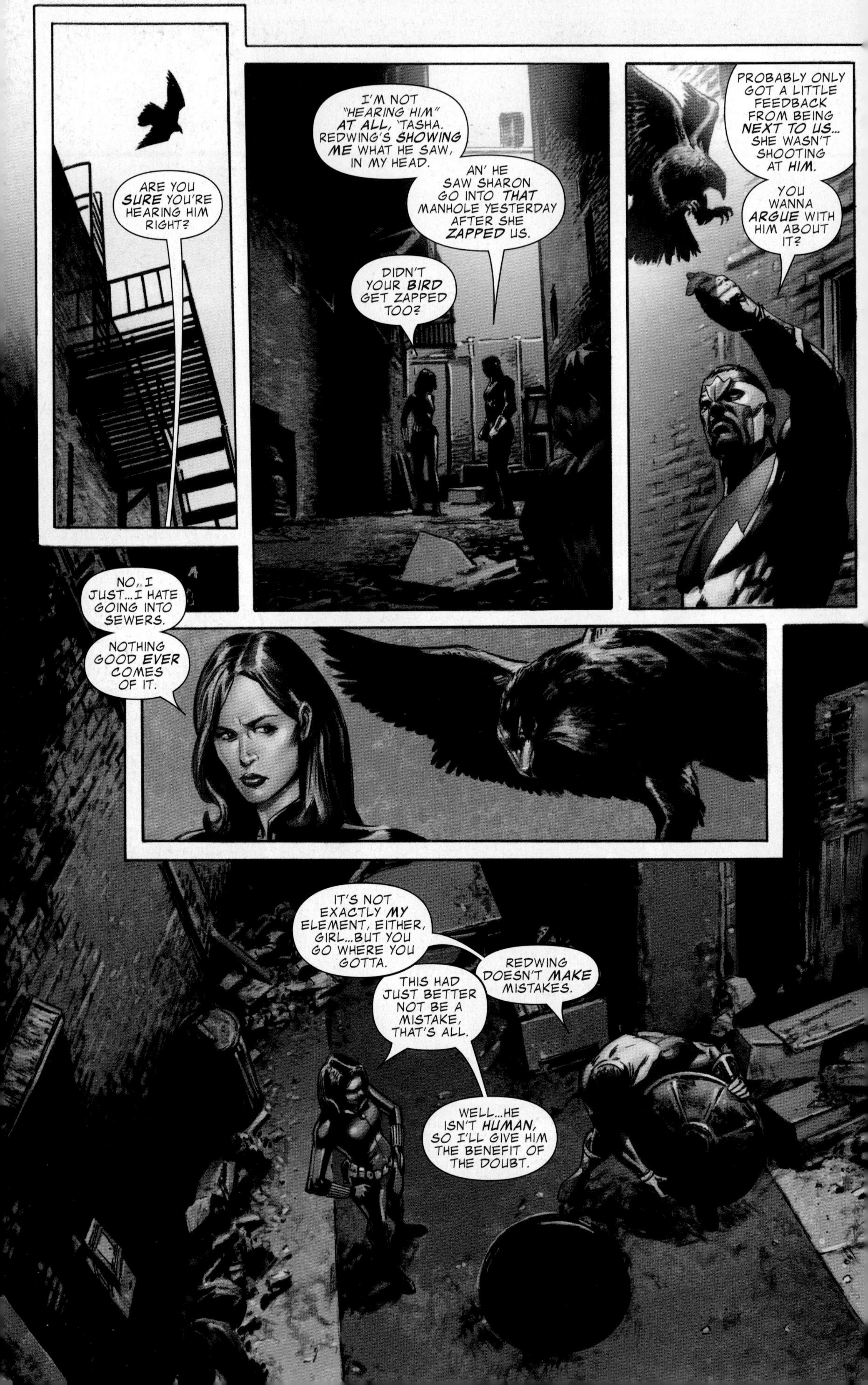
ARE YOU SURE YOU'RE HEARING HIM RIGHT?
I'M NOT "HEARING HIM" AT ALL, 'TASHA. REDWING'S SHOWING ME WHAT HE SAW, IN MY HEAD.
AN' HE SAW SHARON GO INTO THAT MANHOLE YESTERDAY AFTER SHE ZAPPED US.
DIDN'T YOUR BIRD GET ZAPPED TOO?
PROBABLY ONLY GOT A LITTLE FEEDBACK FROM BEING NEXT TO US... SHE WASN'T SHOOTING AT HIM.
YOU WANNA ARGUE WITH HIM ABOUT IT?
NO, I JUST...I HATE GOING INTO SEWERS.
NOTHING GOOD EVER COMES OF IT.
IT'S NOT EXACTLY MY ELEMENT, EITHER, GIRL...BUT YOU GO WHERE YOU GOTTA.
REDWING DOESN'T MAKE MISTAKES.
THIS HAD JUST BETTER NOT BE A MISTAKE, THAT'S ALL.
WELL...HE ISN'T HUMAN, SO I'LL GIVE HIM THE BENEFIT OF THE DOUBT.

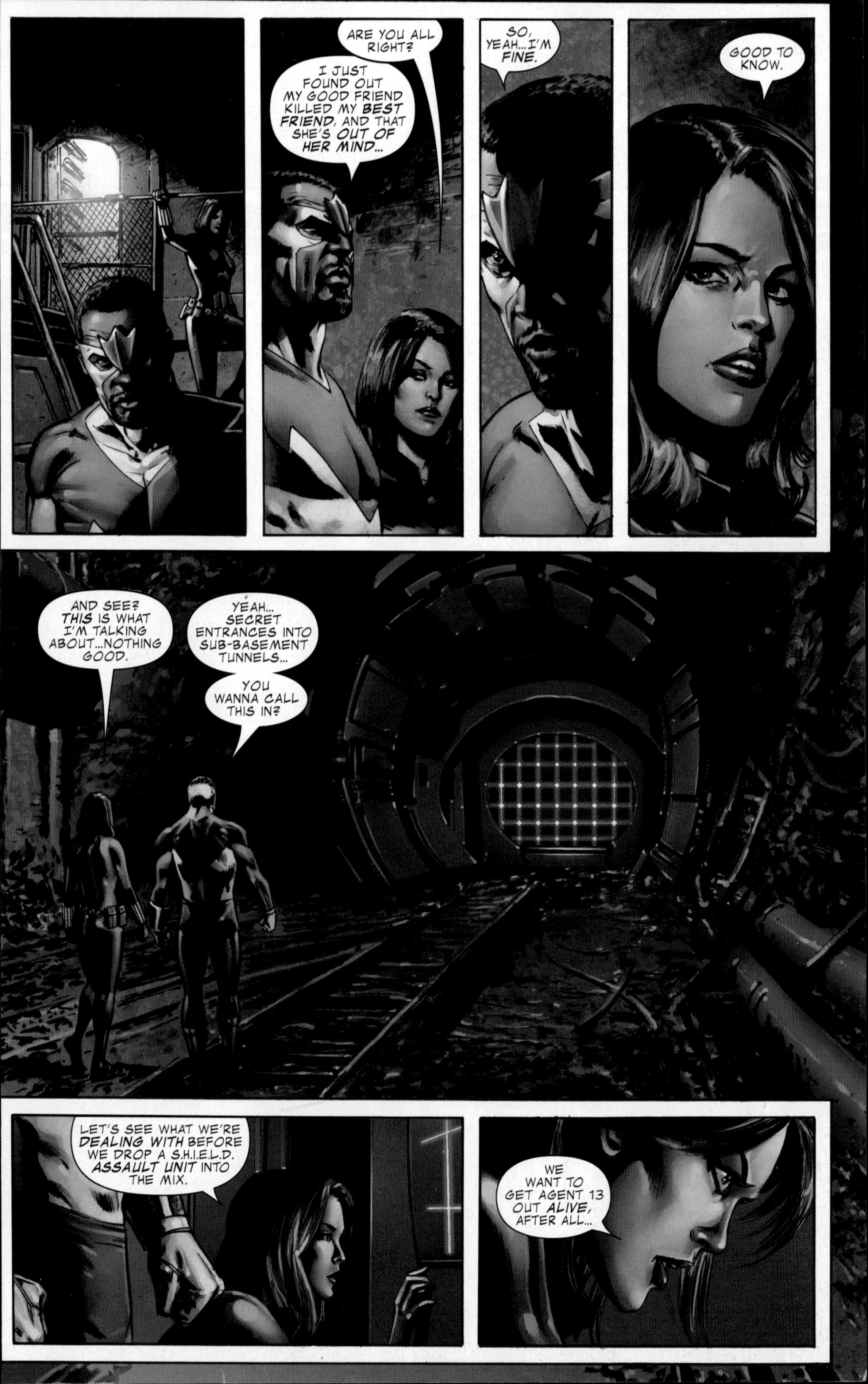
ARE YOU ALL RIGHT?
I JUST FOUND OUT MY GOOD FRIEND KILLED MY BEST FRIEND, AND THAT SHE'S OUT OF HER MIND...
SO, YEAH...I'M FINE.
GOOD TO KNOW.
AND SEE? THIS IS WHAT I'M TALKING ABOUT...NOTHING GOOD.
YEAH... SECRET ENTRANCES INTO SUB-BASEMENT TUNNELS...
YOU WANNA CALL THIS IN?
LET'S SEE WHAT WE'RE DEALING WITH BEFORE WE DROP A S.H.I.E.L.D. ASSAULT UNIT INTO THE MIX.
WE WANT TO GET AGENT 13 OUT ALIVE, AFTER ALL...

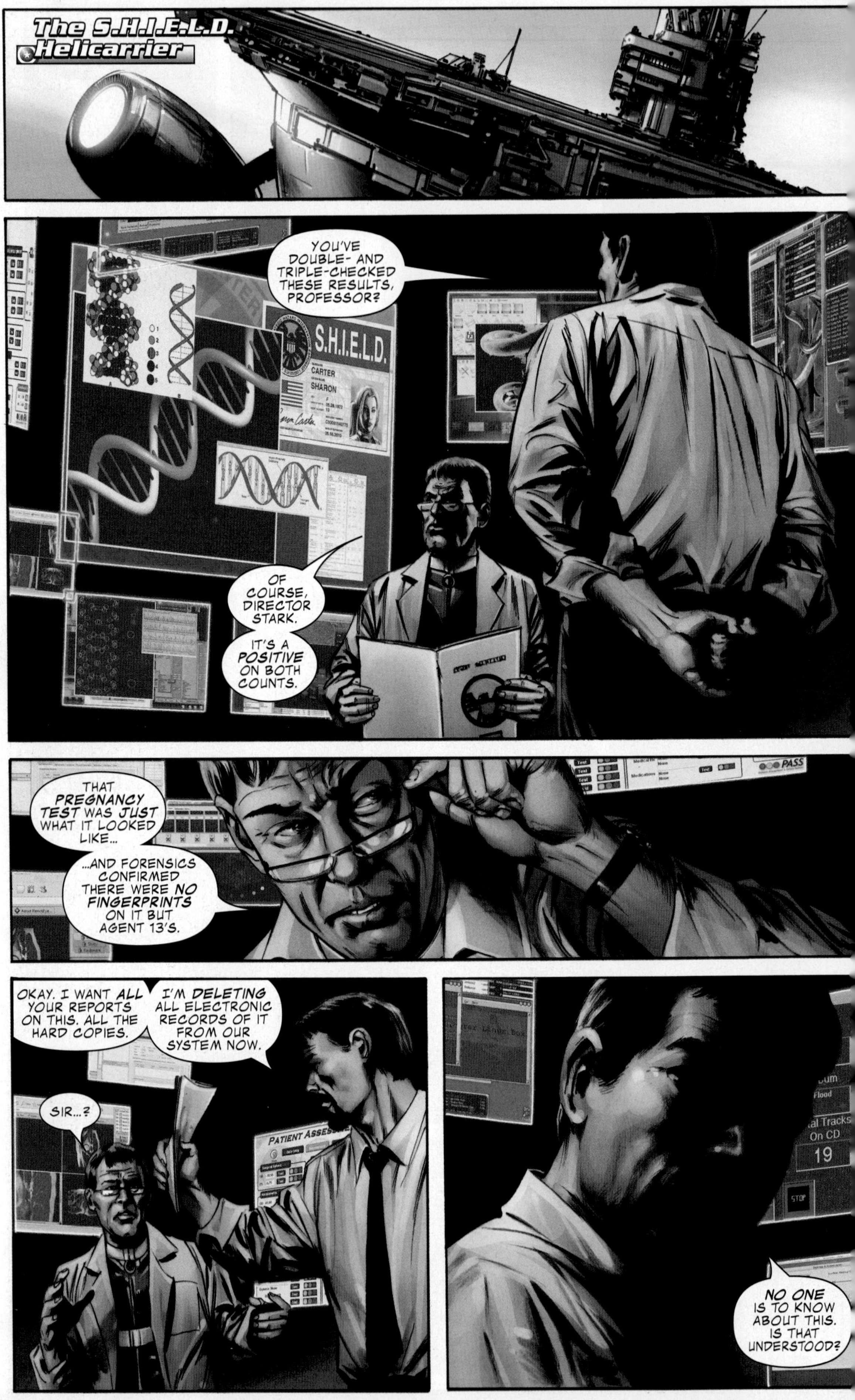
The S.H.I.E.L.D. Helicarrier
YOU'VE DOUBLE- AND TRIPLE-CHECKED THESE RESULTS, PROFESSOR?
S.H.I.E.L.D.
CARTER
SHARON
OF COURSE, DIRECTOR STARK.
IT'S A *POSITIVE* ON BOTH COUNTS.
THAT *PREGNANCY TEST* WAS *JUST* WHAT IT LOOKED LIKE...
...AND FORENSICS CONFIRMED THERE WERE *NO FINGERPRINTS* ON IT BUT AGENT 13'S.
PASS
OKAY. I WANT *ALL* YOUR REPORTS ON THIS. ALL THE HARD COPIES.
I'M *DELETING* ALL ELECTRONIC RECORDS OF IT FROM OUR SYSTEM NOW.
SIR...?
PATIENT ASSESS
Flood
On CD
19
STOP
NO ONE IS TO KNOW ABOUT THIS. IS THAT UNDERSTOOD?

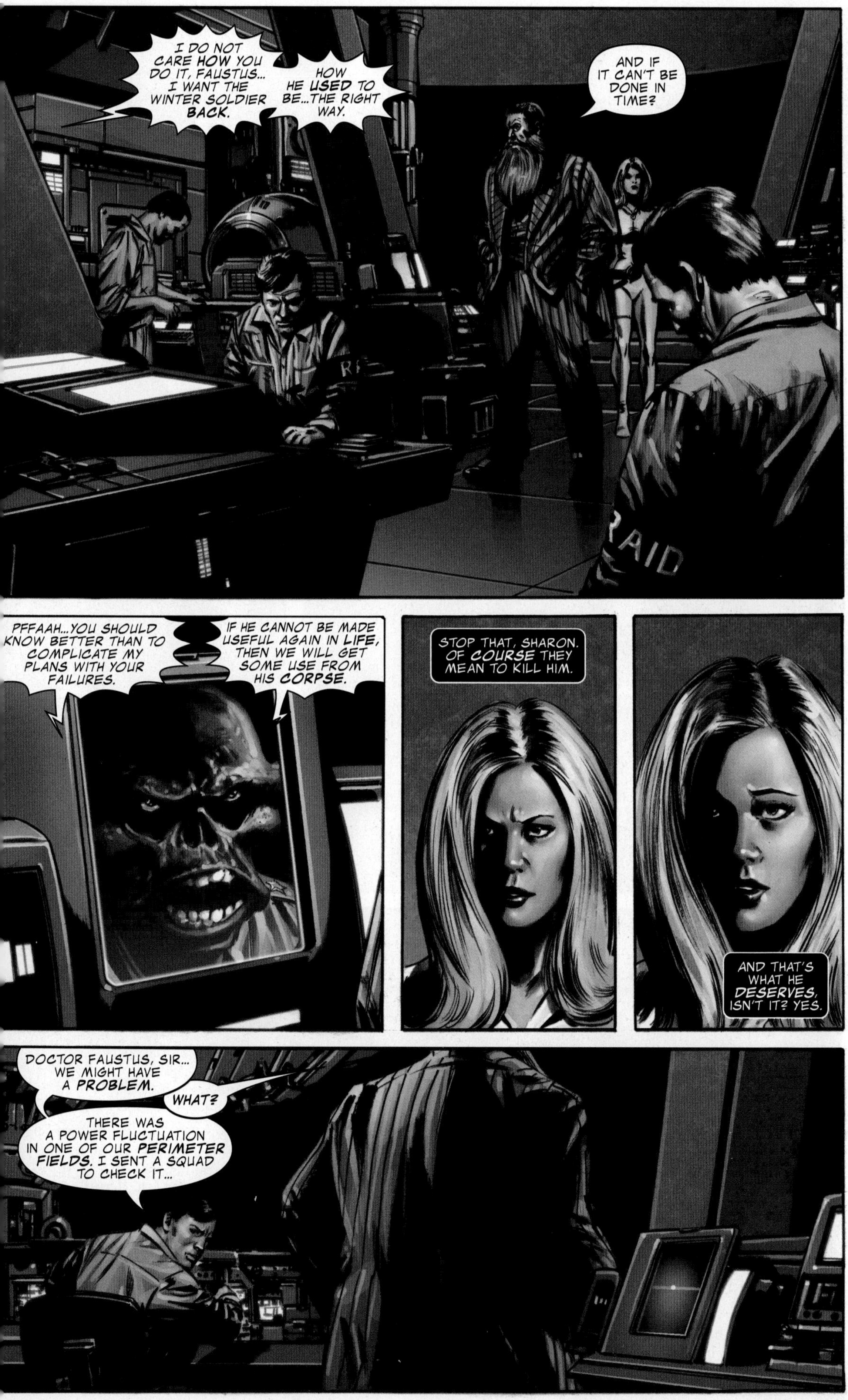
I DO NOT CARE HOW YOU DO IT, FAUSTUS... I WANT THE WINTER SOLDIER BACK.
HOW HE USED TO BE...THE RIGHT WAY.
AND IF IT CAN'T BE DONE IN TIME?
RAID
PFFAAH...YOU SHOULD KNOW BETTER THAN TO COMPLICATE MY PLANS WITH YOUR FAILURES.
IF HE CANNOT BE MADE USEFUL AGAIN IN LIFE, THEN WE WILL GET SOME USE FROM HIS CORPSE.
STOP THAT, SHARON. OF COURSE THEY MEAN TO KILL HIM.
AND THAT'S WHAT HE DESERVES, ISN'T IT? YES.
DOCTOR FAUSTUS, SIR... WE MIGHT HAVE A PROBLEM.
WHAT?
THERE WAS A POWER FLUCTUATION IN ONE OF OUR PERIMETER FIELDS. I SENT A SQUAD TO CHECK IT...

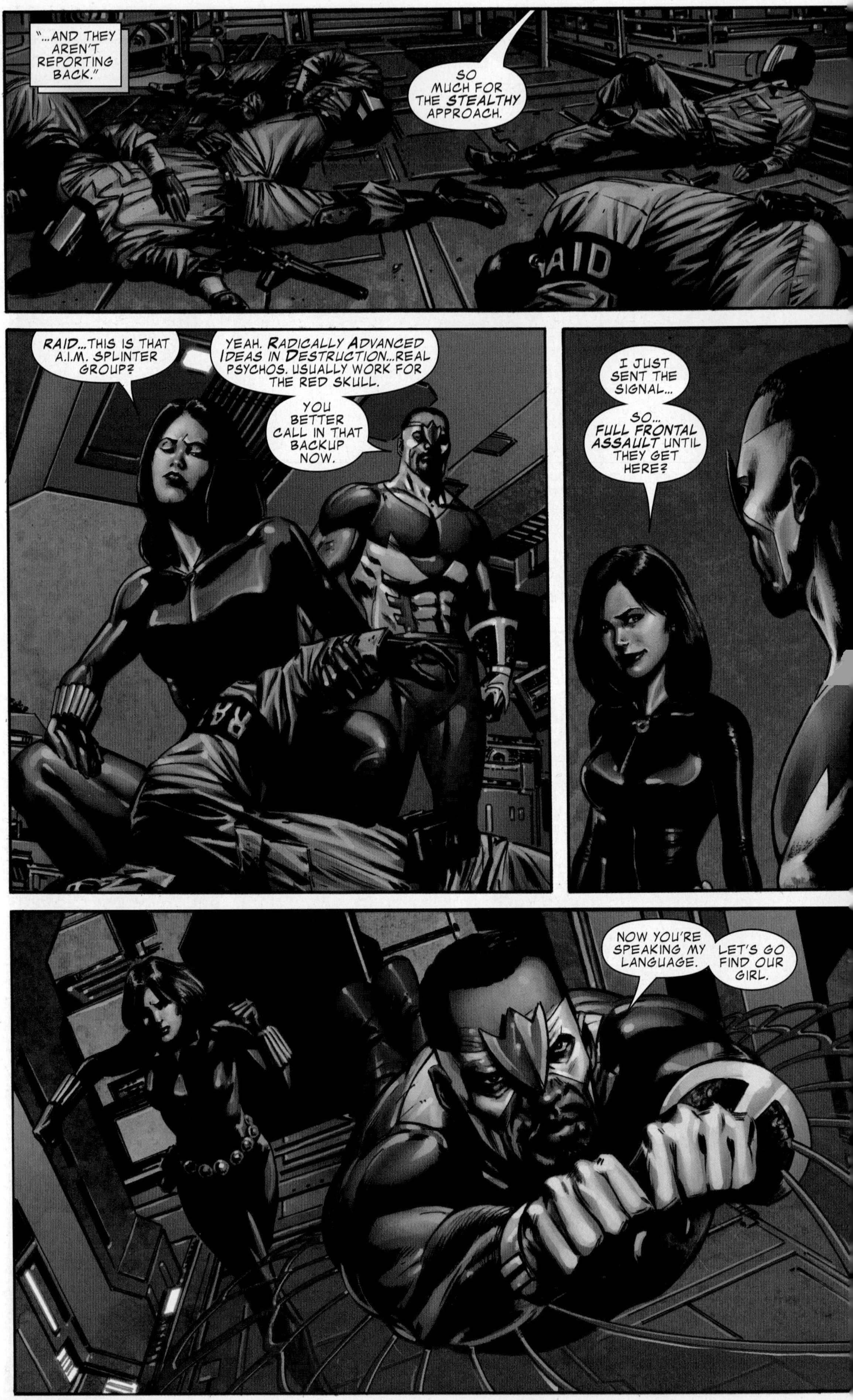
"...AND THEY AREN'T REPORTING BACK."
SO MUCH FOR THE STEALTHY APPROACH.
RAID...THIS IS THAT A.I.M. SPLINTER GROUP?
YEAH. RADICALLY ADVANCED IDEAS IN DESTRUCTION...REAL PSYCHOS. USUALLY WORK FOR THE RED SKULL.
YOU BETTER CALL IN THAT BACKUP NOW.
I JUST SENT THE SIGNAL...
SO... FULL FRONTAL ASSAULT UNTIL THEY GET HERE?
NOW YOU'RE SPEAKING MY LANGUAGE.
LET'S GO FIND OUR GIRL.

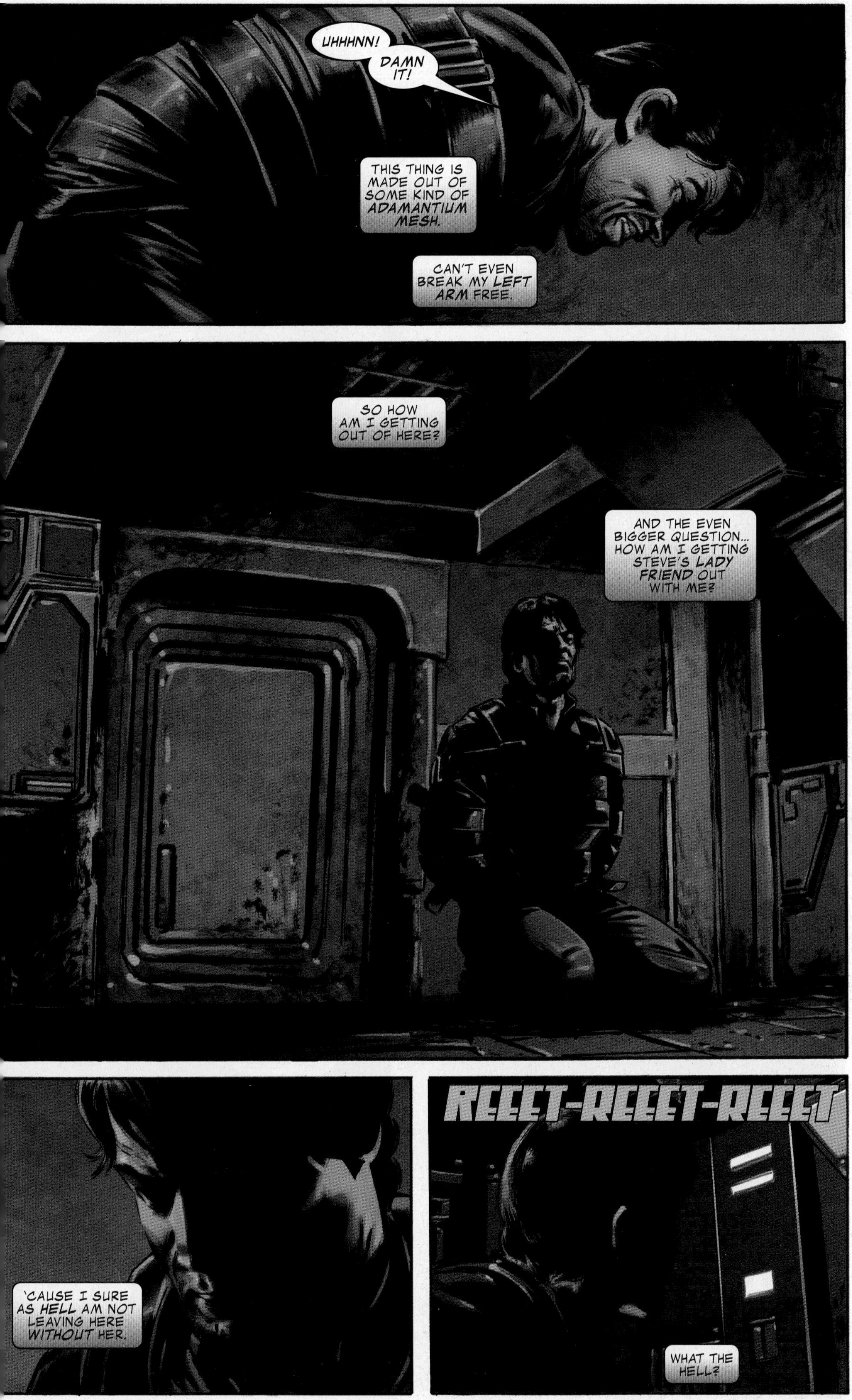
UHHHNN!
DAMN IT!
THIS THING IS MADE OUT OF SOME KIND OF ADAMANTIUM MESH.
CAN'T EVEN BREAK MY LEFT ARM FREE.
SO HOW AM I GETTING OUT OF HERE?
AND THE EVEN BIGGER QUESTION... HOW AM I GETTING STEVE'S LADY FRIEND OUT WITH ME?
'CAUSE I SURE AS HELL AM NOT LEAVING HERE WITHOUT HER.
REEET-REEET-REEET
WHAT THE HELL?

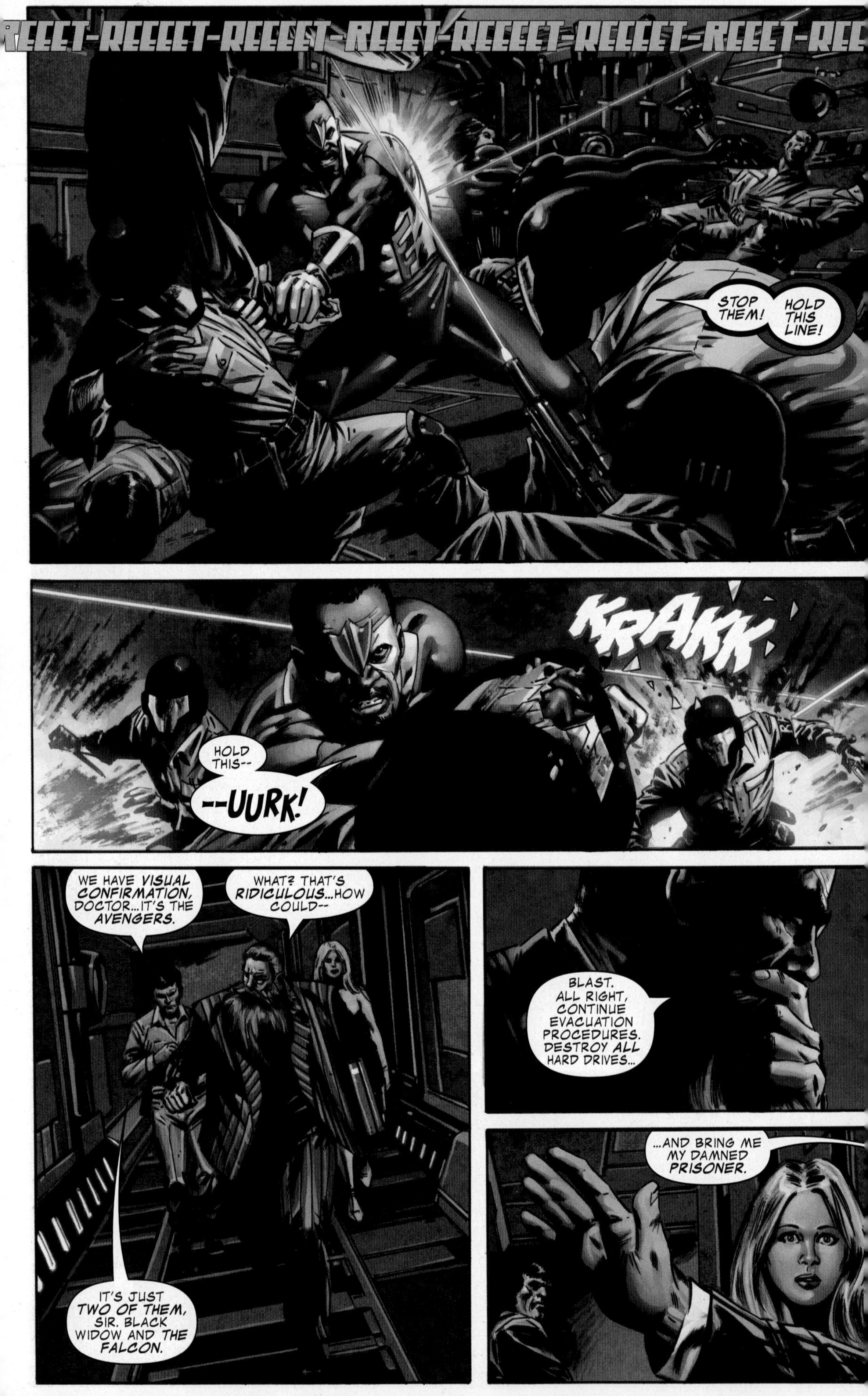
REEET-REEEET-REEEET-REEET-REEEET-REEEET-REEET-REE
STOP THEM!
HOLD THIS LINE!
KRAKK
HOLD THIS--
--UURK!
WE HAVE VISUAL CONFIRMATION, DOCTOR...IT'S THE AVENGERS.
WHAT? THAT'S RIDICULOUS...HOW COULD--
IT'S JUST TWO OF THEM, SIR. BLACK WIDOW AND THE FALCON.
BLAST. ALL RIGHT, CONTINUE EVACUATION PROCEDURES. DESTROY ALL HARD DRIVES...
...AND BRING ME MY DAMNED PRISONER.

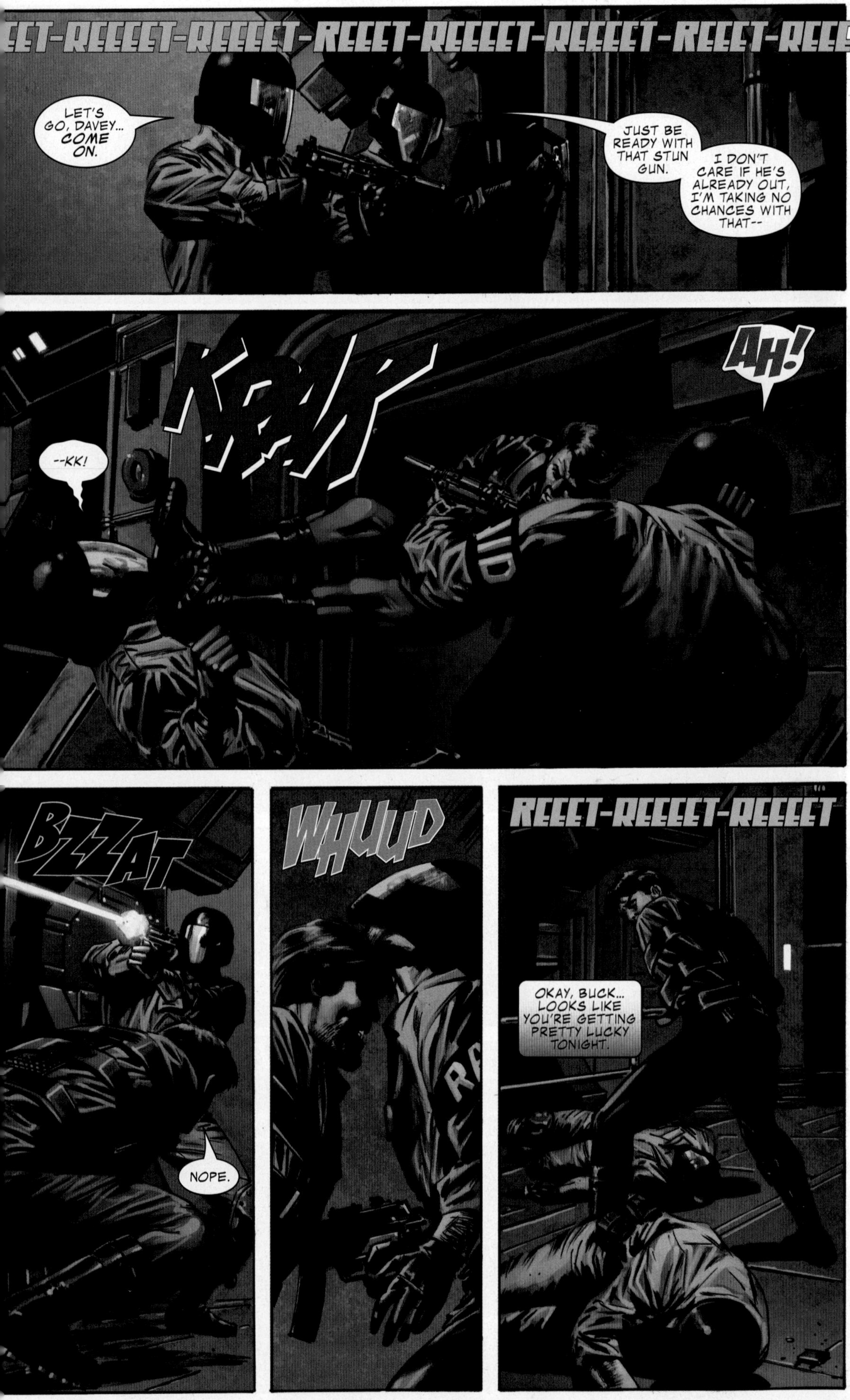
EET-REEEET-REEEET-REEET-REEEET-REEEET-REEET-REEEE
LET'S GO, DAVEY... COME ON.
JUST BE READY WITH THAT STUN GUN.
I DON'T CARE IF HE'S ALREADY OUT, I'M TAKING NO CHANCES WITH THAT--
KRAK
AH!
--KK!
BZZAT
NOPE.
WHUUD
REEET-REEEET-REEEET
OKAY, BUCK... LOOKS LIKE YOU'RE GETTING PRETTY LUCKY TONIGHT.

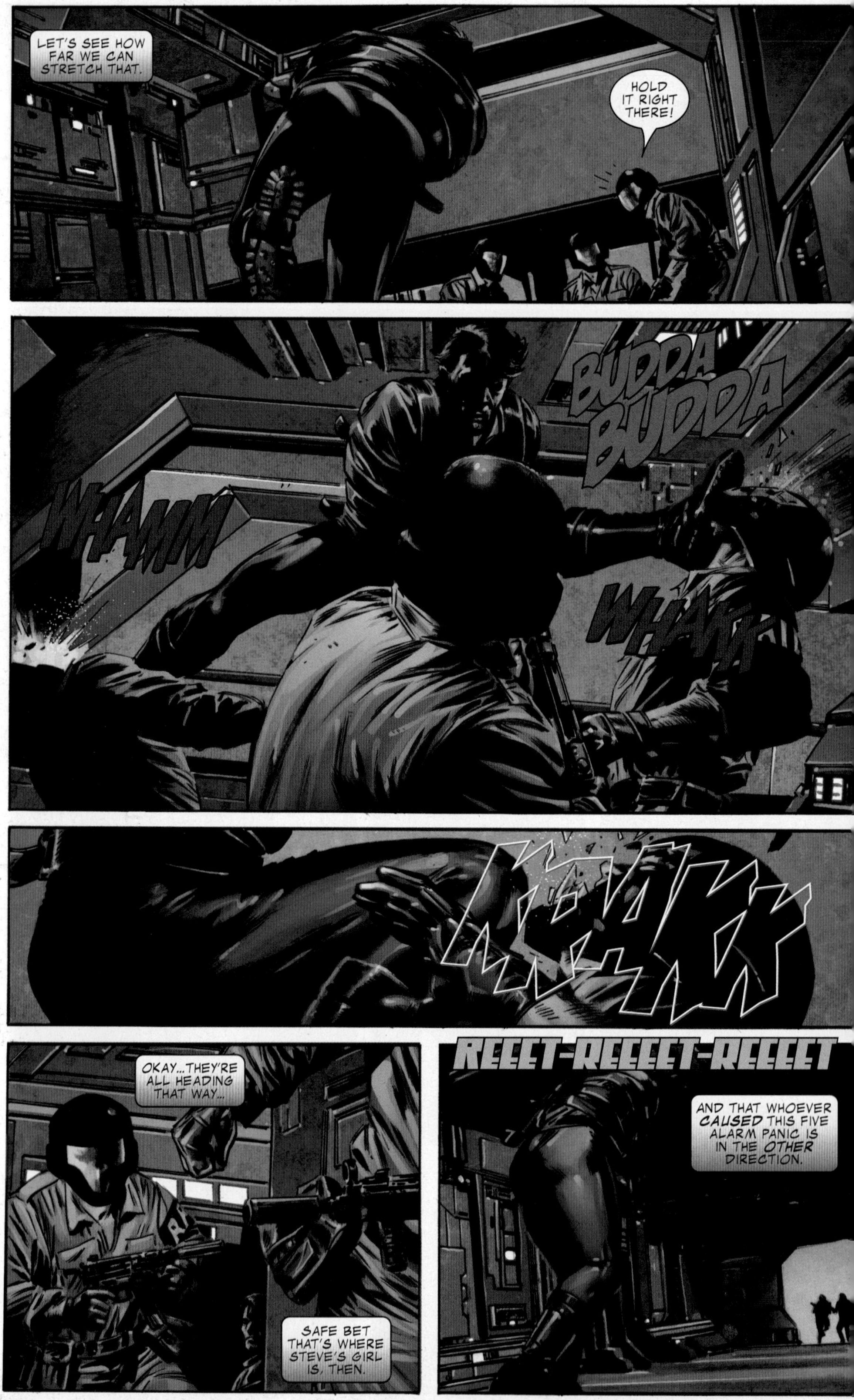
LET'S SEE HOW FAR WE CAN STRETCH THAT.
HOLD IT RIGHT THERE!
BUDDA BUDDA
WHAMM
WHAKK
REEET-REEEET-REEEET
OKAY...THEY'RE ALL HEADING THAT WAY...
SAFE BET THAT'S WHERE STEVE'S GIRL IS, THEN.
AND THAT WHOEVER CAUSED THIS FIVE ALARM PANIC IS IN THE OTHER DIRECTION.

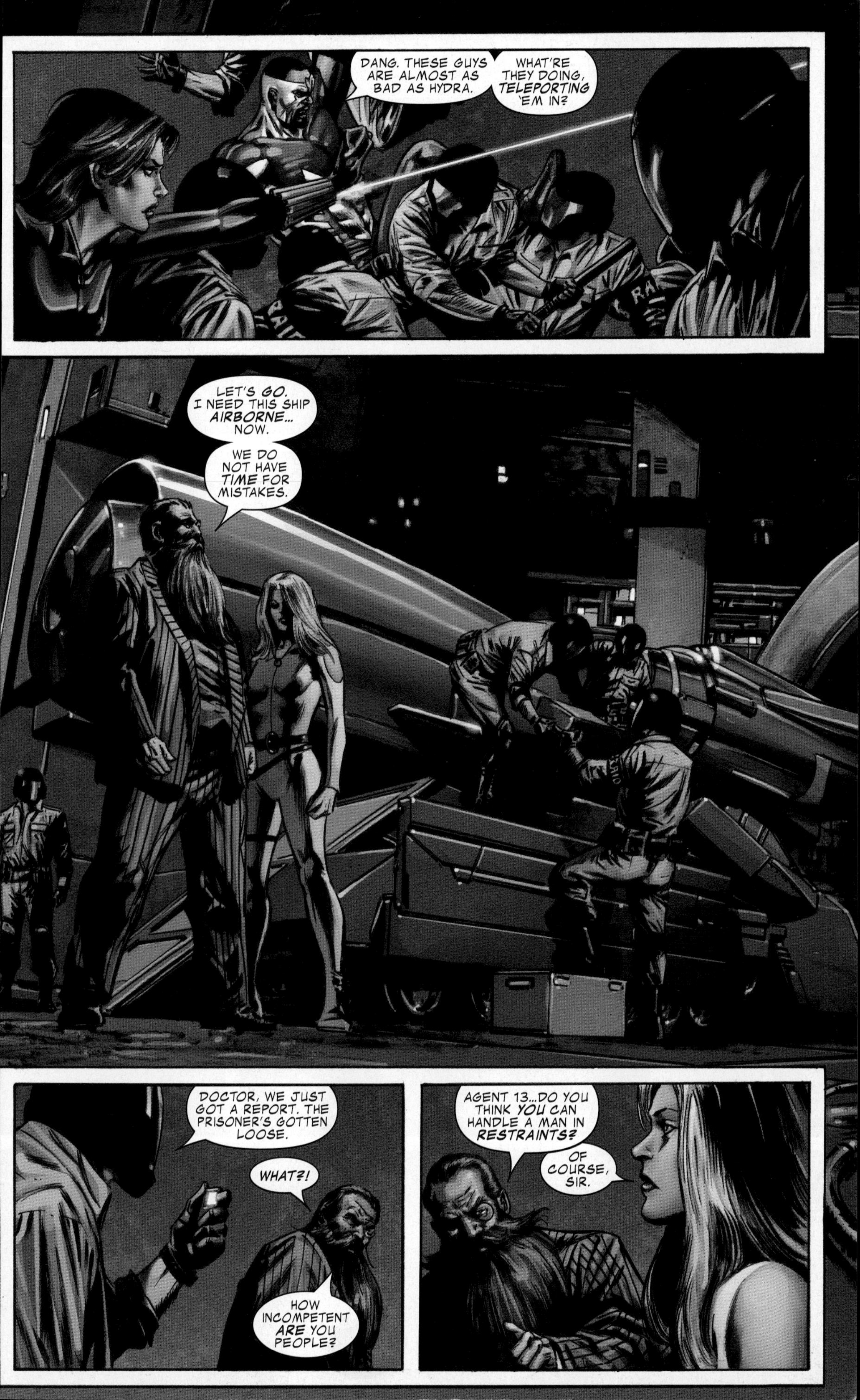
DANG. THESE GUYS ARE ALMOST AS BAD AS HYDRA.
WHAT'RE THEY DOING, TELEPORTING 'EM IN?
LET'S GO. I NEED THIS SHIP AIRBORNE... NOW.
WE DO NOT HAVE TIME FOR MISTAKES.
DOCTOR, WE JUST GOT A REPORT. THE PRISONER'S GOTTEN LOOSE.
WHAT?!
HOW INCOMPETENT ARE YOU PEOPLE?
AGENT 13...DO YOU THINK YOU CAN HANDLE A MAN IN RESTRAINTS?
OF COURSE, SIR.

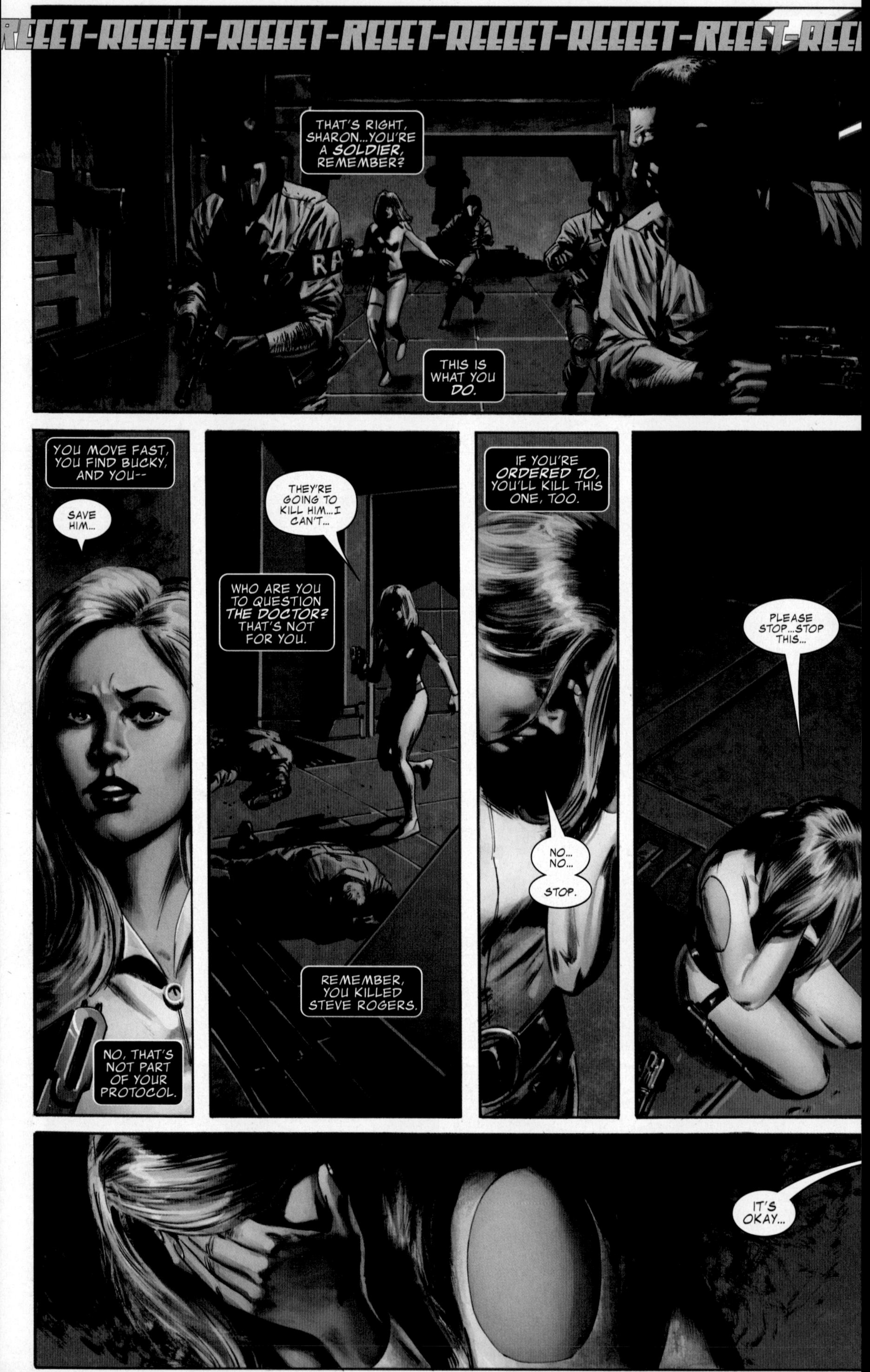
REEEET-REEEEET-REEEEET-REEET-REEEEET-REEEEET-REEET-REE
THAT'S RIGHT, SHARON...YOU'RE A SOLDIER, REMEMBER?
THIS IS WHAT YOU DO.
YOU MOVE FAST, YOU FIND BUCKY, AND YOU--
SAVE HIM...
NO, THAT'S NOT PART OF YOUR PROTOCOL.
THEY'RE GOING TO KILL HIM...I CAN'T...
WHO ARE YOU TO QUESTION THE DOCTOR? THAT'S NOT FOR YOU.
REMEMBER, YOU KILLED STEVE ROGERS.
IF YOU'RE ORDERED TO, YOU'LL KILL THIS ONE, TOO.
NO... NO...
STOP.
PLEASE STOP...STOP THIS...
IT'S OKAY...

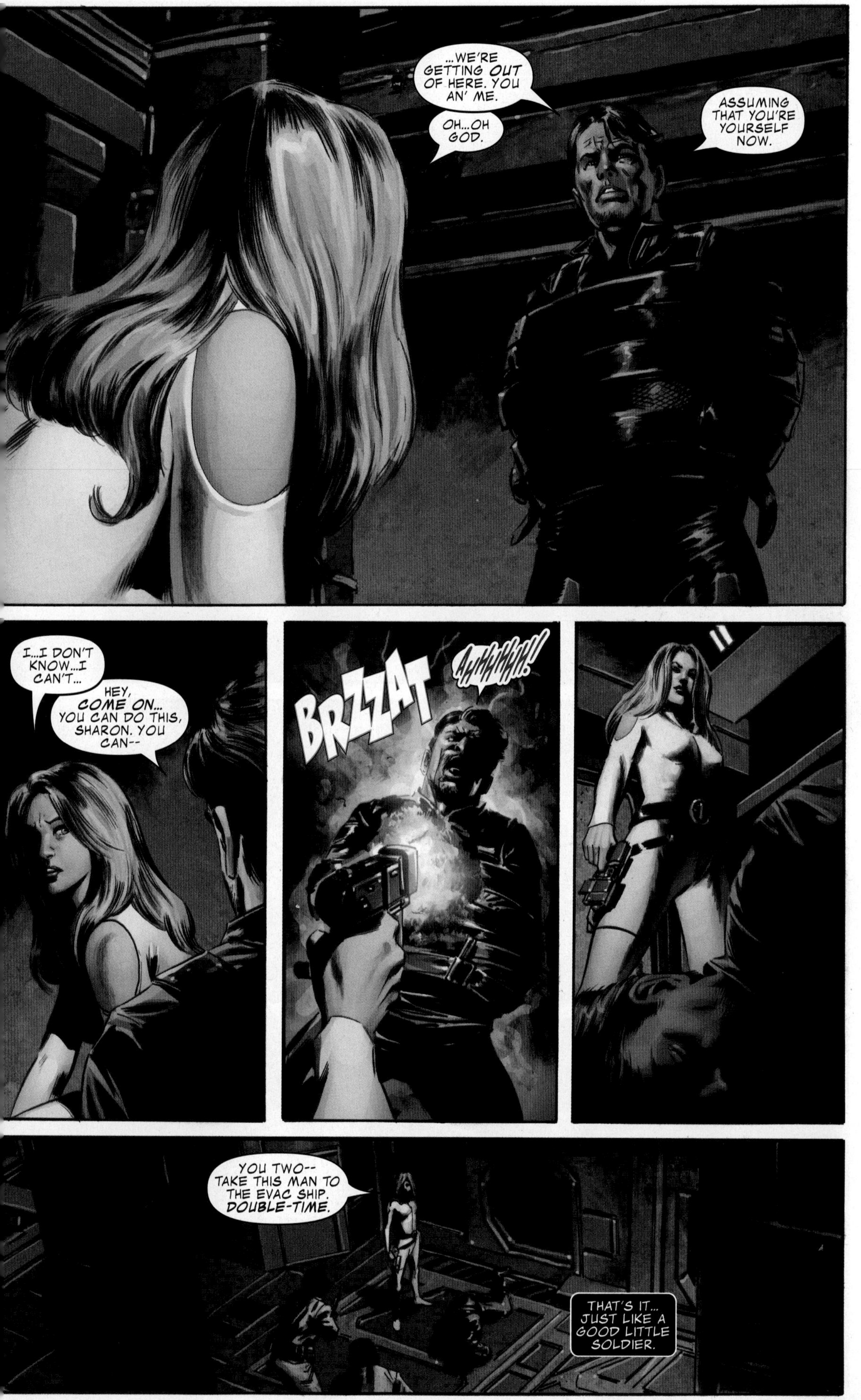
...WE'RE GETTING OUT OF HERE. YOU AN' ME.
OH...OH GOD.
ASSUMING THAT YOU'RE YOURSELF NOW.
I...I DON'T KNOW...I CAN'T...
HEY, COME ON... YOU CAN DO THIS, SHARON. YOU CAN--
BRZZZAT
AHHHHHH!
YOU TWO-- TAKE THIS MAN TO THE EVAC SHIP. DOUBLE-TIME.
THAT'S IT... JUST LIKE A GOOD LITTLE SOLDIER.

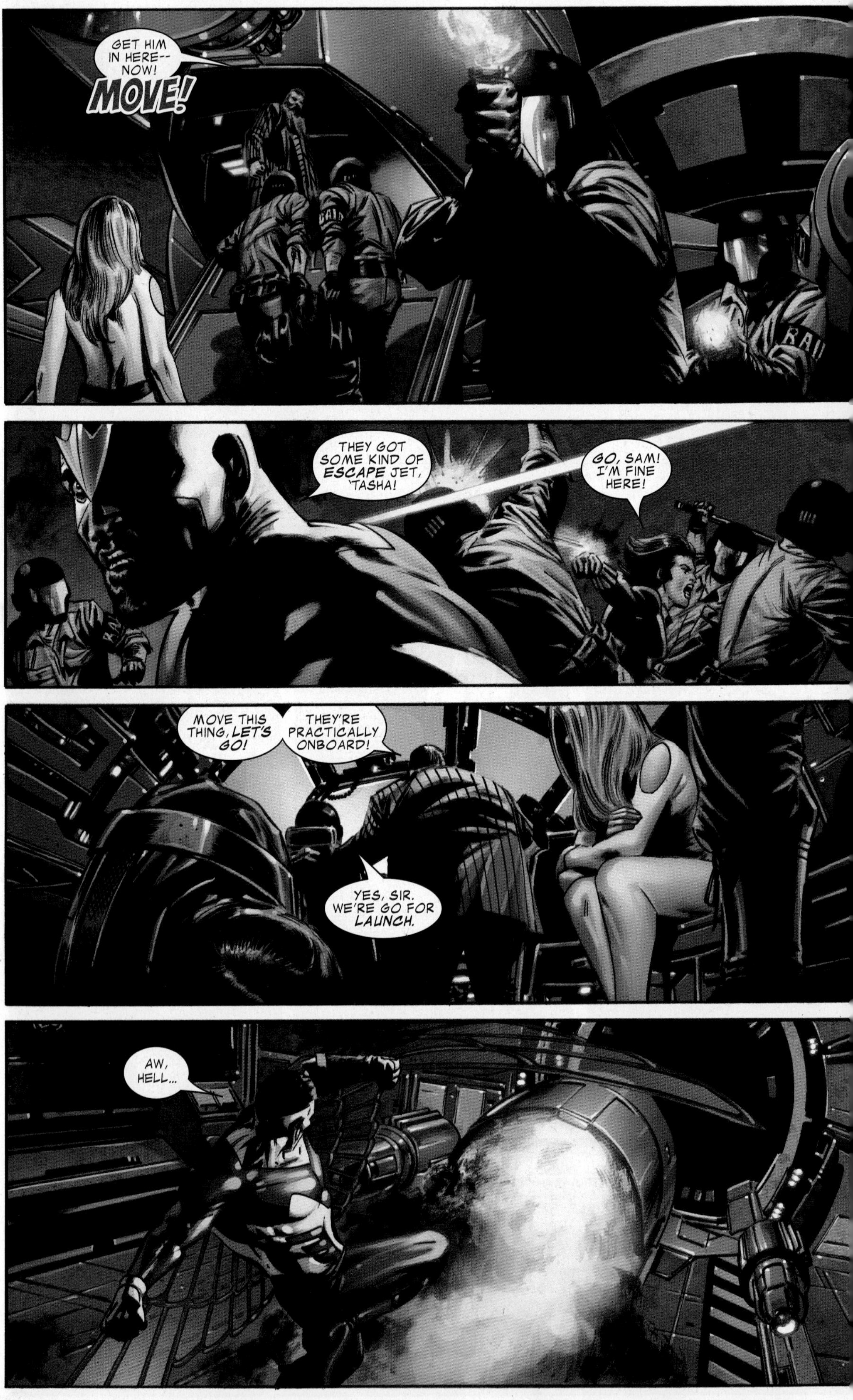
GET HIM IN HERE-- NOW!
MOVE!
THEY GOT SOME KIND OF ESCAPE JET, 'TASHA!
GO, SAM! I'M FINE HERE!
MOVE THIS THING, LET'S GO!
THEY'RE PRACTICALLY ONBOARD!
YES, SIR. WE'RE GO FOR LAUNCH.
AW, HELL...

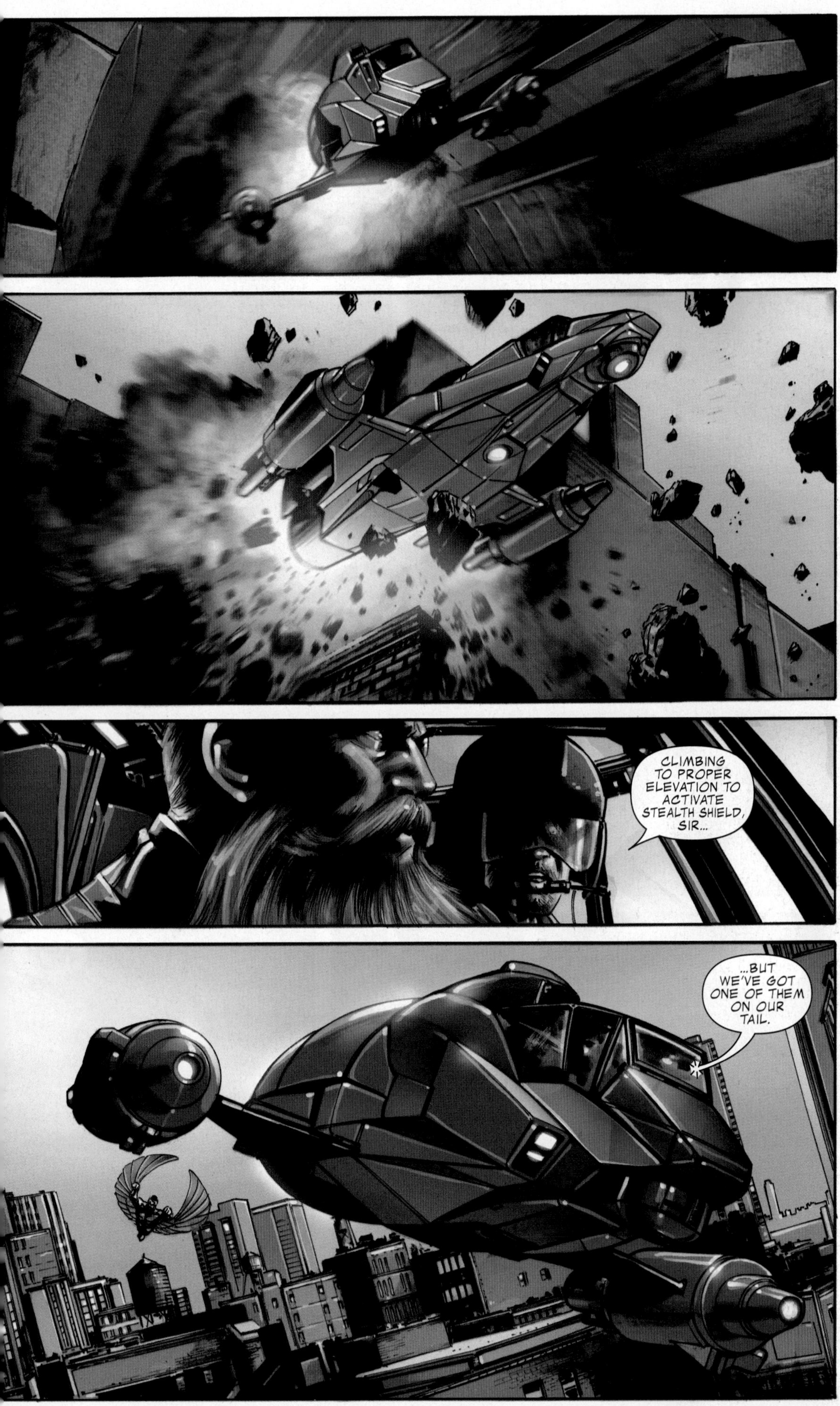
CLIMBING TO PROPER ELEVATION TO ACTIVATE STEALTH SHIELD, SIR...
...BUT WE'VE GOT ONE OF THEM ON OUR TAIL.

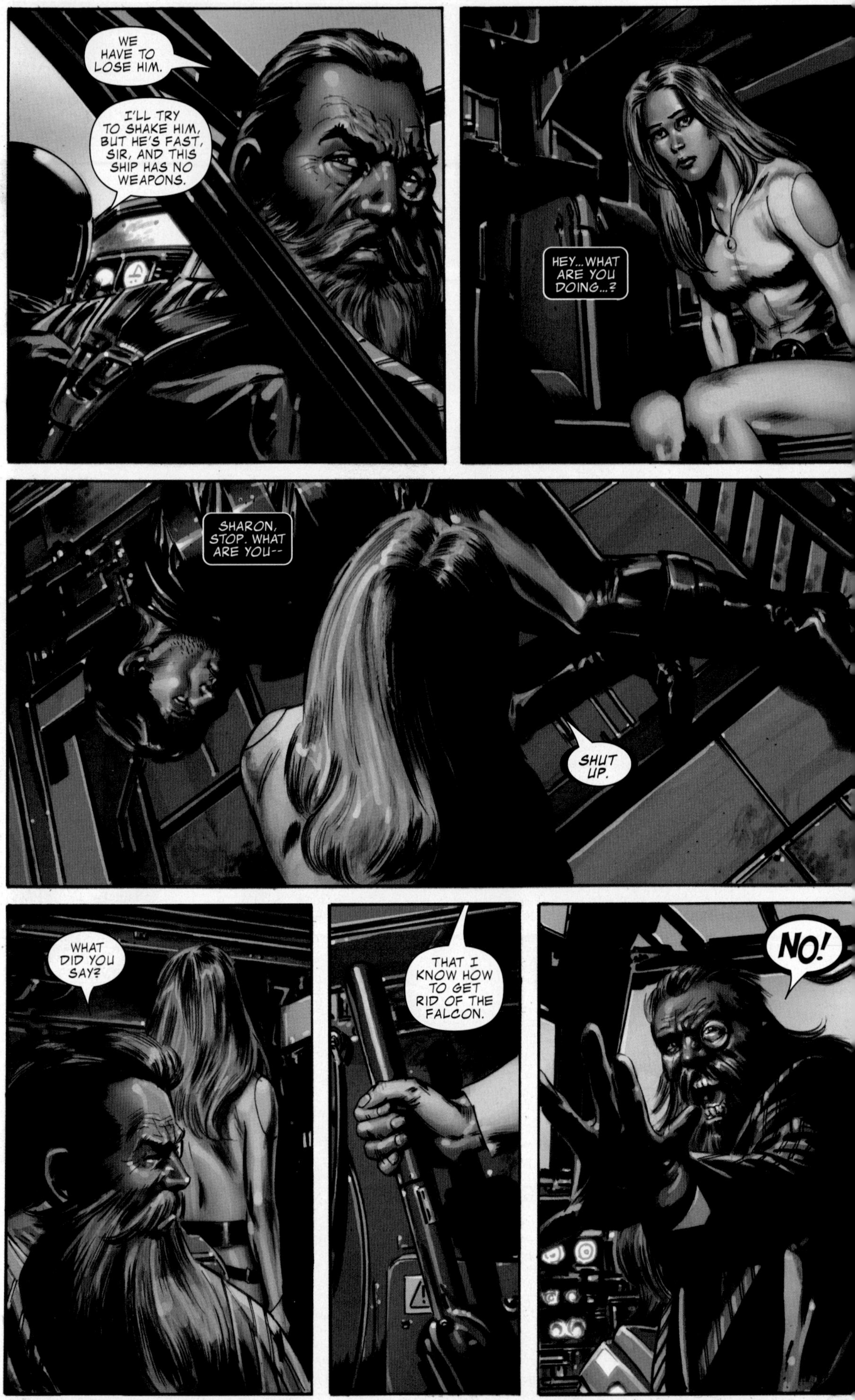
WE HAVE TO LOSE HIM.
I'LL TRY TO SHAKE HIM, BUT HE'S FAST, SIR, AND THIS SHIP HAS NO WEAPONS.
HEY...WHAT ARE YOU DOING...?
SHARON, STOP. WHAT ARE YOU--
SHUT UP.
WHAT DID YOU SAY?
THAT I KNOW HOW TO GET RID OF THE FALCON.
NO!

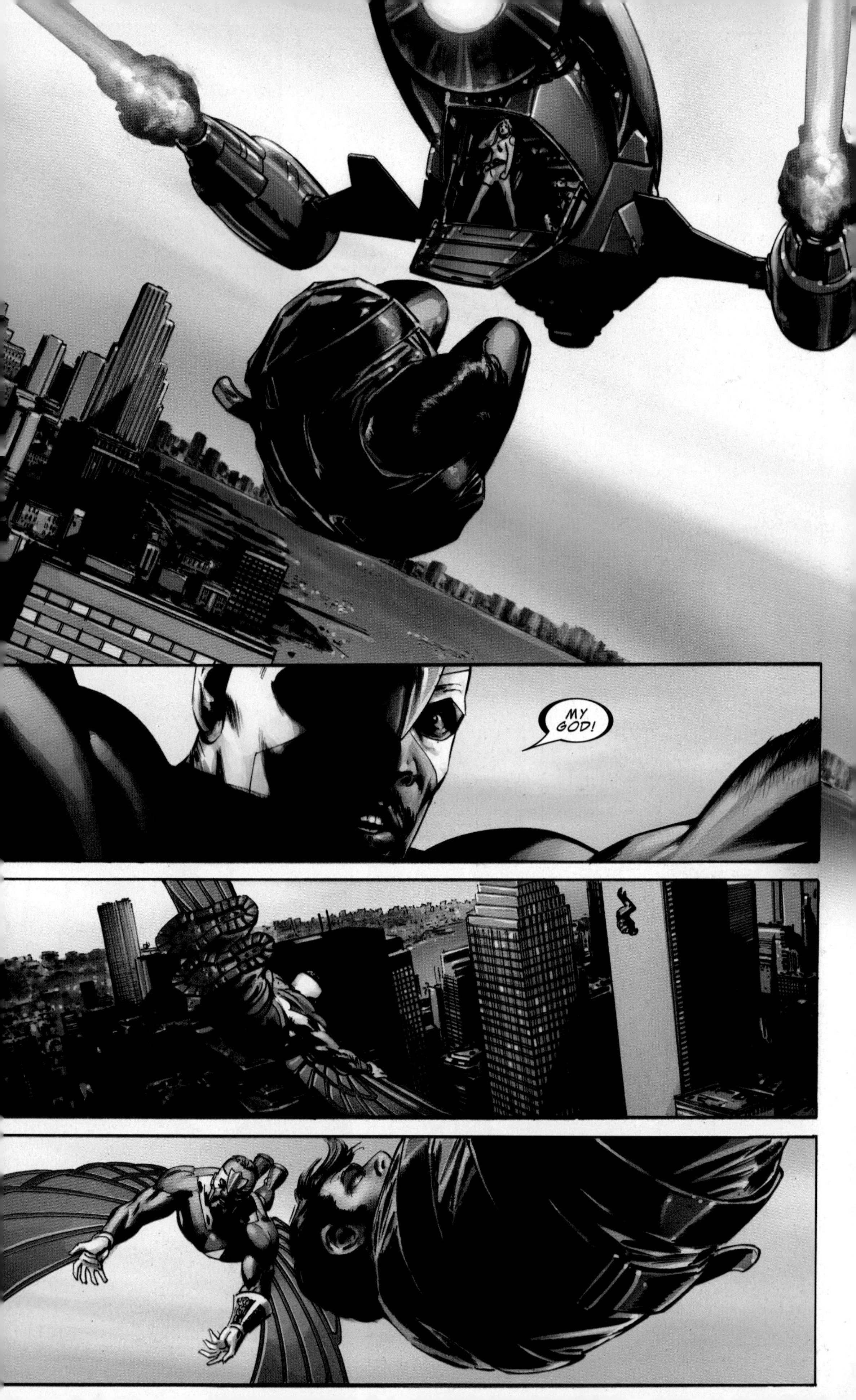
MY GOD!

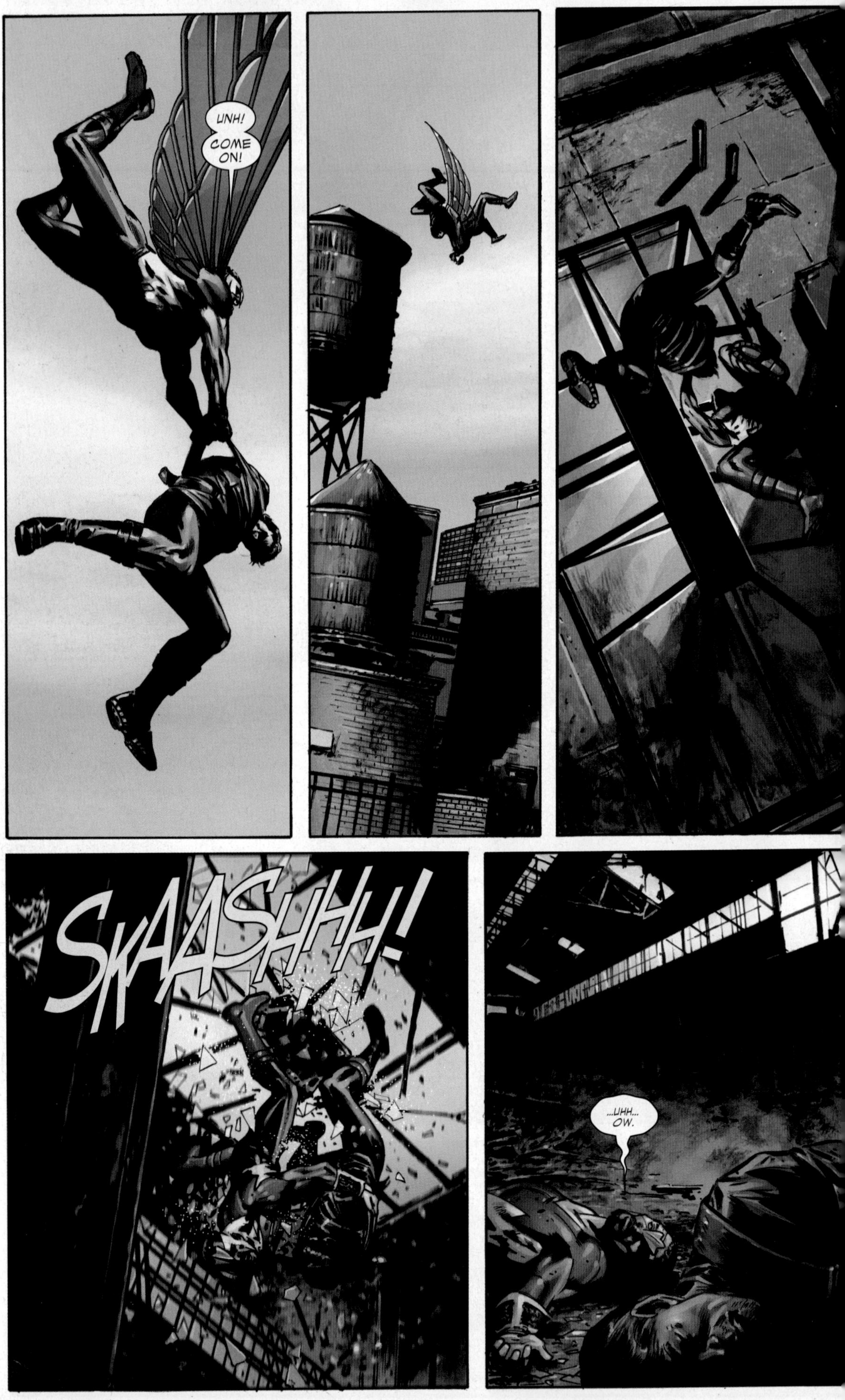
UNH! COME ON!
SKAASHHH!
...UHH... OW.

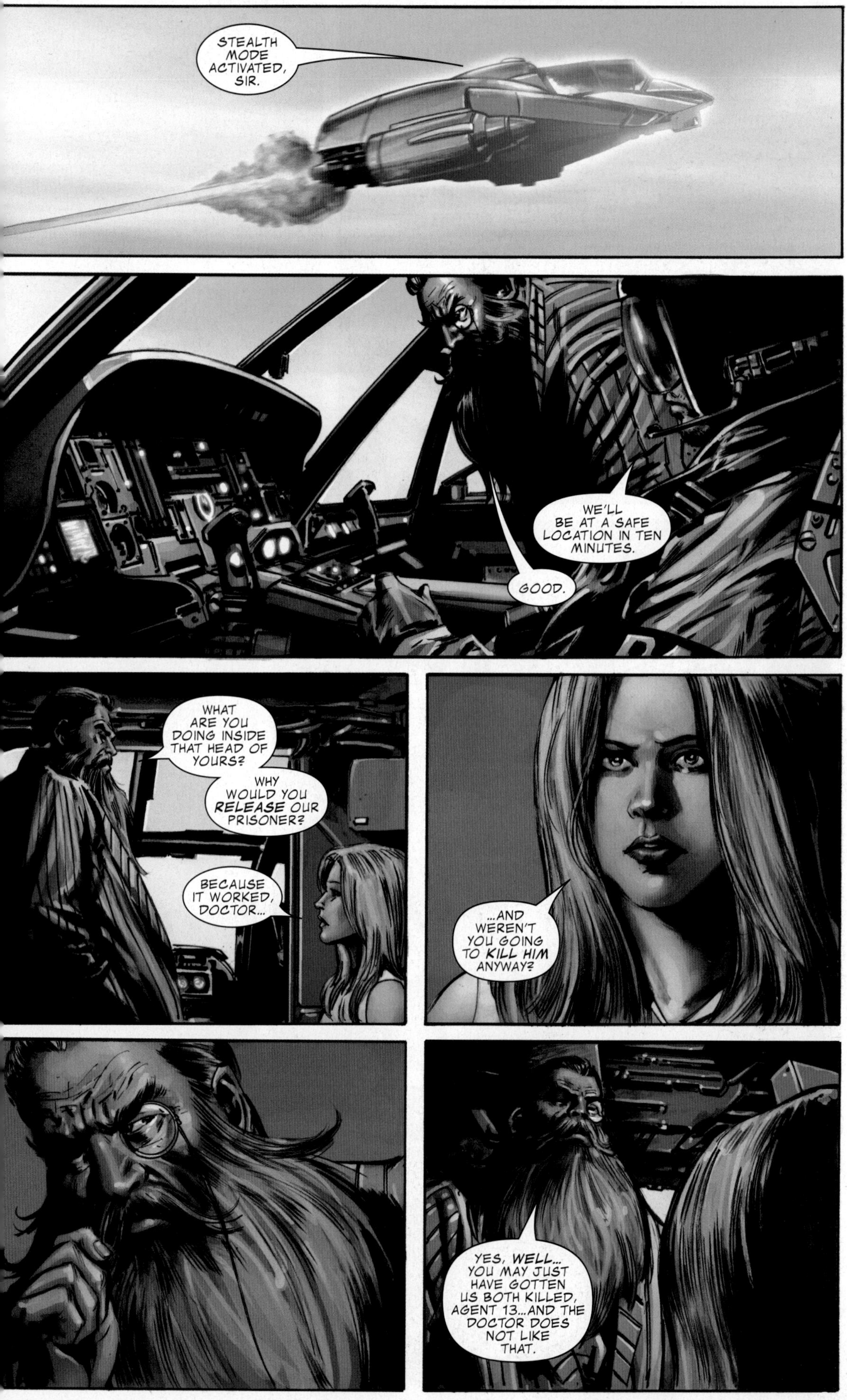
STEALTH MODE ACTIVATED, SIR.
WE'LL BE AT A SAFE LOCATION IN TEN MINUTES.
GOOD.
WHAT ARE YOU DOING INSIDE THAT HEAD OF YOURS?
WHY WOULD YOU *RELEASE* OUR PRISONER?
BECAUSE IT WORKED, DOCTOR...
...AND WEREN'T YOU GOING TO *KILL HIM* ANYWAY?
YES, *WELL*... YOU MAY JUST HAVE GOTTEN US BOTH KILLED, AGENT 13...AND THE DOCTOR DOES NOT LIKE THAT.

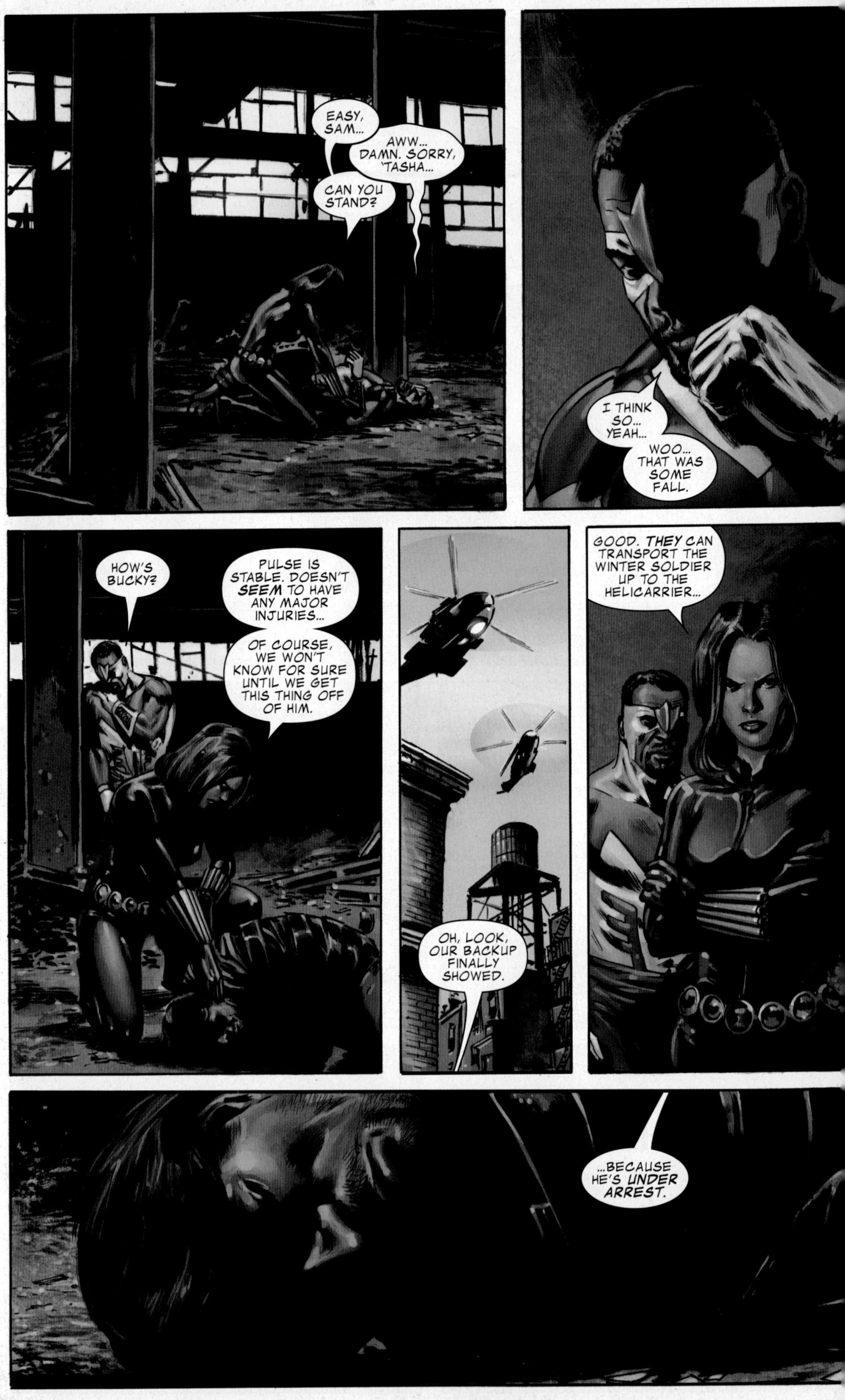
EASY, SAM...
AWW... DAMN. SORRY, 'TASHA...
CAN YOU STAND?
I THINK SO... YEAH...
WOO... THAT WAS SOME FALL.
HOW'S BUCKY?
PULSE IS STABLE. DOESN'T SEEM TO HAVE ANY MAJOR INJURIES...
OF COURSE, WE WON'T KNOW FOR SURE UNTIL WE GET THIS THING OFF OF HIM.
OH, LOOK, OUR BACKUP FINALLY SHOWED.
GOOD. THEY CAN TRANSPORT THE WINTER SOLDIER UP TO THE HELICARRIER...
...BECAUSE HE'S UNDER ARREST.

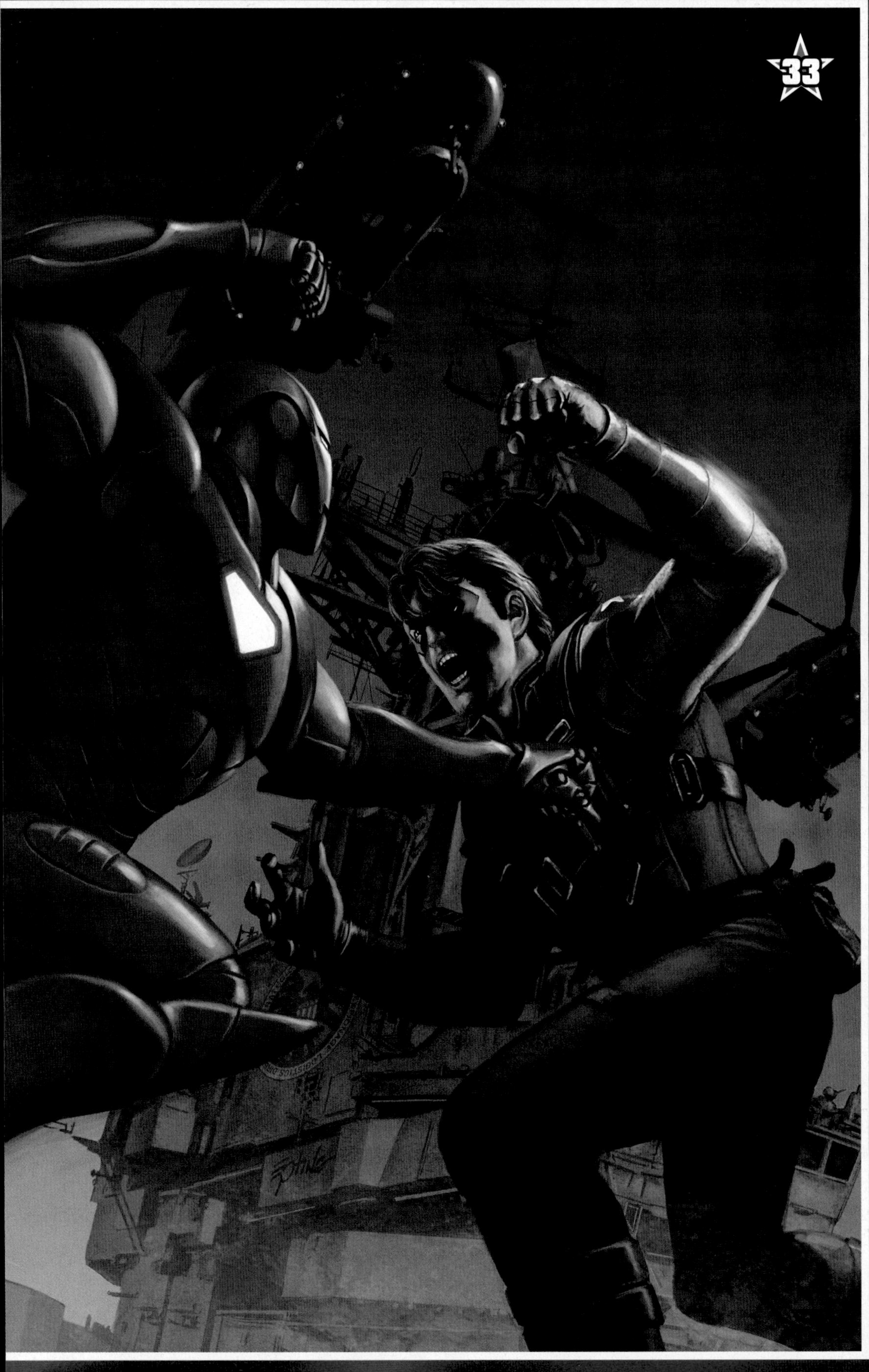

PART THREE

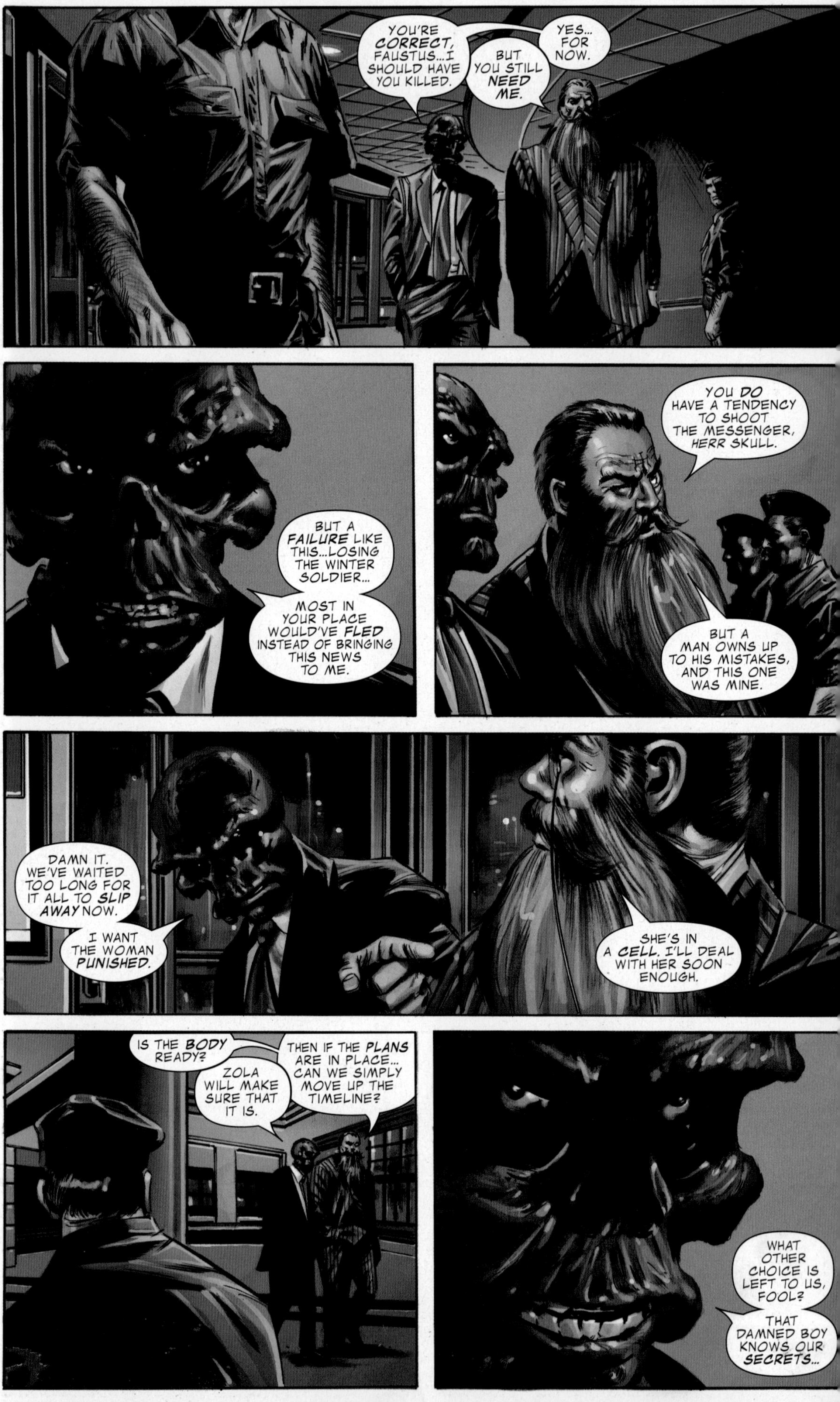
YOU'RE CORRECT, FAUSTUS...I SHOULD HAVE YOU KILLED.
BUT YOU STILL NEED ME.
YES... FOR NOW.
BUT A FAILURE LIKE THIS...LOSING THE WINTER SOLDIER...
MOST IN YOUR PLACE WOULD'VE FLED INSTEAD OF BRINGING THIS NEWS TO ME.
YOU DO HAVE A TENDENCY TO SHOOT THE MESSENGER, HERR SKULL.
BUT A MAN OWNS UP TO HIS MISTAKES, AND THIS ONE WAS MINE.
DAMN IT. WE'VE WAITED TOO LONG FOR IT ALL TO SLIP AWAY NOW.
I WANT THE WOMAN PUNISHED.
SHE'S IN A CELL. I'LL DEAL WITH HER SOON ENOUGH.
IS THE BODY READY?
ZOLA WILL MAKE SURE THAT IT IS.
THEN IF THE PLANS ARE IN PLACE... CAN WE SIMPLY MOVE UP THE TIMELINE?
WHAT OTHER CHOICE IS LEFT TO US, FOOL?
THAT DAMNED BOY KNOWS OUR SECRETS...

"...AND NOW HE'S IN THE HANDS OF THE ENEMY."

THINK IT'S REALLY HIM?

THOUGHT THE GUY WAS A MYTH...FROM, LIKE, THE COLD WAR.

I THINK HE'S KIND OF SEXY.

WHAT IS IT WITH WOMEN? THAT MAN IS A TRAINED KILLER.

OH, AND HALF THE MEN ON BOARD THE HELICARRIER AREN'T?

NOT LIKE THIS ONE.

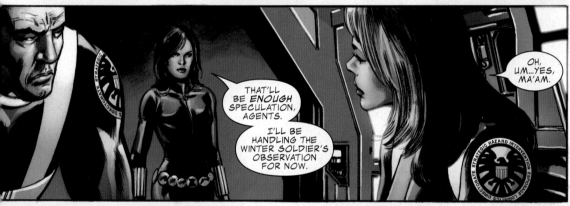

THAT'LL BE ENOUGH SPECULATION, AGENTS.

I'LL BE HANDLING THE WINTER SOLDIER'S OBSERVATION FOR NOW.

OH, UM...YES, MA'AM.

AND OF COURSE, NOW THAT WE'VE GOT YOU HERE, THE REAL QUESTION IS...

...WHAT ON EARTH ARE WE GOING TO DO WITH YOU, MILII MOI?

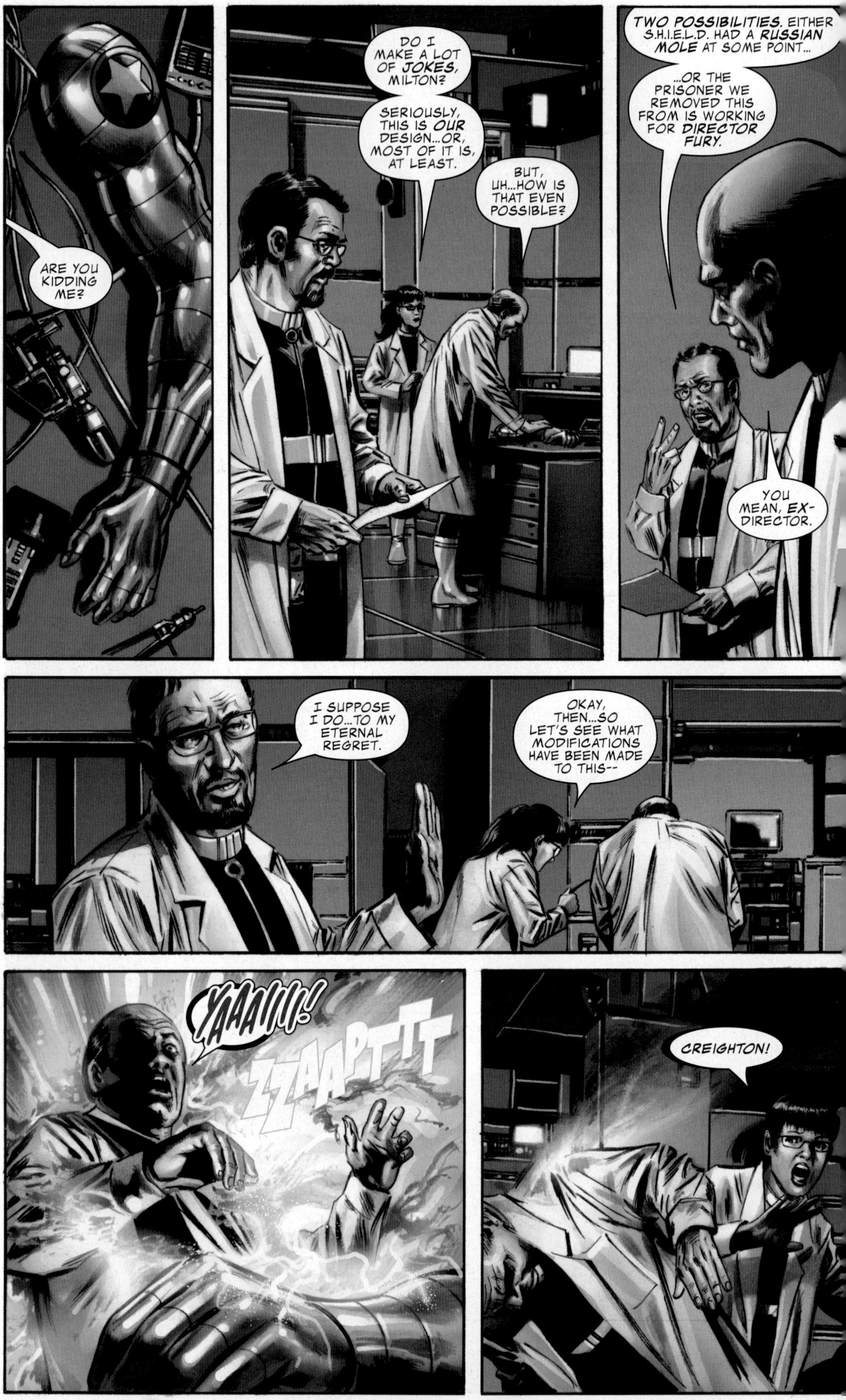
ARE YOU KIDDING ME?
DO I MAKE A LOT OF JOKES, MILTON?
SERIOUSLY, THIS IS OUR DESIGN...OR, MOST OF IT IS, AT LEAST.
BUT, UH...HOW IS THAT EVEN POSSIBLE?
TWO POSSIBILITIES. EITHER S.H.I.E.L.D. HAD A RUSSIAN MOLE AT SOME POINT...
...OR THE PRISONER WE REMOVED THIS FROM IS WORKING FOR DIRECTOR FURY.
YOU MEAN, EX-DIRECTOR.
I SUPPOSE I DO...TO MY ETERNAL REGRET.
OKAY, THEN...SO LET'S SEE WHAT MODIFICATIONS HAVE BEEN MADE TO THIS--
YAAAIIII!
ZZAAPTTT
CREIGHTON!

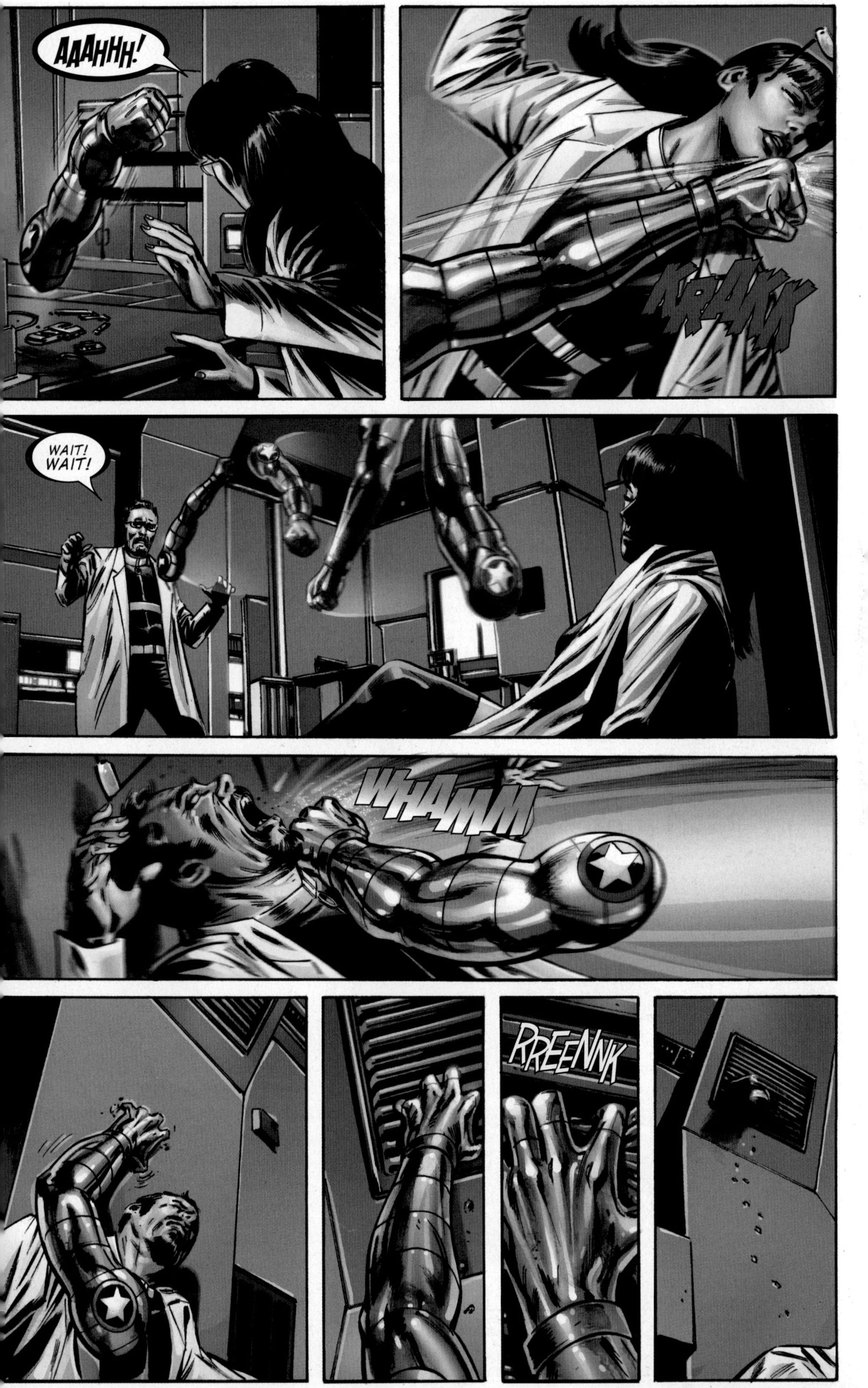
AAAHHH!
KRAKK
WAIT! WAIT!
WHAMM
RREENNK

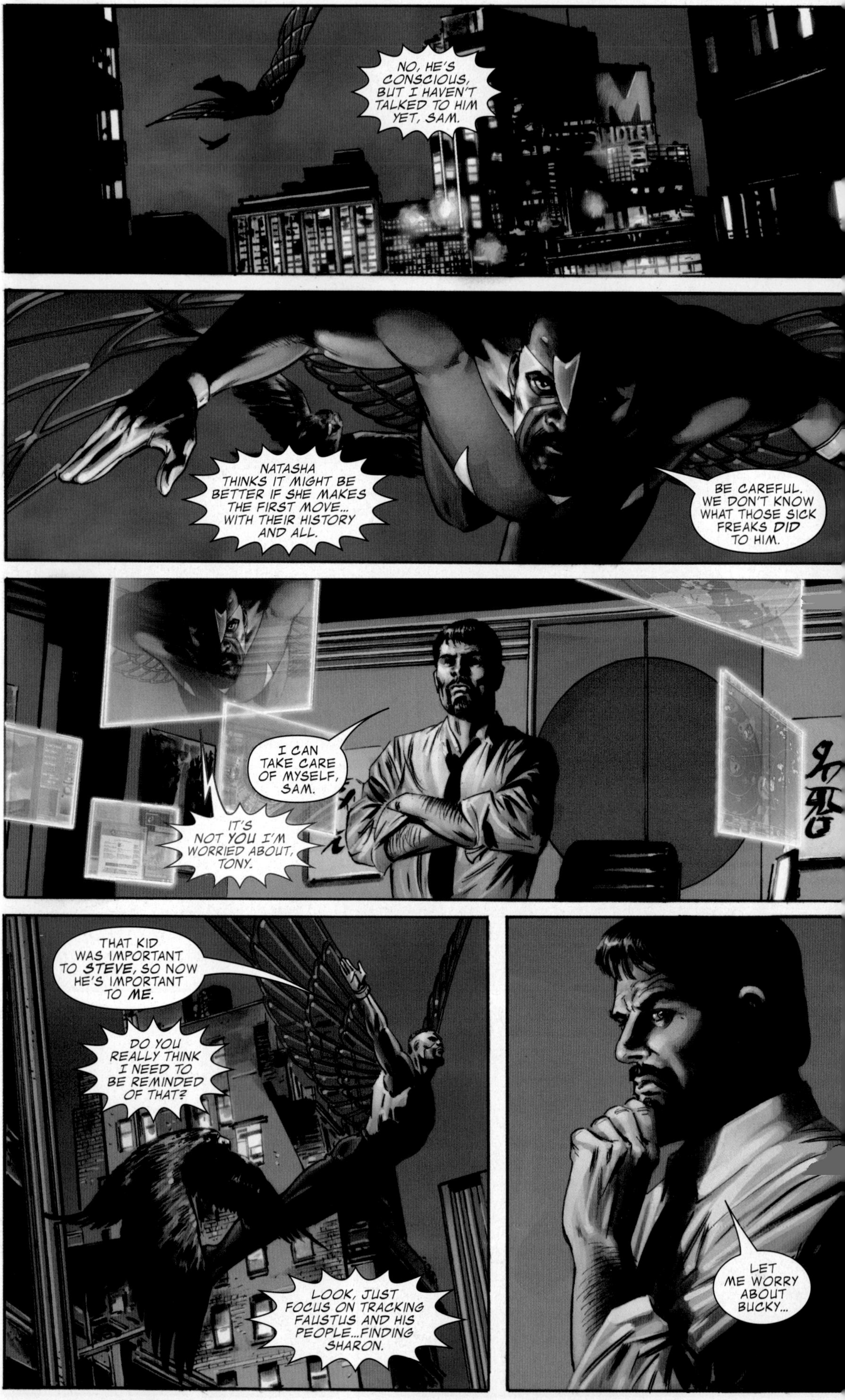

NO, HE'S CONSCIOUS, BUT I HAVEN'T TALKED TO HIM YET, SAM.
NATASHA THINKS IT MIGHT BE BETTER IF SHE MAKES THE FIRST MOVE... WITH THEIR HISTORY AND ALL.
BE CAREFUL. WE DON'T KNOW WHAT THOSE SICK FREAKS DID TO HIM.
I CAN TAKE CARE OF MYSELF, SAM.
IT'S NOT YOU I'M WORRIED ABOUT, TONY.
THAT KID WAS IMPORTANT TO STEVE, SO NOW HE'S IMPORTANT TO ME.
DO YOU REALLY THINK I NEED TO BE REMINDED OF THAT?
LOOK, JUST FOCUS ON TRACKING FAUSTUS AND HIS PEOPLE...FINDING SHARON.
LET ME WORRY ABOUT BUCKY...

POWER GRID FLUCTUATION-- LEVELS TWO, THREE, AND SEVEN.

DAMN IT. NATASHA, WHAT'S GOING ON DOWN THERE?

THE LIGHTS WENT OUT FOR A SECOND AND NOW MY SCREENS ARE ALL STATIC.

COMMS ARE SPOTTY THROUGHOUT THE WHOLE LEVEL. NO VIDEO FEED.

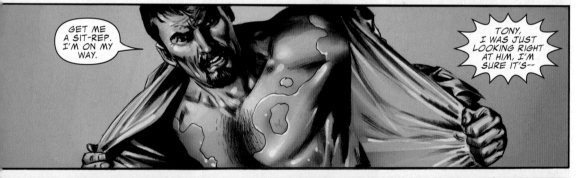

GET ME A SIT-REP. I'M ON MY WAY.

TONY, I WAS JUST LOOKING RIGHT AT HIM, I'M SURE IT'S--

--NOTHING...

LEVEL SEVEN

SECURE HOLDING

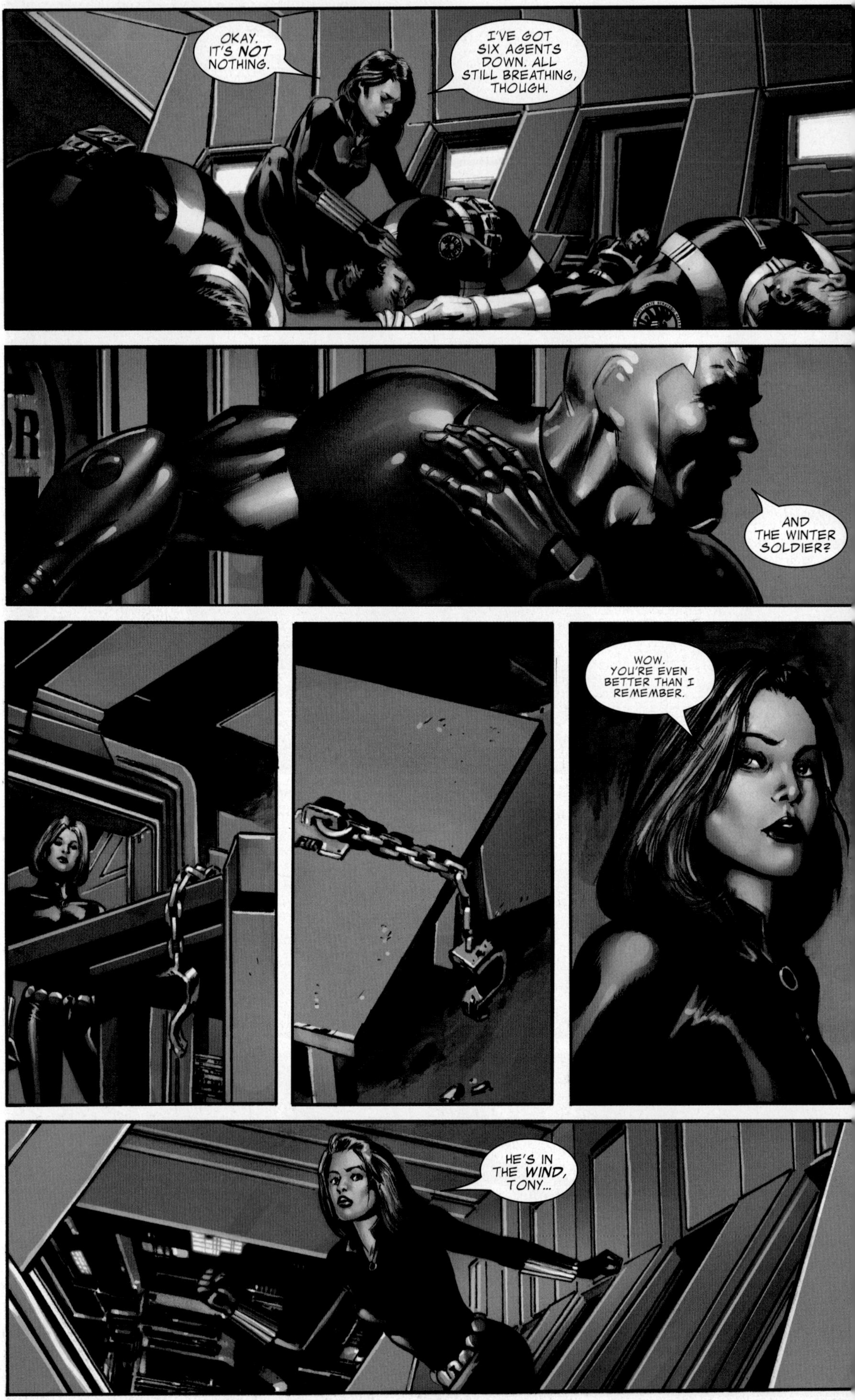
OKAY. IT'S NOT NOTHING.
I'VE GOT SIX AGENTS DOWN. ALL STILL BREATHING, THOUGH.
AND THE WINTER SOLDIER?
WOW. YOU'RE EVEN BETTER THAN I REMEMBER.
HE'S IN THE WIND, TONY...

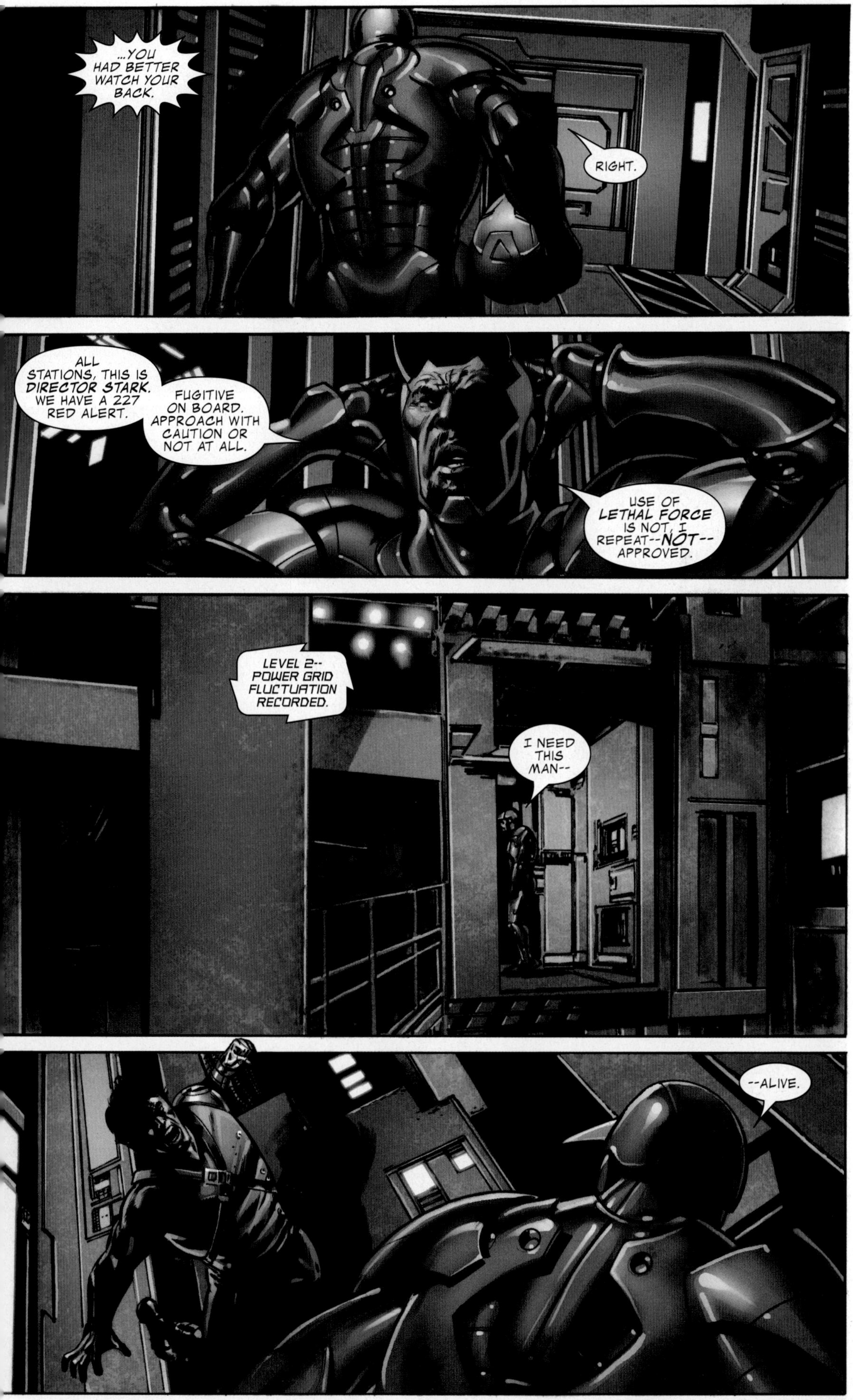
...YOU HAD BETTER WATCH YOUR BACK.
RIGHT.
ALL STATIONS, THIS IS DIRECTOR STARK. WE HAVE A 227 RED ALERT.
FUGITIVE ON BOARD. APPROACH WITH CAUTION OR NOT AT ALL.
USE OF LETHAL FORCE IS NOT, I REPEAT--NOT--APPROVED.
LEVEL 2--POWER GRID FLUCTUATION RECORDED.
I NEED THIS MAN--
--ALIVE.

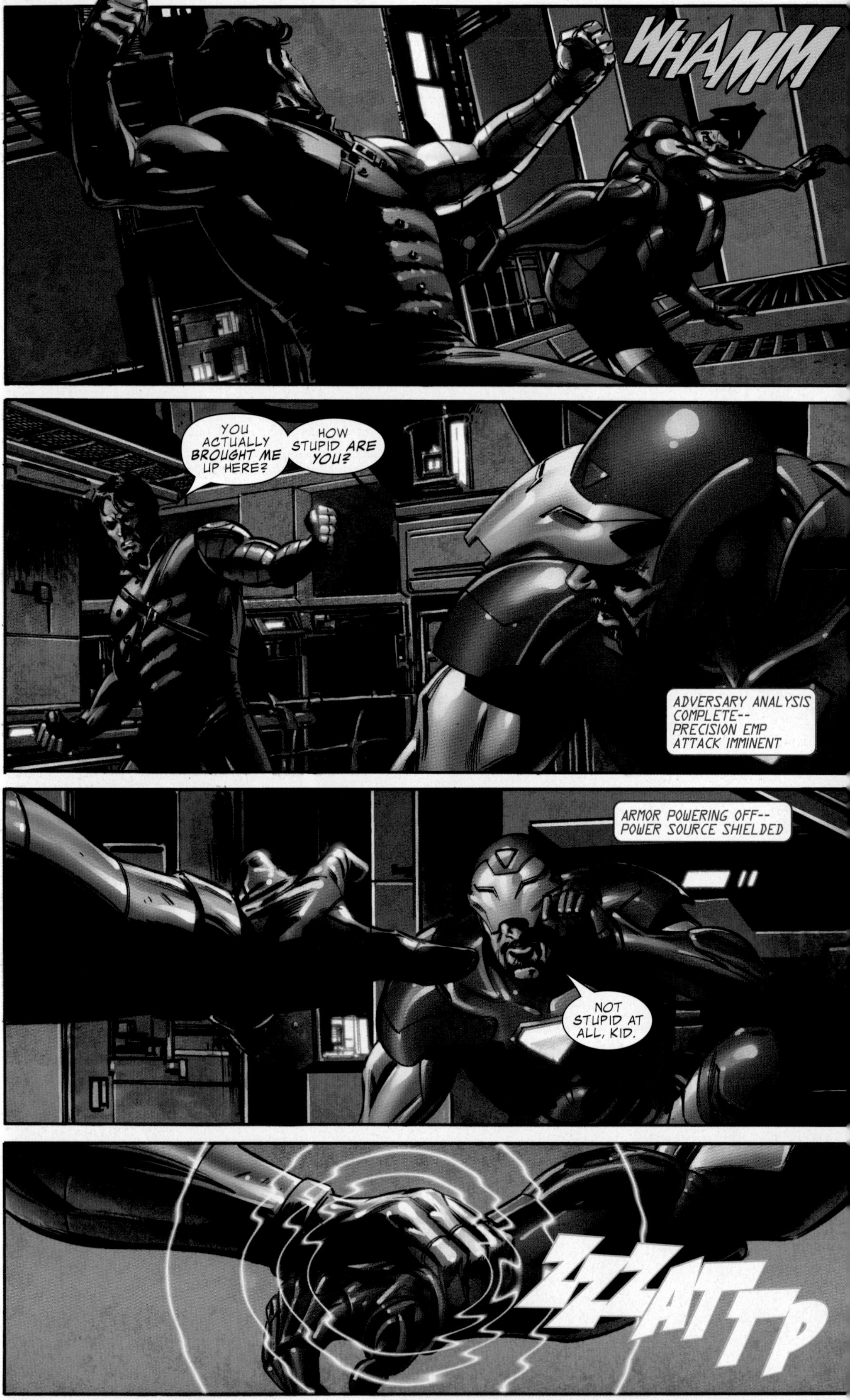
WHAMM
YOU ACTUALLY BROUGHT ME UP HERE?
HOW STUPID ARE YOU?
ADVERSARY ANALYSIS COMPLETE-- PRECISION EMP ATTACK IMMINENT
ARMOR POWERING OFF-- POWER SOURCE SHIELDED
NOT STUPID AT ALL, KID.
ZZZATTTP

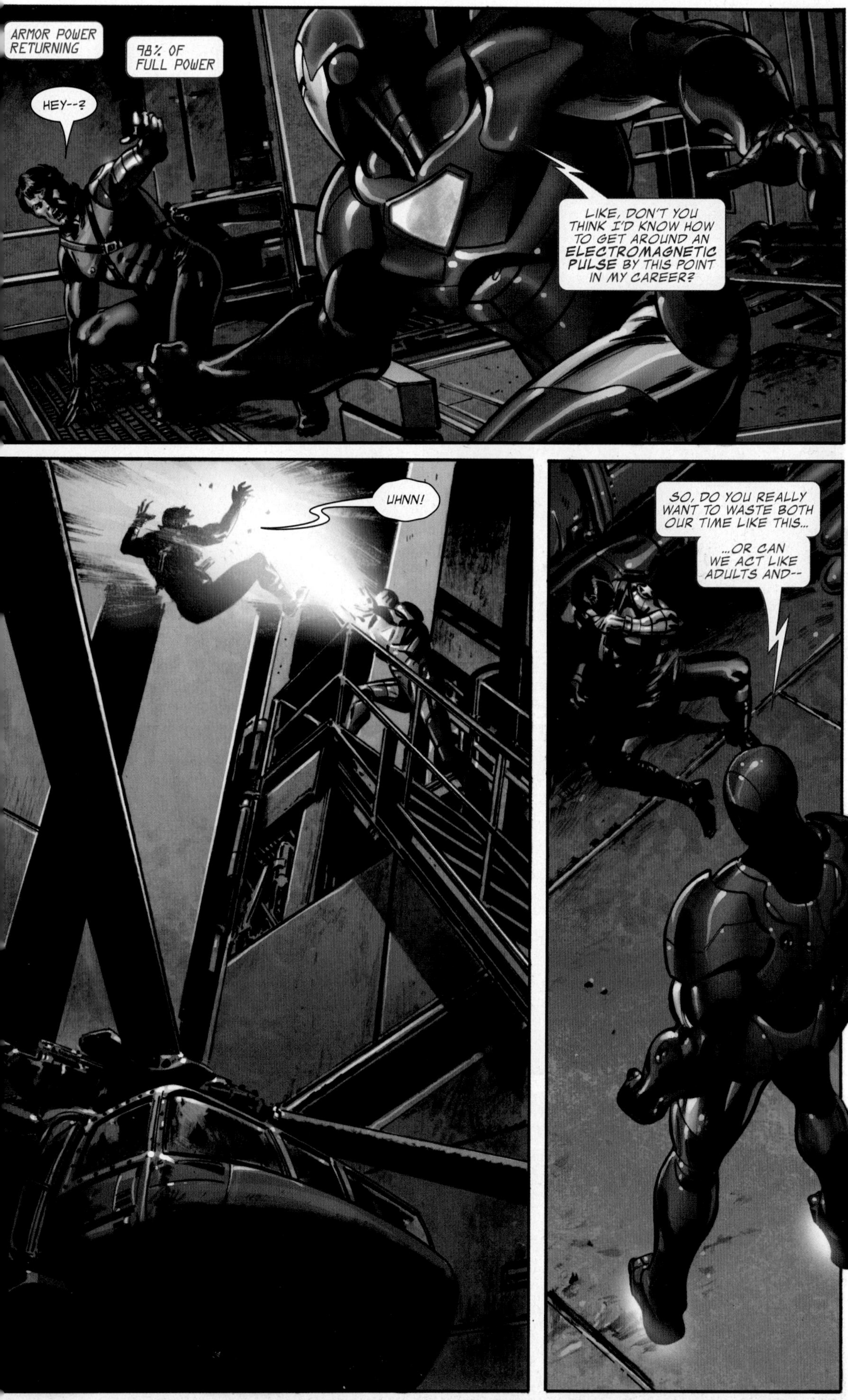
ARMOR POWER RETURNING
98% OF FULL POWER
HEY--?
LIKE, DON'T YOU THINK I'D KNOW HOW TO GET AROUND AN **ELECTROMAGNETIC PULSE** BY THIS POINT IN MY CAREER?
UHNN!
SO, DO YOU REALLY WANT TO WASTE BOTH OUR TIME LIKE THIS...
...OR CAN WE ACT LIKE ADULTS AND--

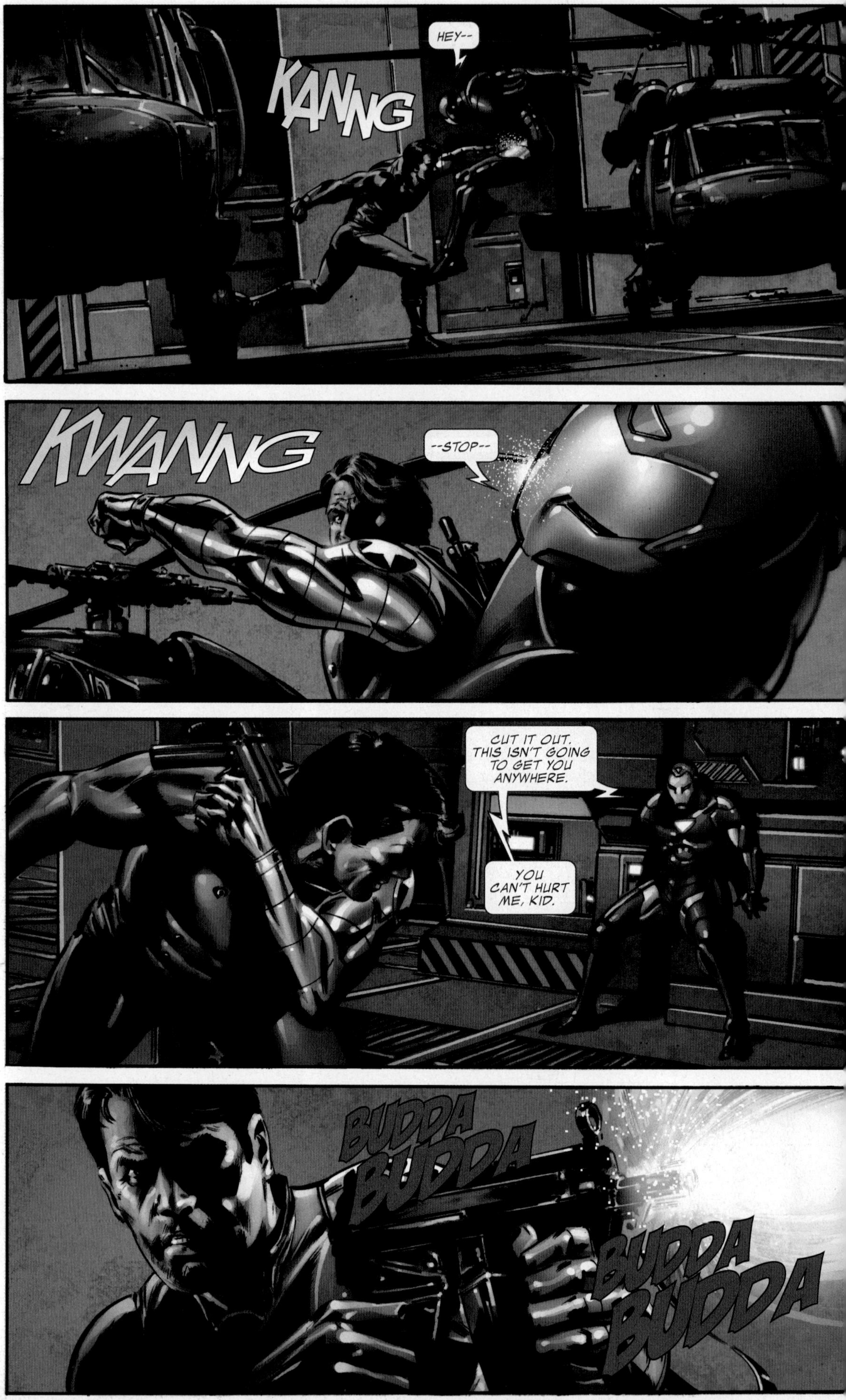
HEY--
KANNG
KWANNG
--STOP--
CUT IT OUT. THIS ISN'T GOING TO GET YOU ANYWHERE.
YOU CAN'T HURT ME, KID.
BUDDA BUDDA
BUDDA BUDDA

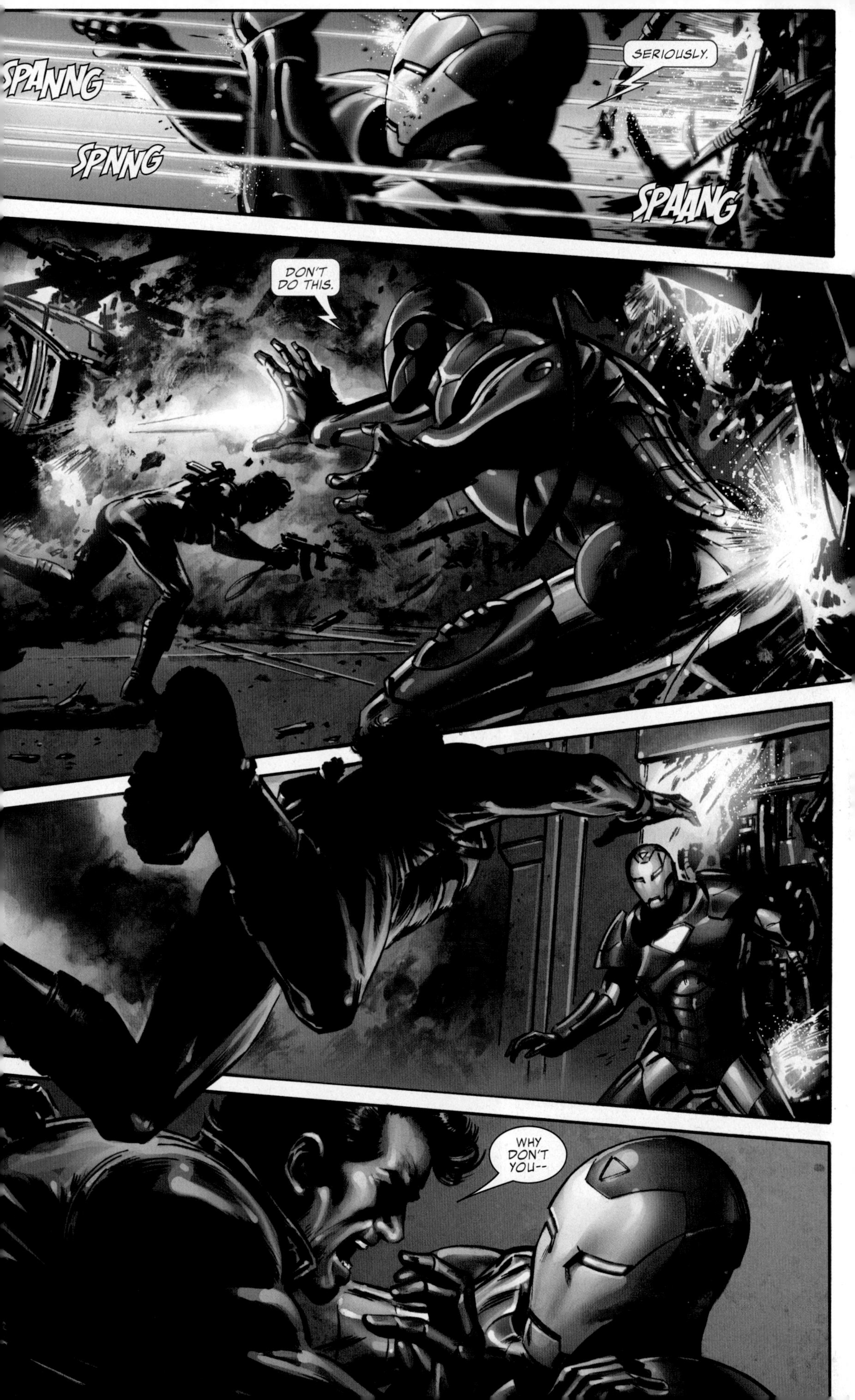
SPANNG
SPNNG
SERIOUSLY.
SPAANG
DON'T DO THIS.
WHY DON'T YOU--

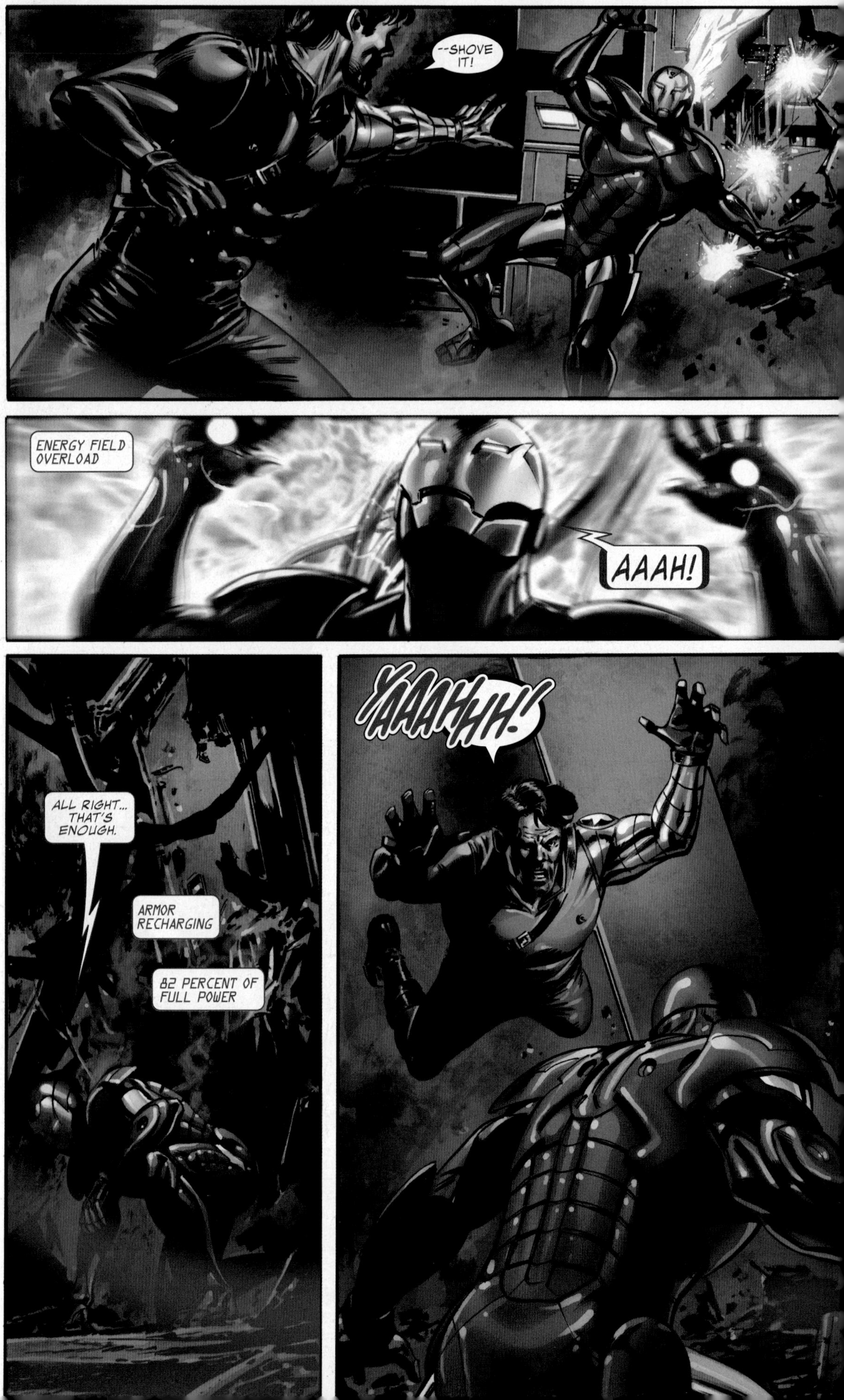
--SHOVE IT!
ENERGY FIELD OVERLOAD
AAAH!
ALL RIGHT... THAT'S ENOUGH.
ARMOR RECHARGING
82 PERCENT OF FULL POWER
YAAAKHH!

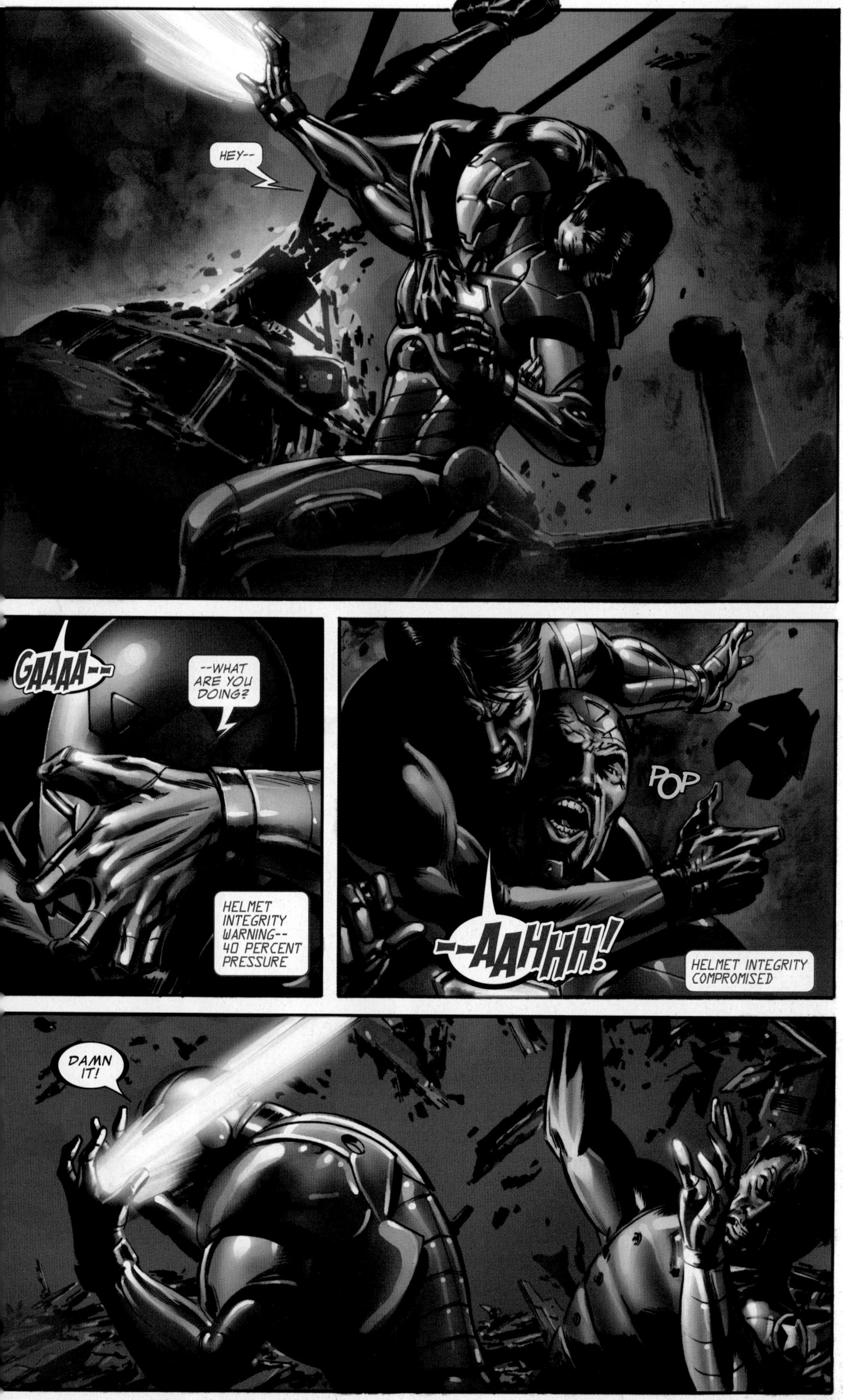
HEY--
GAAAA--
--WHAT ARE YOU DOING?
HELMET INTEGRITY WARNING--40 PERCENT PRESSURE
POP
--AAHHH!
HELMET INTEGRITY COMPROMISED
DAMN IT!

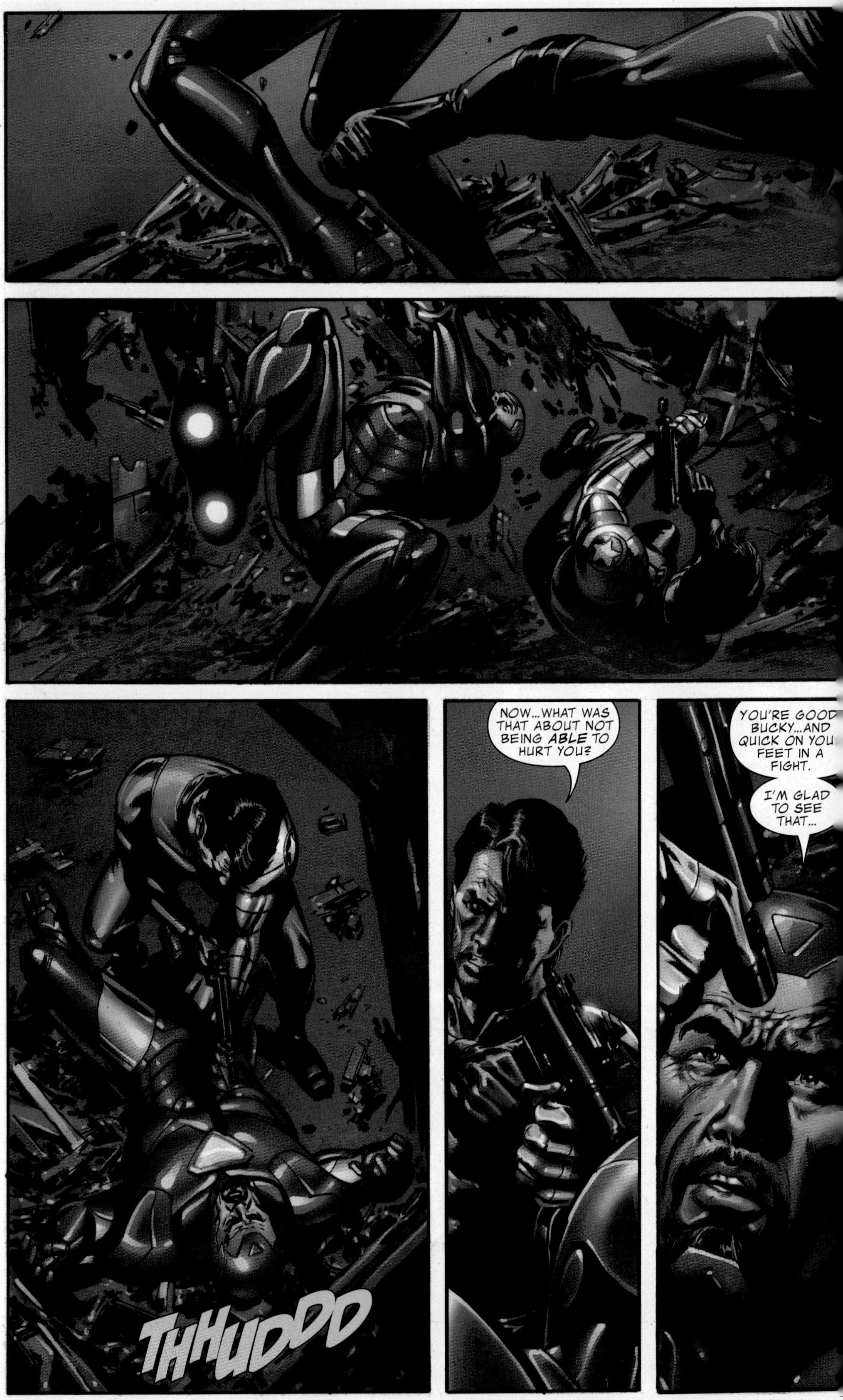
THHUDDD
NOW...WHAT WAS THAT ABOUT NOT BEING ABLE TO HURT YOU?
YOU'RE GOOD BUCKY...AND QUICK ON YOU FEET IN A FIGHT.
I'M GLAD TO SEE THAT...

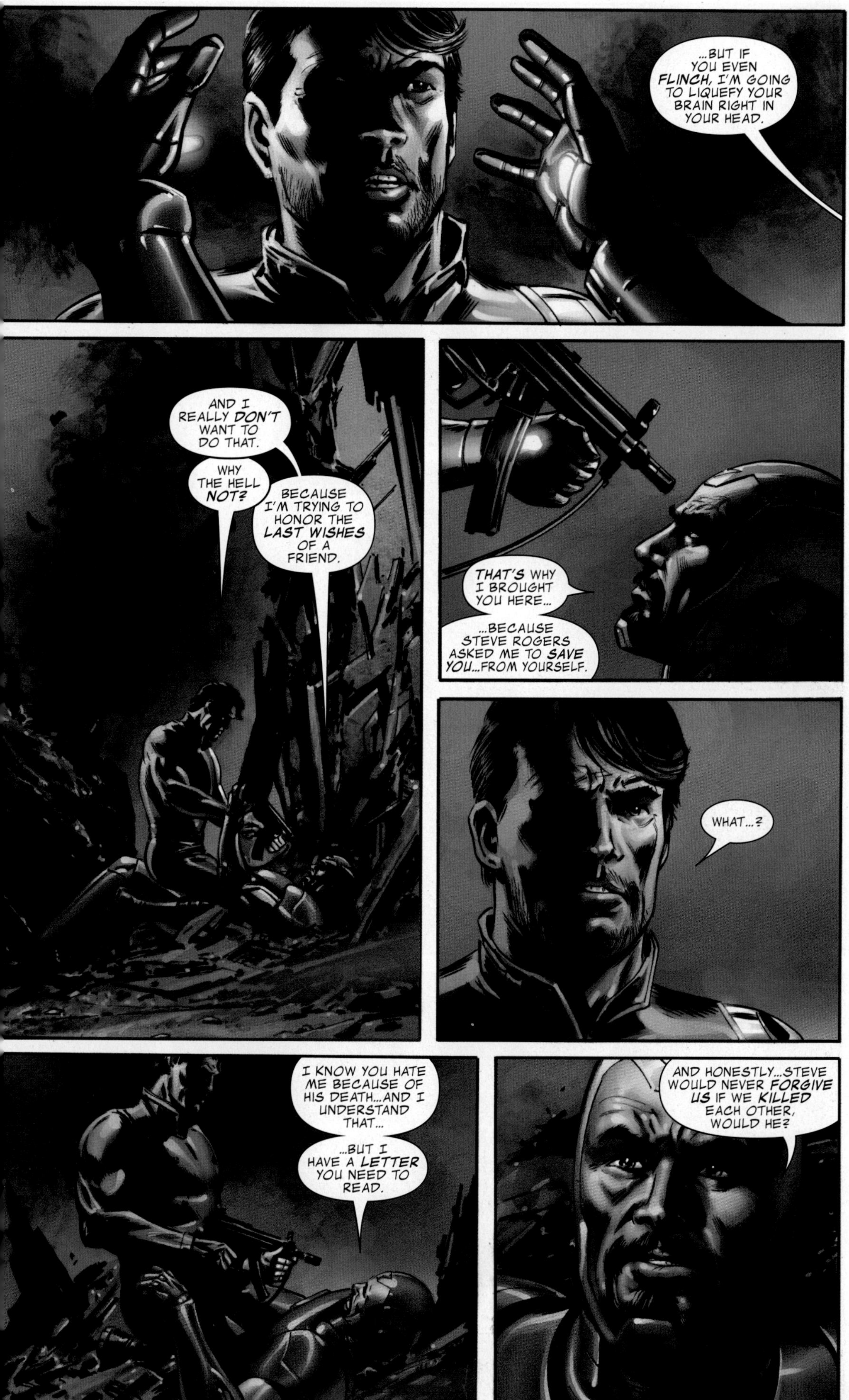
...BUT IF YOU EVEN FLINCH, I'M GOING TO LIQUEFY YOUR BRAIN RIGHT IN YOUR HEAD.
AND I REALLY DON'T WANT TO DO THAT.
WHY THE HELL NOT?
BECAUSE I'M TRYING TO HONOR THE LAST WISHES OF A FRIEND.
THAT'S WHY I BROUGHT YOU HERE...
...BECAUSE STEVE ROGERS ASKED ME TO SAVE YOU...FROM YOURSELF.
WHAT...?
I KNOW YOU HATE ME BECAUSE OF HIS DEATH...AND I UNDERSTAND THAT...
...BUT I HAVE A LETTER YOU NEED TO READ.
AND HONESTLY...STEVE WOULD NEVER FORGIVE US IF WE KILLED EACH OTHER, WOULD HE?

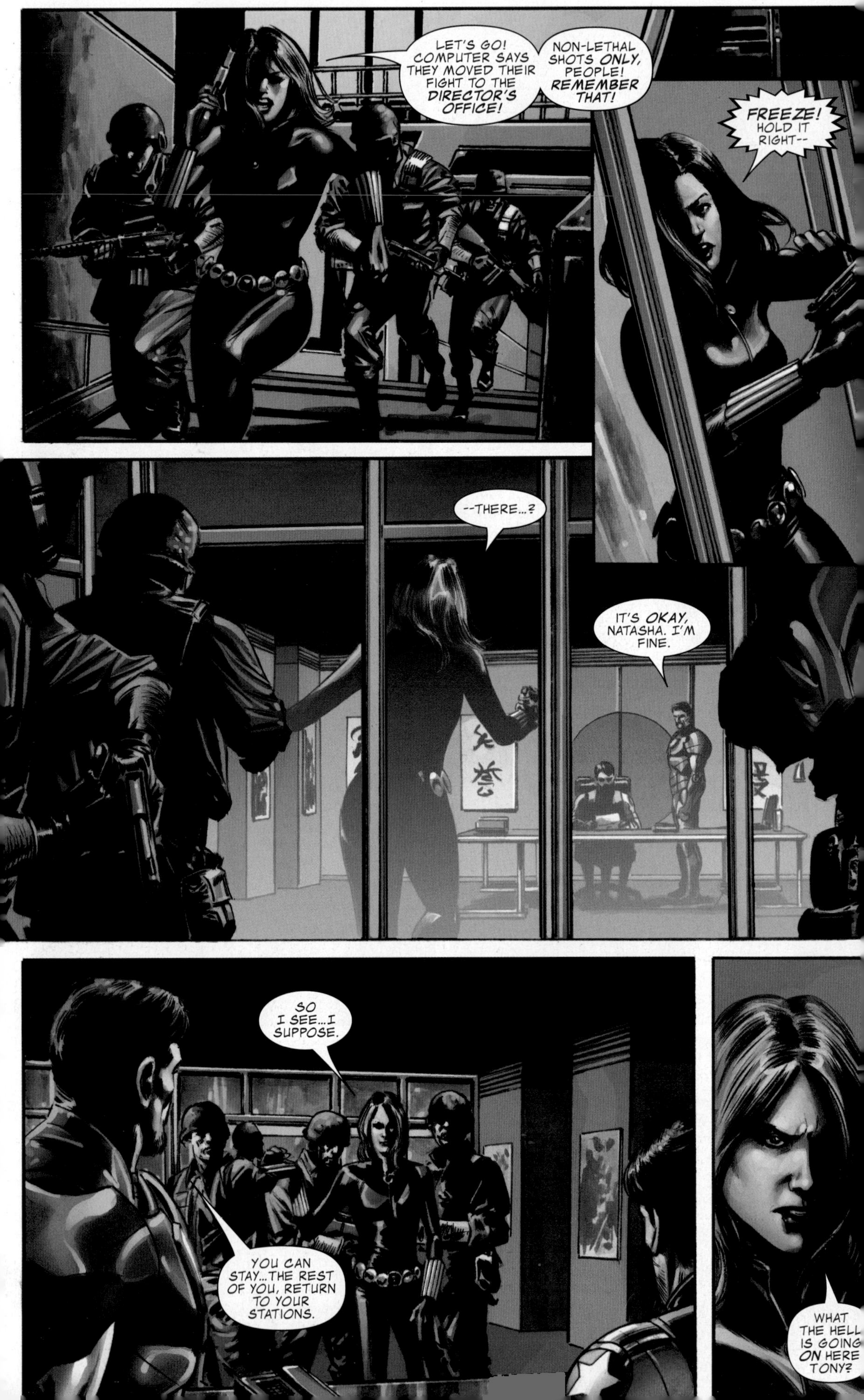
LET'S GO! COMPUTER SAYS THEY MOVED THEIR FIGHT TO THE DIRECTOR'S OFFICE!
NON-LETHAL SHOTS ONLY, PEOPLE! REMEMBER THAT!
FREEZE! HOLD IT RIGHT--
--THERE...?
IT'S OKAY, NATASHA. I'M FINE.
SO I SEE...I SUPPOSE.
YOU CAN STAY...THE REST OF YOU, RETURN TO YOUR STATIONS.
WHAT THE HELL IS GOING ON HERE TONY?

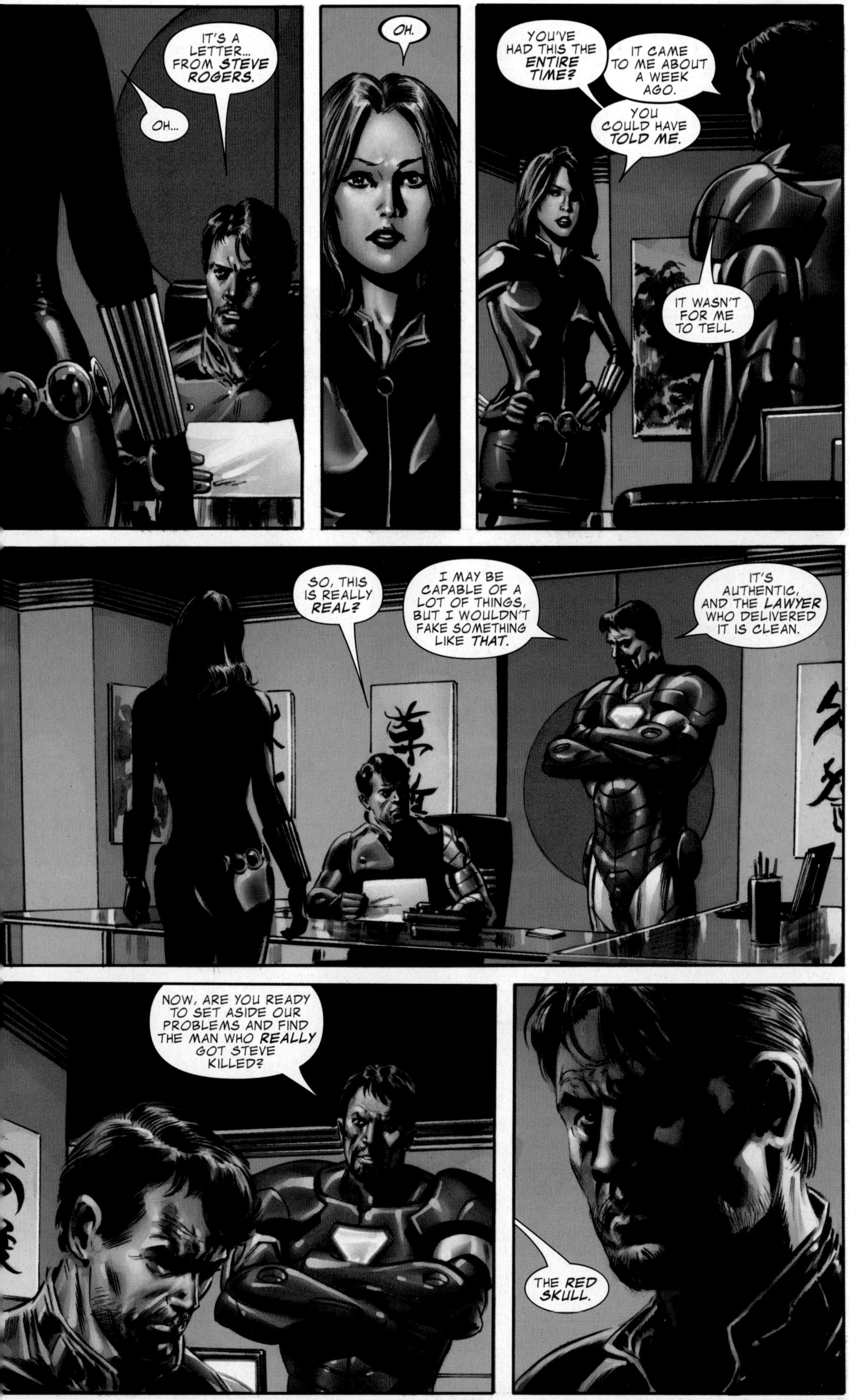

IT'S A LETTER... FROM STEVE ROGERS.
OH...
OH.
YOU'VE HAD THIS THE ENTIRE TIME?
IT CAME TO ME ABOUT A WEEK AGO.
YOU COULD HAVE TOLD ME.
IT WASN'T FOR ME TO TELL.
SO, THIS IS REALLY REAL?
I MAY BE CAPABLE OF A LOT OF THINGS, BUT I WOULDN'T FAKE SOMETHING LIKE THAT.
IT'S AUTHENTIC, AND THE LAWYER WHO DELIVERED IT IS CLEAN.
NOW, ARE YOU READY TO SET ASIDE OUR PROBLEMS AND FIND THE MAN WHO REALLY GOT STEVE KILLED?
THE RED SKULL.

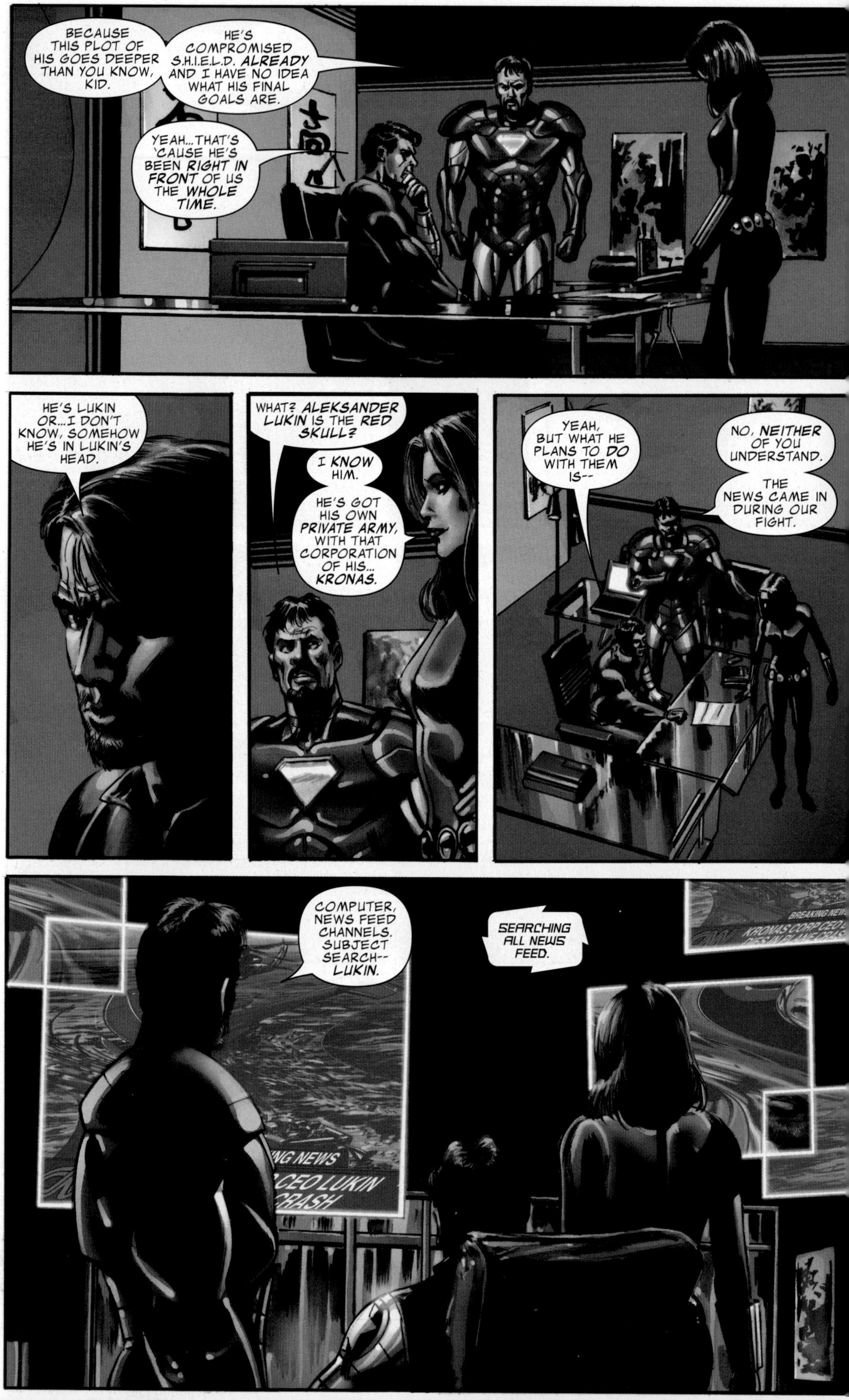
BECAUSE THIS PLOT OF HIS GOES DEEPER THAN YOU KNOW, KID.
HE'S COMPROMISED S.H.I.E.L.D. ALREADY AND I HAVE NO IDEA WHAT HIS FINAL GOALS ARE.
YEAH...THAT'S 'CAUSE HE'S BEEN RIGHT IN FRONT OF US THE WHOLE TIME.
HE'S LUKIN OR...I DON'T KNOW, SOMEHOW HE'S IN LUKIN'S HEAD.
WHAT? ALEKSANDER LUKIN IS THE RED SKULL?
I KNOW HIM.
HE'S GOT HIS OWN PRIVATE ARMY, WITH THAT CORPORATION OF HIS... KRONAS.
YEAH, BUT WHAT HE PLANS TO DO WITH THEM IS--
NO, NEITHER OF YOU UNDERSTAND.
THE NEWS CAME IN DURING OUR FIGHT.
COMPUTER, NEWS FEED CHANNELS. SUBJECT SEARCH-- LUKIN.
SEARCHING ALL NEWS FEED.
BREAKING NEWS
KRONAS CORP CEO L
DIES IN PLANE CRAS
NG NEWS
CEO LUKIN
CRASH

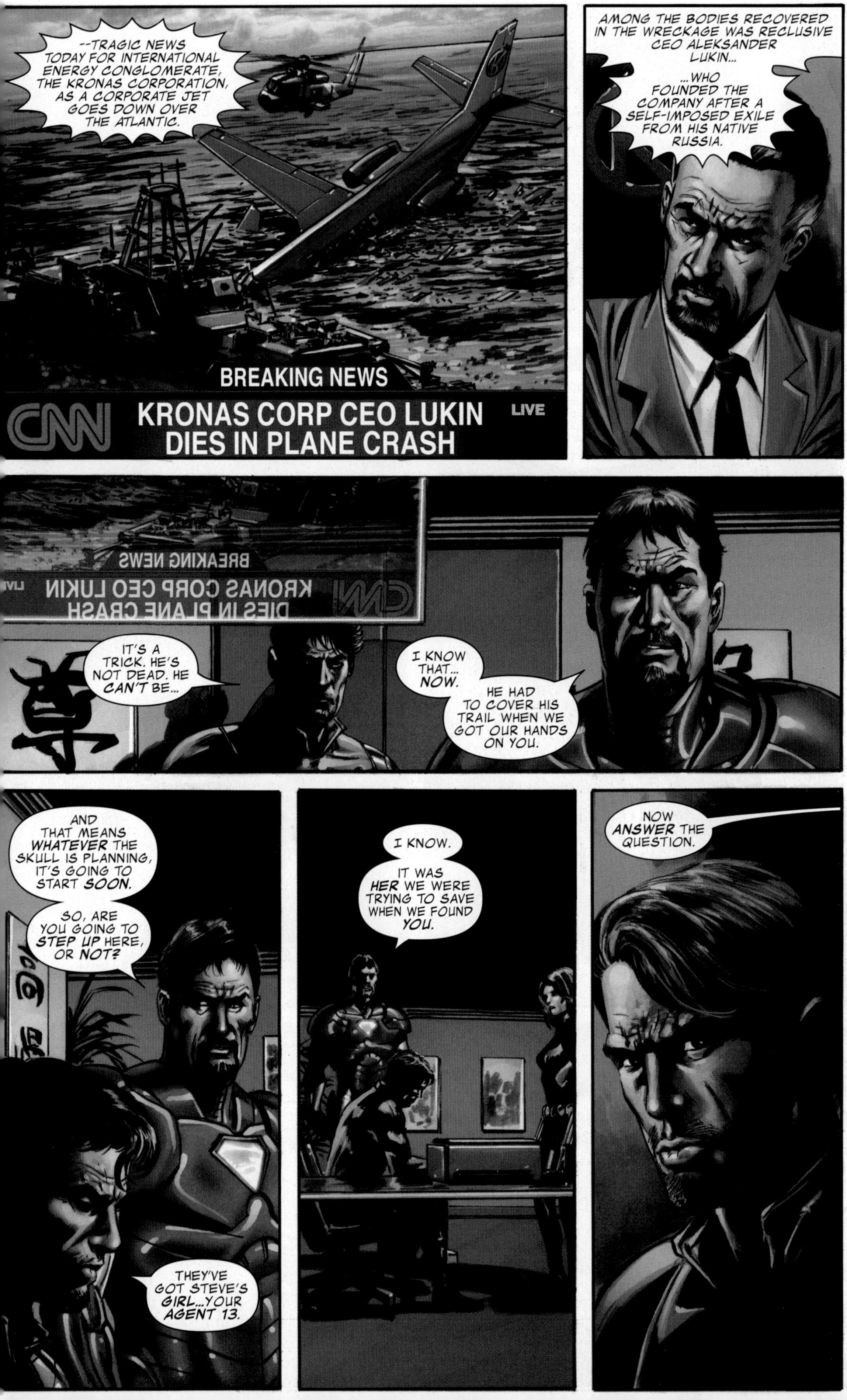
--TRAGIC NEWS TODAY FOR INTERNATIONAL ENERGY CONGLOMERATE, THE KRONAS CORPORATION, AS A CORPORATE JET GOES DOWN OVER THE ATLANTIC.
BREAKING NEWS
CNN
KRONAS CORP CEO LUKIN DIES IN PLANE CRASH
LIVE
AMONG THE BODIES RECOVERED IN THE WRECKAGE WAS RECLUSIVE CEO ALEKSANDER LUKIN...
...WHO FOUNDED THE COMPANY AFTER A SELF-IMPOSED EXILE FROM HIS NATIVE RUSSIA.
IT'S A TRICK. HE'S NOT DEAD. HE CAN'T BE...
I KNOW THAT... NOW.
HE HAD TO COVER HIS TRAIL WHEN WE GOT OUR HANDS ON YOU.
AND THAT MEANS WHATEVER THE SKULL IS PLANNING, IT'S GOING TO START SOON.
SO, ARE YOU GOING TO STEP UP HERE, OR NOT?
THEY'VE GOT STEVE'S GIRL...YOUR AGENT 13.
I KNOW.
IT WAS HER WE WERE TRYING TO SAVE WHEN WE FOUND YOU.
NOW ANSWER THE QUESTION.

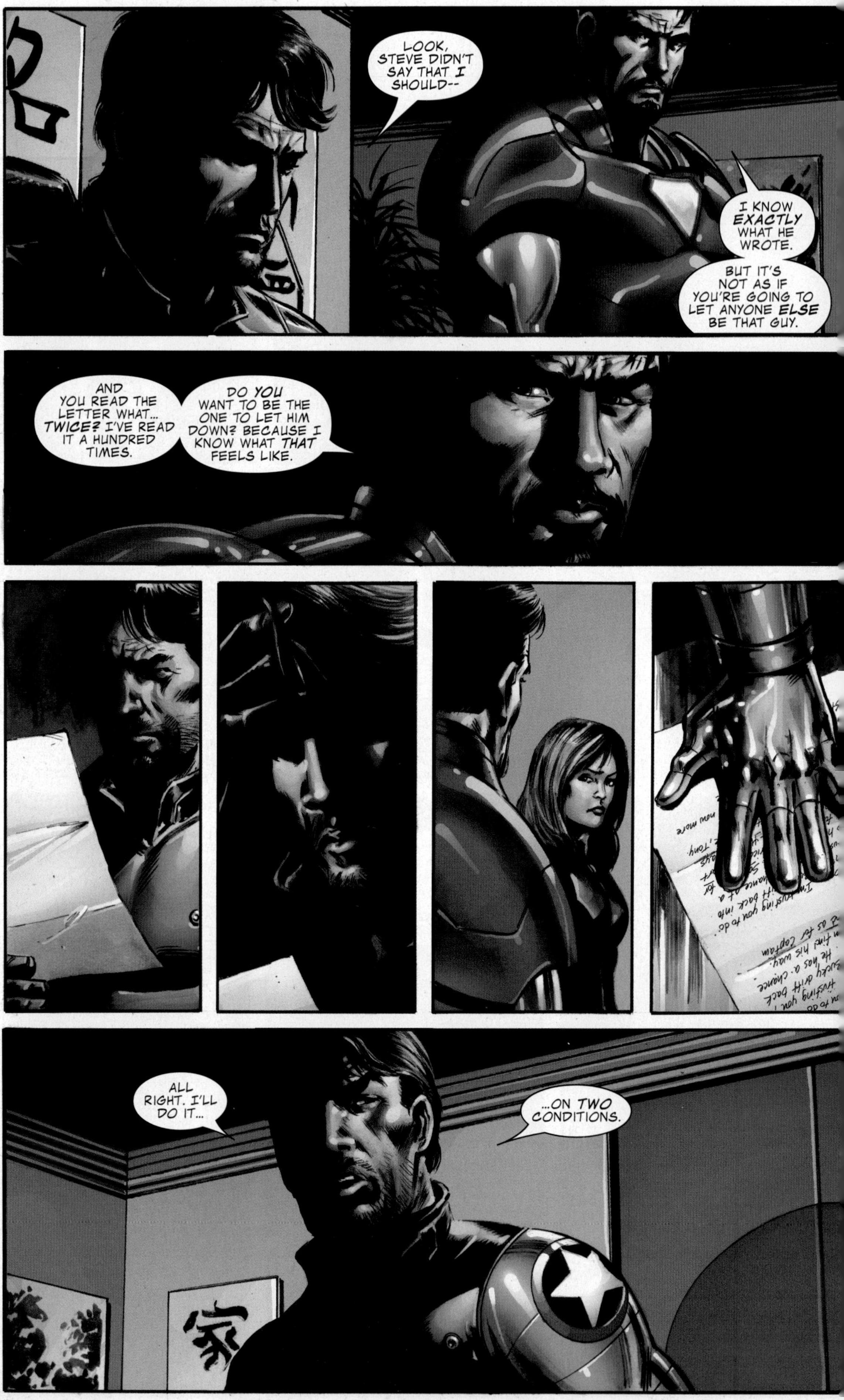

LOOK, STEVE DIDN'T SAY THAT I SHOULD--
I KNOW EXACTLY WHAT HE WROTE.
BUT IT'S NOT AS IF YOU'RE GOING TO LET ANYONE ELSE BE THAT GUY.
AND YOU READ THE LETTER WHAT... TWICE? I'VE READ IT A HUNDRED TIMES.
DO YOU WANT TO BE THE ONE TO LET HIM DOWN? BECAUSE I KNOW WHAT THAT FEELS LIKE.
ALL RIGHT. I'LL DO IT...
...ON TWO CONDITIONS.

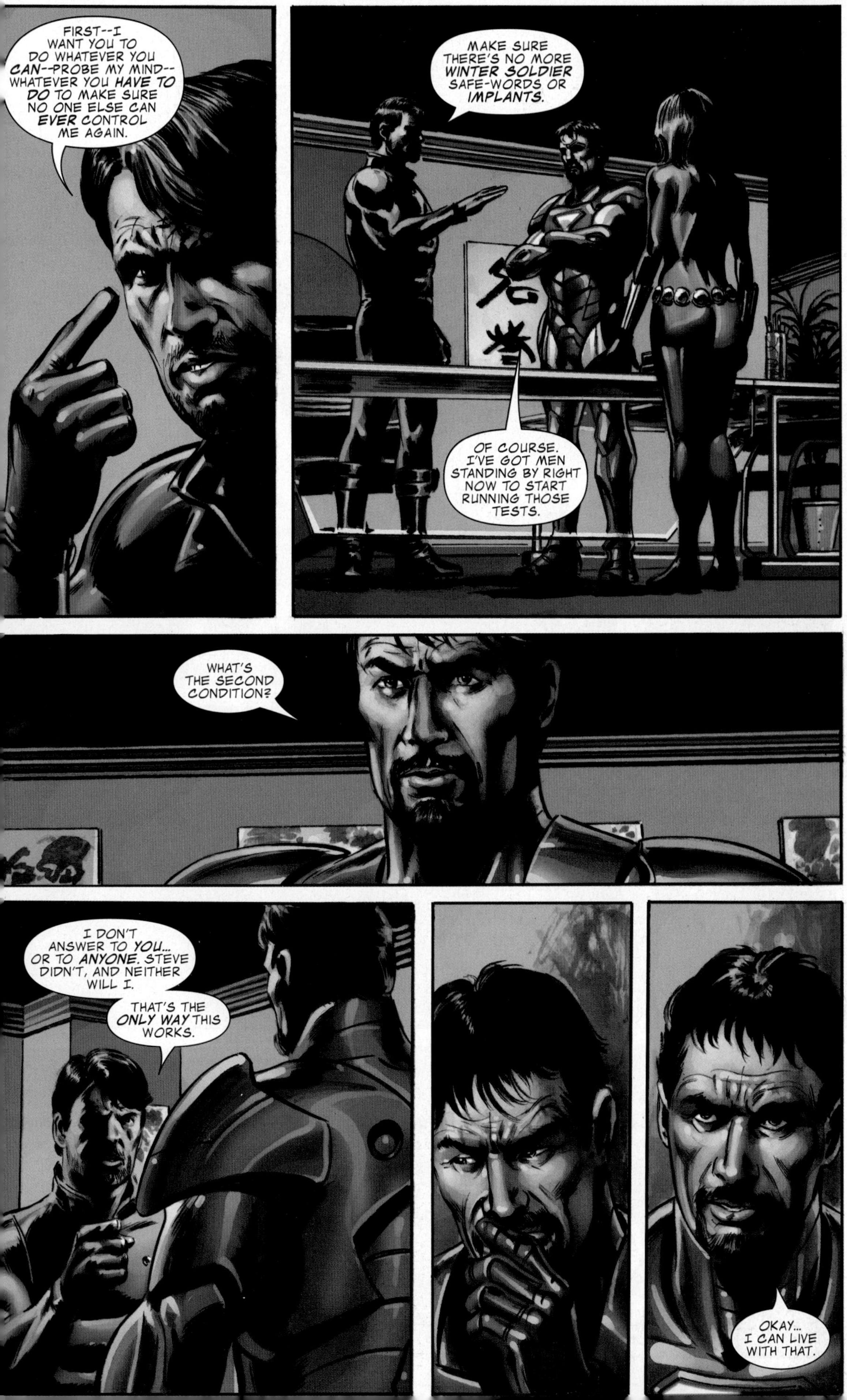
FIRST--I WANT YOU TO DO WHATEVER YOU CAN--PROBE MY MIND--WHATEVER YOU HAVE TO DO TO MAKE SURE NO ONE ELSE CAN EVER CONTROL ME AGAIN.
MAKE SURE THERE'S NO MORE WINTER SOLDIER SAFE-WORDS OR IMPLANTS.
OF COURSE. I'VE GOT MEN STANDING BY RIGHT NOW TO START RUNNING THOSE TESTS.
WHAT'S THE SECOND CONDITION?
I DON'T ANSWER TO YOU... OR TO ANYONE. STEVE DIDN'T, AND NEITHER WILL I.
THAT'S THE ONLY WAY THIS WORKS.
OKAY... I CAN LIVE WITH THAT.

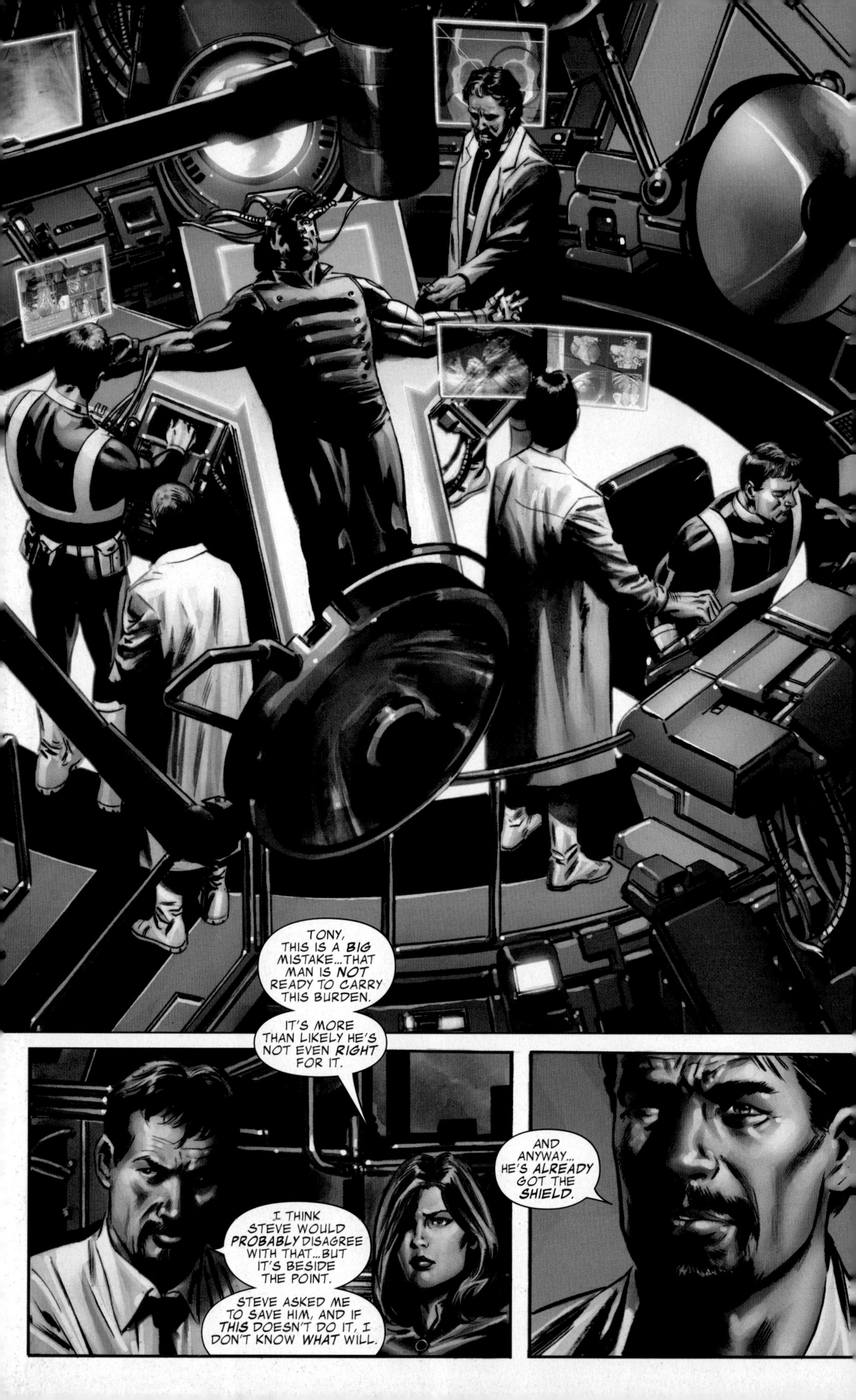

TONY, THIS IS A BIG MISTAKE...THAT MAN IS NOT READY TO CARRY THIS BURDEN.
IT'S MORE THAN LIKELY HE'S NOT EVEN RIGHT FOR IT.
I THINK STEVE WOULD PROBABLY DISAGREE WITH THAT...BUT IT'S BESIDE THE POINT.
STEVE ASKED ME TO SAVE HIM, AND IF THIS DOESN'T DO IT, I DON'T KNOW WHAT WILL.
AND ANYWAY... HE'S ALREADY GOT THE SHIELD.

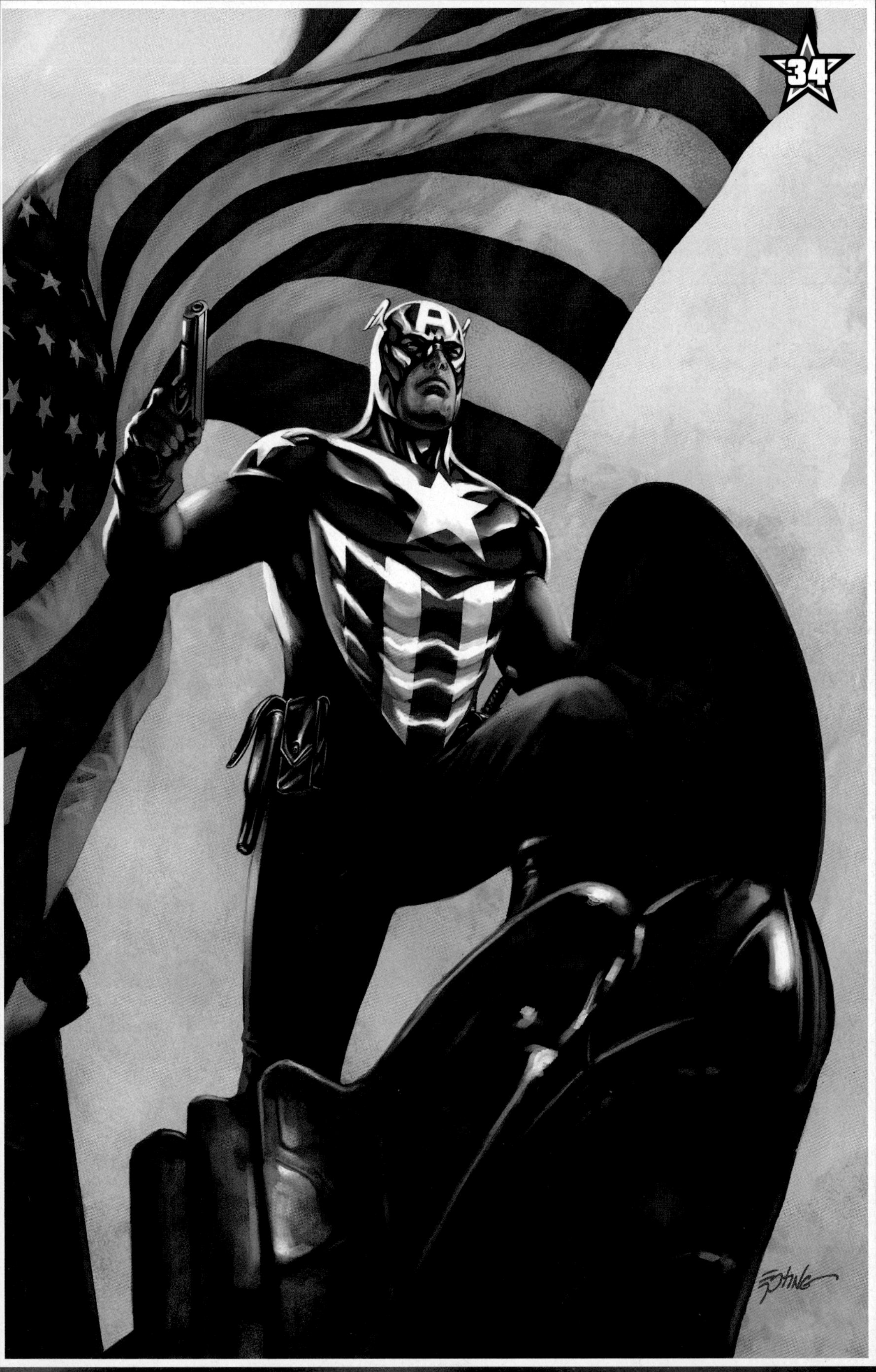
34

PART FOUR

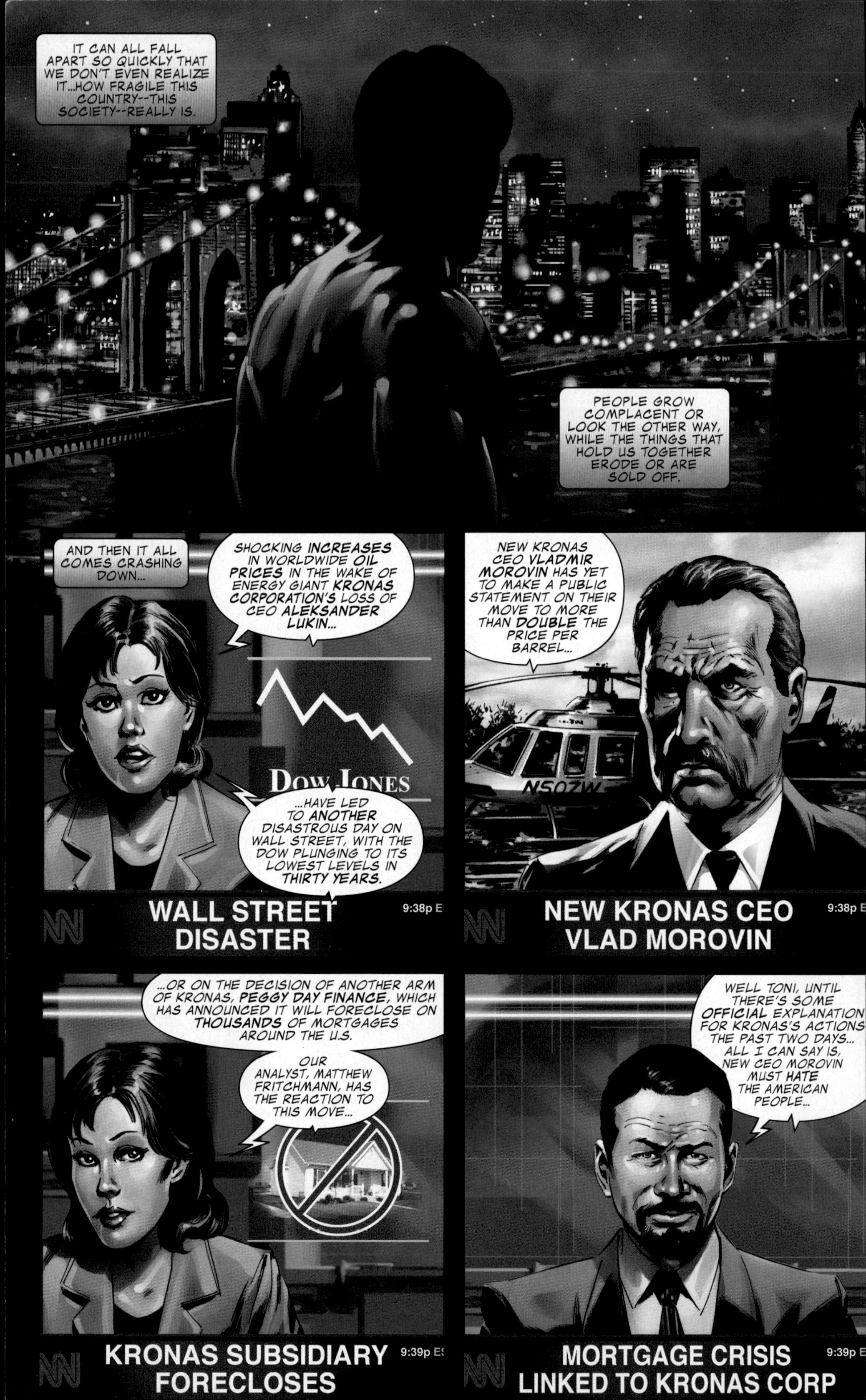
IT CAN ALL FALL APART SO QUICKLY THAT WE DON'T EVEN REALIZE IT...HOW FRAGILE THIS COUNTRY--THIS SOCIETY--REALLY IS.
PEOPLE GROW COMPLACENT OR LOOK THE OTHER WAY, WHILE THE THINGS THAT HOLD US TOGETHER ERODE OR ARE SOLD OFF.
AND THEN IT ALL COMES CRASHING DOWN...
SHOCKING INCREASES IN WORLDWIDE OIL PRICES IN THE WAKE OF ENERGY GIANT KRONAS CORPORATION'S LOSS OF CEO ALEKSANDER LUKIN...
DOW JONES
...HAVE LED TO ANOTHER DISASTROUS DAY ON WALL STREET, WITH THE DOW PLUNGING TO ITS LOWEST LEVELS IN THIRTY YEARS.
WALL STREET DISASTER
9:38p E
NEW KRONAS CEO VLADMIR MOROVIN HAS YET TO MAKE A PUBLIC STATEMENT ON THEIR MOVE TO MORE THAN DOUBLE THE PRICE PER BARREL...
N507W
NEW KRONAS CEO VLAD MOROVIN
9:38p E
...OR ON THE DECISION OF ANOTHER ARM OF KRONAS, PEGGY DAY FINANCE, WHICH HAS ANNOUNCED IT WILL FORECLOSE ON THOUSANDS OF MORTGAGES AROUND THE U.S.
OUR ANALYST, MATTHEW FRITCHMANN, HAS THE REACTION TO THIS MOVE...
KRONAS SUBSIDIARY FORECLOSES
9:39p E
WELL TONI, UNTIL THERE'S SOME OFFICIAL EXPLANATION FOR KRONAS'S ACTIONS THE PAST TWO DAYS... ALL I CAN SAY IS, NEW CEO MOROVIN MUST HATE THE AMERICAN PEOPLE...
MORTGAGE CRISIS LINKED TO KRONAS CORP
9:39p E

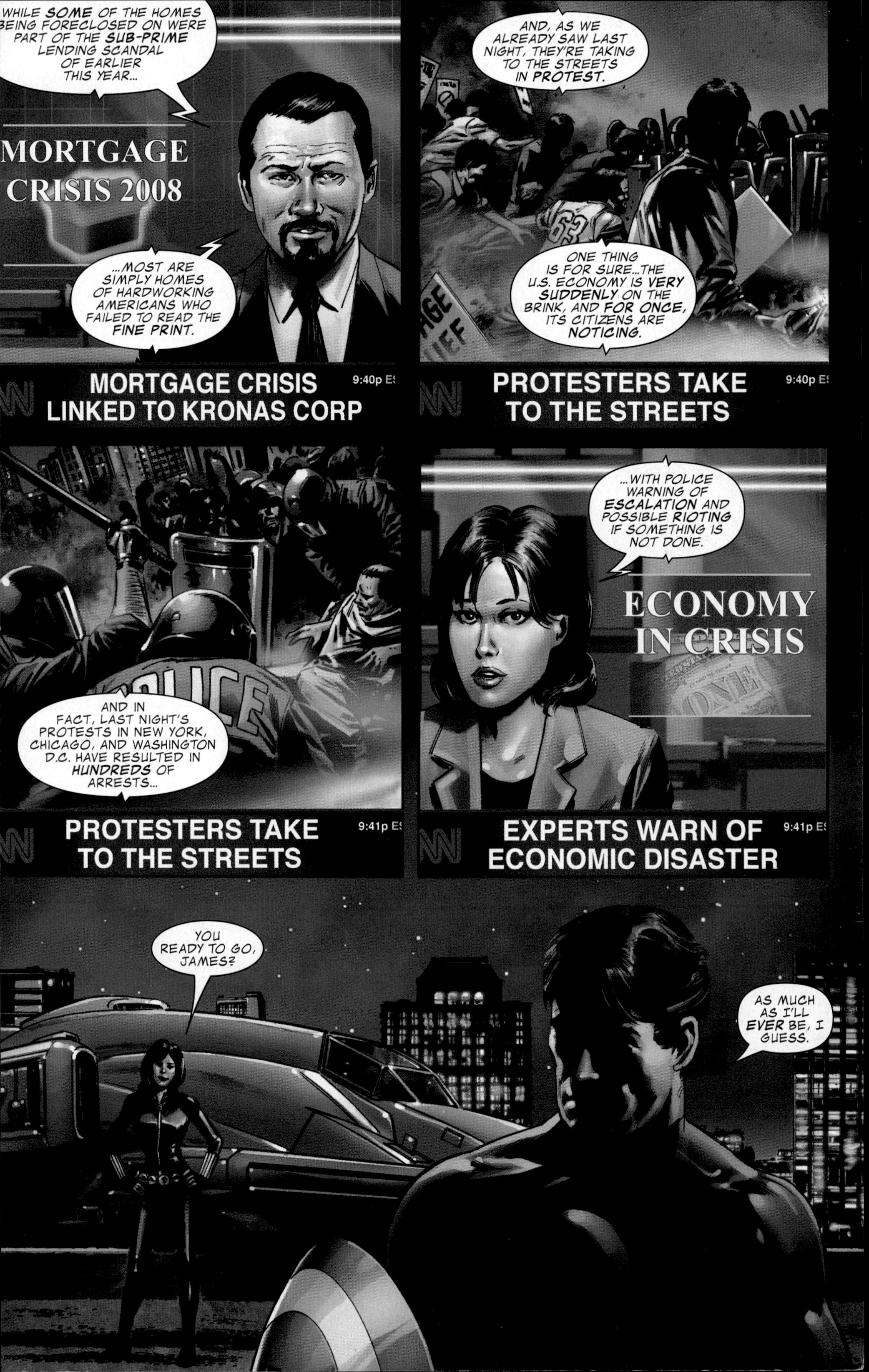

WHILE SOME OF THE HOMES BEING FORECLOSED ON WERE PART OF THE SUB-PRIME LENDING SCANDAL OF EARLIER THIS YEAR...
MORTGAGE CRISIS 2008
...MOST ARE SIMPLY HOMES OF HARDWORKING AMERICANS WHO FAILED TO READ THE FINE PRINT.
MORTGAGE CRISIS LINKED TO KRONAS CORP
9:40p
AND, AS WE ALREADY SAW LAST NIGHT, THEY'RE TAKING TO THE STREETS IN PROTEST.
ONE THING IS FOR SURE...THE U.S. ECONOMY IS VERY SUDDENLY ON THE BRINK, AND FOR ONCE, ITS CITIZENS ARE NOTICING.
PROTESTERS TAKE TO THE STREETS
9:40p
AND IN FACT, LAST NIGHT'S PROTESTS IN NEW YORK, CHICAGO, AND WASHINGTON D.C. HAVE RESULTED IN HUNDREDS OF ARRESTS...
PROTESTERS TAKE TO THE STREETS
9:41p
...WITH POLICE WARNING OF ESCALATION AND POSSIBLE RIOTING IF SOMETHING IS NOT DONE.
ECONOMY IN CRISIS
EXPERTS WARN OF ECONOMIC DISASTER
9:41p
YOU READY TO GO, JAMES?
AS MUCH AS I'LL EVER BE, I GUESS.

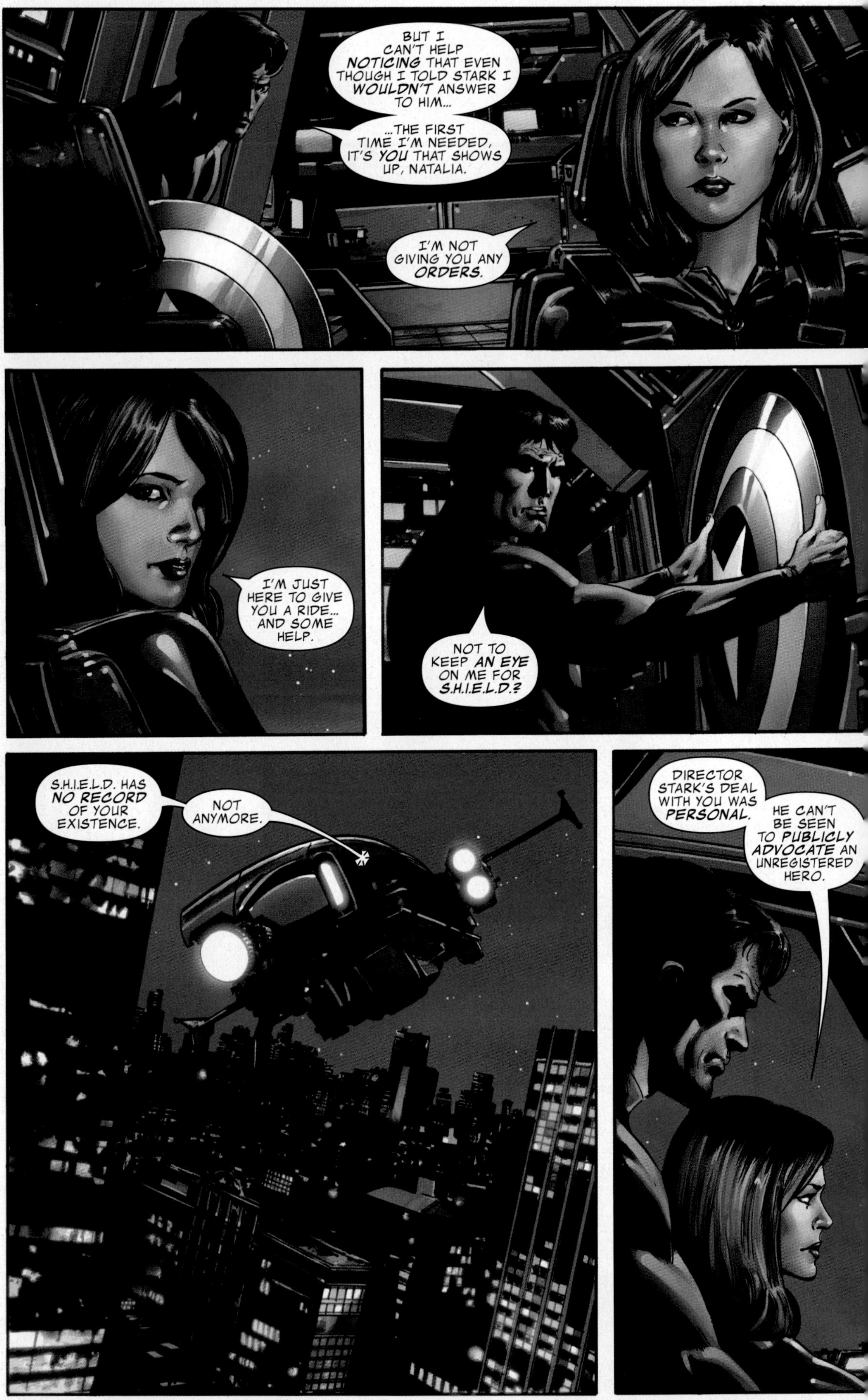
BUT I CAN'T HELP NOTICING THAT EVEN THOUGH I TOLD STARK I WOULDN'T ANSWER TO HIM...
...THE FIRST TIME I'M NEEDED, IT'S YOU THAT SHOWS UP, NATALIA.
I'M NOT GIVING YOU ANY ORDERS.
I'M JUST HERE TO GIVE YOU A RIDE... AND SOME HELP.
NOT TO KEEP AN EYE ON ME FOR S.H.I.E.L.D.?
S.H.I.E.L.D. HAS NO RECORD OF YOUR EXISTENCE.
NOT ANYMORE.
DIRECTOR STARK'S DEAL WITH YOU WAS PERSONAL.
HE CAN'T BE SEEN TO PUBLICLY ADVOCATE AN UNREGISTERED HERO.

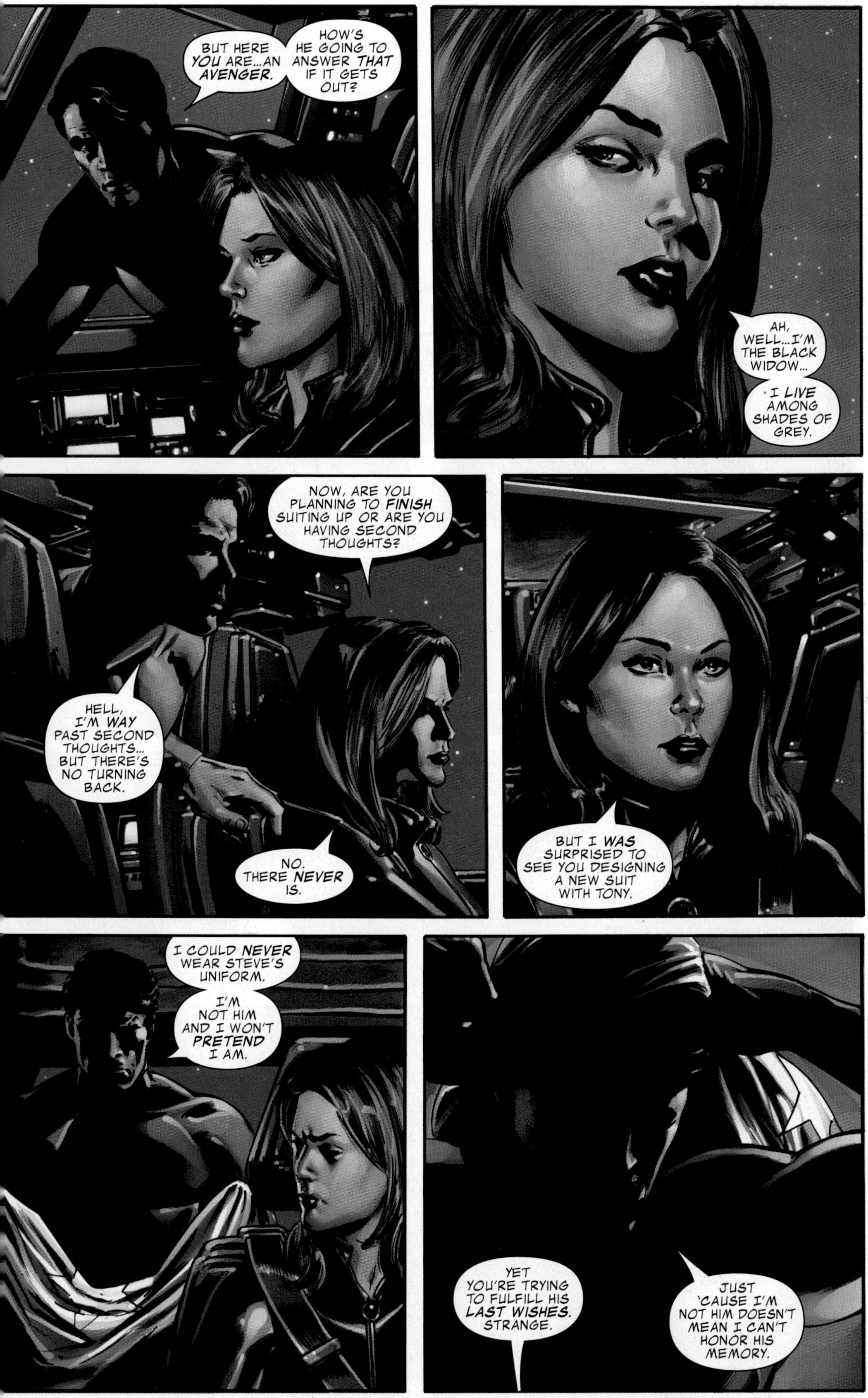
BUT HERE YOU ARE...AN AVENGER.
HOW'S HE GOING TO ANSWER THAT IF IT GETS OUT?
AH, WELL...I'M THE BLACK WIDOW...
I LIVE AMONG SHADES OF GREY.
NOW, ARE YOU PLANNING TO FINISH SUITING UP OR ARE YOU HAVING SECOND THOUGHTS?
HELL, I'M WAY PAST SECOND THOUGHTS... BUT THERE'S NO TURNING BACK.
NO. THERE NEVER IS.
BUT I WAS SURPRISED TO SEE YOU DESIGNING A NEW SUIT WITH TONY.
I COULD NEVER WEAR STEVE'S UNIFORM.
I'M NOT HIM AND I WON'T PRETEND I AM.
YET YOU'RE TRYING TO FULFILL HIS LAST WISHES. STRANGE.
JUST 'CAUSE I'M NOT HIM DOESN'T MEAN I CAN'T HONOR HIS MEMORY.

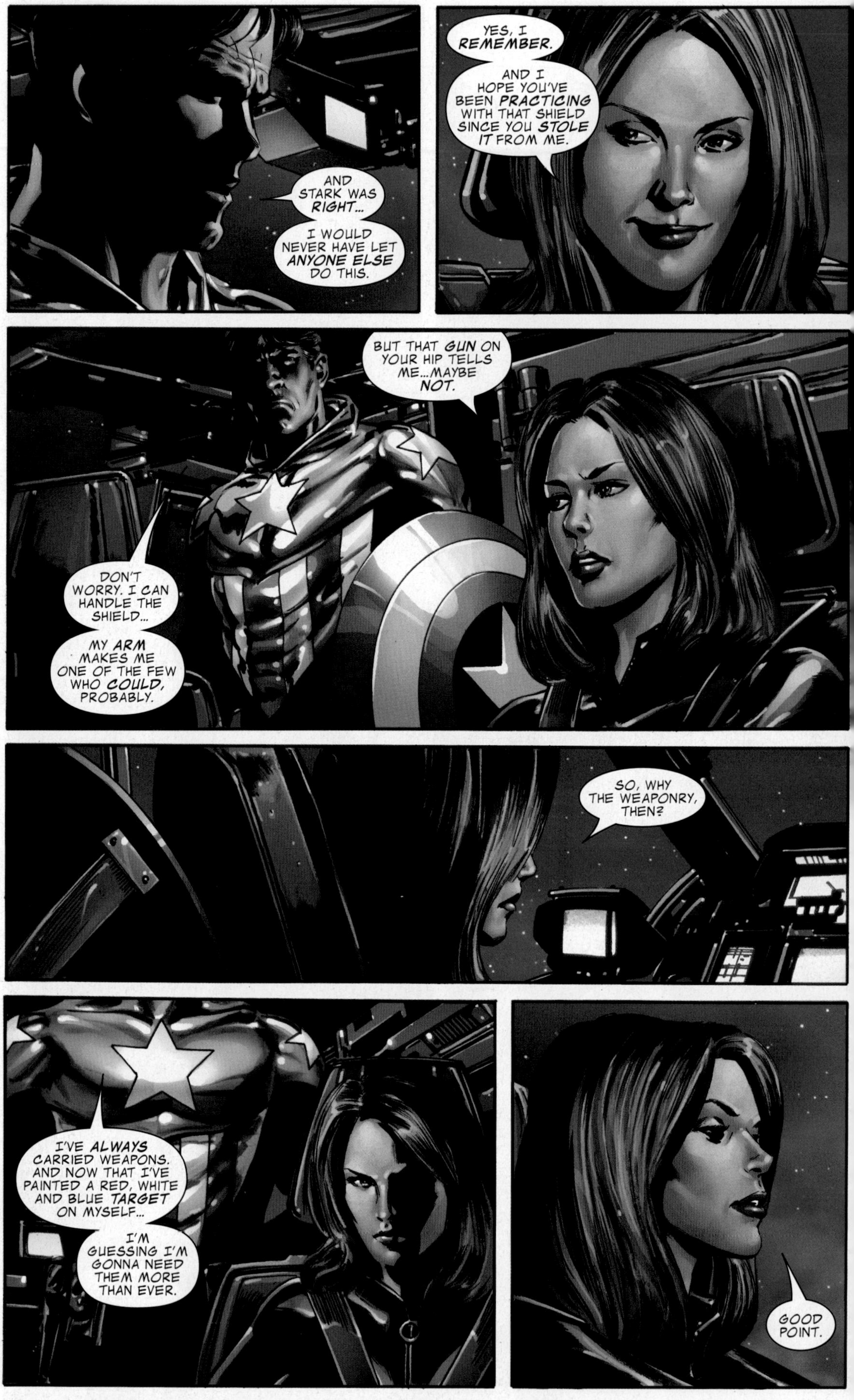
AND STARK WAS RIGHT...
I WOULD NEVER HAVE LET ANYONE ELSE DO THIS.
YES, I REMEMBER.
AND I HOPE YOU'VE BEEN PRACTICING WITH THAT SHIELD SINCE YOU STOLE IT FROM ME.
BUT THAT GUN ON YOUR HIP TELLS ME...MAYBE NOT.
DON'T WORRY. I CAN HANDLE THE SHIELD...
MY ARM MAKES ME ONE OF THE FEW WHO COULD, PROBABLY.
SO, WHY THE WEAPONRY, THEN?
I'VE ALWAYS CARRIED WEAPONS. AND NOW THAT I'VE PAINTED A RED, WHITE AND BLUE TARGET ON MYSELF...
I'M GUESSING I'M GONNA NEED THEM MORE THAN EVER.
GOOD POINT.

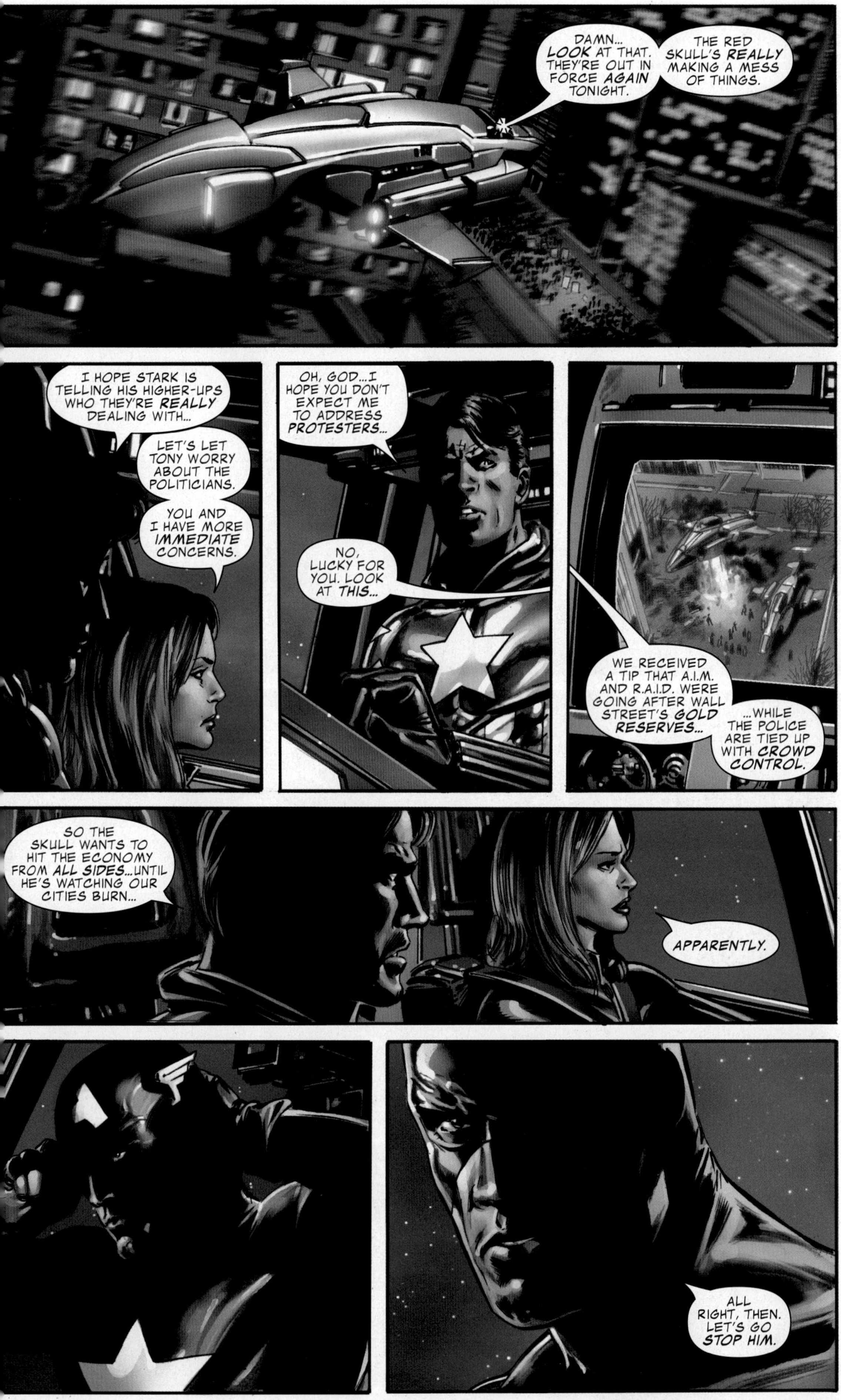
DAMN... LOOK AT THAT. THEY'RE OUT IN FORCE AGAIN TONIGHT.
THE RED SKULL'S REALLY MAKING A MESS OF THINGS.
I HOPE STARK IS TELLING HIS HIGHER-UPS WHO THEY'RE REALLY DEALING WITH...
LET'S LET TONY WORRY ABOUT THE POLITICIANS.
YOU AND I HAVE MORE IMMEDIATE CONCERNS.
OH, GOD...I HOPE YOU DON'T EXPECT ME TO ADDRESS PROTESTERS...
NO, LUCKY FOR YOU. LOOK AT THIS...
WE RECEIVED A TIP THAT A.I.M. AND R.A.I.D. WERE GOING AFTER WALL STREET'S GOLD RESERVES...
...WHILE THE POLICE ARE TIED UP WITH CROWD CONTROL.
SO THE SKULL WANTS TO HIT THE ECONOMY FROM ALL SIDES...UNTIL HE'S WATCHING OUR CITIES BURN...
APPARENTLY.
ALL RIGHT, THEN. LET'S GO STOP HIM.

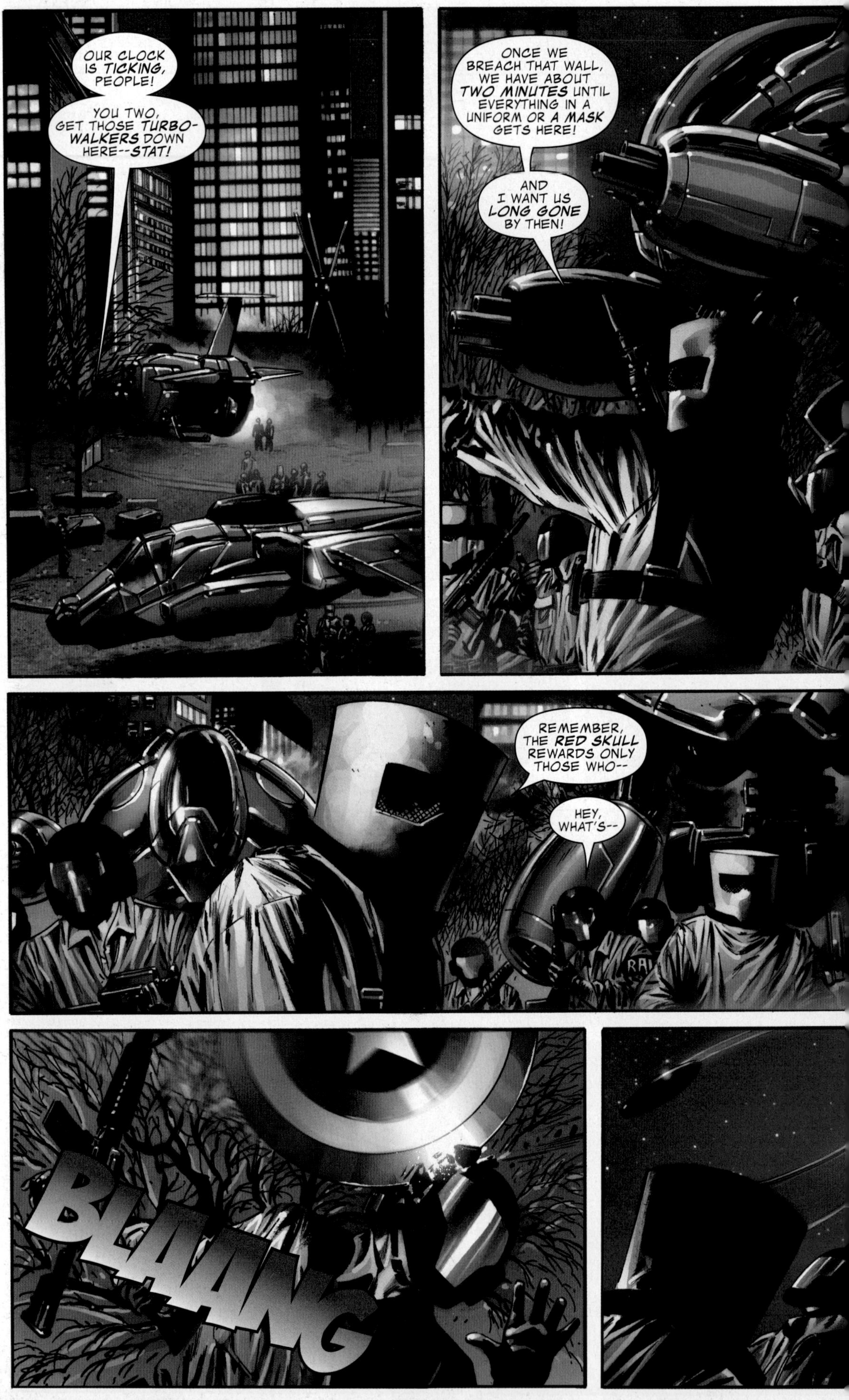
OUR CLOCK IS TICKING, PEOPLE!
YOU TWO, GET THOSE TURBO-WALKERS DOWN HERE--STAT!
ONCE WE BREACH THAT WALL, WE HAVE ABOUT TWO MINUTES UNTIL EVERYTHING IN A UNIFORM OR A MASK GETS HERE!
AND I WANT US LONG GONE BY THEN!
REMEMBER, THE RED SKULL REWARDS ONLY THOSE WHO--
HEY, WHAT'S--
BLAAANG

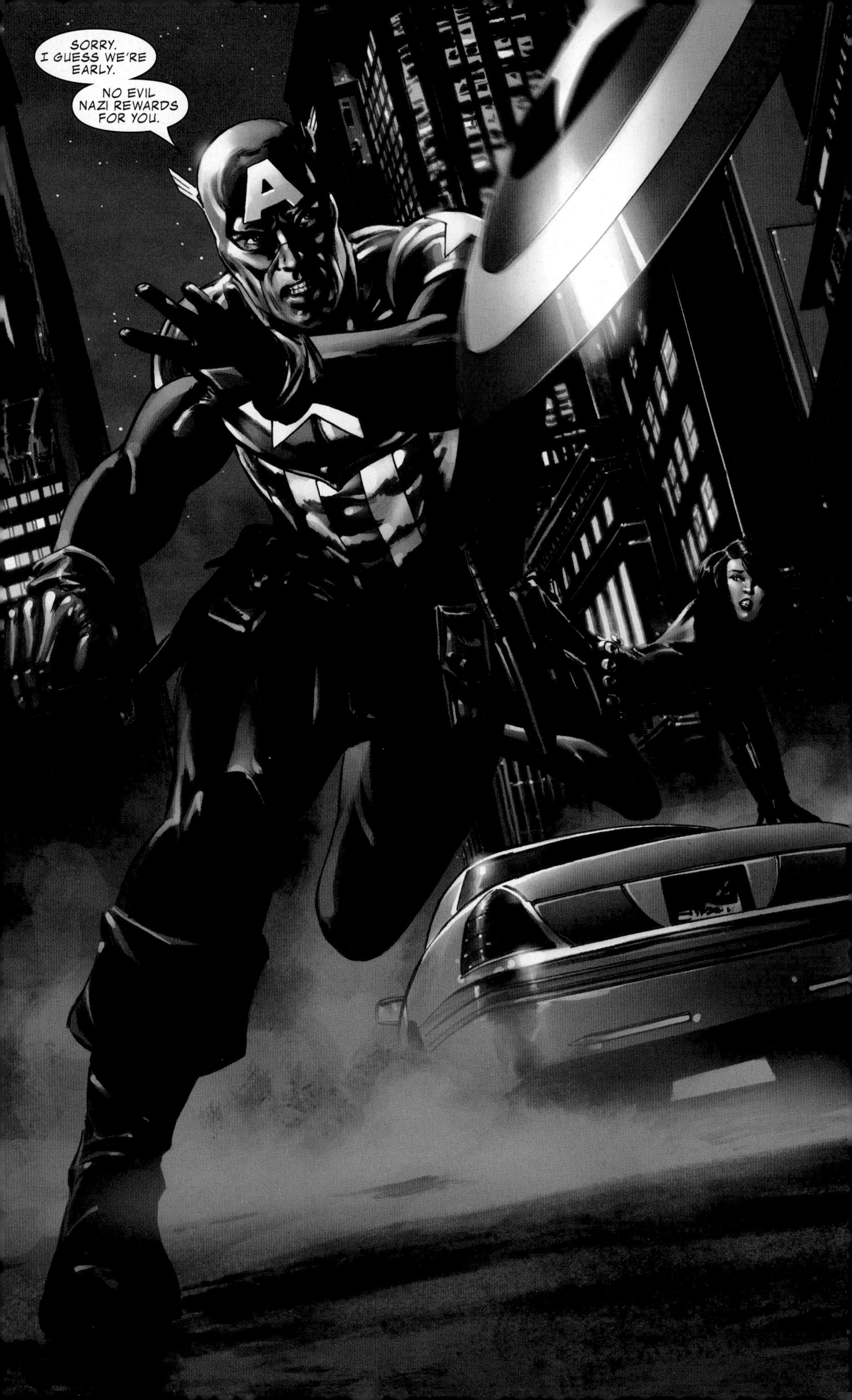
SORRY. I GUESS WE'RE EARLY.
NO EVIL NAZI REWARDS FOR YOU.

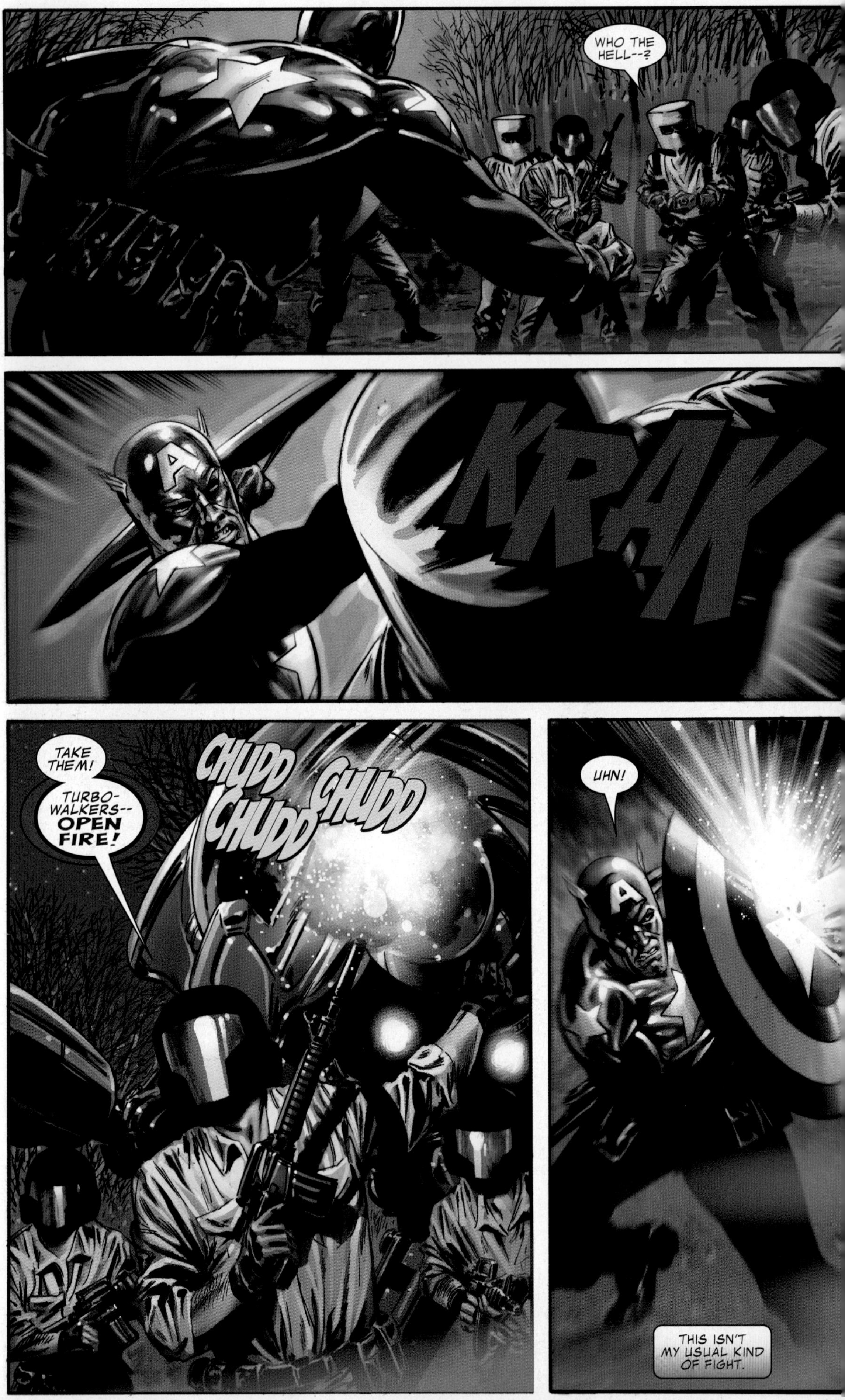
WHO THE HELL--?
KRAK
TAKE THEM!
TURBO-WALKERS-- OPEN FIRE!
CHUDD CHUDD CHUDD
UHN!
THIS ISN'T MY USUAL KIND OF FIGHT.

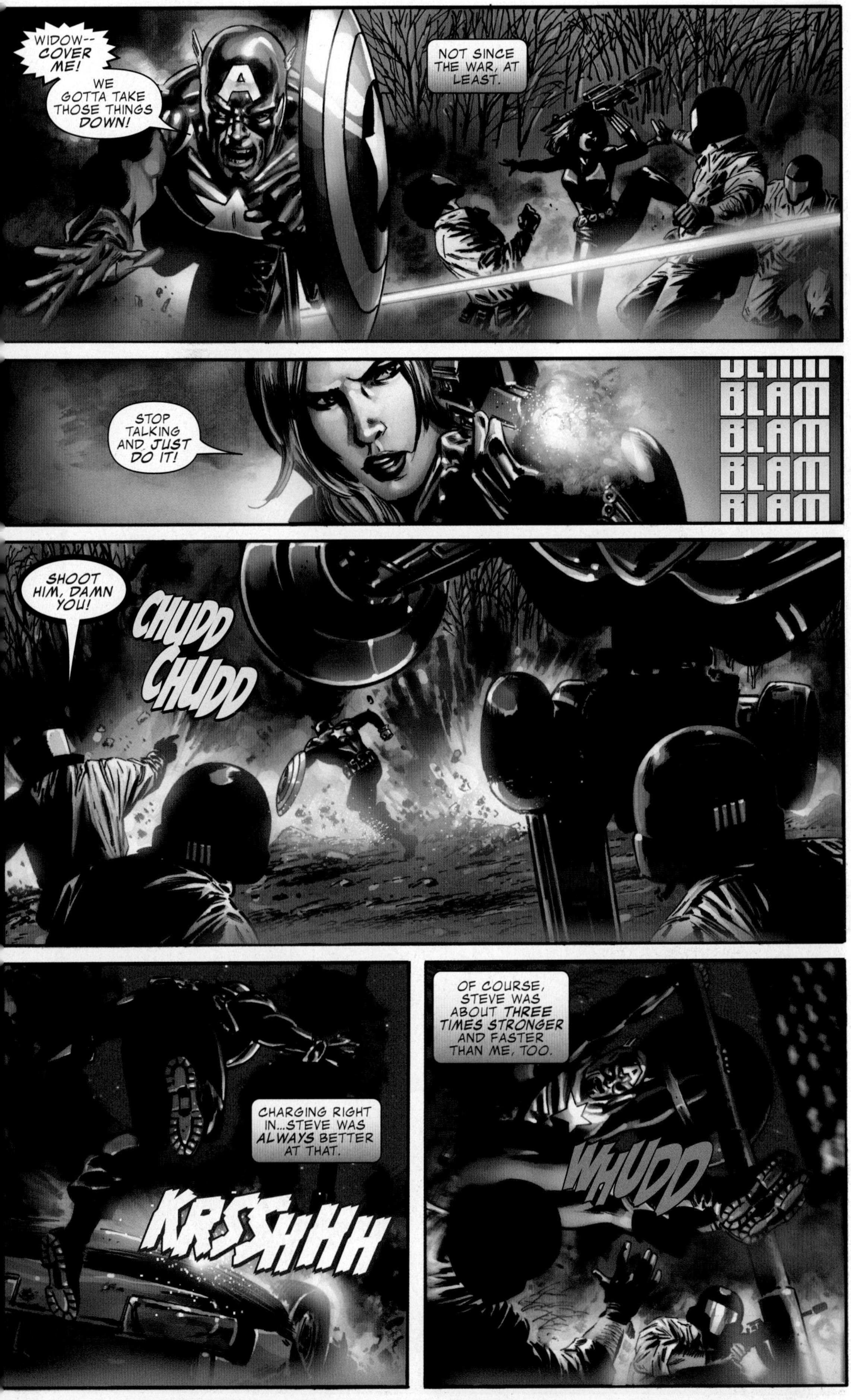

WIDOW-- COVER ME!
WE GOTTA TAKE THOSE THINGS DOWN!
NOT SINCE THE WAR, AT LEAST.
STOP TALKING AND JUST DO IT!
BLAM
BLAM
BLAM
SHOOT HIM, DAMN YOU!
CHUDD CHUDD
CHARGING RIGHT IN...STEVE WAS ALWAYS BETTER AT THAT.
KRSSHHH
OF COURSE, STEVE WAS ABOUT THREE TIMES STRONGER AND FASTER THAN ME, TOO.
WHUDD

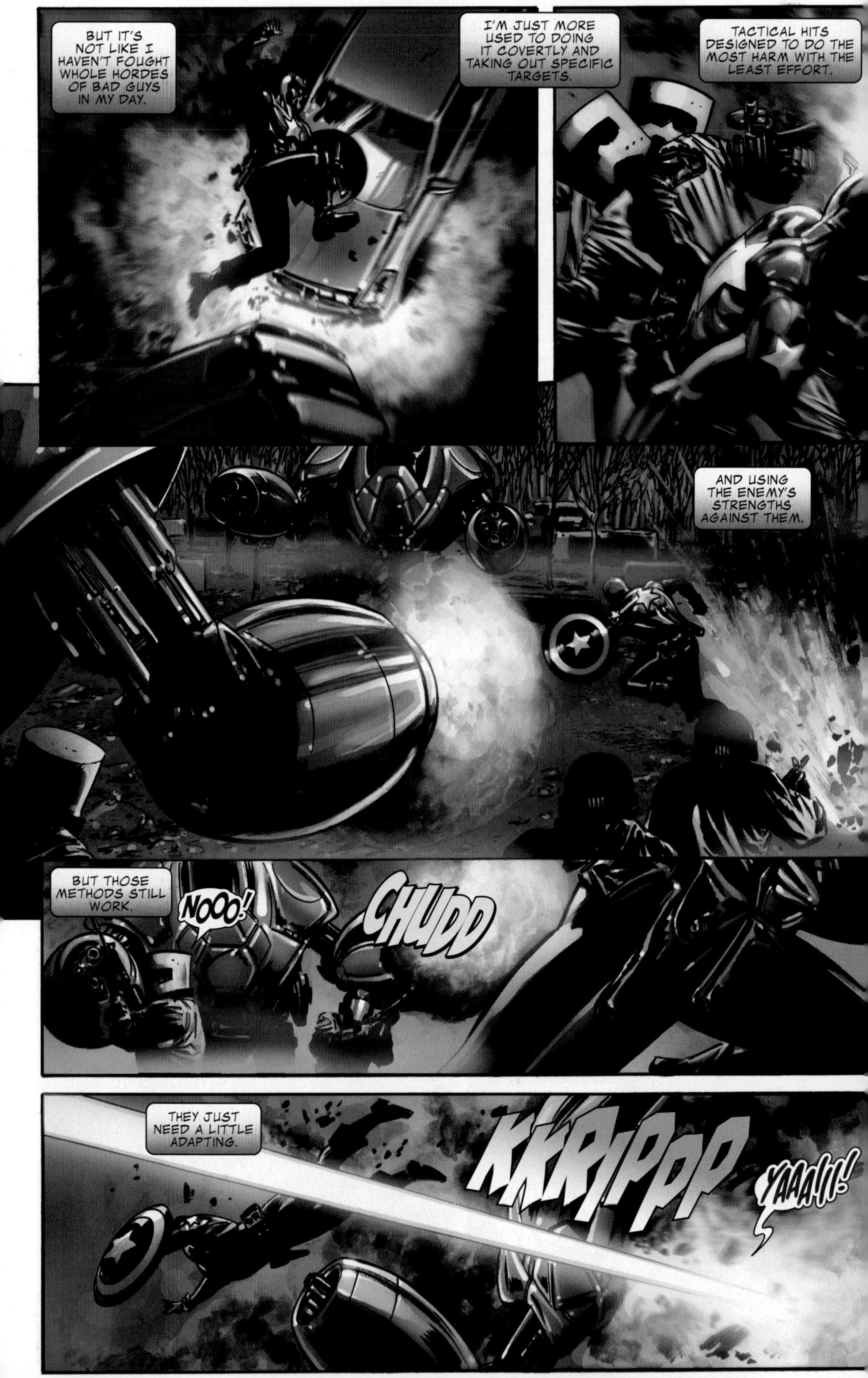
BUT IT'S NOT LIKE I HAVEN'T FOUGHT WHOLE HORDES OF BAD GUYS IN MY DAY.
I'M JUST MORE USED TO DOING IT COVERTLY AND TAKING OUT SPECIFIC TARGETS.
TACTICAL HITS DESIGNED TO DO THE MOST HARM WITH THE LEAST EFFORT.
AND USING THE ENEMY'S STRENGTHS AGAINST THEM.
BUT THOSE METHODS STILL WORK.
NOOO!
CHUDD
THEY JUST NEED A LITTLE ADAPTING.
KKRIPPP
YAAAIII!

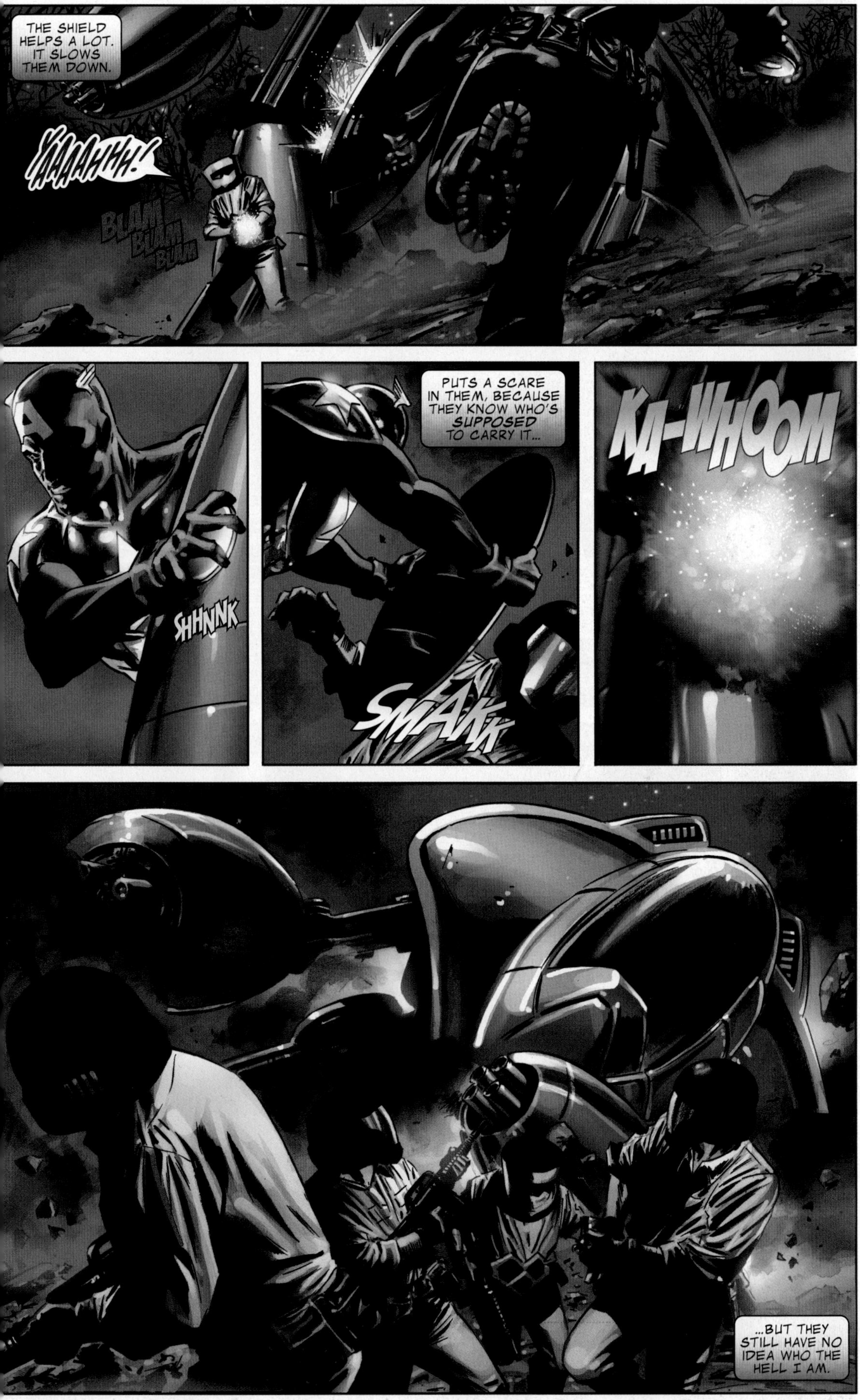
THE SHIELD HELPS A LOT. IT SLOWS THEM DOWN.
YAAAAHHH!
BLAM BLAM BLAM
SHHNNK
PUTS A SCARE IN THEM, BECAUSE THEY KNOW WHO'S SUPPOSED TO CARRY IT...
SMAKK
KA-WHOOM
...BUT THEY STILL HAVE NO IDEA WHO THE HELL I AM.

MR. SECRETARY, I DON'T CARE *WHAT* REPORTS YOU'VE SEEN...

The S.H.I.E.L.D. Helicarrier
Currently Hovering
Above Washington D.C.

...I HAVE *RELIABLE INTEL* THAT THE BODY FOUND IN THAT PLANE CRASH WAS *NOT ALEKSANDER LUKIN*.

I'VE BEEN TELLING YOU PEOPLE THIS FOR *DAYS*, BUT IT SEEMS *NO ONE* WILL HEAR ME.

DR. JACK SHEPHARD. THE LOST... ARE FOUND

DETAILS CAN BE FOUND AT FIND815.COM

DON'T TAKE A *TONE* WITH ME, DIRECTOR STARK.

THIS COUNTRY IS IN THE MIDST OF A *MAJOR CRISIS*...

SO YOUR *UNFOUNDED ALLEGATIONS* ABOUT *DEAD MEN* ARE GOING TO HAVE TO WAIT UNTIL IT'S RESOLVED.

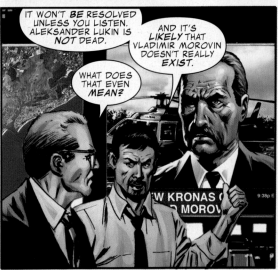

IT WON'T *BE* RESOLVED UNLESS YOU LISTEN. ALEKSANDER LUKIN IS *NOT DEAD*.

AND IT'S *LIKELY* THAT VLADIMIR MOROVIN DOESN'T REALLY *EXIST*.

WHAT DOES THAT EVEN *MEAN?*

W KRONAS
D MOROV

9:38p E

THAT THIS *ENTIRE CRISIS* IS AN *ORCHESTRATED ATTACK* ON THE U.S. BY THE KRONAS CORPORATION...

BECAUSE THEY'RE REALLY BEING RUN BY THE *RED SKULL*.

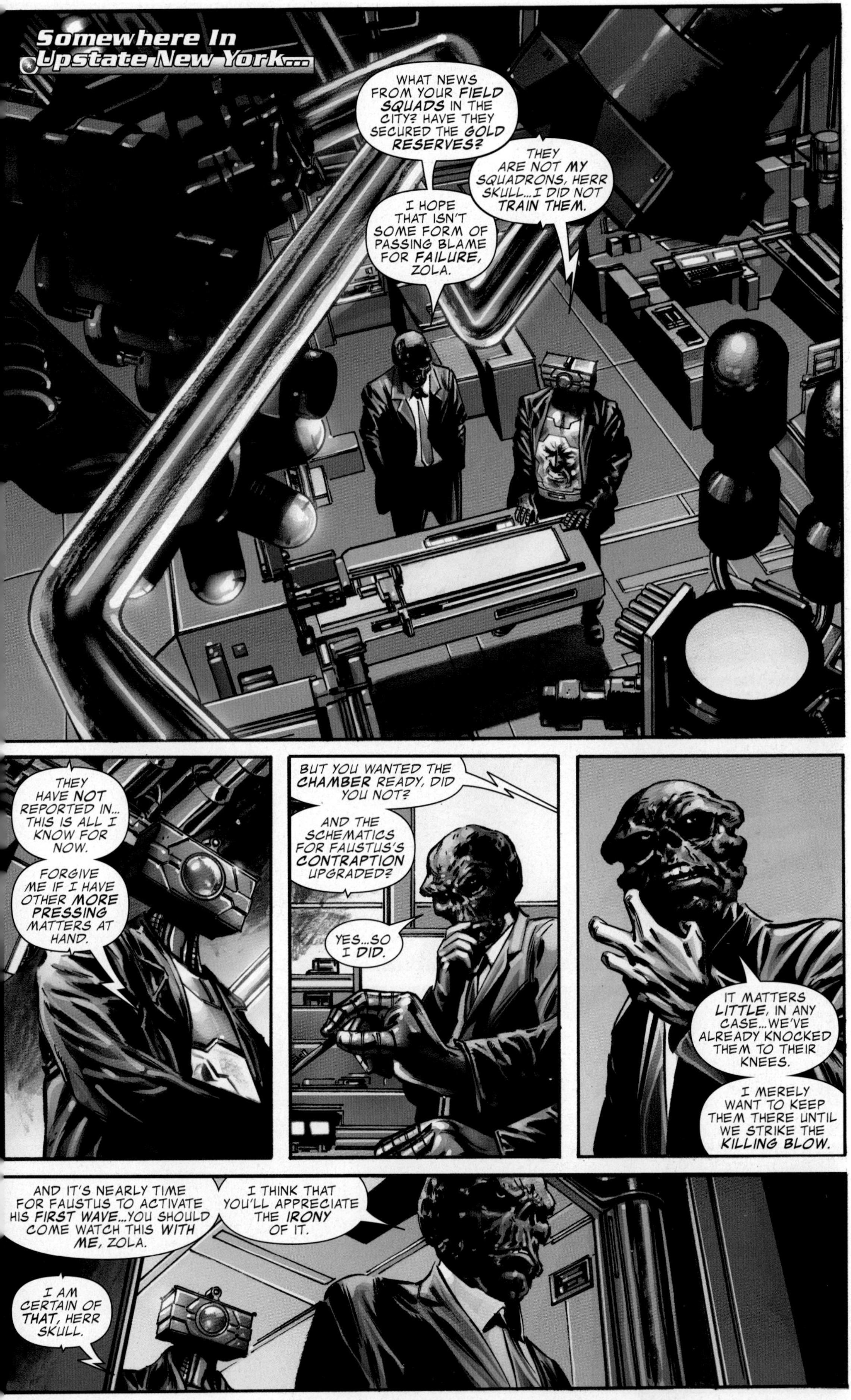
Somewhere In Upstate New York...
WHAT NEWS FROM YOUR FIELD SQUADS IN THE CITY? HAVE THEY SECURED THE GOLD RESERVES?
THEY ARE NOT MY SQUADRONS, HERR SKULL...I DID NOT TRAIN THEM.
I HOPE THAT ISN'T SOME FORM OF PASSING BLAME FOR FAILURE, ZOLA.
THEY HAVE NOT REPORTED IN... THIS IS ALL I KNOW FOR NOW.
FORGIVE ME IF I HAVE OTHER MORE PRESSING MATTERS AT HAND.
BUT YOU WANTED THE CHAMBER READY, DID YOU NOT?
AND THE SCHEMATICS FOR FAUSTUS'S CONTRAPTION UPGRADED?
YES...SO I DID.
IT MATTERS LITTLE, IN ANY CASE...WE'VE ALREADY KNOCKED THEM TO THEIR KNEES.
I MERELY WANT TO KEEP THEM THERE UNTIL WE STRIKE THE KILLING BLOW.
AND IT'S NEARLY TIME FOR FAUSTUS TO ACTIVATE HIS FIRST WAVE...YOU SHOULD COME WATCH THIS WITH ME, ZOLA.
I THINK THAT YOU'LL APPRECIATE THE IRONY OF IT.
I AM CERTAIN OF THAT, HERR SKULL.

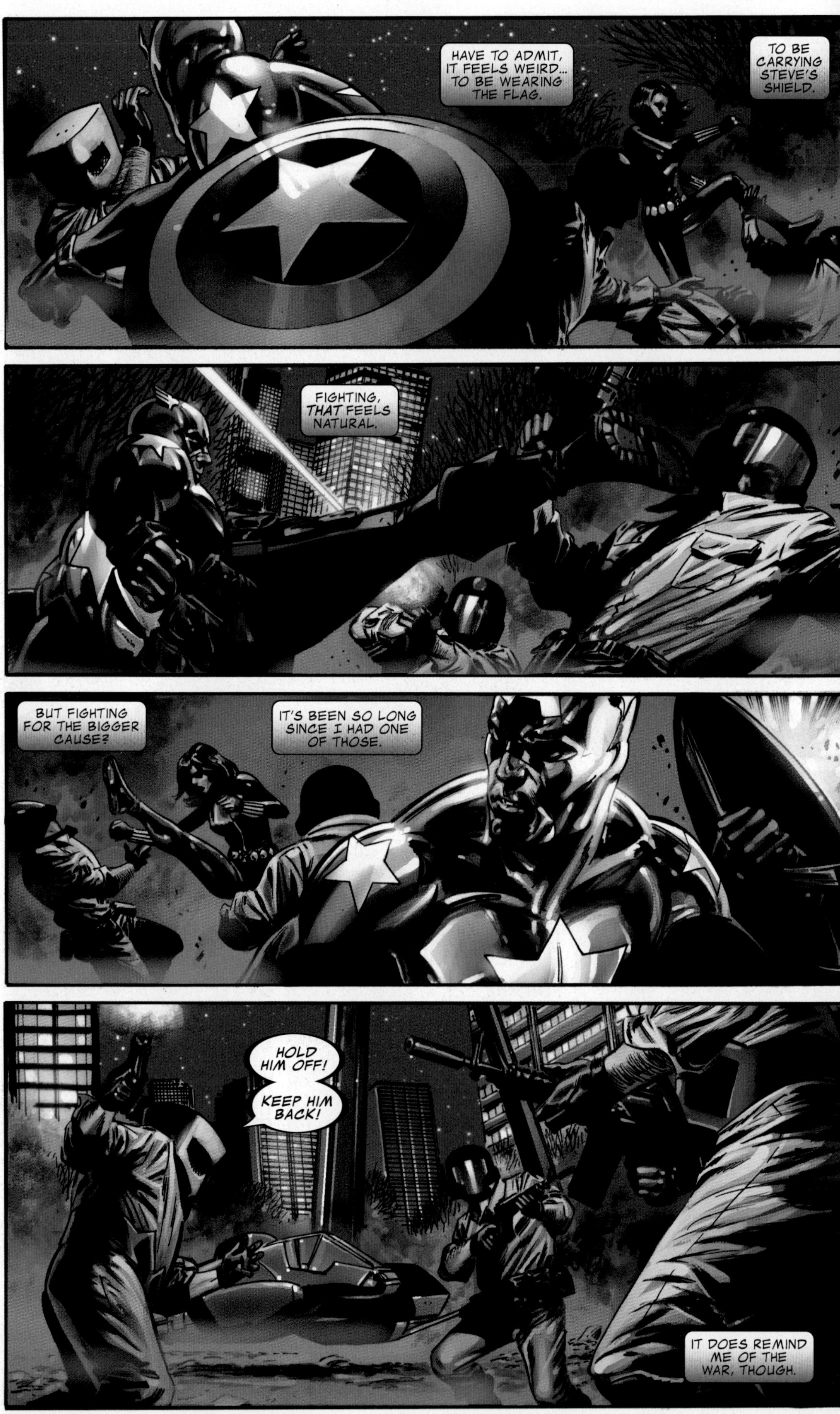
HAVE TO ADMIT, IT FEELS WEIRD... TO BE WEARING THE FLAG.
TO BE CARRYING STEVE'S SHIELD.
FIGHTING, *THAT* FEELS NATURAL.
BUT FIGHTING FOR THE BIGGER CAUSE?
IT'S BEEN SO LONG SINCE I HAD ONE OF THOSE.
HOLD HIM OFF!
KEEP HIM BACK!
IT DOES REMIND ME OF THE WAR, THOUGH.

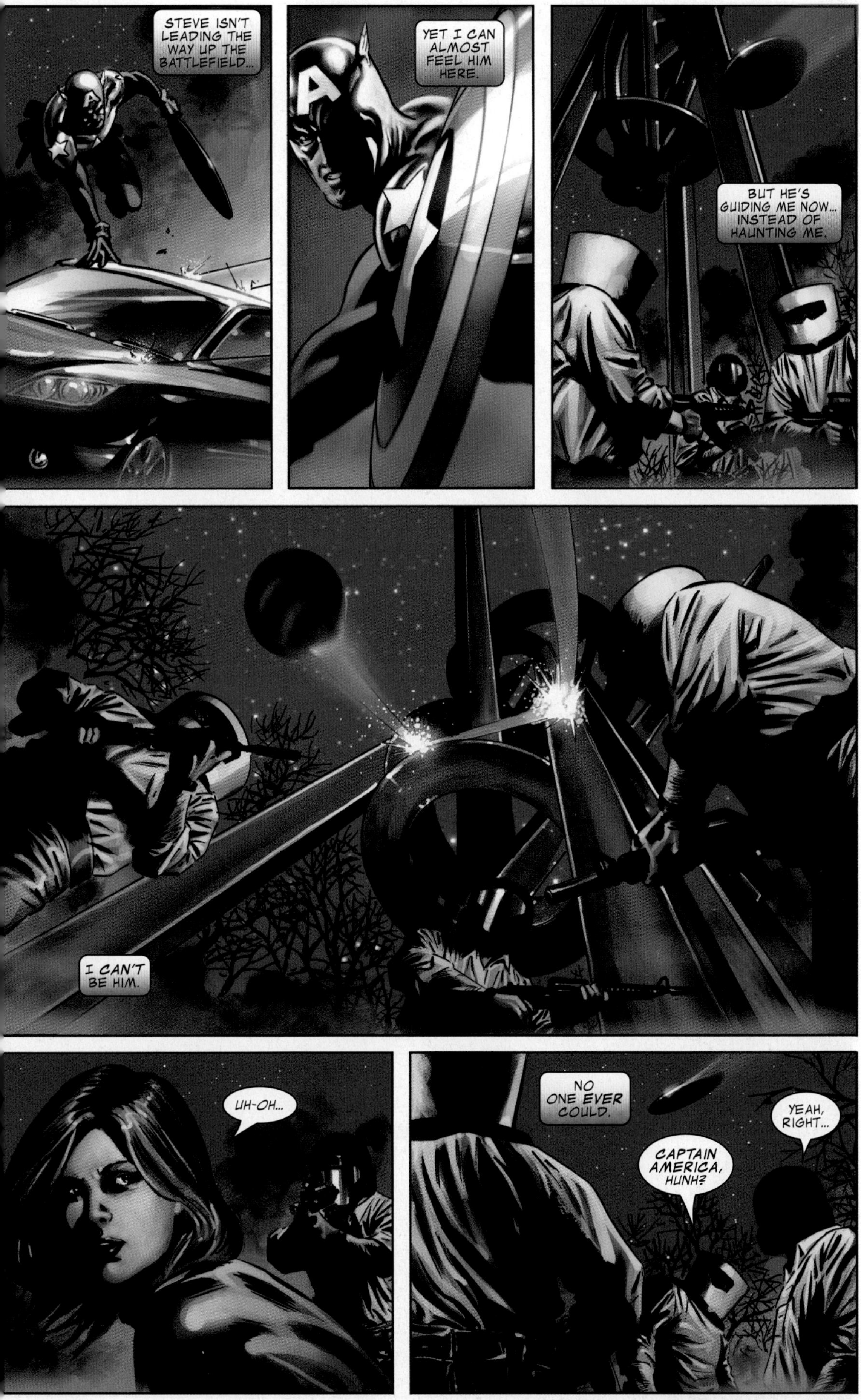
STEVE ISN'T LEADING THE WAY UP THE BATTLEFIELD...
YET I CAN ALMOST FEEL HIM HERE.
BUT HE'S GUIDING ME NOW... INSTEAD OF HAUNTING ME.
I CAN'T BE HIM.
UH-OH...
NO ONE EVER COULD.
CAPTAIN AMERICA, HUNH?
YEAH, RIGHT...

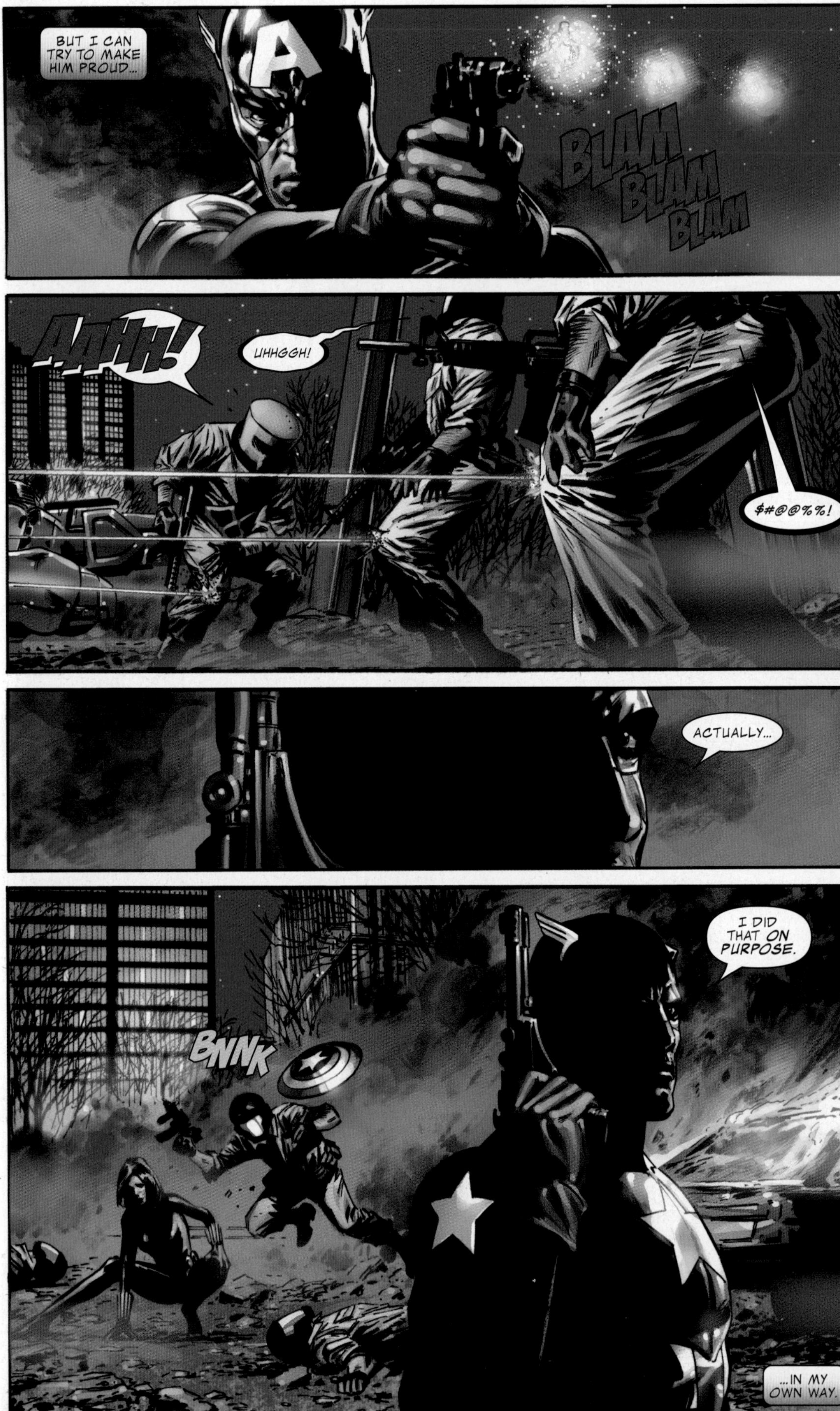

BUT I CAN TRY TO MAKE HIM PROUD...
BLAM BLAM BLAM
AAHH!
UHHGGH!
$#@@%%!
ACTUALLY...
I DID THAT ON PURPOSE.
BNNK
...IN MY OWN WAY.

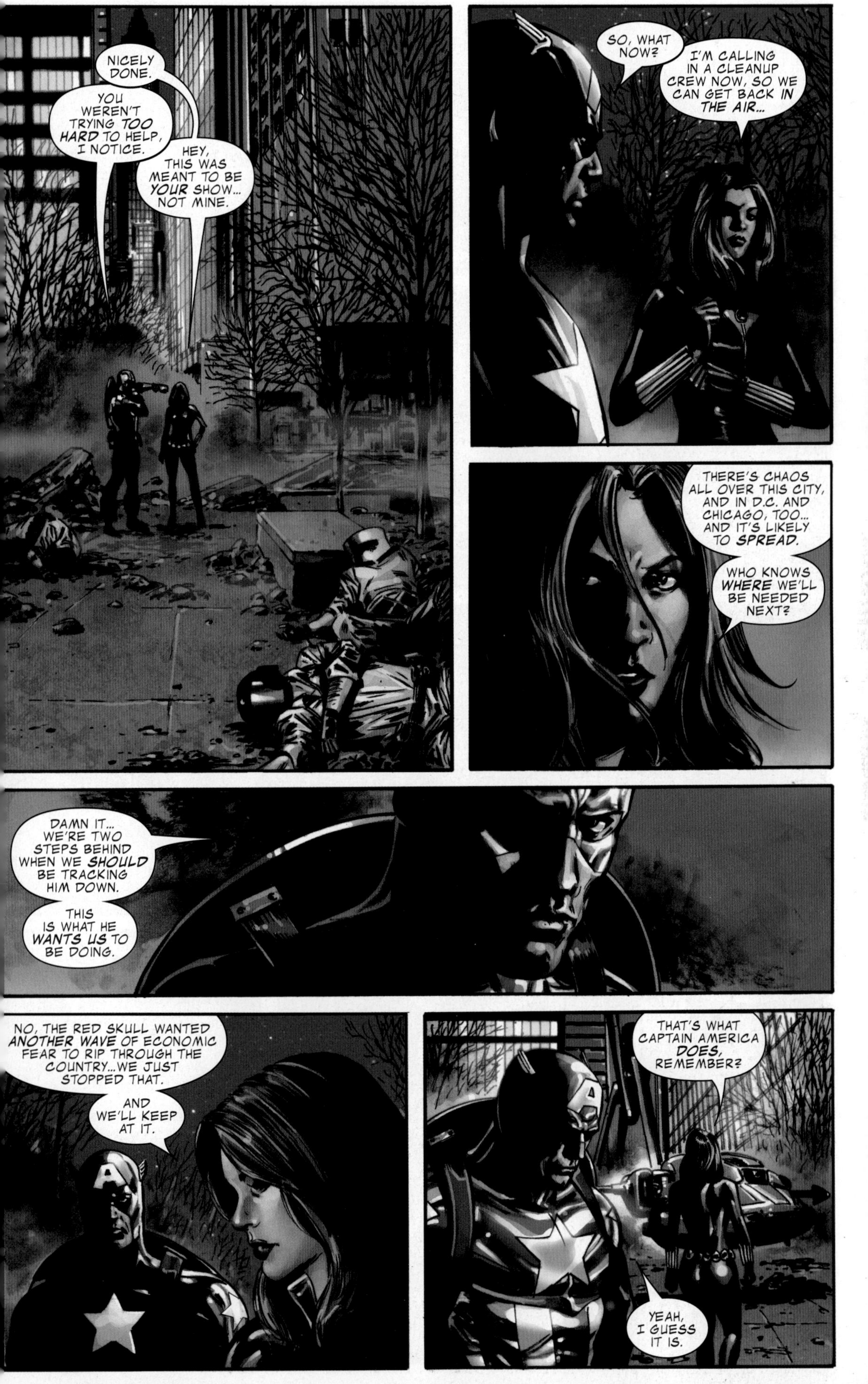
NICELY DONE.
YOU WEREN'T TRYING TOO HARD TO HELP, I NOTICE.
HEY, THIS WAS MEANT TO BE YOUR SHOW... NOT MINE.
SO, WHAT NOW?
I'M CALLING IN A CLEANUP CREW NOW, SO WE CAN GET BACK IN THE AIR...
THERE'S CHAOS ALL OVER THIS CITY, AND IN D.C. AND CHICAGO, TOO... AND IT'S LIKELY TO SPREAD.
WHO KNOWS WHERE WE'LL BE NEEDED NEXT?
DAMN IT... WE'RE TWO STEPS BEHIND WHEN WE SHOULD BE TRACKING HIM DOWN.
THIS IS WHAT HE WANTS US TO BE DOING.
NO, THE RED SKULL WANTED ANOTHER WAVE OF ECONOMIC FEAR TO RIP THROUGH THE COUNTRY...WE JUST STOPPED THAT.
AND WE'LL KEEP AT IT.
THAT'S WHAT CAPTAIN AMERICA DOES, REMEMBER?
YEAH, I GUESS IT IS.

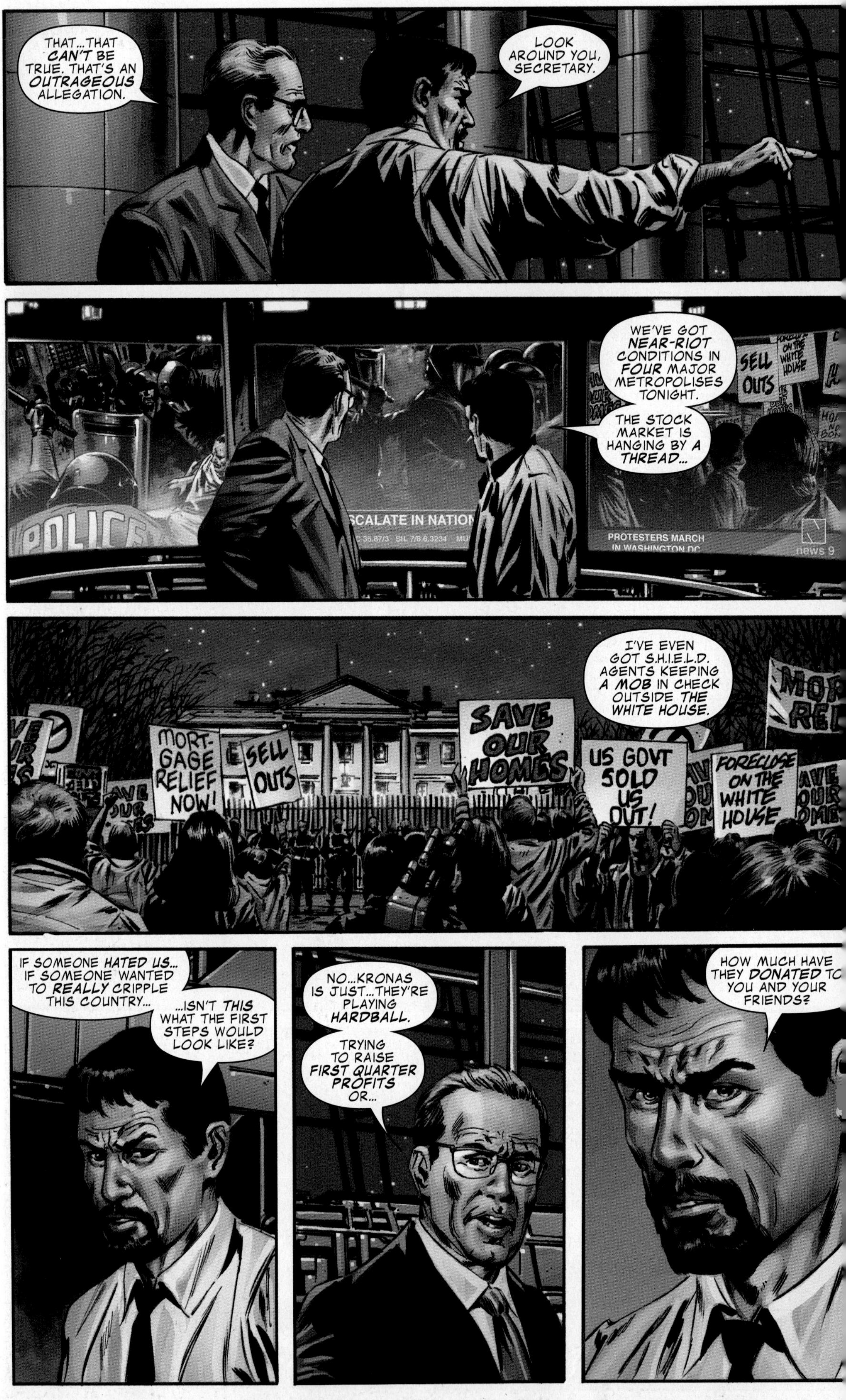
THAT...THAT CAN'T BE TRUE. THAT'S AN OUTRAGEOUS ALLEGATION.
LOOK AROUND YOU, SECRETARY.
POLICE
PROTESTERS MARCH IN WASHINGTON DC
news 9
SELL OUTS
WE'VE GOT NEAR-RIOT CONDITIONS IN FOUR MAJOR METROPOLISES TONIGHT.
THE STOCK MARKET IS HANGING BY A THREAD...
I'VE EVEN GOT S.H.I.E.L.D. AGENTS KEEPING A MOB IN CHECK OUTSIDE THE WHITE HOUSE.
MORT-GAGE RELIEF NOW!
SELL OUTS
SAVE OUR HOMES
US GOVT SOLD US OUT!
FORECLOSE ON THE WHITE HOUSE
IF SOMEONE HATED US... IF SOMEONE WANTED TO REALLY CRIPPLE THIS COUNTRY...
...ISN'T THIS WHAT THE FIRST STEPS WOULD LOOK LIKE?
NO...KRONAS IS JUST...THEY'RE PLAYING HARDBALL.
TRYING TO RAISE FIRST QUARTER PROFITS OR...
HOW MUCH HAVE THEY DONATED TO YOU AND YOUR FRIENDS?

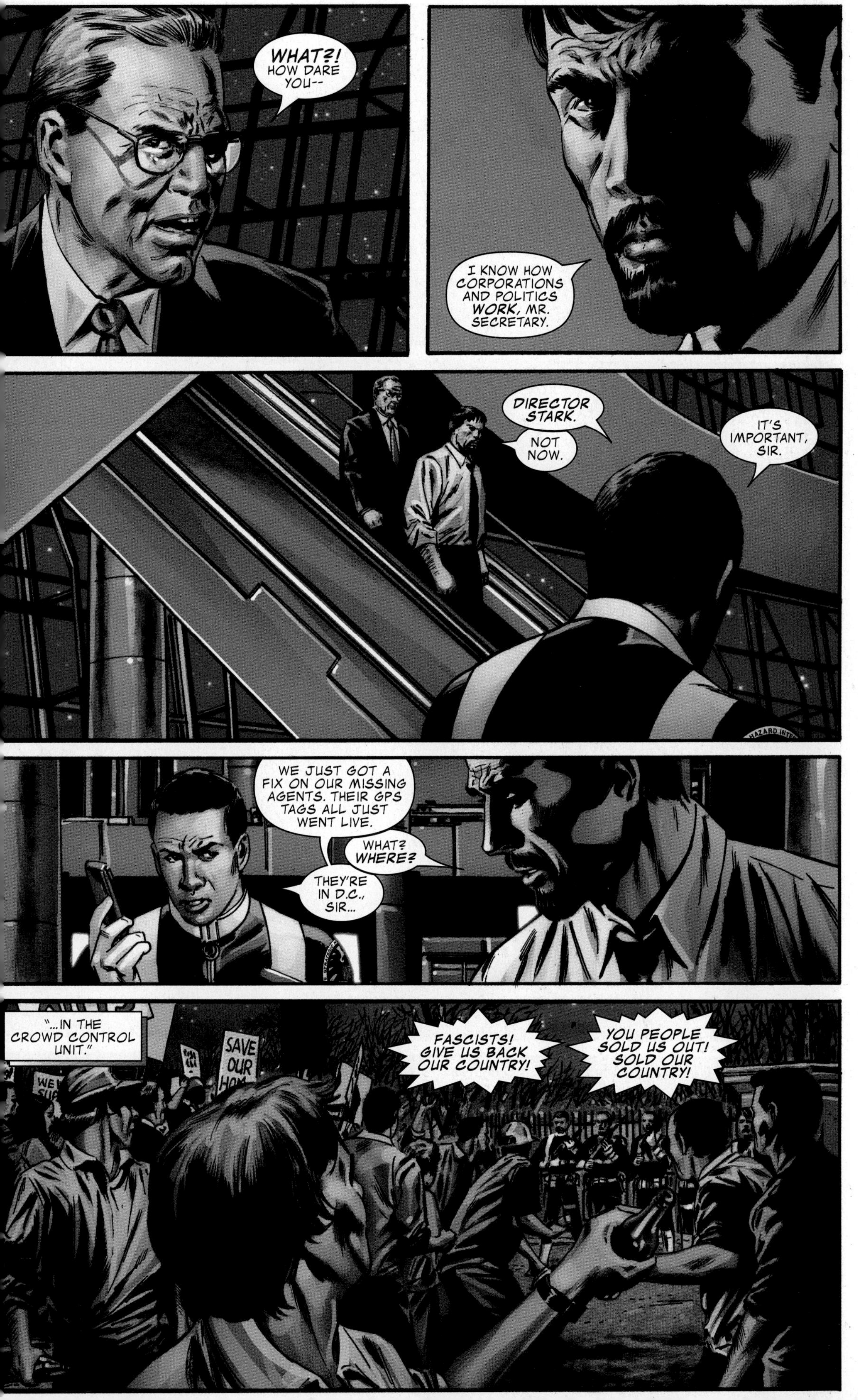
WHAT?! HOW DARE YOU--
I KNOW HOW CORPORATIONS AND POLITICS WORK, MR. SECRETARY.
DIRECTOR STARK.
NOT NOW.
IT'S IMPORTANT, SIR.
WE JUST GOT A FIX ON OUR MISSING AGENTS. THEIR GPS TAGS ALL JUST WENT LIVE.
WHAT? WHERE?
THEY'RE IN D.C., SIR...
"...IN THE CROWD CONTROL UNIT."
SAVE OUR HOM
FASCISTS! GIVE US BACK OUR COUNTRY!
YOU PEOPLE SOLD US OUT! SOLD OUR COUNTRY!

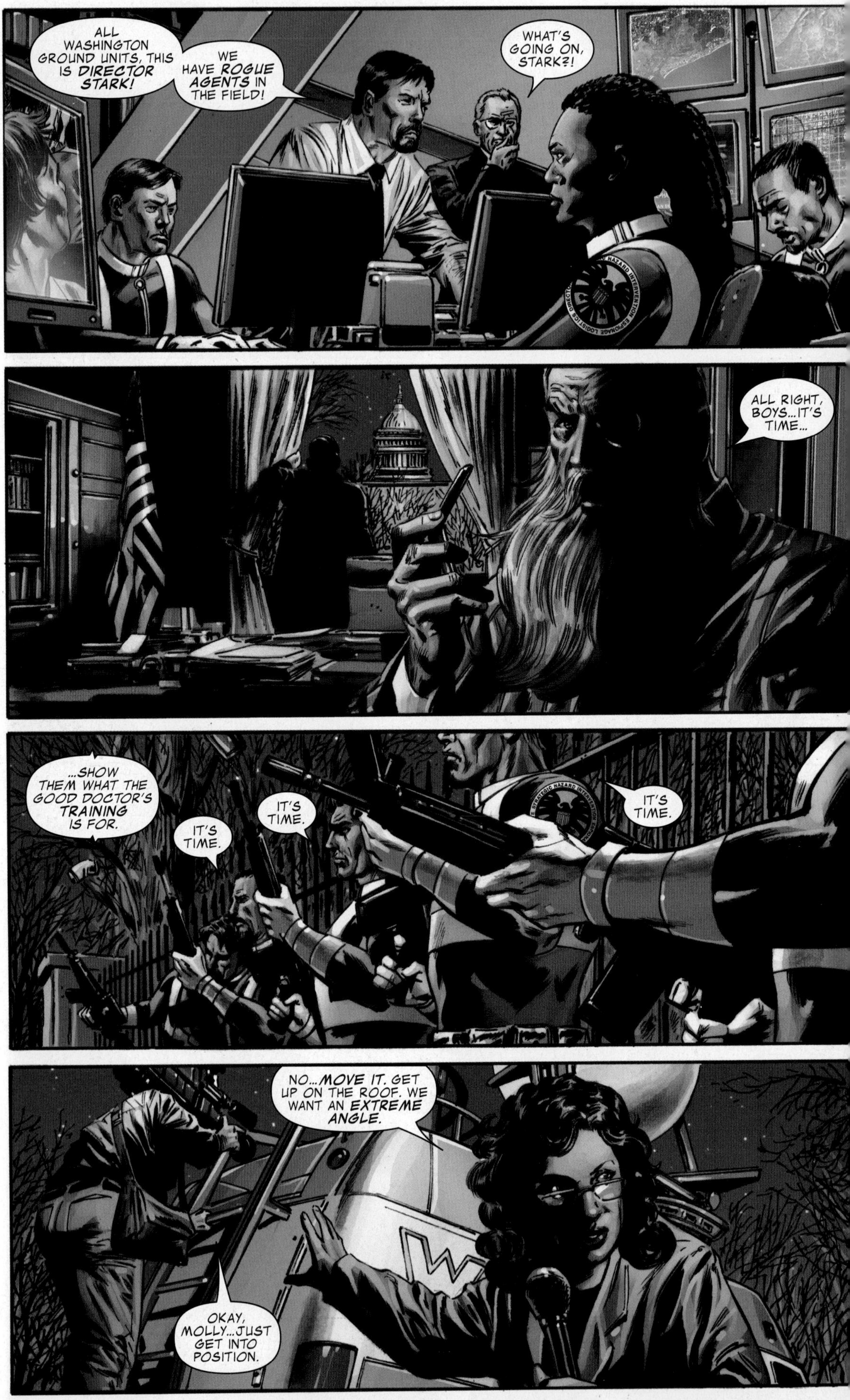
ALL WASHINGTON GROUND UNITS, THIS IS DIRECTOR STARK!
WE HAVE ROGUE AGENTS IN THE FIELD!
WHAT'S GOING ON, STARK?!
ALL RIGHT, BOYS...IT'S TIME...
...SHOW THEM WHAT THE GOOD DOCTOR'S TRAINING IS FOR.
IT'S TIME.
IT'S TIME.
IT'S TIME.
NO...MOVE IT. GET UP ON THE ROOF. WE WANT AN EXTREME ANGLE.
OKAY, MOLLY...JUST GET INTO POSITION.

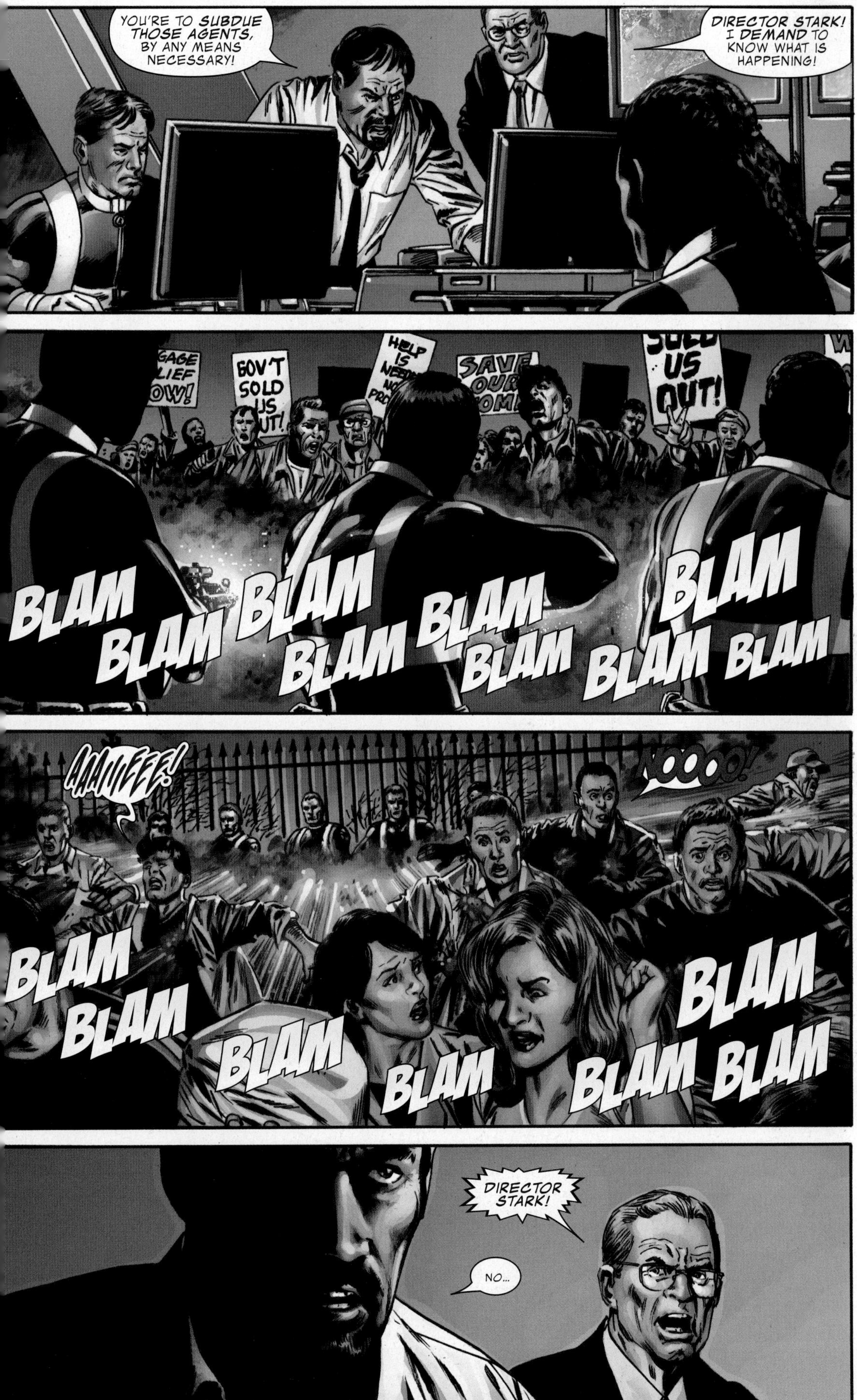
YOU'RE TO SUBDUE THOSE AGENTS, BY ANY MEANS NECESSARY!
DIRECTOR STARK! I DEMAND TO KNOW WHAT IS HAPPENING!
GOV'T SOLD US OUT!
US OUT!
BLAM BLAM BLAM BLAM BLAM BLAM BLAM BLAM BLAM
AAAIIEEE!
NOOOO!
BLAM BLAM BLAM BLAM BLAM BLAM BLAM
DIRECTOR STARK!
NO...

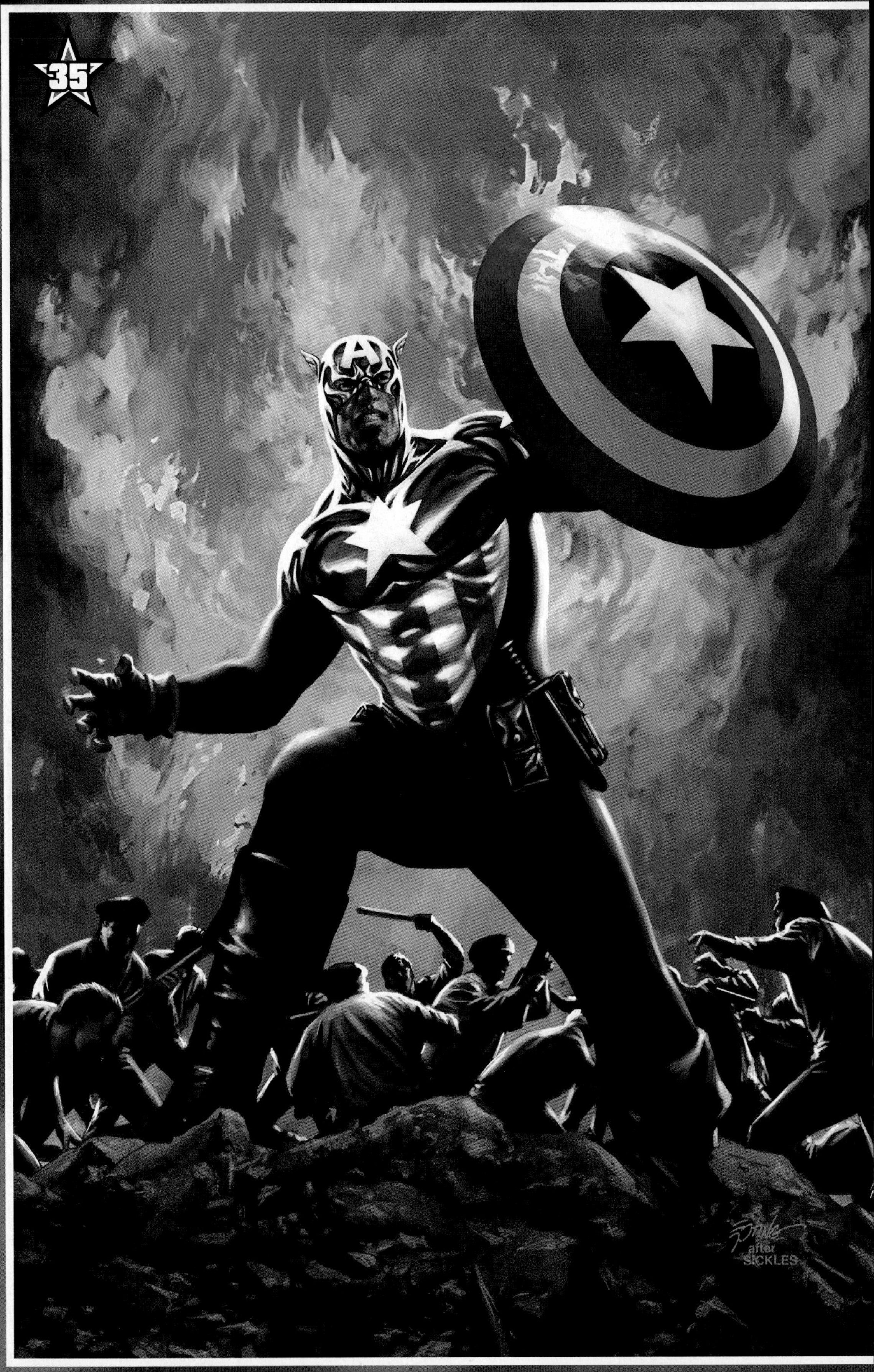
35
after
SICKLES

PART FIVE

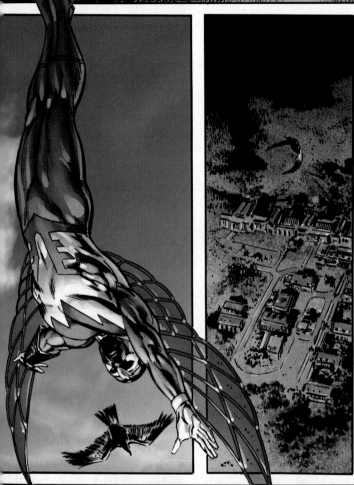

TONY, THINK I *GOT* SOMETHING.

WHAT IS IT, *SAM?*

LOOKS LIKE AN ABANDONED *REHAB CLINIC* OR SOMETHING... FEW HOURS UPSTATE.

AND ACCORDING TO MY *SOURCES,* DR. FAUSTUS WAS HERE RECENTLY...

ANY SIGN OF AGENT 13?

NO, BUT HE WASN'T ON HIS OWN.

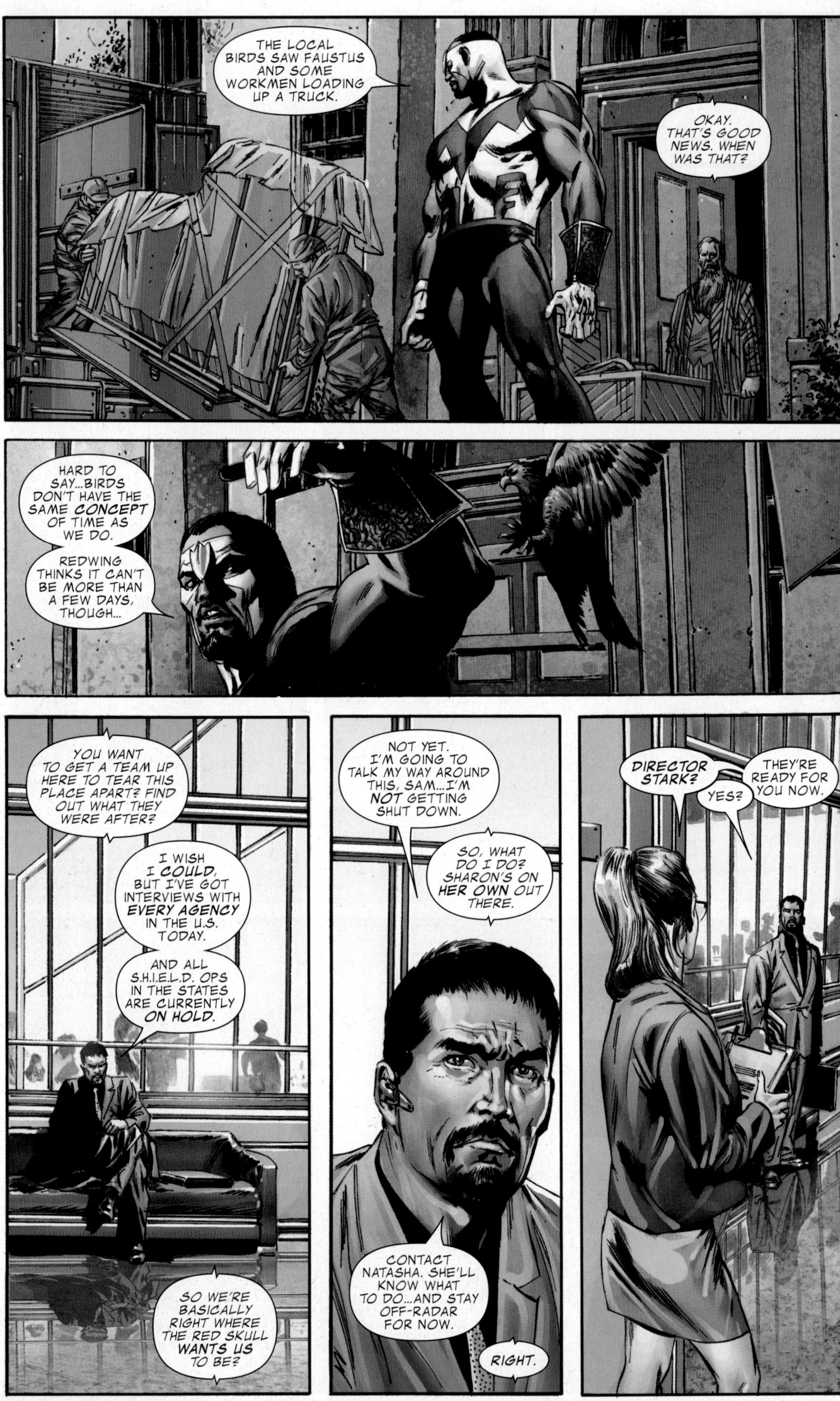
THE LOCAL BIRDS SAW FAUSTUS AND SOME WORKMEN LOADING UP A TRUCK.
OKAY. THAT'S GOOD NEWS. WHEN WAS THAT?
HARD TO SAY...BIRDS DON'T HAVE THE SAME CONCEPT OF TIME AS WE DO.
REDWING THINKS IT CAN'T BE MORE THAN A FEW DAYS, THOUGH...
YOU WANT TO GET A TEAM UP HERE TO TEAR THIS PLACE APART? FIND OUT WHAT THEY WERE AFTER?
I WISH I COULD, BUT I'VE GOT INTERVIEWS WITH EVERY AGENCY IN THE U.S. TODAY.
AND ALL S.H.I.E.L.D. OPS IN THE STATES ARE CURRENTLY ON HOLD.
SO WE'RE BASICALLY RIGHT WHERE THE RED SKULL WANTS US TO BE?
NOT YET. I'M GOING TO TALK MY WAY AROUND THIS, SAM...I'M NOT GETTING SHUT DOWN.
SO, WHAT DO I DO? SHARON'S ON HER OWN OUT THERE.
CONTACT NATASHA. SHE'LL KNOW WHAT TO DO...AND STAY OFF-RADAR FOR NOW.
RIGHT.
DIRECTOR STARK?
YES?
THEY'RE READY FOR YOU NOW.

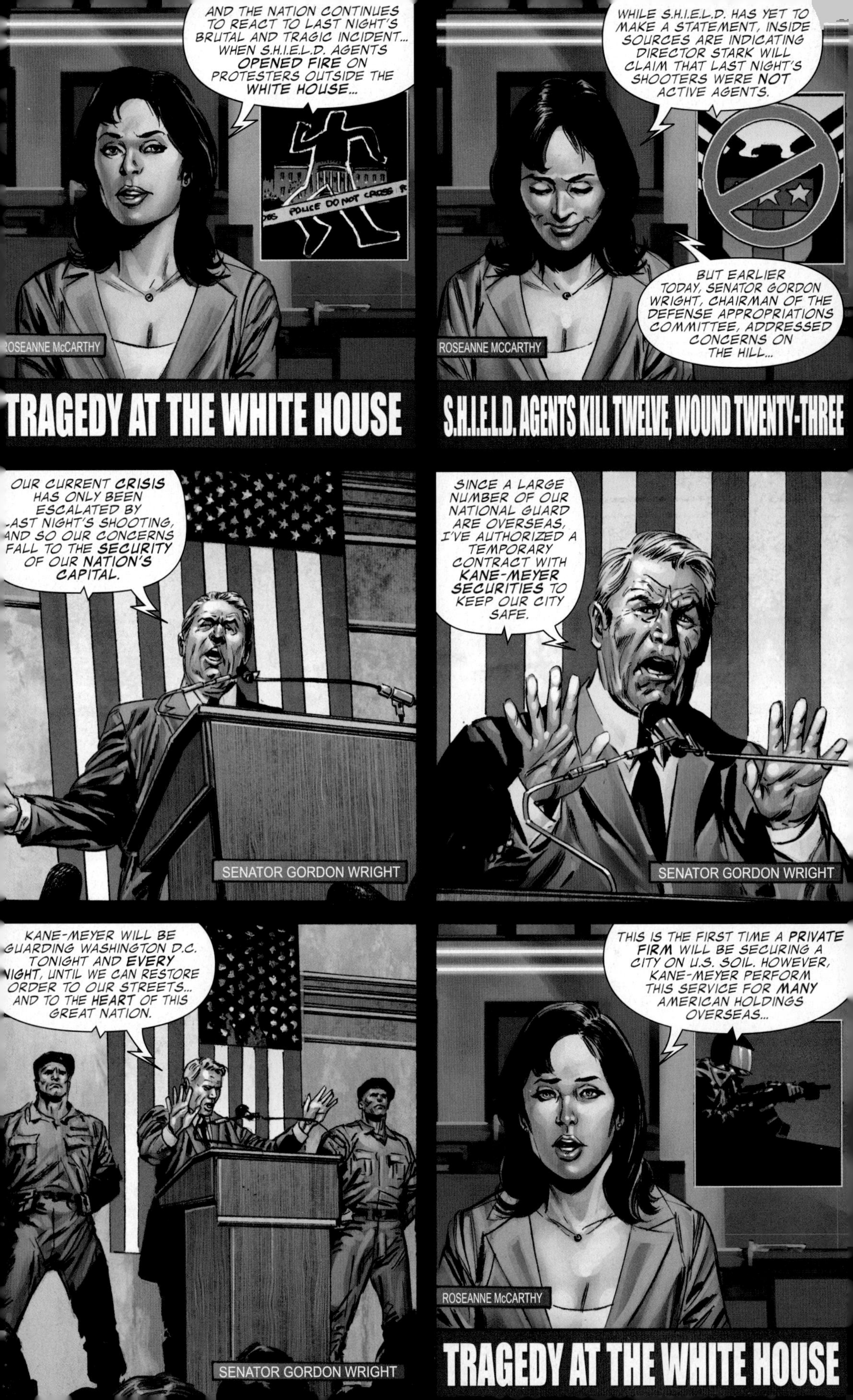

AND THE NATION CONTINUES TO REACT TO LAST NIGHT'S BRUTAL AND TRAGIC INCIDENT... WHEN S.H.I.E.L.D. AGENTS OPENED FIRE ON PROTESTERS OUTSIDE THE WHITE HOUSE...
POLICE DO NOT CROSS
ROSEANNE McCARTHY
TRAGEDY AT THE WHITE HOUSE
WHILE S.H.I.E.L.D. HAS YET TO MAKE A STATEMENT, INSIDE SOURCES ARE INDICATING DIRECTOR STARK WILL CLAIM THAT LAST NIGHT'S SHOOTERS WERE NOT ACTIVE AGENTS.
BUT EARLIER TODAY, SENATOR GORDON WRIGHT, CHAIRMAN OF THE DEFENSE APPROPRIATIONS COMMITTEE, ADDRESSED CONCERNS ON THE HILL...
ROSEANNE McCARTHY
S.H.I.E.L.D. AGENTS KILL TWELVE, WOUND TWENTY-THREE
OUR CURRENT CRISIS HAS ONLY BEEN ESCALATED BY LAST NIGHT'S SHOOTING, AND SO OUR CONCERNS FALL TO THE SECURITY OF OUR NATION'S CAPITAL.
SENATOR GORDON WRIGHT
SINCE A LARGE NUMBER OF OUR NATIONAL GUARD ARE OVERSEAS, I'VE AUTHORIZED A TEMPORARY CONTRACT WITH KANE-MEYER SECURITIES TO KEEP OUR CITY SAFE.
SENATOR GORDON WRIGHT
KANE-MEYER WILL BE GUARDING WASHINGTON D.C. TONIGHT AND EVERY NIGHT, UNTIL WE CAN RESTORE ORDER TO OUR STREETS... AND TO THE HEART OF THIS GREAT NATION.
SENATOR GORDON WRIGHT
THIS IS THE FIRST TIME A PRIVATE FIRM WILL BE SECURING A CITY ON U.S. SOIL. HOWEVER, KANE-MEYER PERFORM THIS SERVICE FOR MANY AMERICAN HOLDINGS OVERSEAS...
ROSEANNE McCARTHY
TRAGEDY AT THE WHITE HOUSE

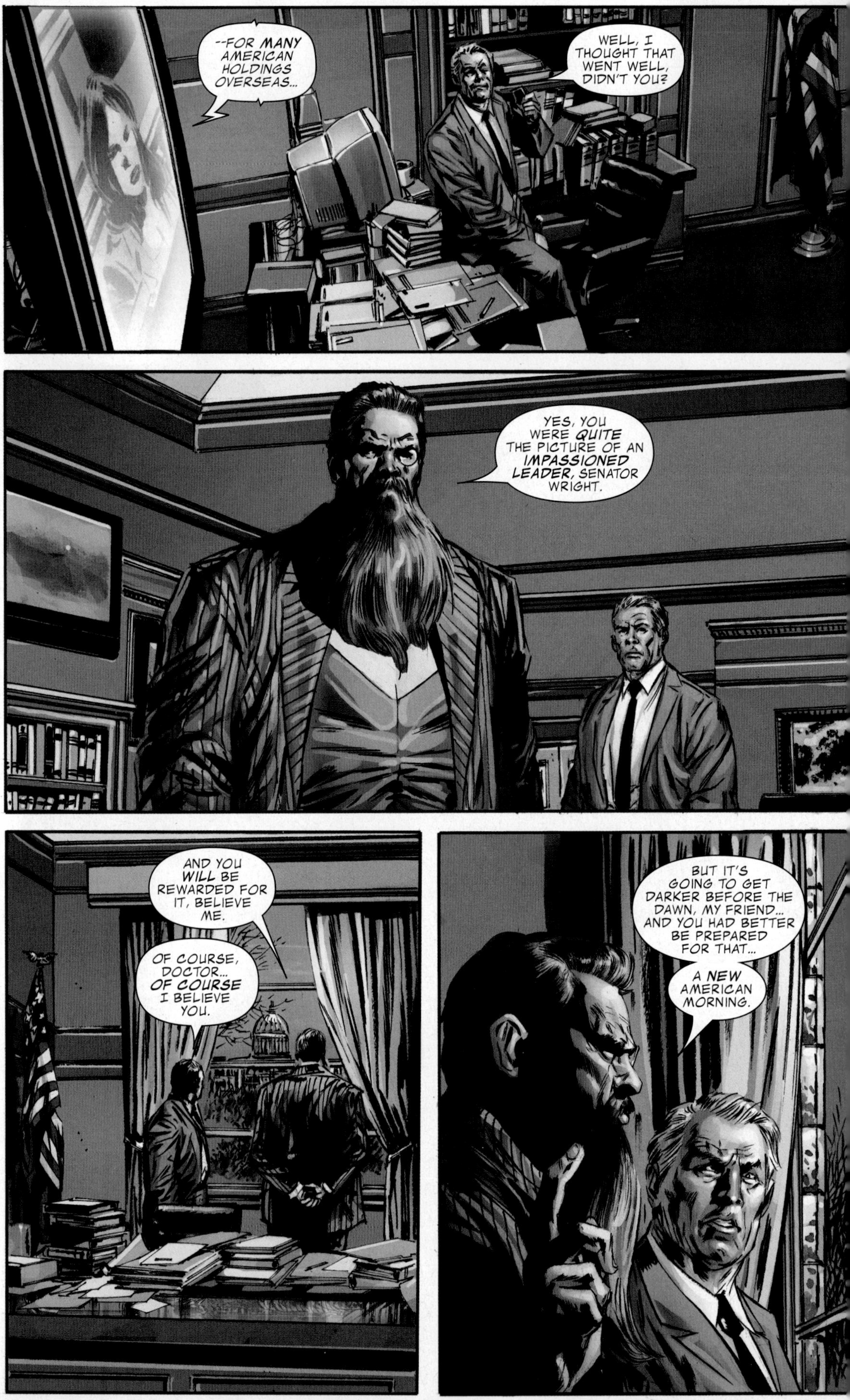
--FOR MANY AMERICAN HOLDINGS OVERSEAS...
WELL, I THOUGHT THAT WENT WELL, DIDN'T YOU?
YES, YOU WERE QUITE THE PICTURE OF AN IMPASSIONED LEADER, SENATOR WRIGHT.
AND YOU WILL BE REWARDED FOR IT, BELIEVE ME.
OF COURSE, DOCTOR... OF COURSE I BELIEVE YOU.
BUT IT'S GOING TO GET DARKER BEFORE THE DAWN, MY FRIEND... AND YOU HAD BETTER BE PREPARED FOR THAT...
A NEW AMERICAN MORNING.

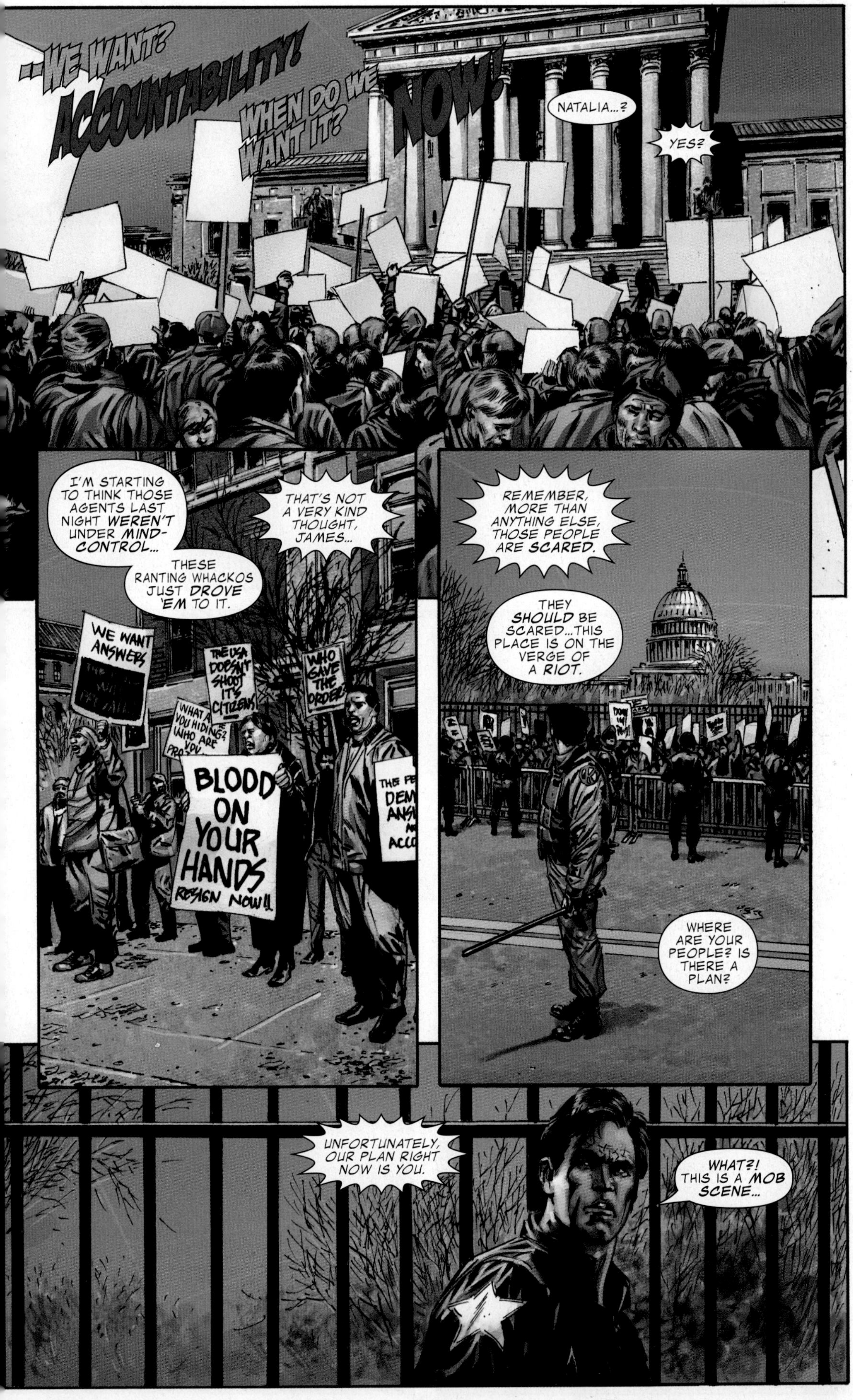

..WE WANT?
ACCOUNTABILITY!
WHEN DO WE WANT IT?
NOW!
NATALIA...?
YES?
I'M STARTING TO THINK THOSE AGENTS LAST NIGHT WEREN'T UNDER MIND-CONTROL...
THESE RANTING WHACKOS JUST DROVE 'EM TO IT.
THAT'S NOT A VERY KIND THOUGHT, JAMES...
WE WANT ANSWERS
THE USA DOESN'T SHOOT IT'S CITIZENS!
WHO GAVE THE ORDER?
BLOOD ON YOUR HANDS RESIGN NOW!!
REMEMBER, MORE THAN ANYTHING ELSE, THOSE PEOPLE ARE SCARED.
THEY SHOULD BE SCARED...THIS PLACE IS ON THE VERGE OF A RIOT.
WHERE ARE YOUR PEOPLE? IS THERE A PLAN?
UNFORTUNATELY, OUR PLAN RIGHT NOW IS YOU.
WHAT?! THIS IS A MOB SCENE...

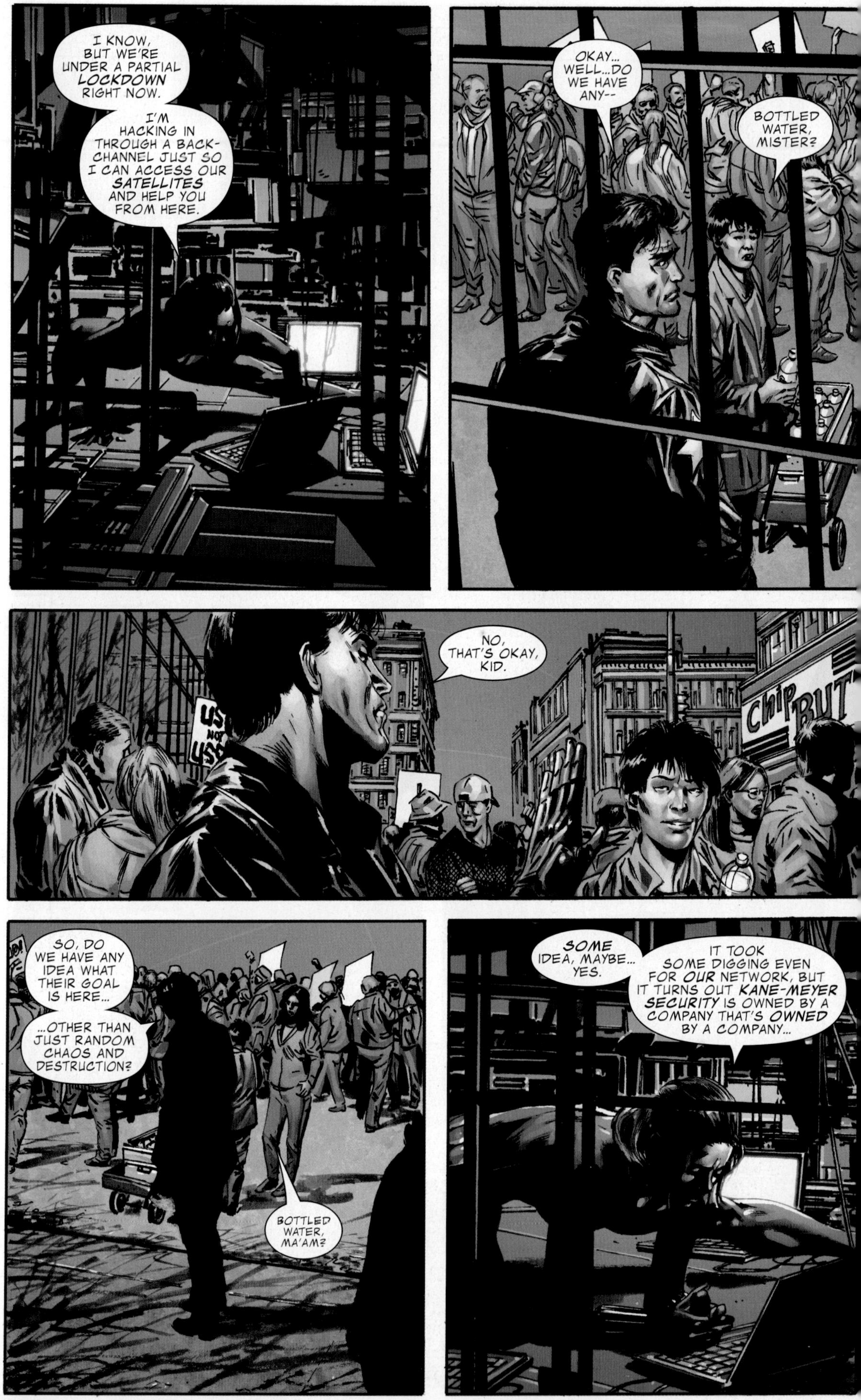
I KNOW, BUT WE'RE UNDER A PARTIAL LOCKDOWN RIGHT NOW.
I'M HACKING IN THROUGH A BACK-CHANNEL JUST SO I CAN ACCESS OUR SATELLITES AND HELP YOU FROM HERE.
OKAY... WELL...DO WE HAVE ANY--
BOTTLED WATER, MISTER?
NO, THAT'S OKAY, KID.
Chip BUT
SO, DO WE HAVE ANY IDEA WHAT THEIR GOAL IS HERE...
...OTHER THAN JUST RANDOM CHAOS AND DESTRUCTION?
BOTTLED WATER, MA'AM?
SOME IDEA, MAYBE... YES.
IT TOOK SOME DIGGING EVEN FOR OUR NETWORK, BUT IT TURNS OUT KANE-MEYER SECURITY IS OWNED BY A COMPANY THAT'S OWNED BY A COMPANY...

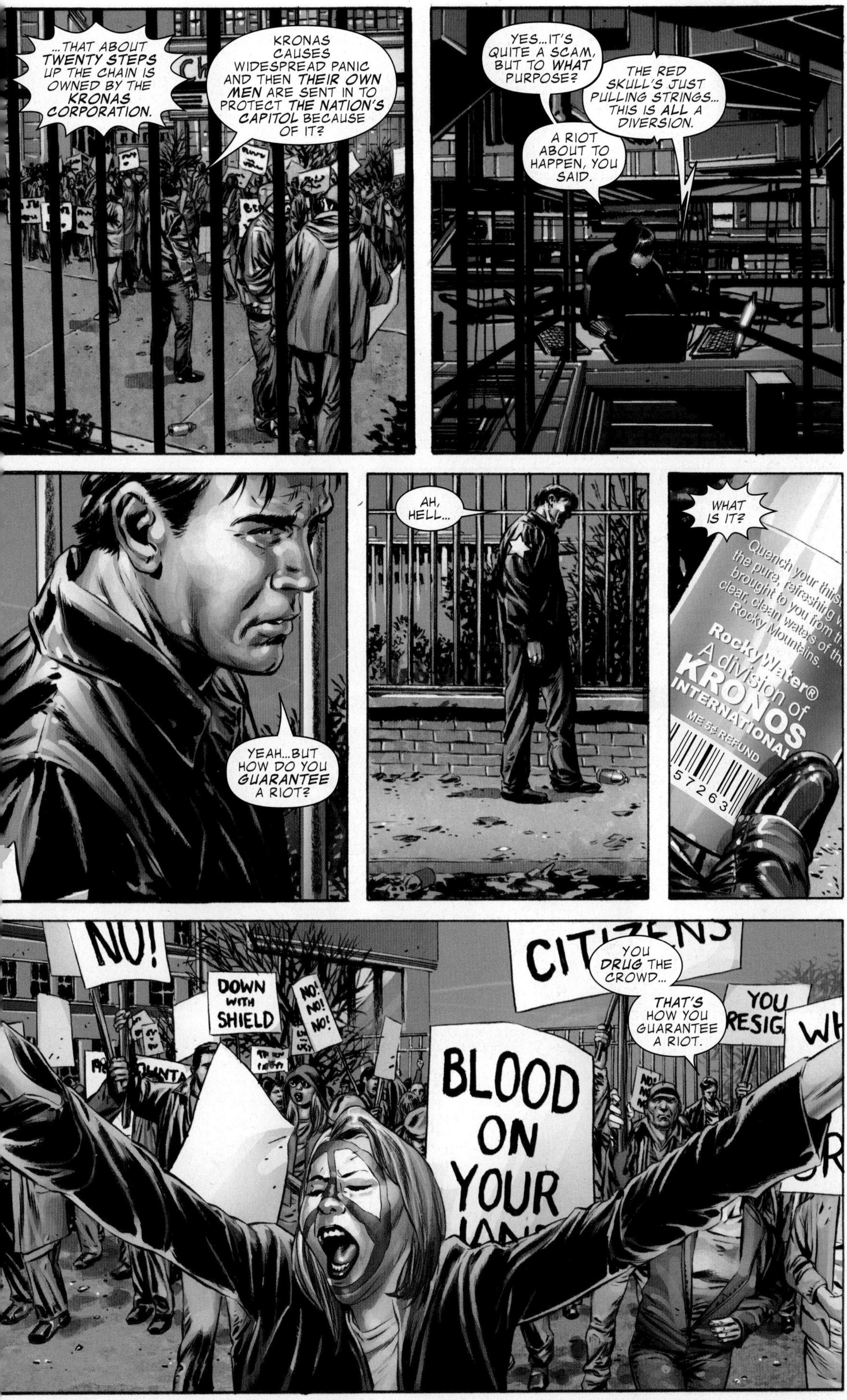
...THAT ABOUT TWENTY STEPS UP THE CHAIN IS OWNED BY THE KRONAS CORPORATION.
KRONAS CAUSES WIDESPREAD PANIC AND THEN THEIR OWN MEN ARE SENT IN TO PROTECT THE NATION'S CAPITOL BECAUSE OF IT?
YES...IT'S QUITE A SCAM, BUT TO WHAT PURPOSE?
A RIOT ABOUT TO HAPPEN, YOU SAID.
THE RED SKULL'S JUST PULLING STRINGS... THIS IS ALL A DIVERSION.
YEAH...BUT HOW DO YOU GUARANTEE A RIOT?
AH, HELL...
WHAT IS IT?
Quench your thirs
the pure, refreshing w
brought to you from th
clear, clean waters of th
Rocky Mountains.
RockyWater®
A division of
KRONOS
INTERNATIONAL
ME 5¢ REFUND
57263
NO!
DOWN WITH SHIELD
NO! NO! NO!
CITIZENS
BLOOD ON YOUR
YOU DRUG THE CROWD...
THAT'S HOW YOU GUARANTEE A RIOT.
YOU RESIG
WH

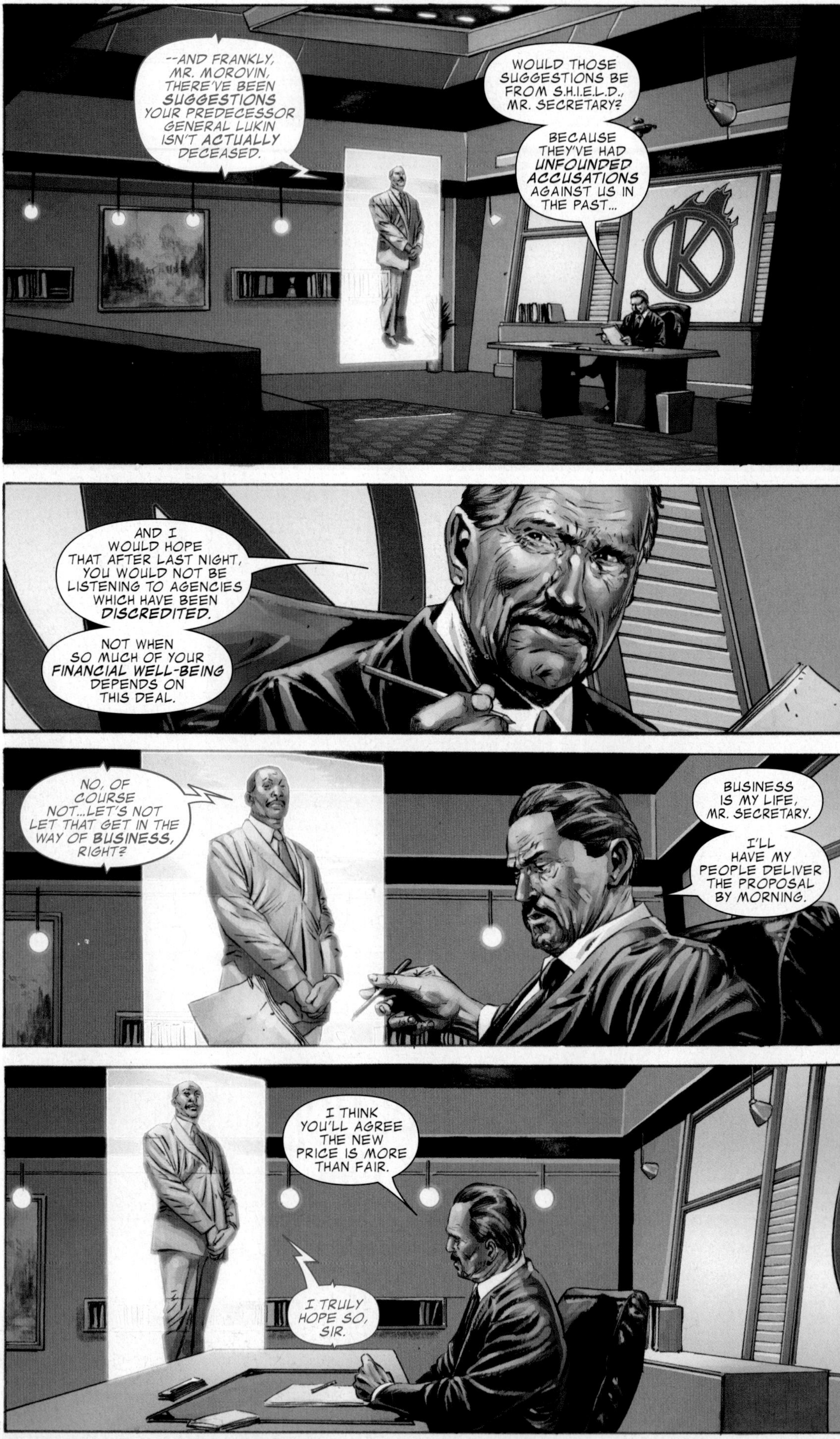
--AND FRANKLY, MR. MOROVIN, THERE'VE BEEN SUGGESTIONS YOUR PREDECESSOR GENERAL LUKIN ISN'T ACTUALLY DECEASED.
WOULD THOSE SUGGESTIONS BE FROM S.H.I.E.L.D., MR. SECRETARY?
BECAUSE THEY'VE HAD UNFOUNDED ACCUSATIONS AGAINST US IN THE PAST...
AND I WOULD HOPE THAT AFTER LAST NIGHT, YOU WOULD NOT BE LISTENING TO AGENCIES WHICH HAVE BEEN DISCREDITED.
NOT WHEN SO MUCH OF YOUR FINANCIAL WELL-BEING DEPENDS ON THIS DEAL.
NO, OF COURSE NOT...LET'S NOT LET THAT GET IN THE WAY OF BUSINESS, RIGHT?
BUSINESS IS MY LIFE, MR. SECRETARY.
I'LL HAVE MY PEOPLE DELIVER THE PROPOSAL BY MORNING.
I THINK YOU'LL AGREE THE NEW PRICE IS MORE THAN FAIR.
I TRULY HOPE SO, SIR.

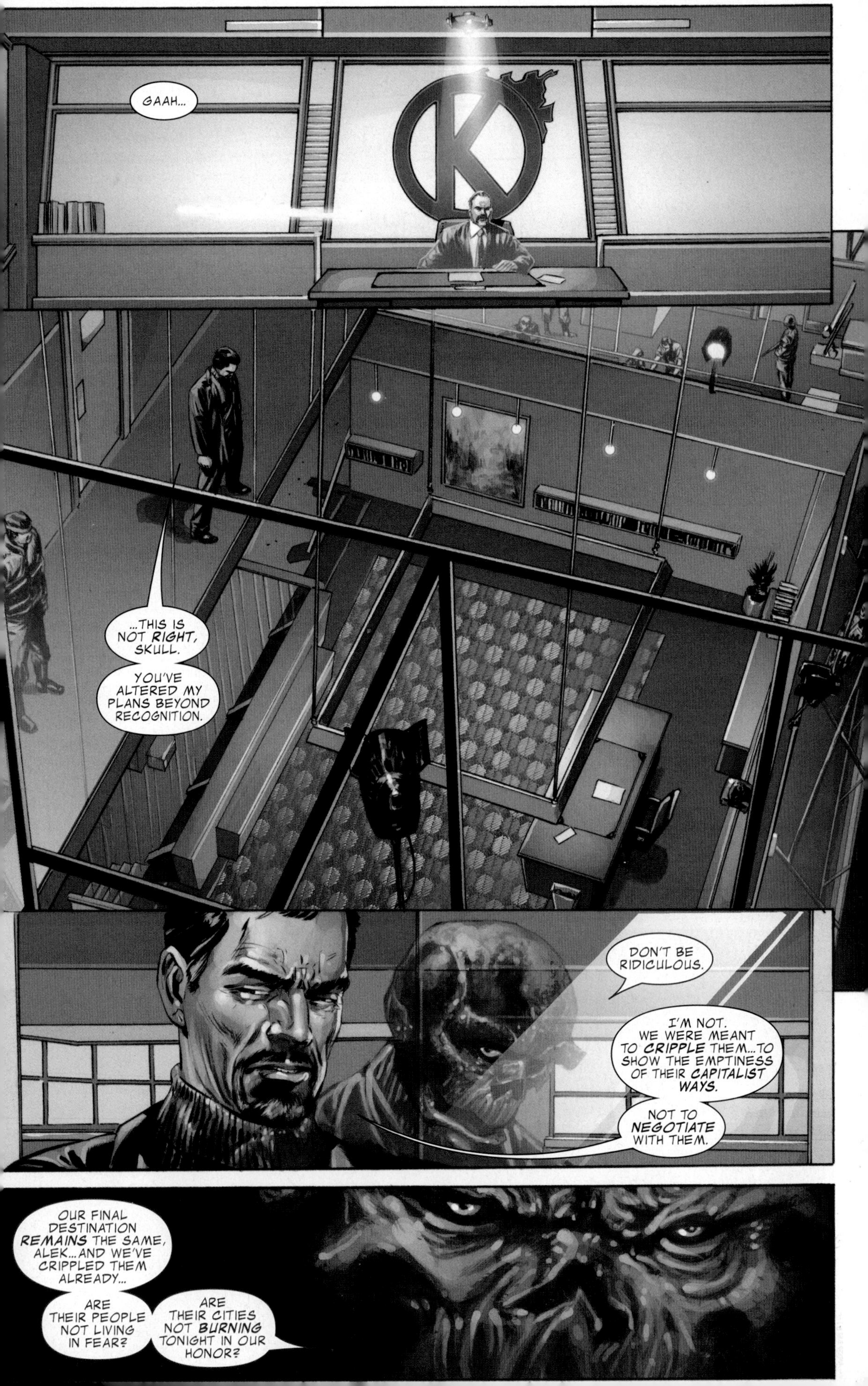
GAAH...
...THIS IS NOT RIGHT, SKULL.
YOU'VE ALTERED MY PLANS BEYOND RECOGNITION.
DON'T BE RIDICULOUS.
I'M NOT. WE WERE MEANT TO CRIPPLE THEM...TO SHOW THE EMPTINESS OF THEIR CAPITALIST WAYS.
NOT TO NEGOTIATE WITH THEM.
OUR FINAL DESTINATION REMAINS THE SAME, ALEK...AND WE'VE CRIPPLED THEM ALREADY...
ARE THEIR PEOPLE NOT LIVING IN FEAR?
ARE THEIR CITIES NOT BURNING TONIGHT IN OUR HONOR?

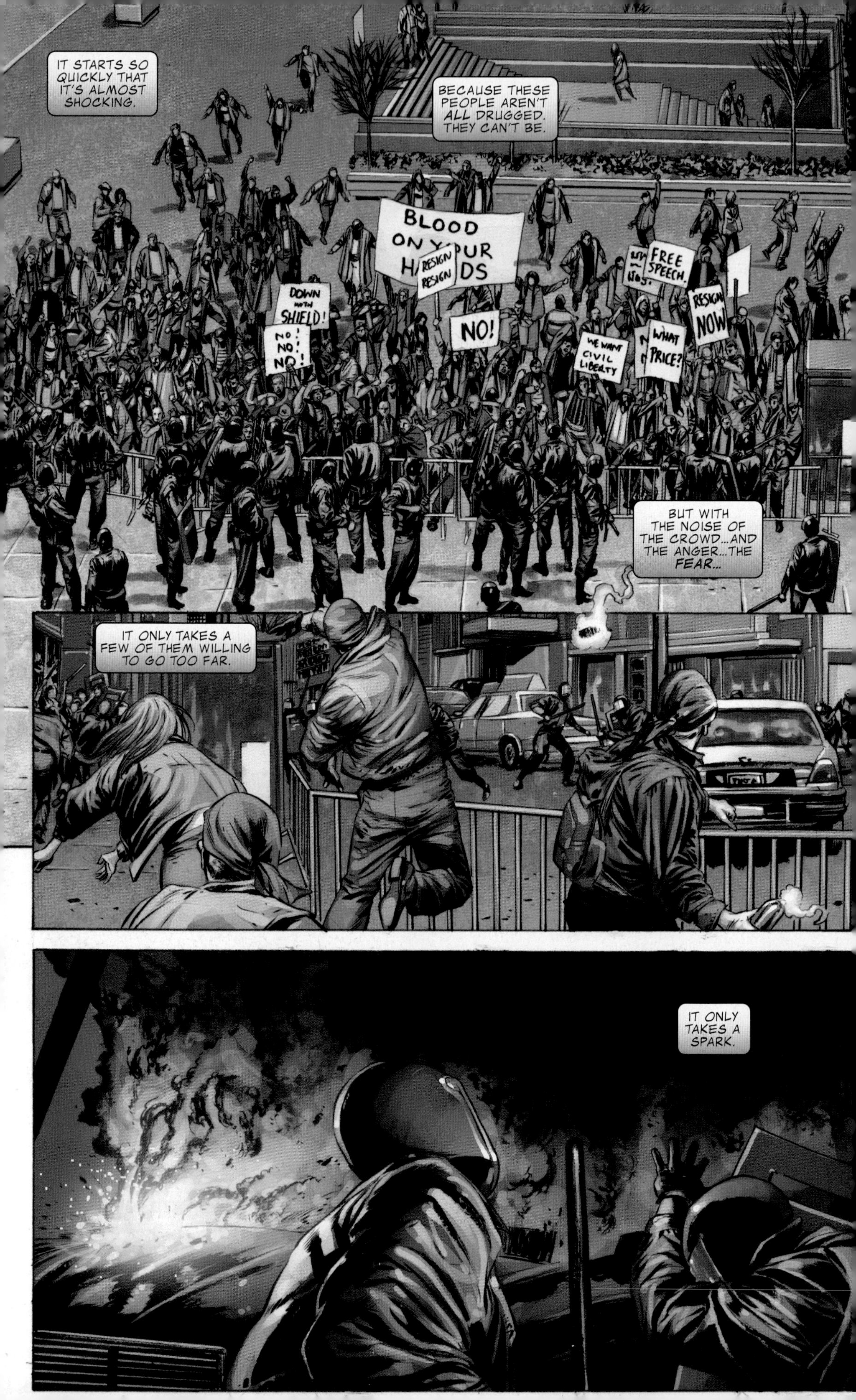
IT STARTS SO QUICKLY THAT IT'S ALMOST SHOCKING.
BECAUSE THESE PEOPLE AREN'T ALL DRUGGED. THEY CAN'T BE.
BLOOD
RESIGN RESIGN
DOWN WITH SHIELD!
NO! NO! NO!
NO!
FREE SPEECH.
RESIGN NOW
WE WANT CIVIL LIBERTY
WHAT PRICE?
BUT WITH THE NOISE OF THE CROWD...AND THE ANGER...THE FEAR...
IT ONLY TAKES A FEW OF THEM WILLING TO GO TOO FAR.
IT ONLY TAKES A SPARK.

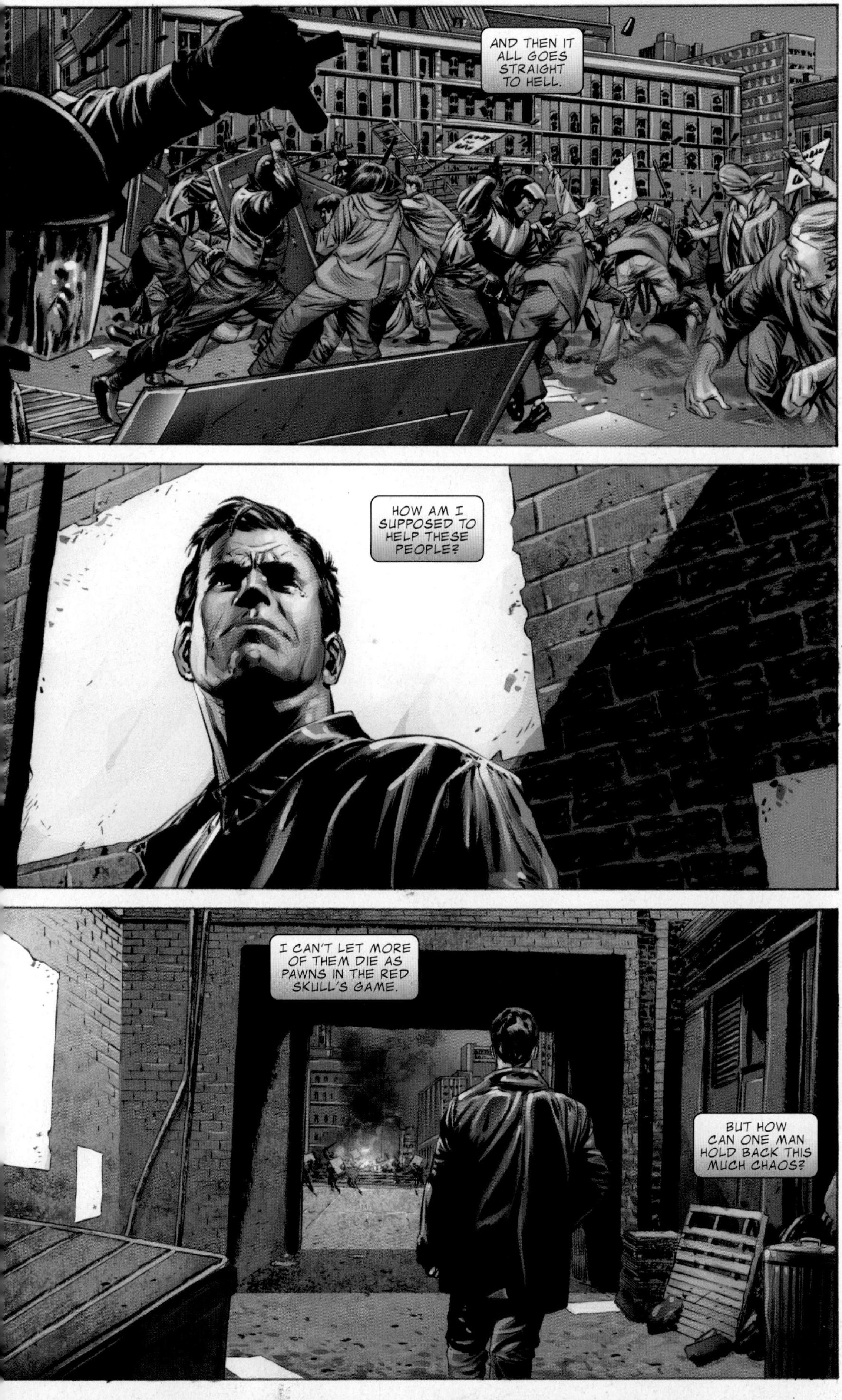
AND THEN IT ALL GOES STRAIGHT TO HELL.
HOW AM I SUPPOSED TO HELP THESE PEOPLE?
I CAN'T LET MORE OF THEM DIE AS PAWNS IN THE RED SKULL'S GAME.
BUT HOW CAN ONE MAN HOLD BACK THIS MUCH CHAOS?

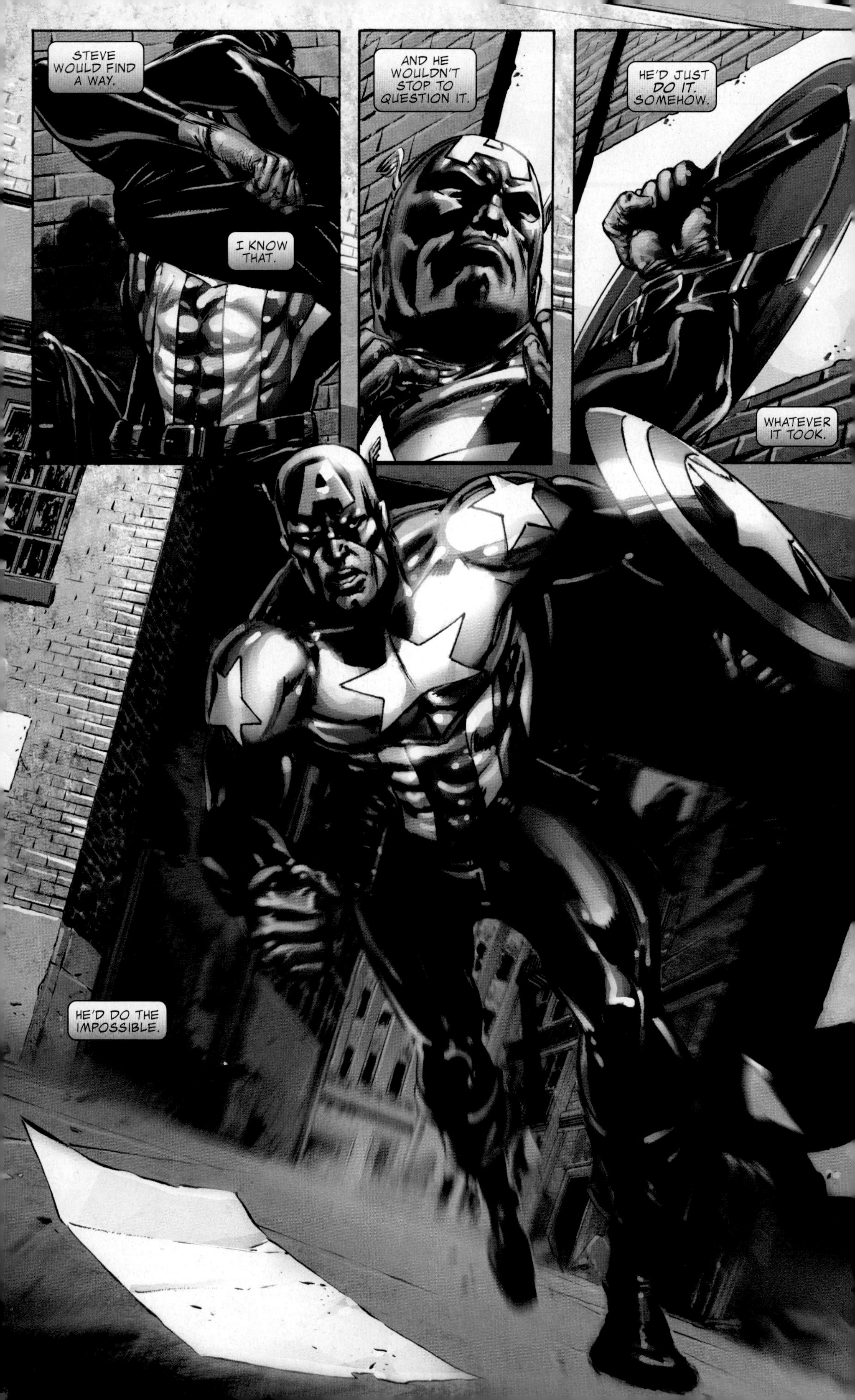
STEVE WOULD FIND A WAY.
I KNOW THAT.
AND HE WOULDN'T STOP TO QUESTION IT.
HE'D JUST DO IT. SOMEHOW.
WHATEVER IT TOOK.
HE'D DO THE IMPOSSIBLE.

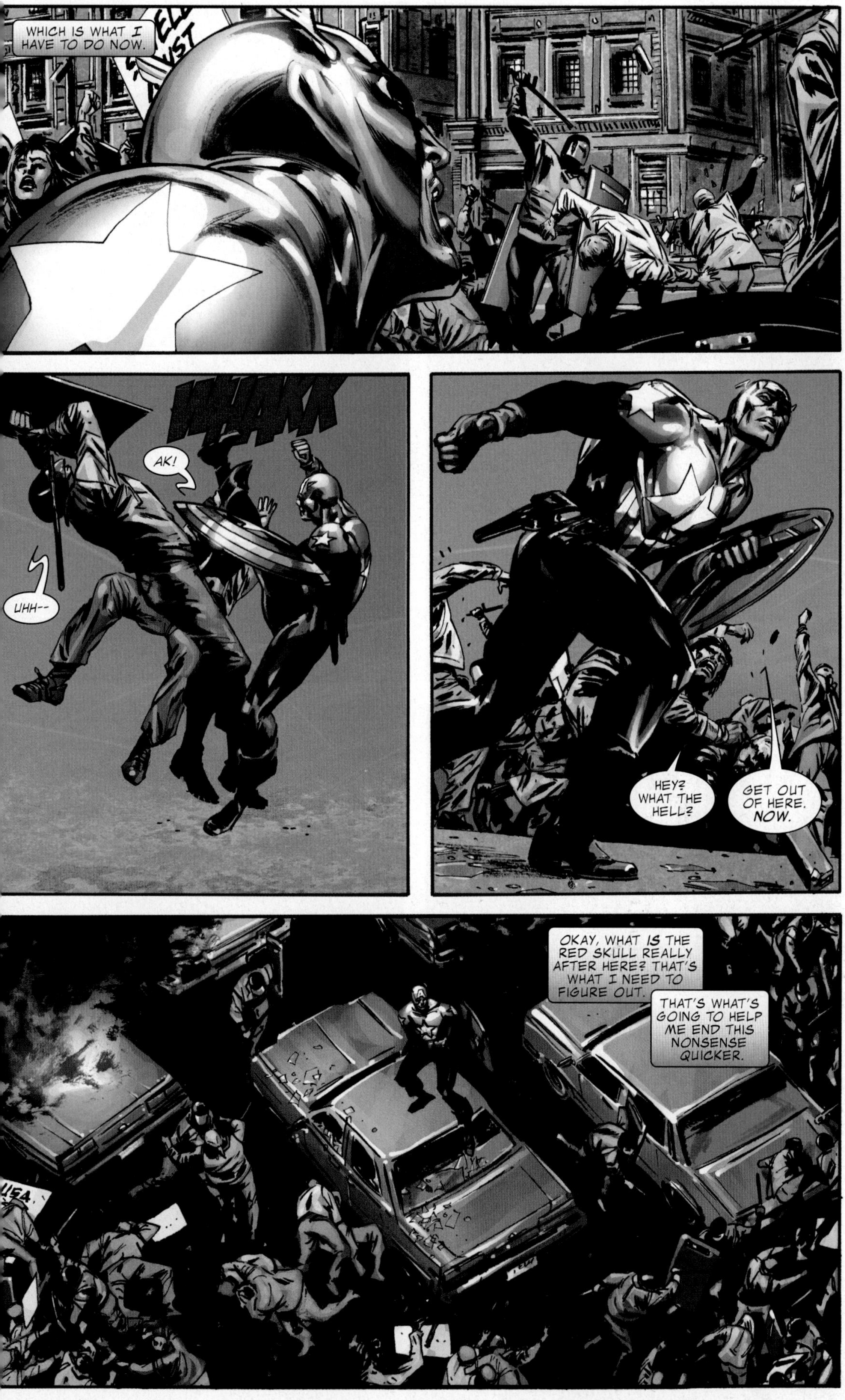
WHICH IS WHAT I HAVE TO DO NOW.
WHAKK
AK!
UHH--
HEY? WHAT THE HELL?
GET OUT OF HERE. NOW.
OKAY, WHAT IS THE RED SKULL REALLY AFTER HERE? THAT'S WHAT I NEED TO FIGURE OUT.
THAT'S WHAT'S GOING TO HELP ME END THIS NONSENSE QUICKER.

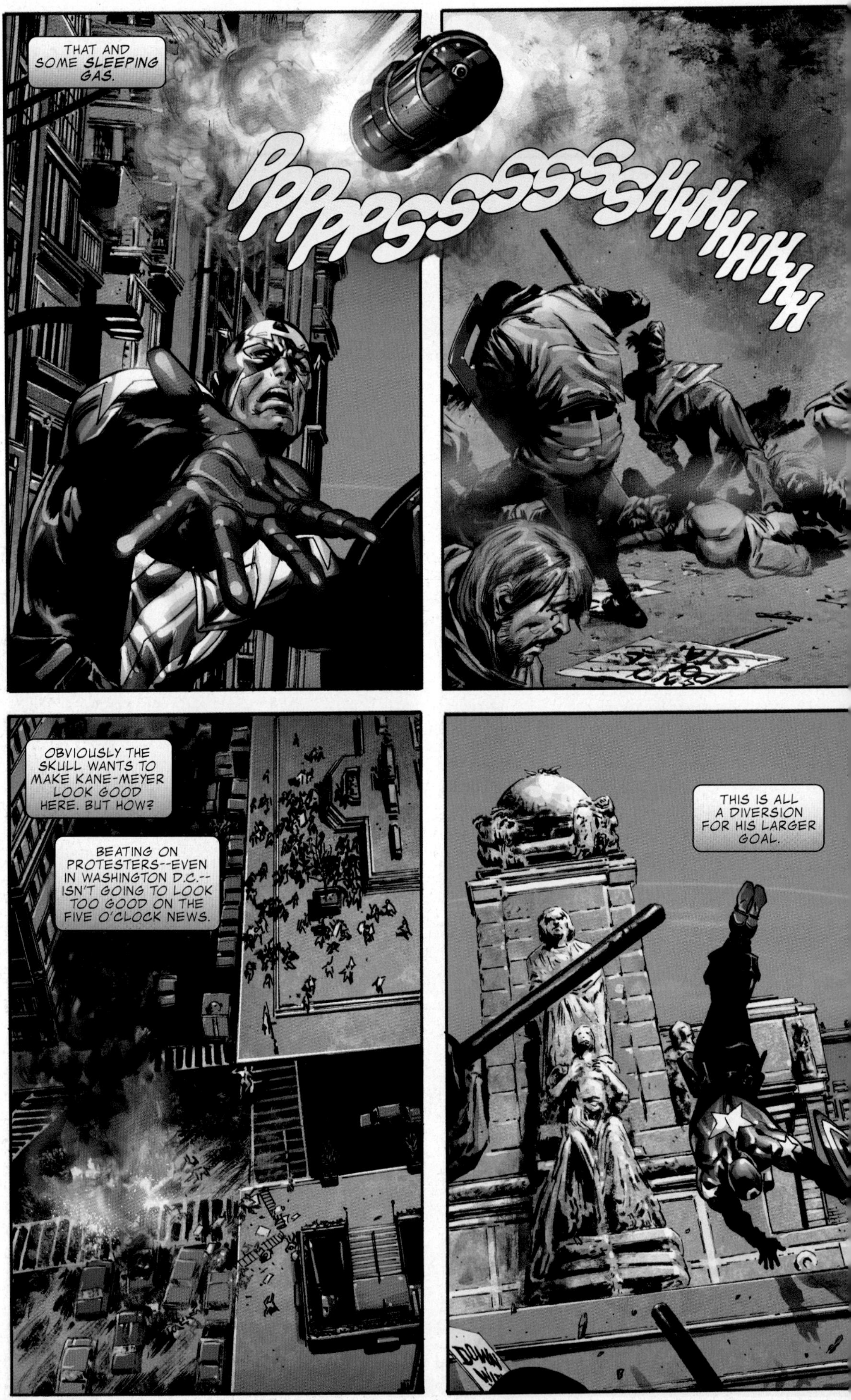
THAT AND SOME SLEEPING GAS.
PPPPPSSSSSSSSSHHHHHHHH
OBVIOUSLY THE SKULL WANTS TO MAKE KANE-MEYER LOOK GOOD HERE. BUT HOW?
BEATING ON PROTESTERS--EVEN IN WASHINGTON D.C.--ISN'T GOING TO LOOK TOO GOOD ON THE FIVE O'CLOCK NEWS.
THIS IS ALL A DIVERSION FOR HIS LARGER GOAL.

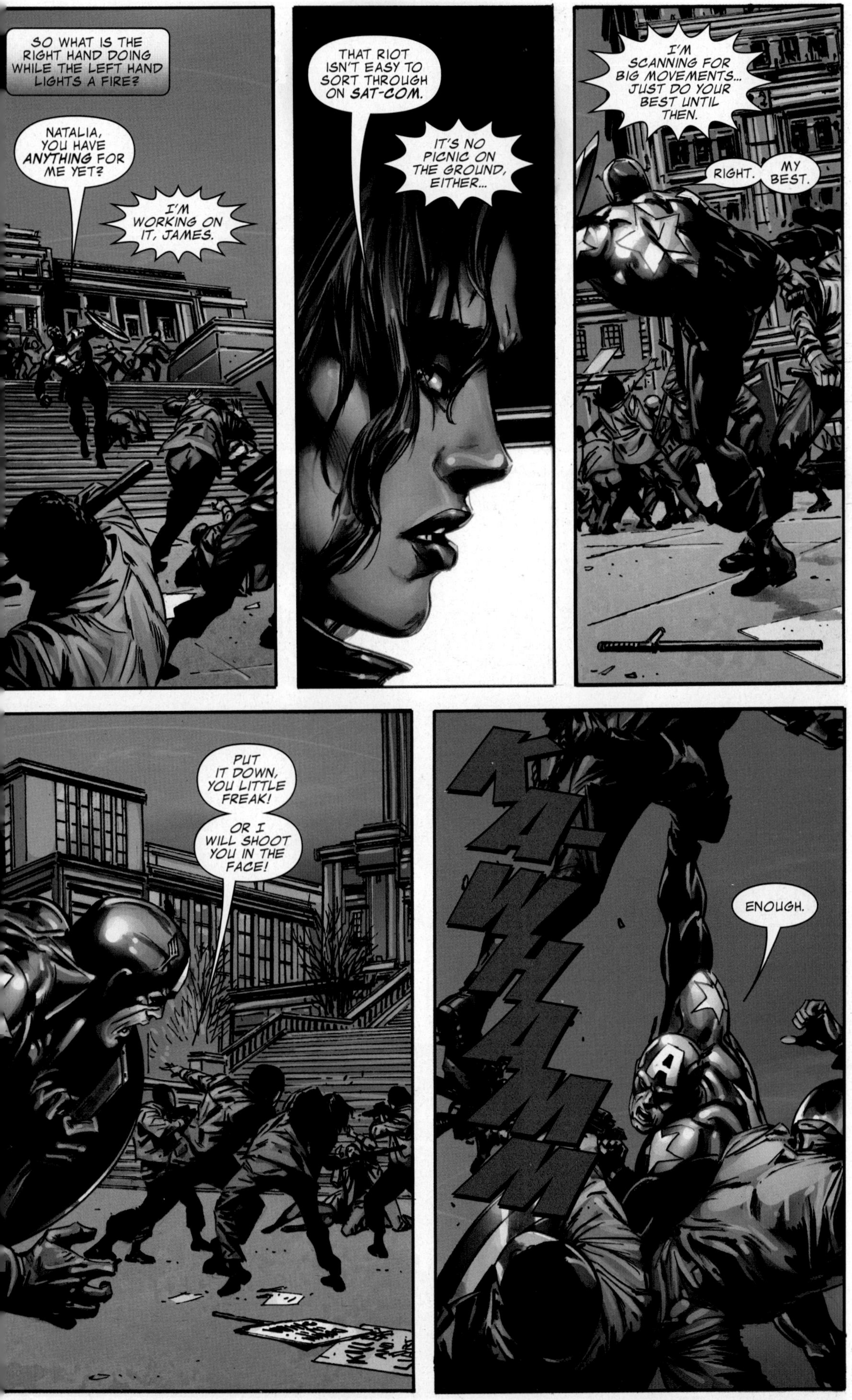
SO WHAT IS THE RIGHT HAND DOING WHILE THE LEFT HAND LIGHTS A FIRE?
NATALIA, YOU HAVE ANYTHING FOR ME YET?
I'M WORKING ON IT, JAMES.
THAT RIOT ISN'T EASY TO SORT THROUGH ON SAT-COM.
IT'S NO PICNIC ON THE GROUND, EITHER...
I'M SCANNING FOR BIG MOVEMENTS... JUST DO YOUR BEST UNTIL THEN.
RIGHT.
MY BEST.
PUT IT DOWN, YOU LITTLE FREAK!
OR I WILL SHOOT YOU IN THE FACE!
KA-WHAMM
ENOUGH.

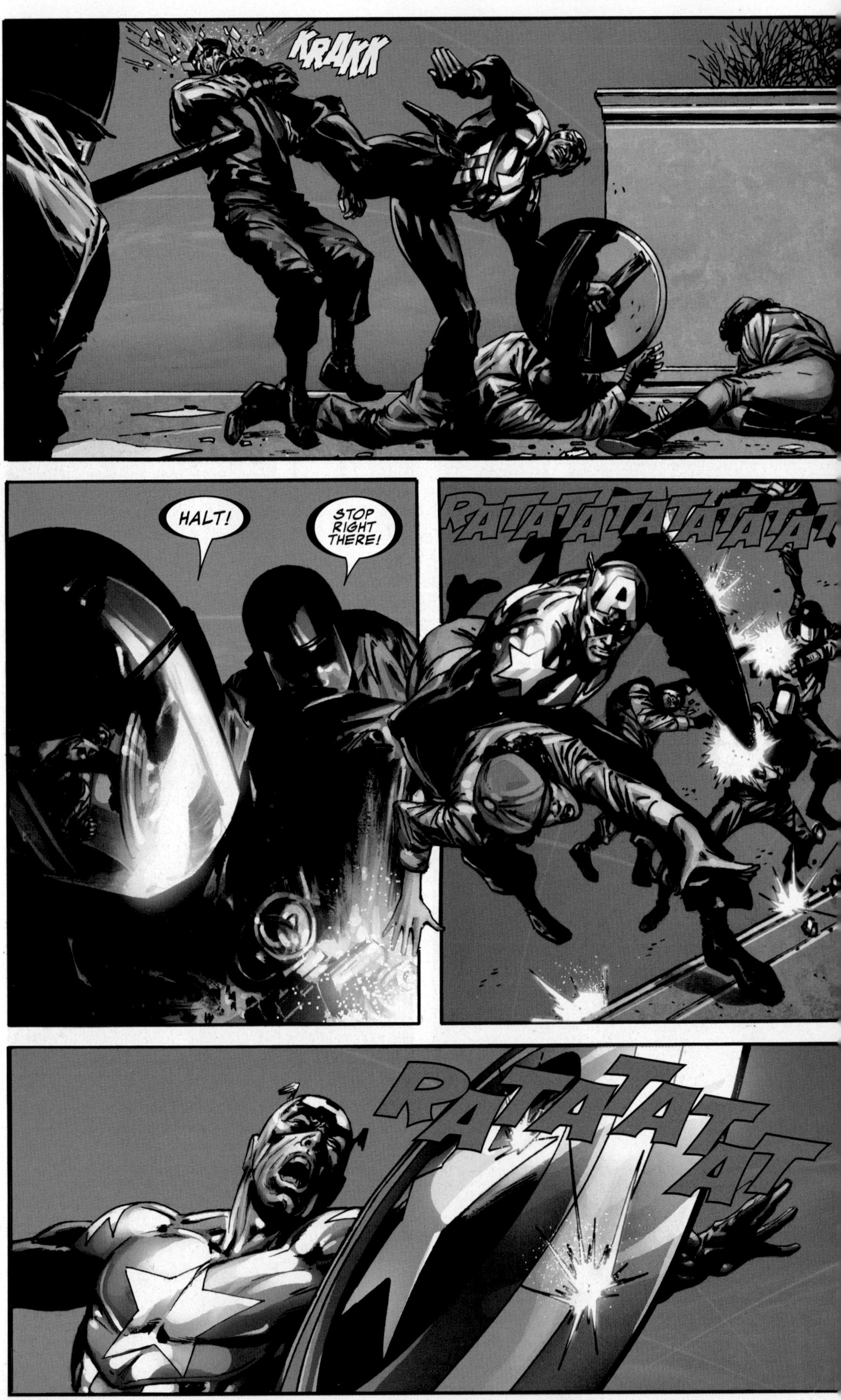
KRAKK
HALT!
STOP RIGHT THERE!
RATATATATATATAT
RATATATAT

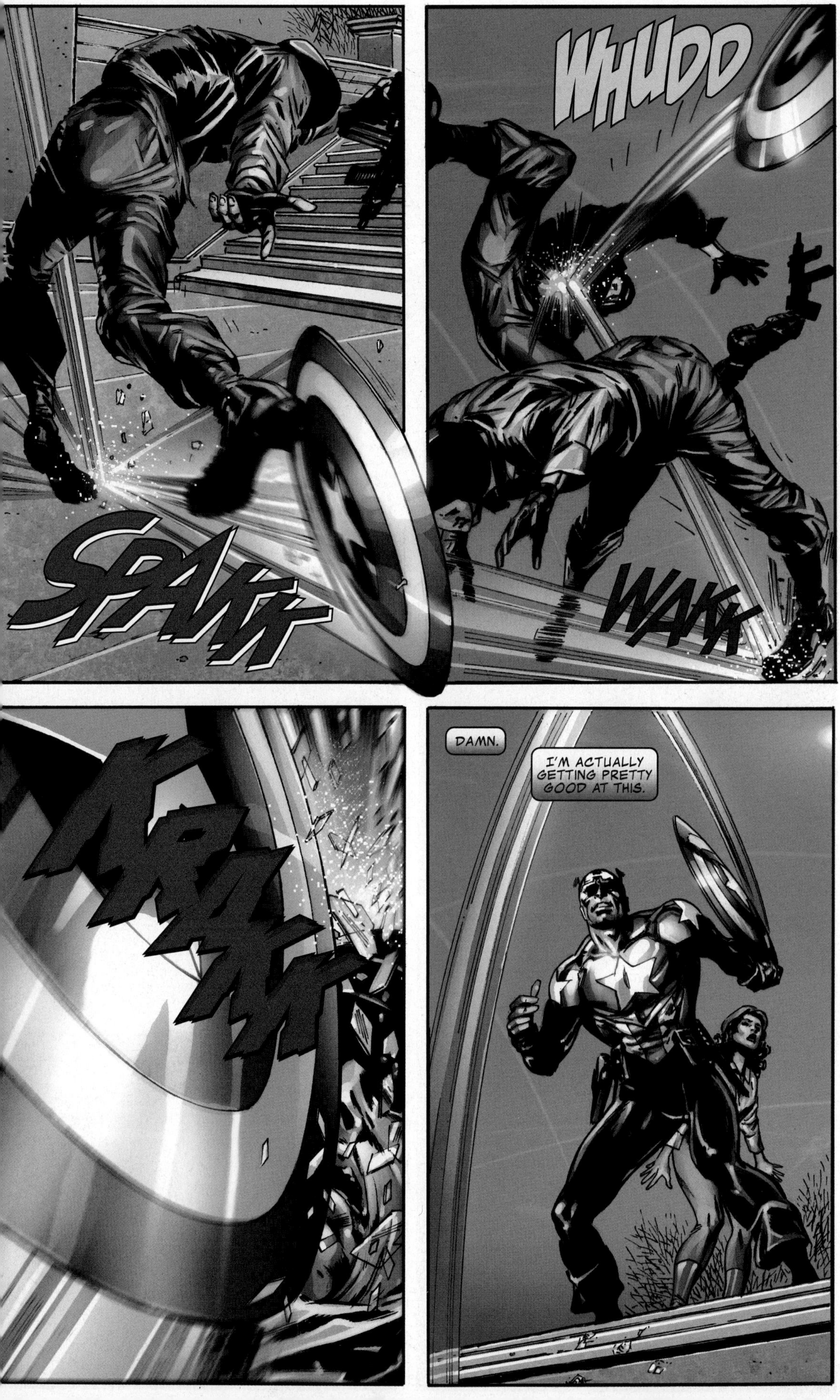
SPAKK
WHUDD
WAKK
KRAKK
DAMN.
I'M ACTUALLY GETTING PRETTY GOOD AT THIS.

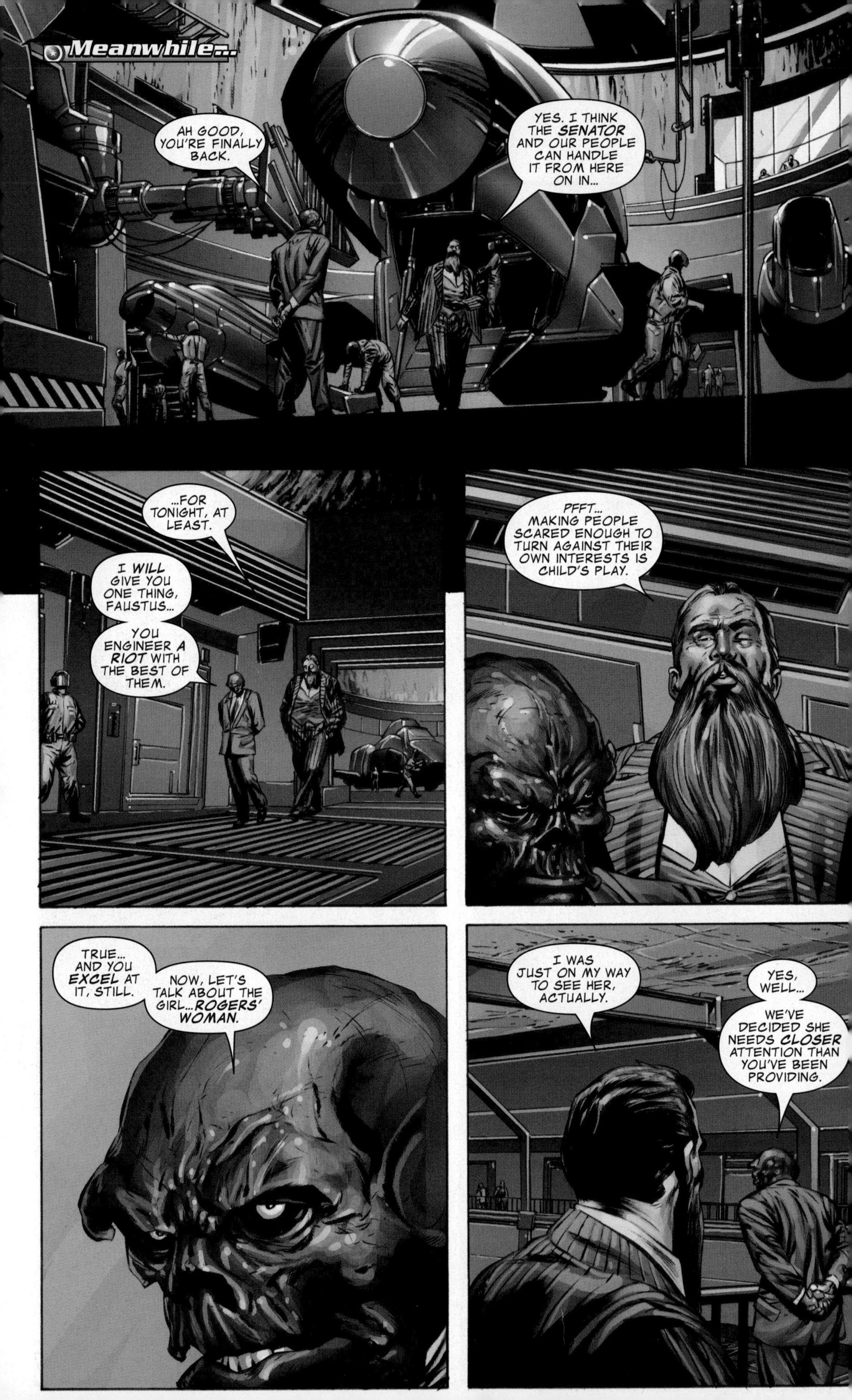
Meanwhile...
AH GOOD, YOU'RE FINALLY BACK.
YES. I THINK THE SENATOR AND OUR PEOPLE CAN HANDLE IT FROM HERE ON IN...
...FOR TONIGHT, AT LEAST.
I WILL GIVE YOU ONE THING, FAUSTUS...
YOU ENGINEER A RIOT WITH THE BEST OF THEM.
PFFT... MAKING PEOPLE SCARED ENOUGH TO TURN AGAINST THEIR OWN INTERESTS IS CHILD'S PLAY.
TRUE... AND YOU EXCEL AT IT, STILL.
NOW, LET'S TALK ABOUT THE GIRL... ROGERS' WOMAN.
I WAS JUST ON MY WAY TO SEE HER, ACTUALLY.
YES, WELL...
WE'VE DECIDED SHE NEEDS CLOSER ATTENTION THAN YOU'VE BEEN PROVIDING.

JAMES-- I MAY HAVE SOMETHING.

GOOD. WHAT IS IT?

I FEEL LIKE I'M SWATTING FLIES OUT HERE.

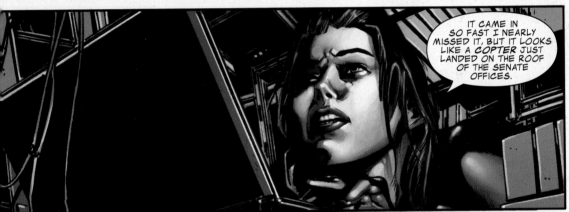

IT CAME IN SO FAST I NEARLY MISSED IT, BUT IT LOOKS LIKE A COPTER JUST LANDED ON THE ROOF OF THE SENATE OFFICES.

THAT'S GOT TO BE PART OF THE SKULL'S PLAN.

YEAH...IT'S A BIGGER TARGET. THAT'S FOR SURE.

KRAKK

SCAN THE SENATE COMM. SYSTEM...I'M ON MY WAY...

BUT IT'D BE NICE TO KNOW WHAT I'M RUSHING INTO.

I'M ALREADY HACKING THROUGH THEIR SECURITY.

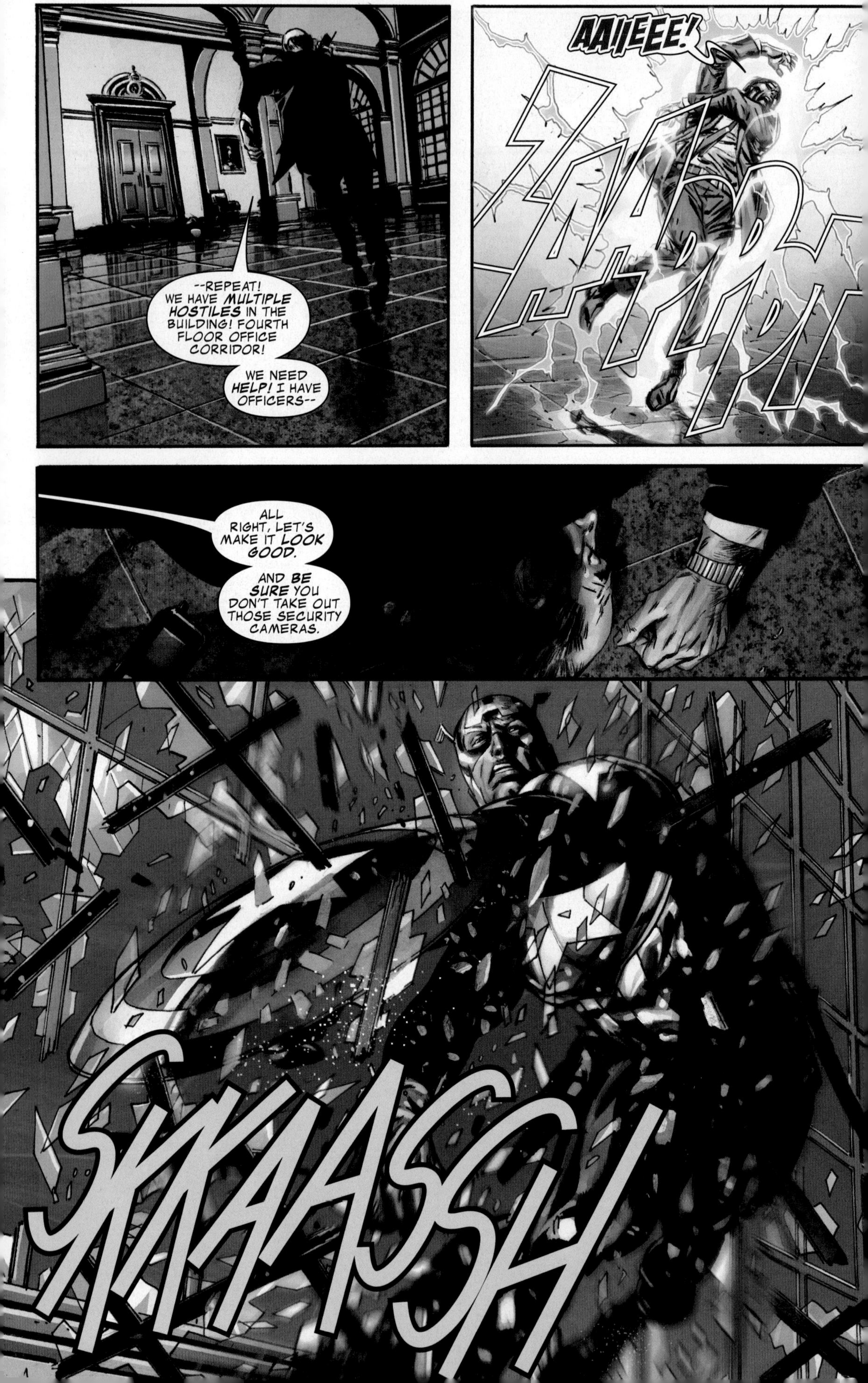
--REPEAT! WE HAVE MULTIPLE HOSTILES IN THE BUILDING! FOURTH FLOOR OFFICE CORRIDOR!
WE NEED HELP! I HAVE OFFICERS--
AAIIEEE!
ALL RIGHT, LET'S MAKE IT LOOK GOOD.
AND BE SURE YOU DON'T TAKE OUT THOSE SECURITY CAMERAS.
SKKAASH

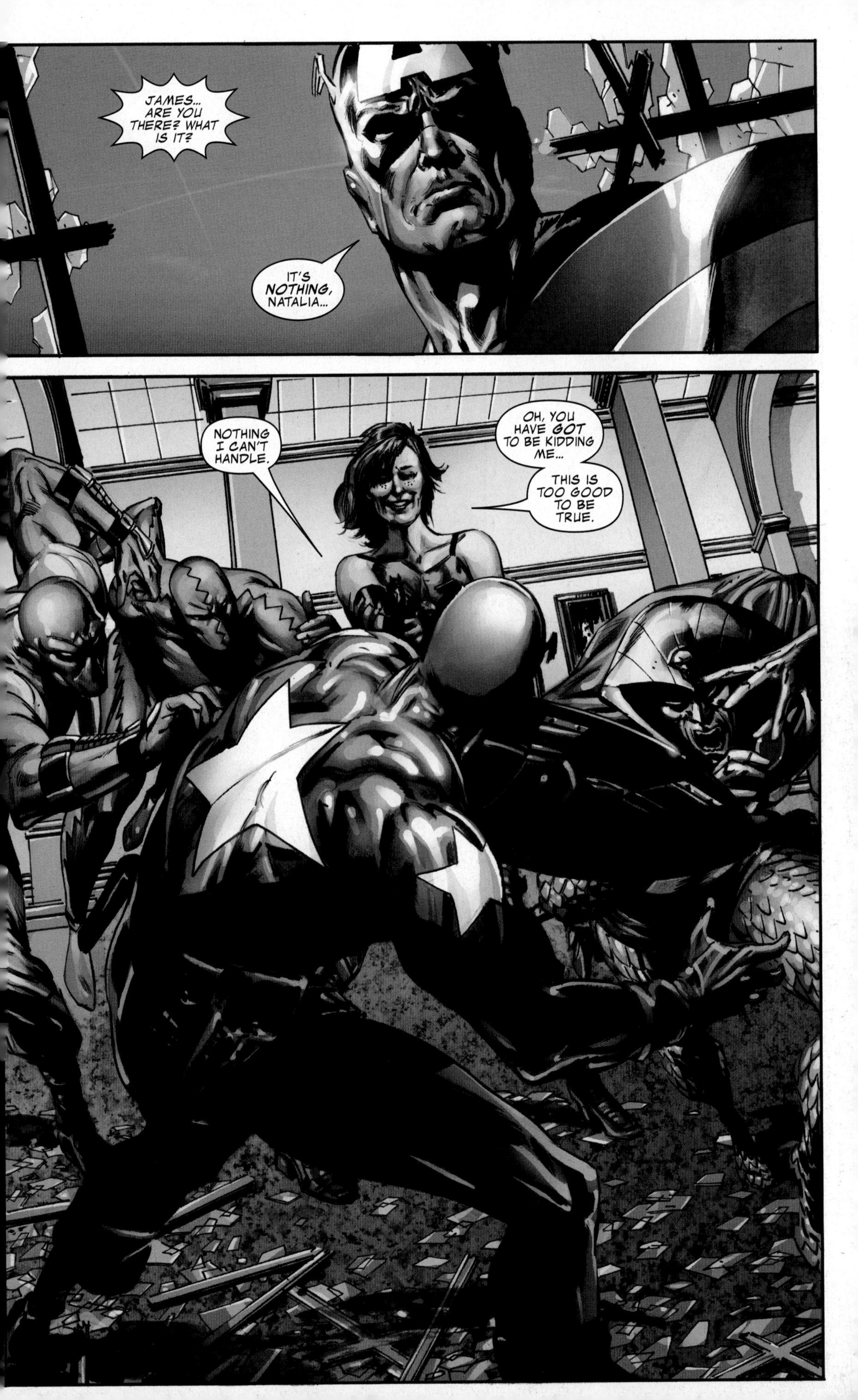
JAMES... ARE YOU THERE? WHAT IS IT?
IT'S NOTHING, NATALIA...
NOTHING I CAN'T HANDLE.
OH, YOU HAVE GOT TO BE KIDDING ME...
THIS IS TOO GOOD TO BE TRUE.

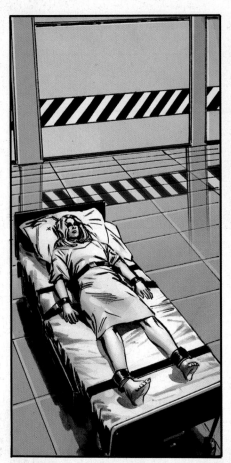

WHA...?

WHAT'S-- HEY...WHAT IS THIS?

JUST RELAX, WOMAN...THERE'S NO NEED TO STRUGGLE.

ARNIM ZOLA IS A DOCTOR, TOO...

STOP IT, SHARON. STOP BEING SCARED.

REMEMBER, YOU WORK FOR THEM NOW.

...BUT A DIFFERENT VARIETY THAN YOUR FRIEND FAUSTUS.

AND HOW LONG DID YOU REALLY THINK YOU COULD HIDE THIS PREGNANCY?

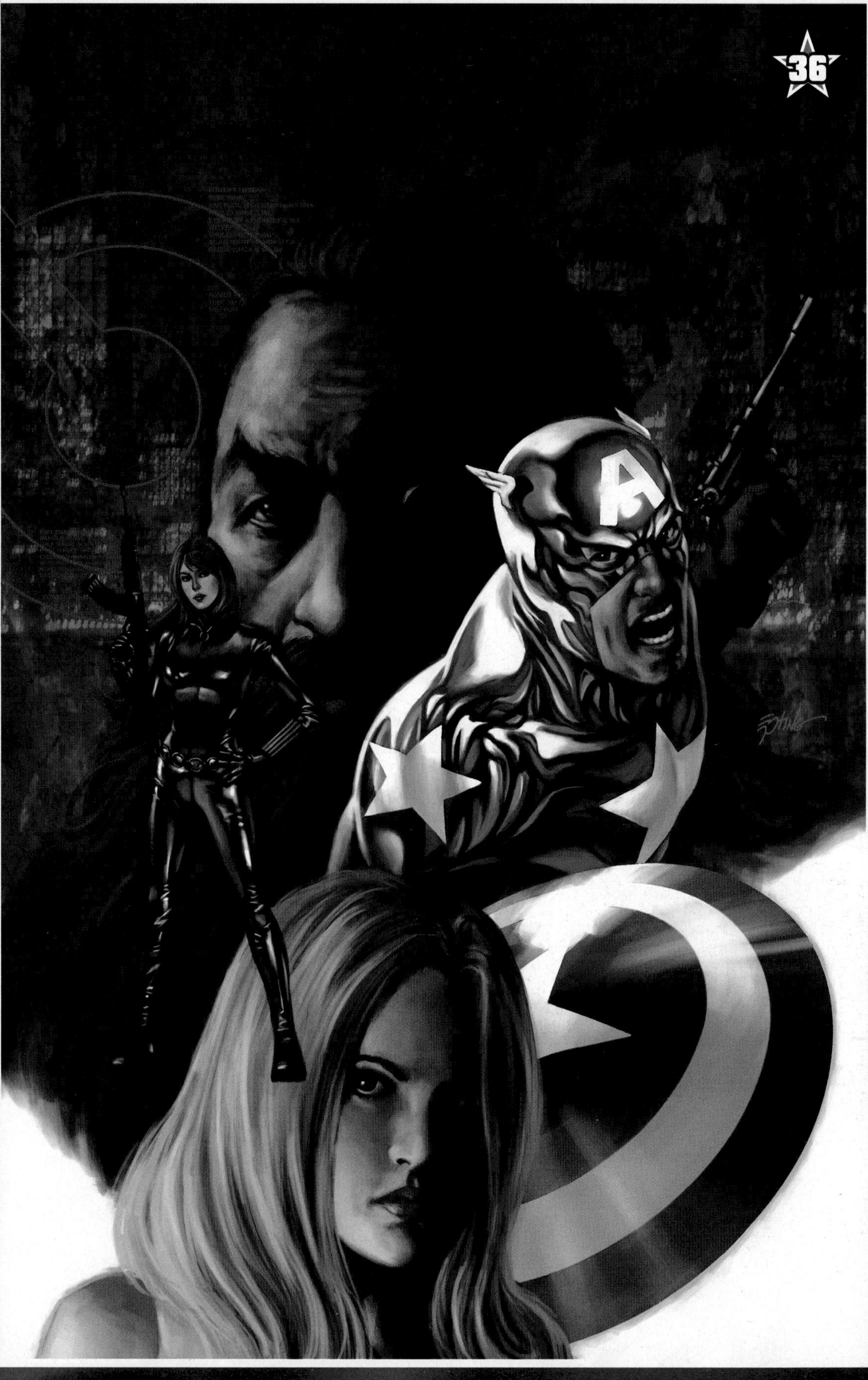
36

PART SIX

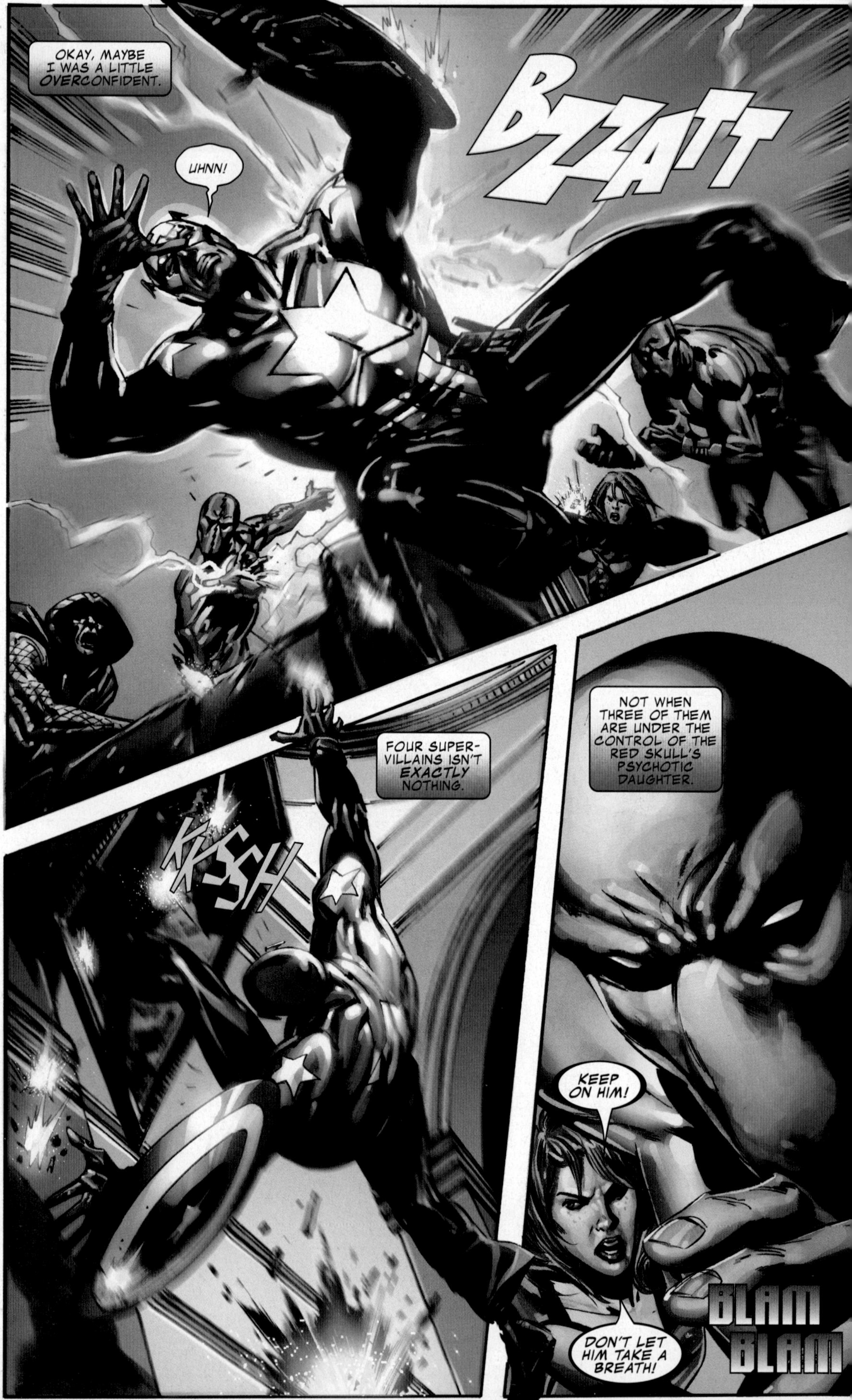
OKAY, MAYBE I WAS A LITTLE OVERCONFIDENT.
UHNN!
BZZATT
FOUR SUPER-VILLAINS ISN'T EXACTLY NOTHING.
KKSSH
NOT WHEN THREE OF THEM ARE UNDER THE CONTROL OF THE RED SKULL'S PSYCHOTIC DAUGHTER.
KEEP ON HIM!
DON'T LET HIM TAKE A BREATH!
BLAM BLAM

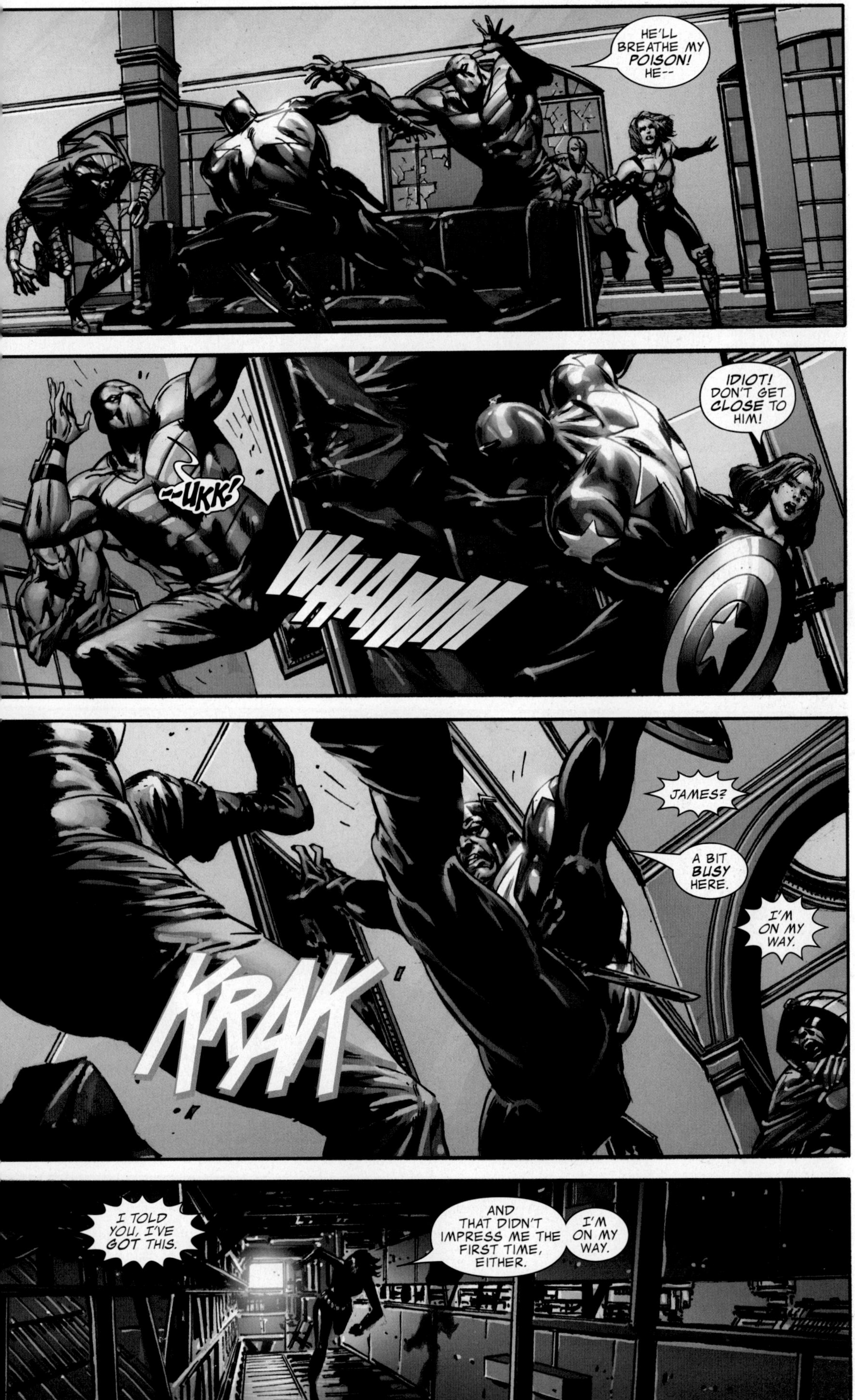
HE'LL BREATHE MY POISON! HE--
--UKK!
WHAMM
IDIOT! DON'T GET CLOSE TO HIM!
KRAK
JAMES?
A BIT BUSY HERE.
I'M ON MY WAY.
I TOLD YOU, I'VE GOT THIS.
AND THAT DIDN'T IMPRESS ME THE FIRST TIME, EITHER.
I'M ON MY WAY.

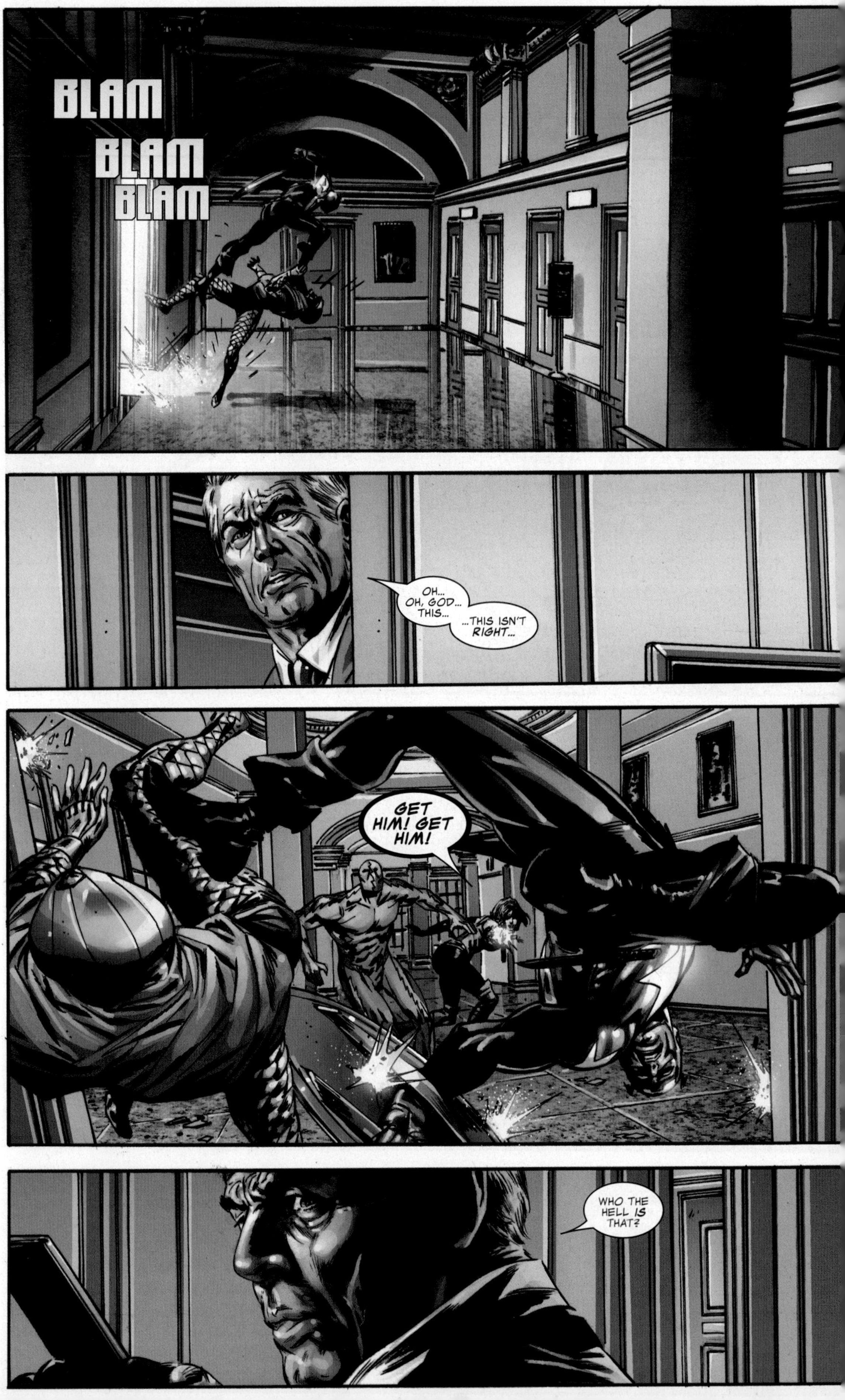
BLAM
BLAM
BLAM
OH... OH, GOD... THIS...
...THIS ISN'T RIGHT...
GET HIM! GET HIM!
WHO THE HELL IS THAT?

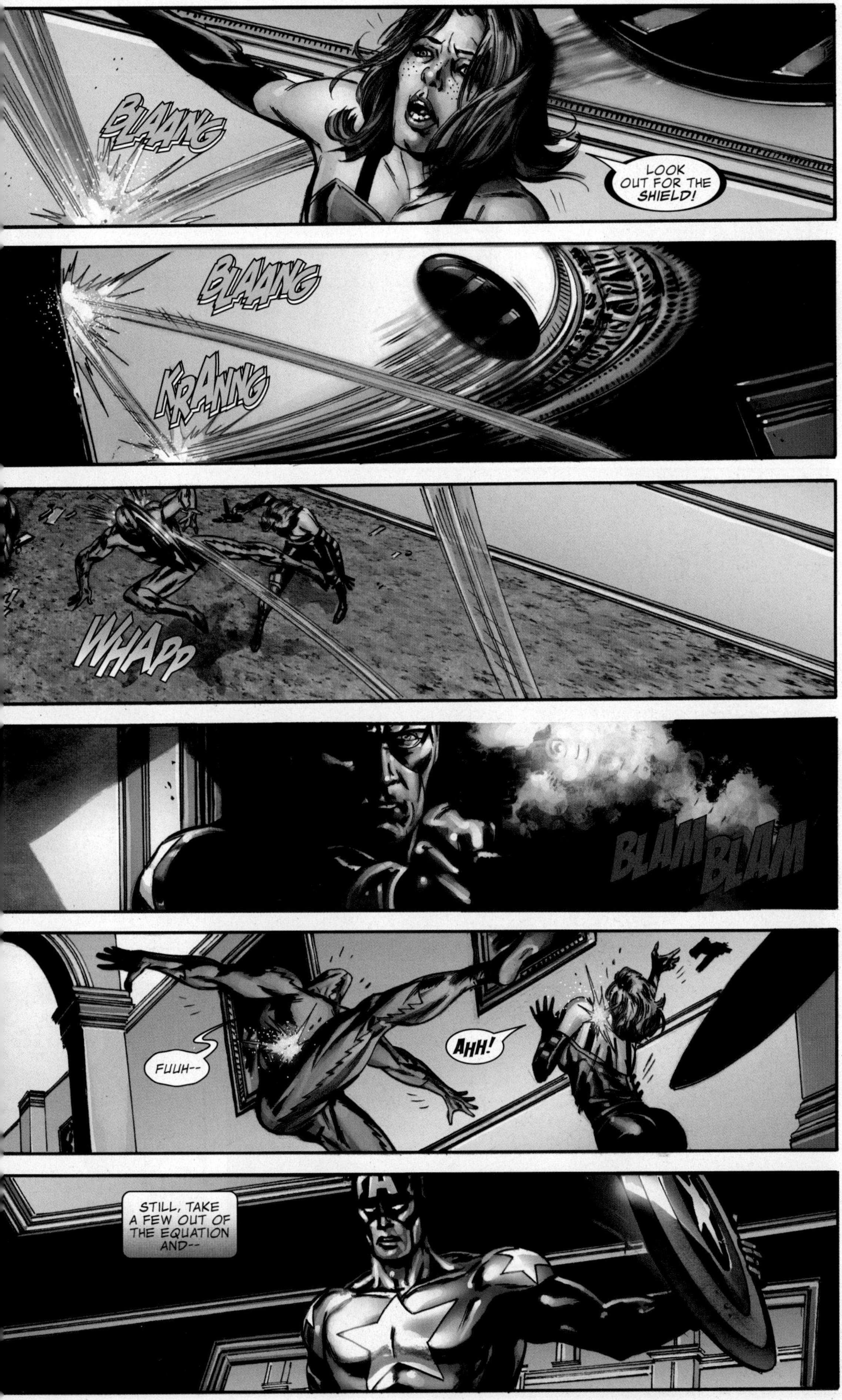
BLAANG
LOOK OUT FOR THE SHIELD!
BLAANG
KRANNG
WHAPP
BLAM
BLAM
FUUH--
AHH!
STILL, TAKE A FEW OUT OF THE EQUATION AND--

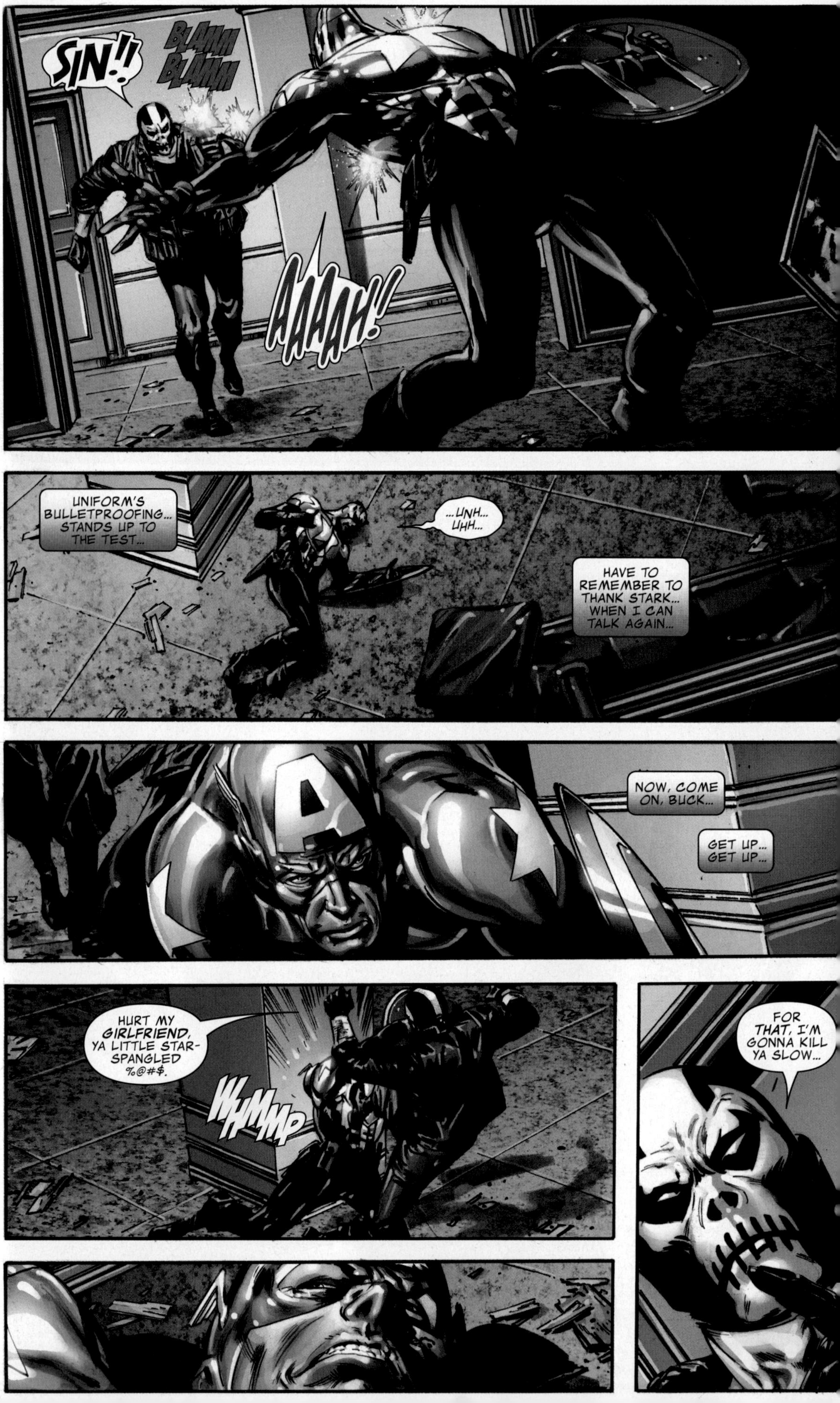
SIN!!
BLAMM BLAMM
AAAAH!
UNIFORM'S BULLETPROOFING... STANDS UP TO THE TEST...
...UNH... UHH...
HAVE TO REMEMBER TO THANK STARK... WHEN I CAN TALK AGAIN...
NOW, COME ON, BUCK...
GET UP... GET UP...
HURT MY GIRLFRIEND, YA LITTLE STAR-SPANGLED %@#$.
WHMMP
FOR THAT, I'M GONNA KILL YA SLOW...

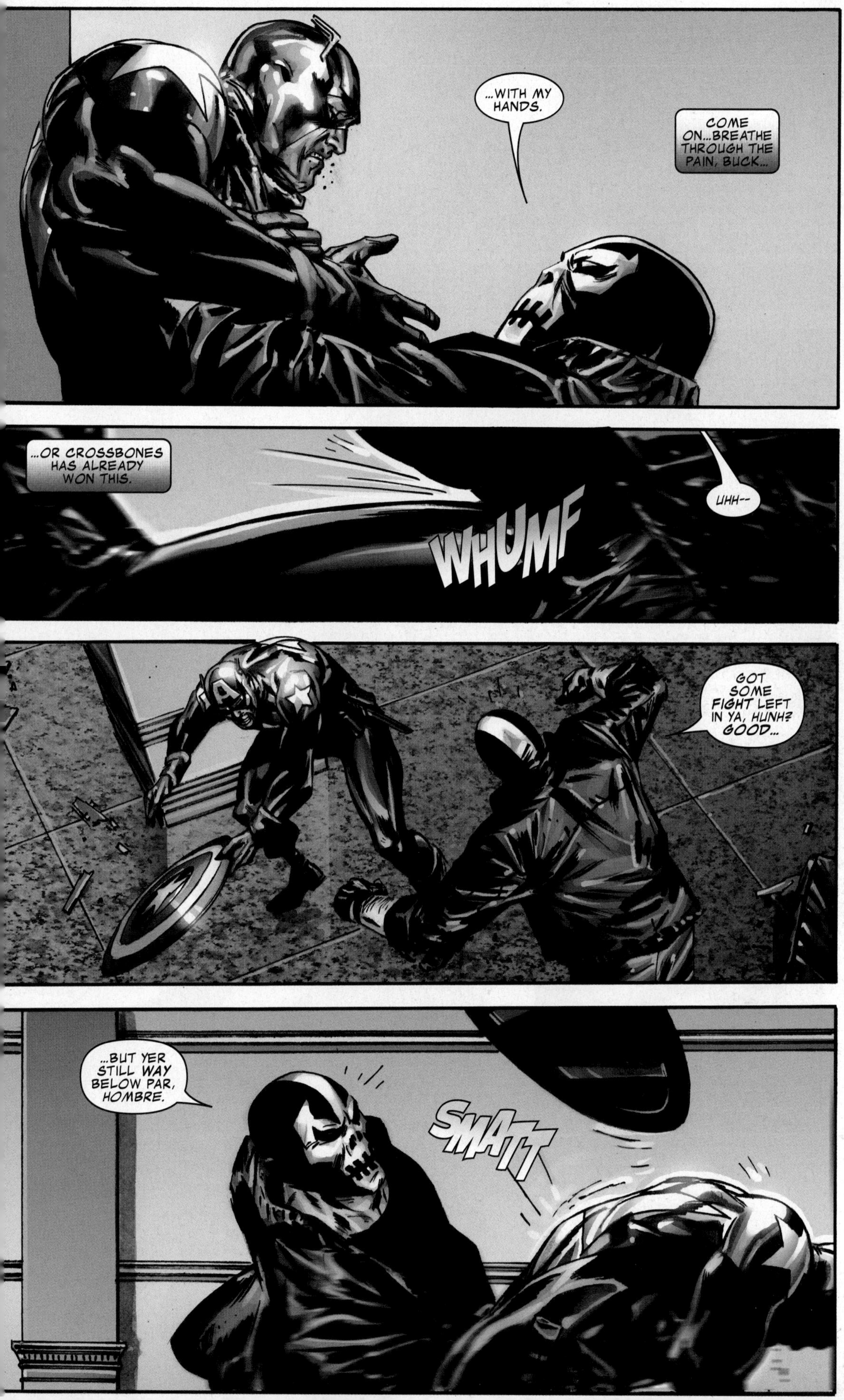
...WITH MY HANDS.
COME ON...BREATHE THROUGH THE PAIN, BUCK...
...OR CROSSBONES HAS ALREADY WON THIS.
UHH--
WHUMF
GOT SOME FIGHT LEFT IN YA, HUNH? GOOD...
...BUT YER STILL WAY BELOW PAR, HOMBRE.
SMATT

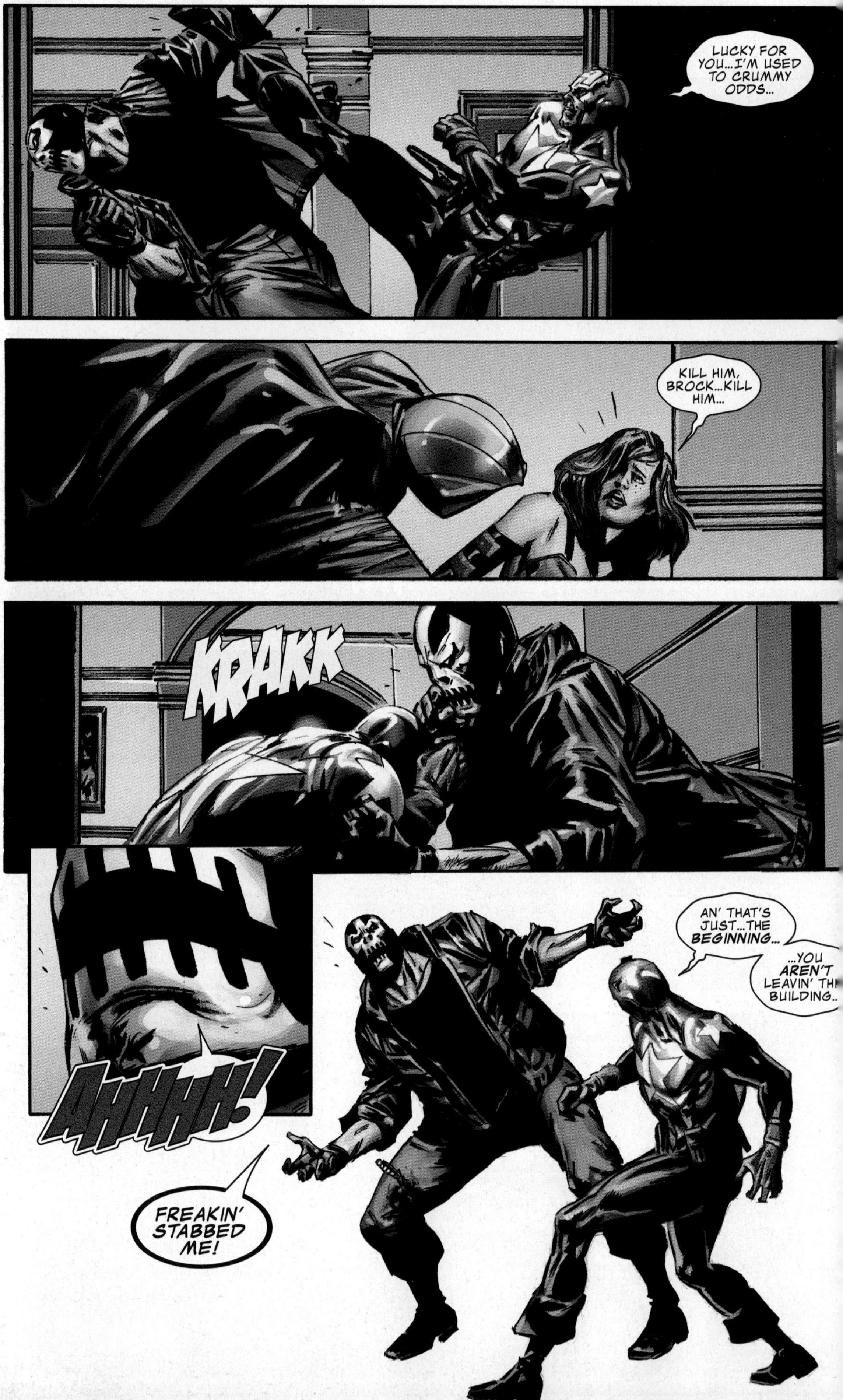

LUCKY FOR YOU...I'M USED TO CRUMMY ODDS...
KILL HIM, BROCK...KILL HIM...
KRAKK
AHHHH!
FREAKIN' STABBED ME!
AN' THAT'S JUST...THE BEGINNING...
...YOU AREN'T LEAVIN' TH BUILDING..

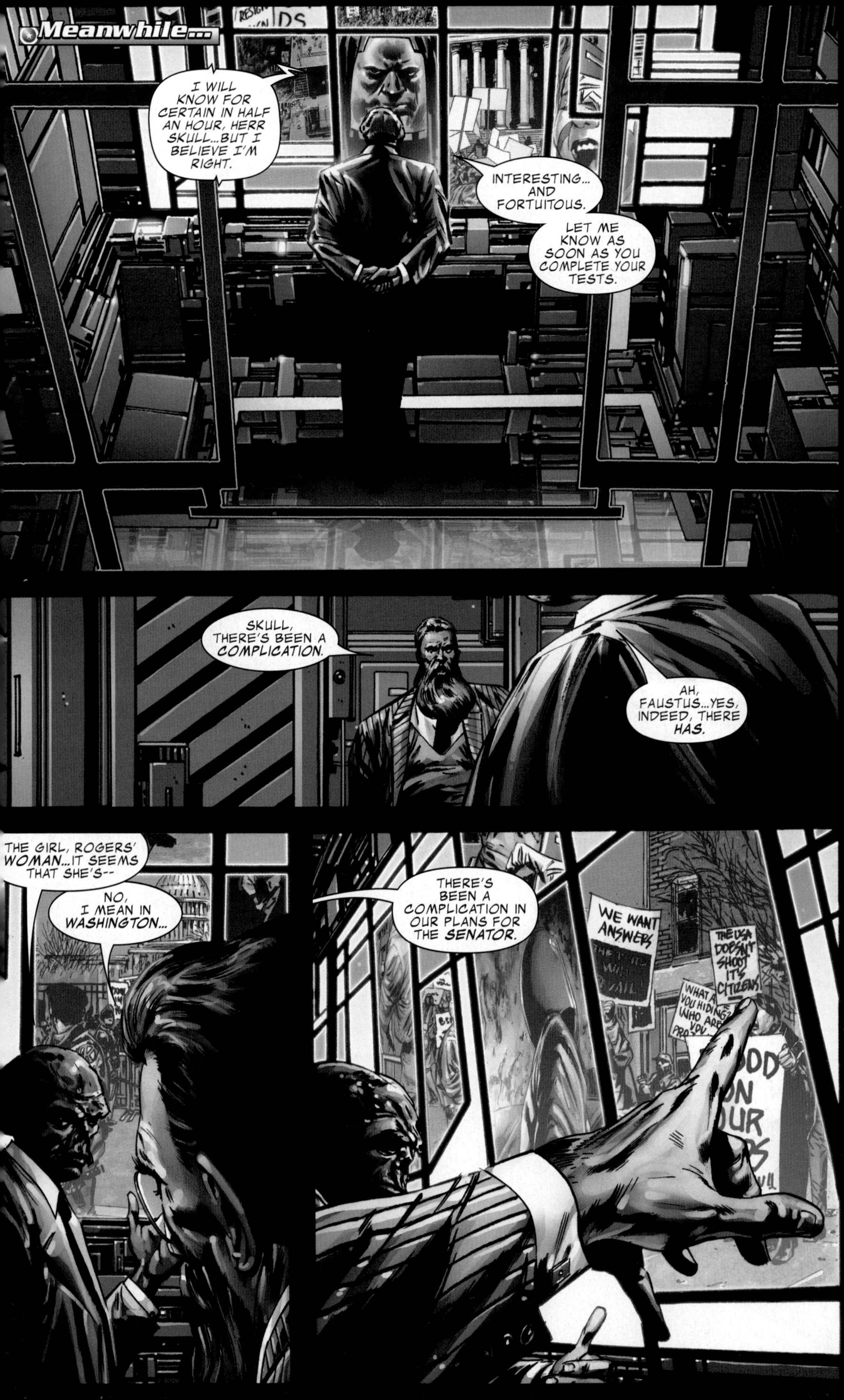
Meanwhile...
I WILL KNOW FOR CERTAIN IN HALF AN HOUR, HERR SKULL...BUT I BELIEVE I'M RIGHT.
INTERESTING... AND FORTUITOUS.
LET ME KNOW AS SOON AS YOU COMPLETE YOUR TESTS.
SKULL, THERE'S BEEN A COMPLICATION.
AH, FAUSTUS...YES, INDEED, THERE HAS.
THE GIRL, ROGERS' WOMAN...IT SEEMS THAT SHE'S--
NO, I MEAN IN WASHINGTON...
THERE'S BEEN A COMPLICATION IN OUR PLANS FOR THE SENATOR.
WE WANT ANSWERS
THE USA DOESN'T SHOOT IT'S CITIZENS

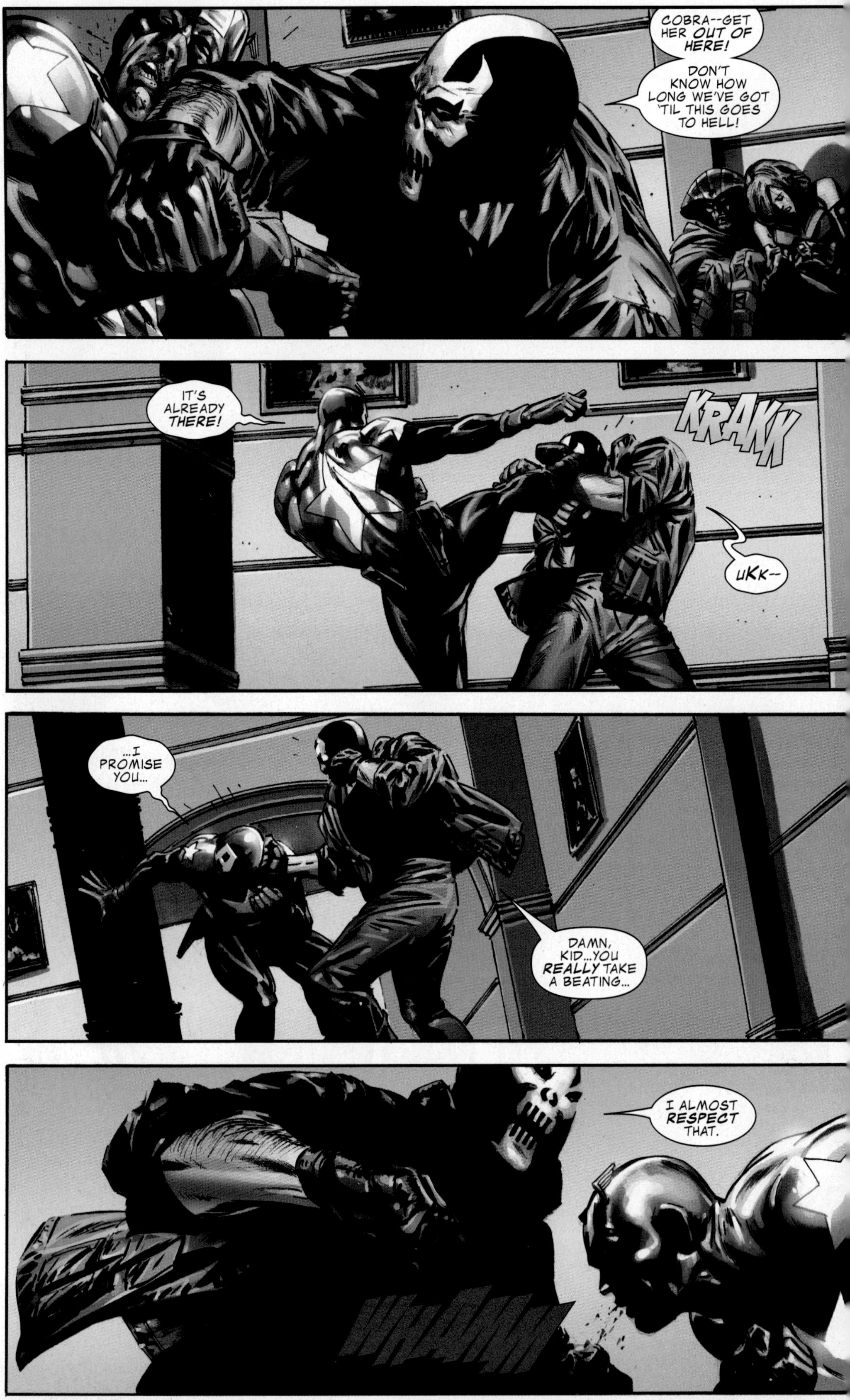
COBRA--GET HER OUT OF HERE!
DON'T KNOW HOW LONG WE'VE GOT 'TIL THIS GOES TO HELL!
IT'S ALREADY THERE!
KRAKK
UKK--
...I PROMISE YOU...
DAMN, KID...YOU REALLY TAKE A BEATING...
I ALMOST RESPECT THAT.

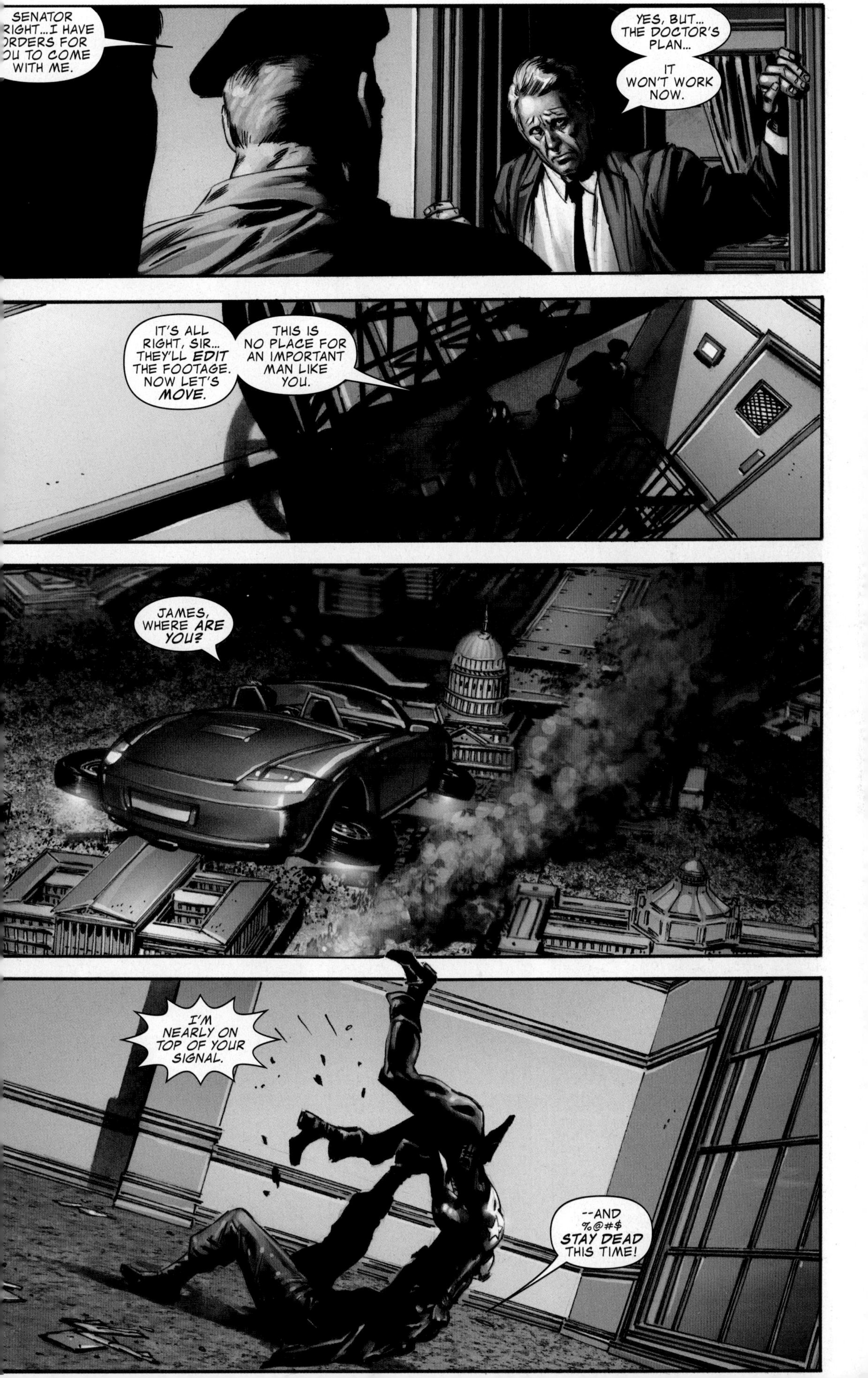
SENATOR
RIGHT...I HAVE
ORDERS FOR
OU TO COME
WITH ME.
YES, BUT... THE DOCTOR'S PLAN...
IT WON'T WORK NOW.
IT'S ALL RIGHT, SIR... THEY'LL EDIT THE FOOTAGE. NOW LET'S MOVE.
THIS IS NO PLACE FOR AN IMPORTANT MAN LIKE YOU.
JAMES, WHERE ARE YOU?
I'M NEARLY ON TOP OF YOUR SIGNAL.
--AND %@#$ STAY DEAD THIS TIME!

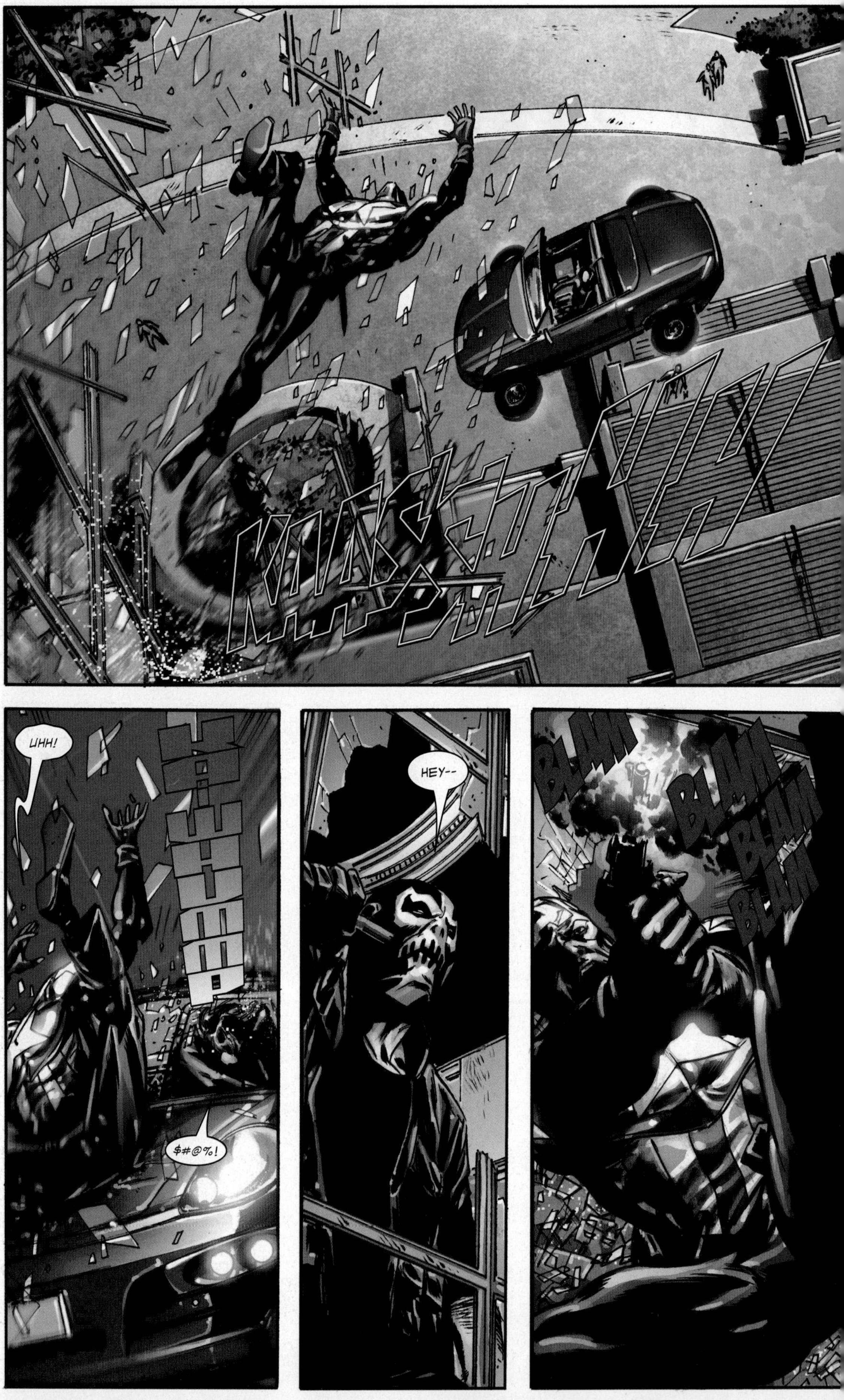
UHH!
$#@%!
HEY--
BLAM
BLAM
BLAM
BLAM

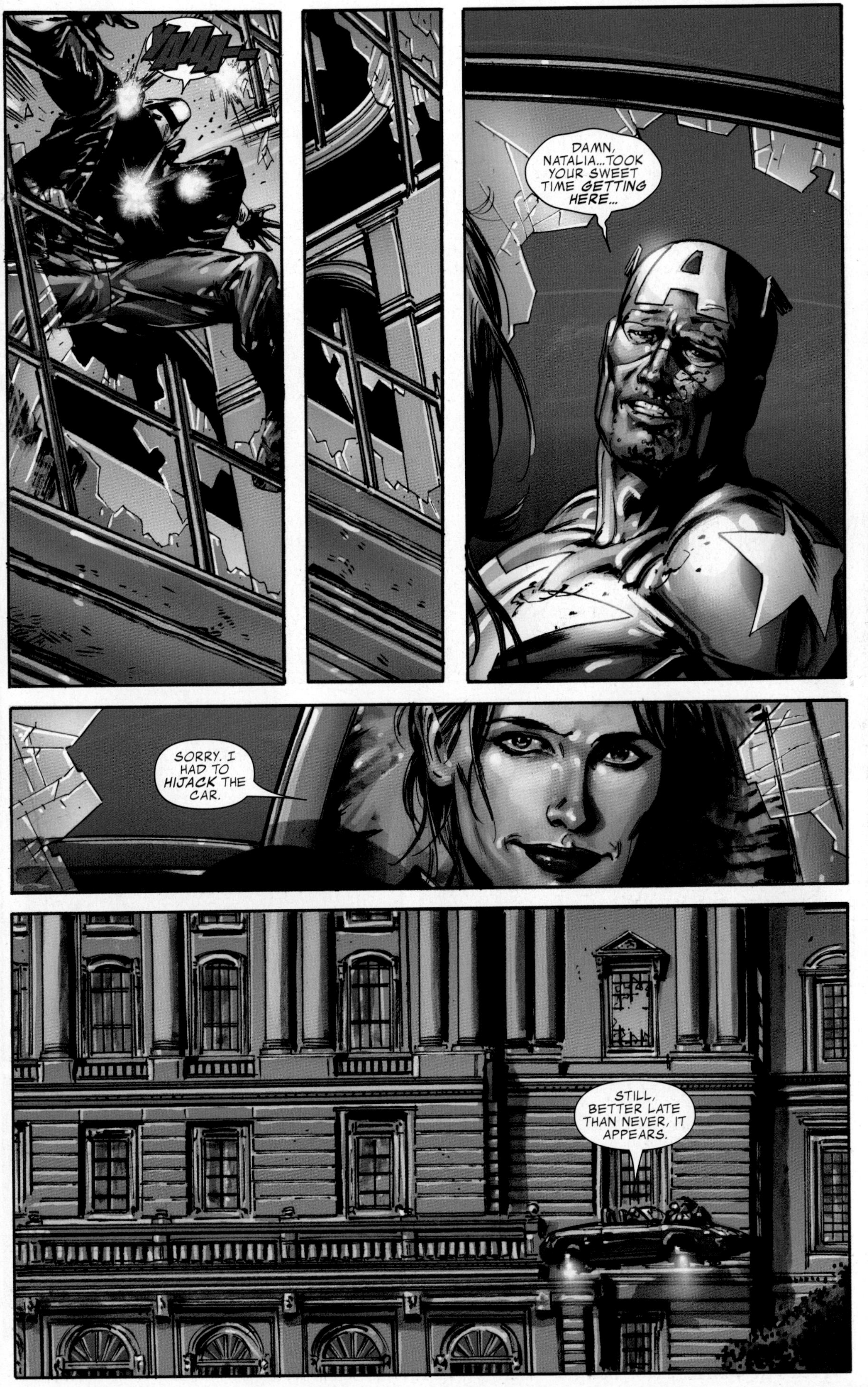
YAAA--!
DAMN, NATALIA...TOOK YOUR SWEET TIME GETTING HERE...
SORRY. I HAD TO HIJACK THE CAR.
STILL, BETTER LATE THAN NEVER, IT APPEARS.

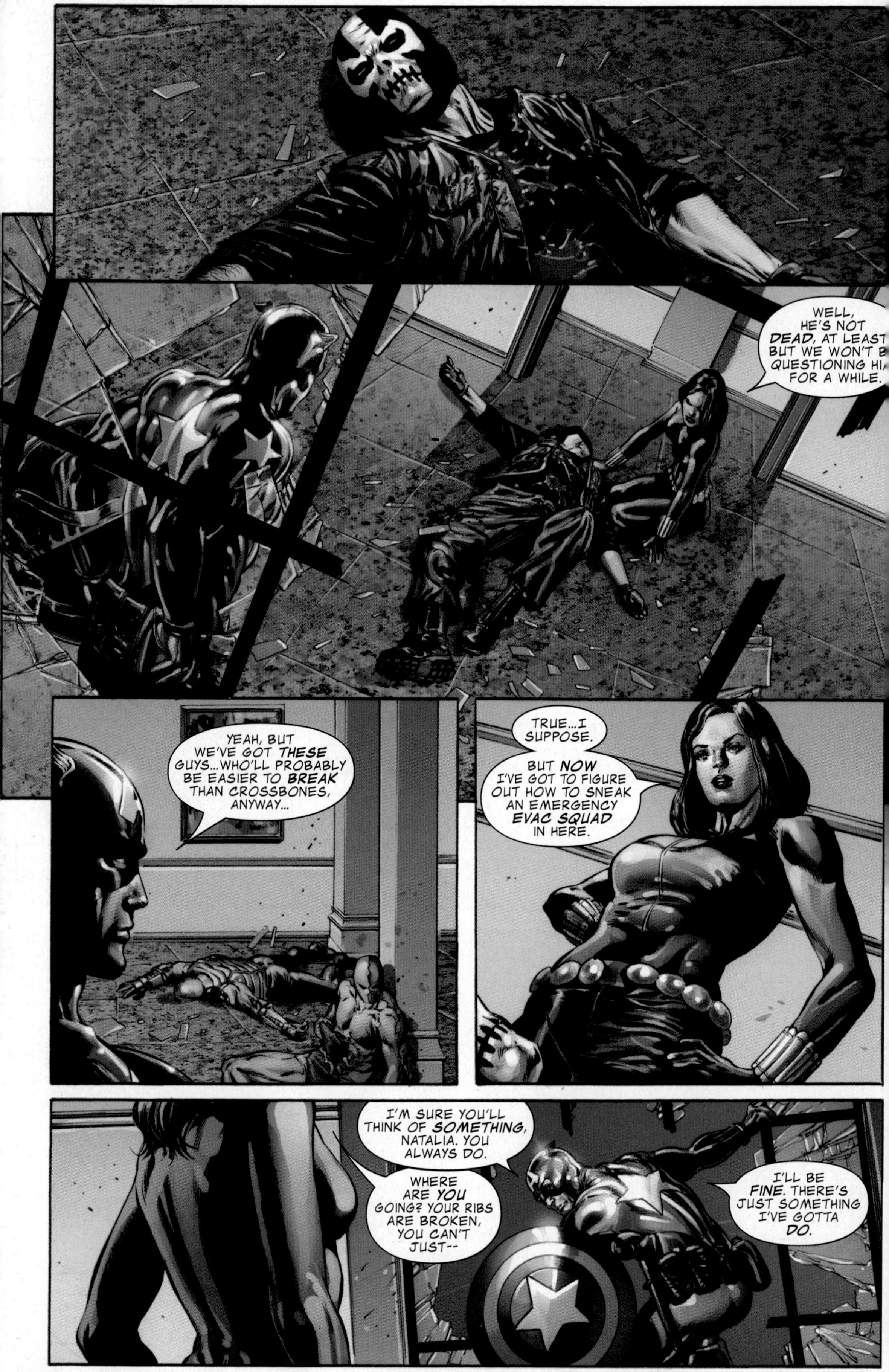
WELL, HE'S NOT DEAD, AT LEAST BUT WE WON'T B QUESTIONING HI FOR A WHILE.
YEAH, BUT WE'VE GOT THESE GUYS...WHO'LL PROBABLY BE EASIER TO BREAK THAN CROSSBONES, ANYWAY...
TRUE...I SUPPOSE.
BUT NOW I'VE GOT TO FIGURE OUT HOW TO SNEAK AN EMERGENCY EVAC SQUAD IN HERE.
I'M SURE YOU'LL THINK OF SOMETHING, NATALIA. YOU ALWAYS DO.
WHERE ARE YOU GOING? YOUR RIBS ARE BROKEN, YOU CAN'T JUST--
I'LL BE FINE. THERE'S JUST SOMETHING I'VE GOTTA DO.

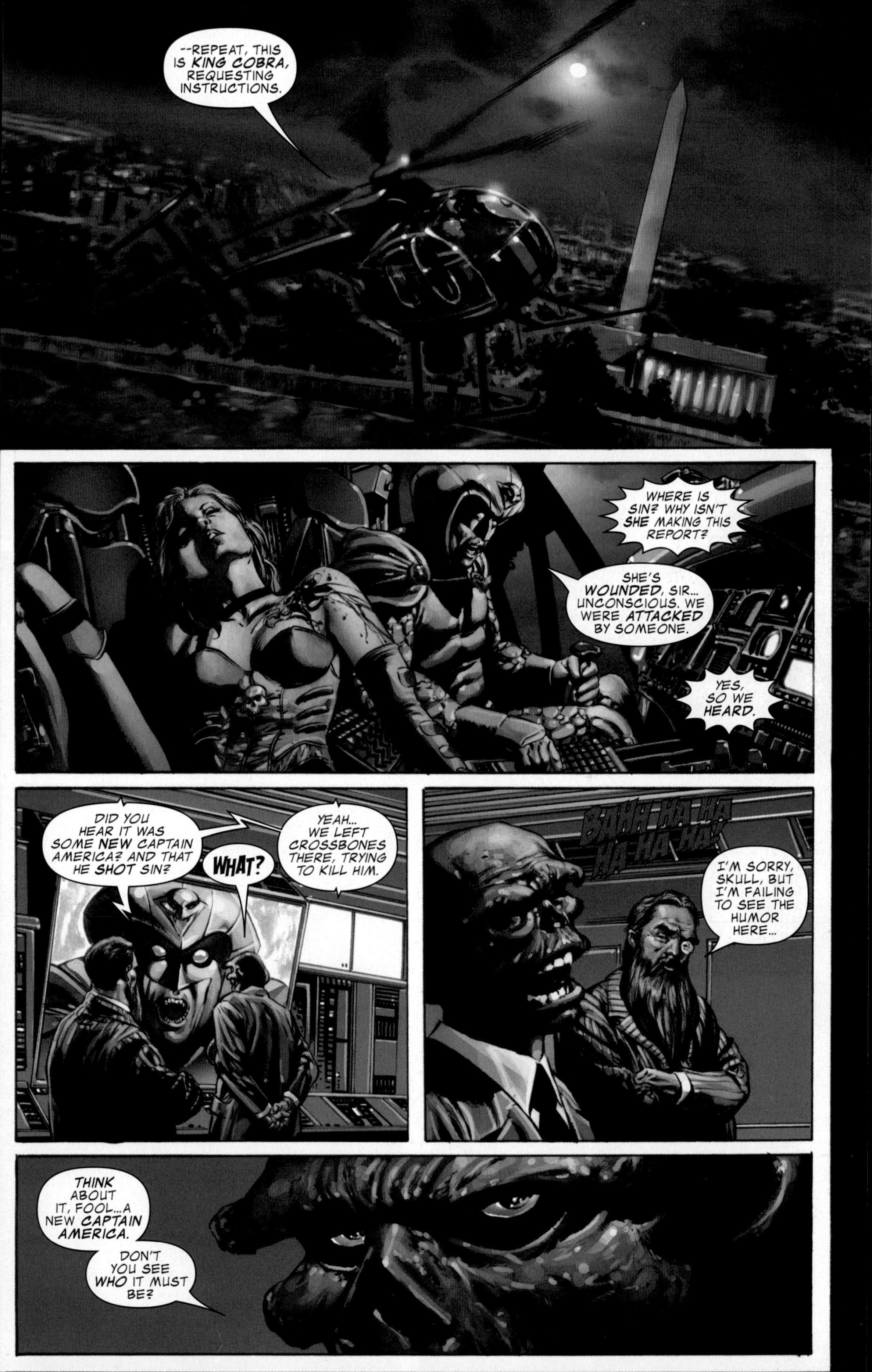
--REPEAT, THIS IS KING COBRA, REQUESTING INSTRUCTIONS.
WHERE IS SIN? WHY ISN'T SHE MAKING THIS REPORT?
SHE'S WOUNDED, SIR... UNCONSCIOUS. WE WERE ATTACKED BY SOMEONE.
YES, SO WE HEARD.
DID YOU HEAR IT WAS SOME NEW CAPTAIN AMERICA? AND THAT HE SHOT SIN?
WHAT?
YEAH... WE LEFT CROSSBONES THERE, TRYING TO KILL HIM.
BAHH HA HA HA HA HA!
I'M SORRY, SKULL, BUT I'M FAILING TO SEE THE HUMOR HERE...
THINK ABOUT IT, FOOL...A NEW CAPTAIN AMERICA.
DON'T YOU SEE WHO IT MUST BE?

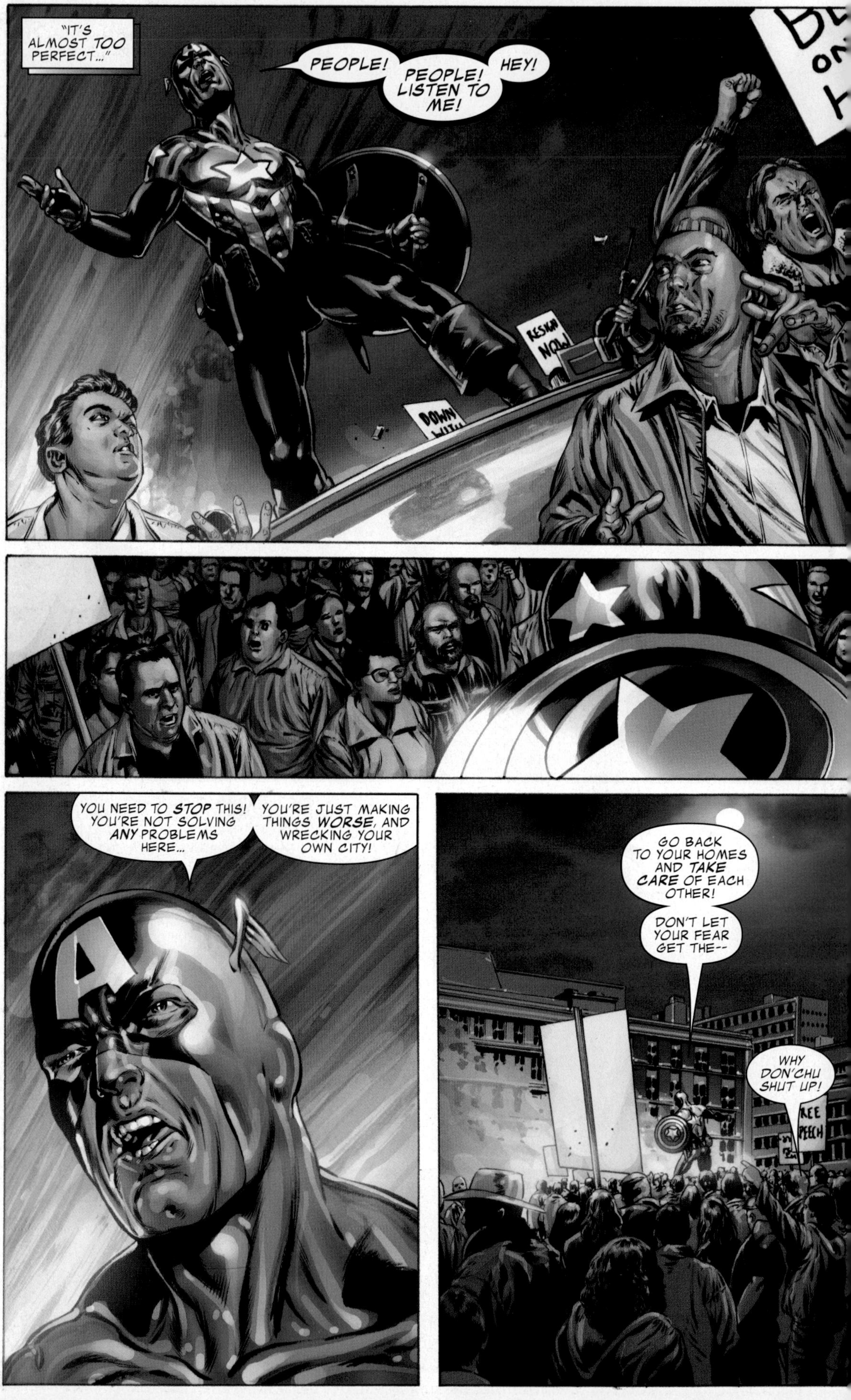
"IT'S ALMOST TOO PERFECT..."
PEOPLE!
PEOPLE! LISTEN TO ME!
HEY!
RESIGN NOW
YOU NEED TO STOP THIS! YOU'RE NOT SOLVING ANY PROBLEMS HERE...
YOU'RE JUST MAKING THINGS WORSE, AND WRECKING YOUR OWN CITY!
GO BACK TO YOUR HOMES AND TAKE CARE OF EACH OTHER!
DON'T LET YOUR FEAR GET THE--
WHY DON'CHU SHUT UP!

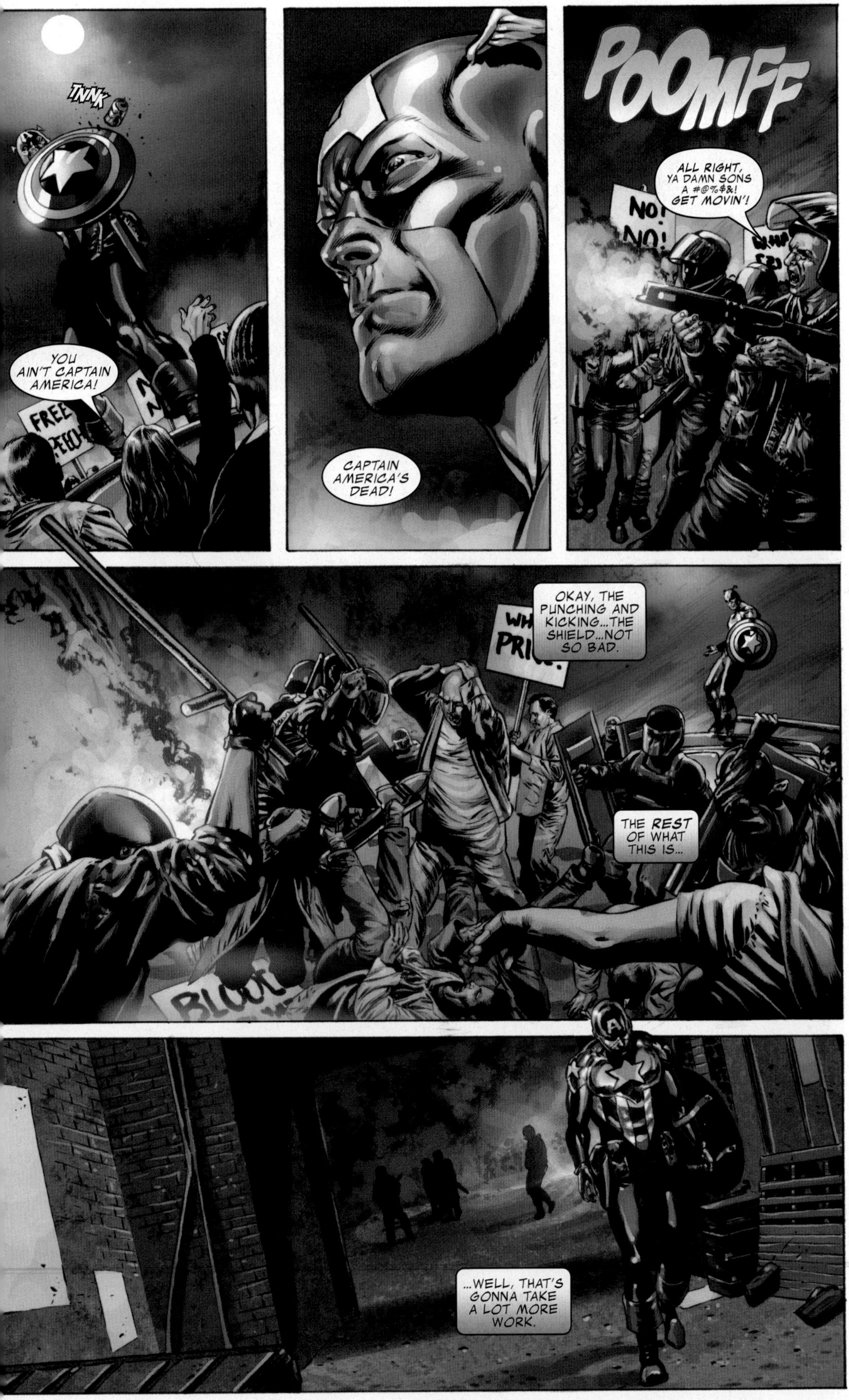
TNNK
YOU AIN'T CAPTAIN AMERICA!
CAPTAIN AMERICA'S DEAD!
POOMFF
ALL RIGHT, YA DAMN SONS A #@%$&! GET MOVIN'!
OKAY, THE PUNCHING AND KICKING...THE SHIELD...NOT SO BAD.
THE REST OF WHAT THIS IS...
...WELL, THAT'S GONNA TAKE A LOT MORE WORK.

--AND YOU CAN SEE A MAN IN WHAT *APPEARS* TO BE A CAPTAIN AMERICA UNIFORM OF SOME KIND...

IS THERE A NEW CAPTAIN AMERICA?

5:23 p ES

...ALTHOUGH *BOTH* AUTHORITIES FROM THE GOVERNMENT AND S.H.I.E.L.D. DIRECTOR TONY STARK HAVE DECLINED TO COMMENT AT THIS POINT.

DID YOU SEE THE NEW CAP? CALL: 888-555-MASK

5:23 p ES

OTHER SHOCKING NEWS FROM LAST NIGHT'S RIOT WAS THE DRAMATIC RESCUE OF *SENATOR GORDON WRIGHT* FROM SUPER-POWERED TERRORISTS...

SENATOR RESCUED FROM TERRORISTS

5:23 p ES

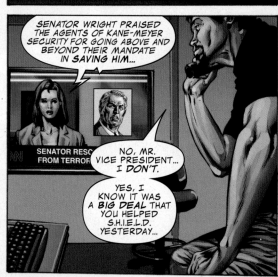

SENATOR WRIGHT PRAISED THE AGENTS OF KANE-MEYER SECURITY FOR GOING ABOVE AND BEYOND THEIR MANDATE IN *SAVING HIM...*

SENATOR RESC FROM TERROR

NO, MR. VICE PRESIDENT... I *DON'T.*

YES, I KNOW IT WAS A *BIG DEAL* THAT YOU HELPED S.H.I.E.L.D. YESTERDAY...

YES, SIR...I *DO* UNDERSTAND THAT.

BUT I *PROMISE* YOU, I DON'T KNOW *ANYTHING* ABOUT THIS NEW CAPTAIN AMERICA...

SHOULDN'T YOU BE *RESTING* OR SOMETHING?

NAH. I'M A QUICK HEALER...

RIGHT.

DID YOU GET ANYTHING FROM THE SKULL'S GOONS YET?

NOT MUCH... CROSSBONES IS STILL *UNCONSCIOUS* AFTER SURGERY...

AND THE OTHERS DON'T *KNOW* ANYTHING. NOT REALLY.

THEY WERE HOLED UP HERE IN THE CITY, AND ONLY *SIN* COMMUNICATED WITH HER FATHER.

BUT YOU GOT THE LOCATION OF THEIR *SAFE HOUSE?*

YES, AND WE HAVE A TEAM GOING OVER EVERY *INCH* OF IT.

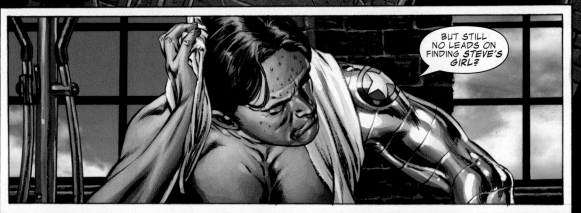

BUT STILL NO LEADS ON FINDING *STEVE'S GIRL?*

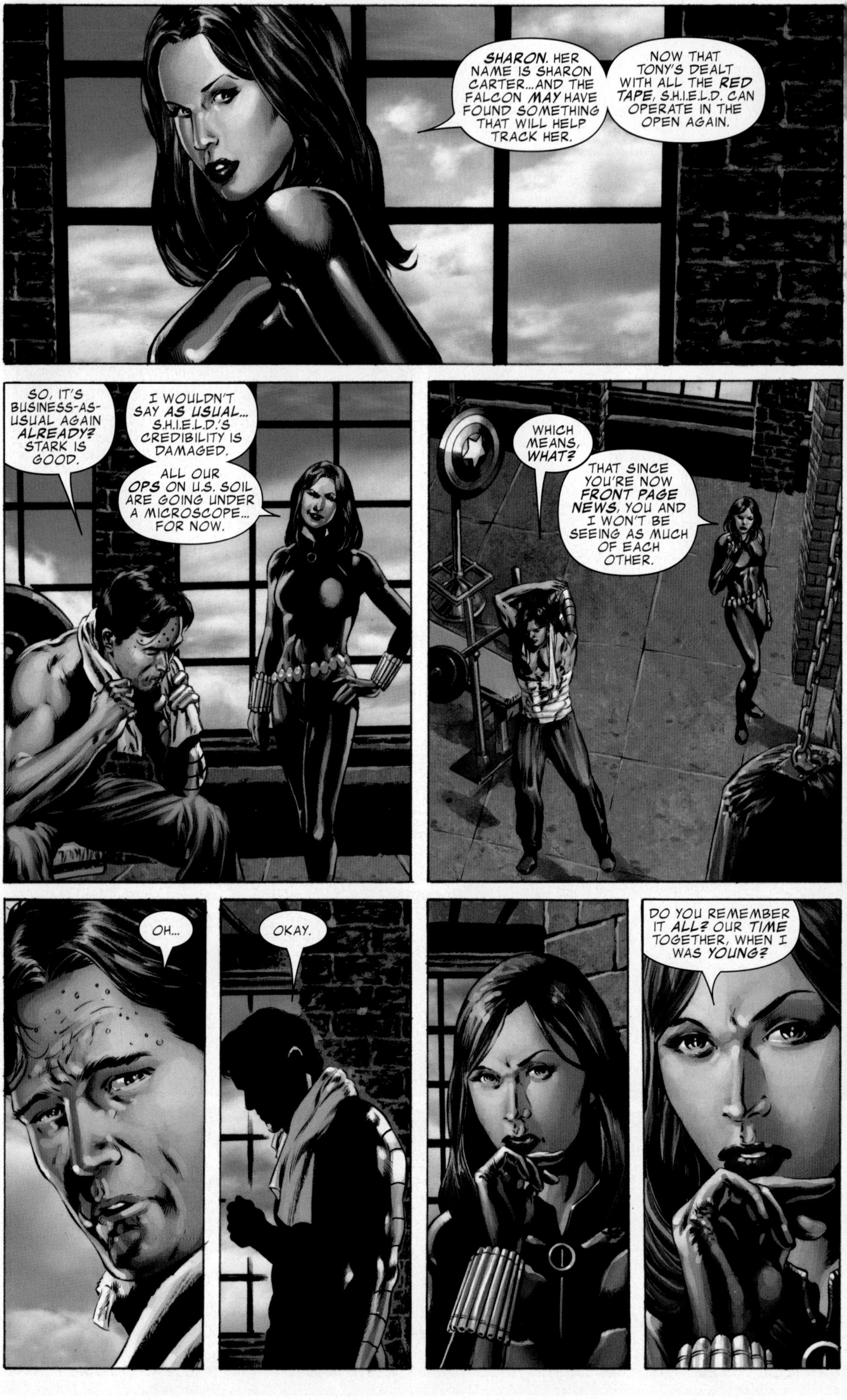
SHARON. HER NAME IS SHARON CARTER...AND THE FALCON MAY HAVE FOUND SOMETHING THAT WILL HELP TRACK HER.
NOW THAT TONY'S DEALT WITH ALL THE RED TAPE, S.H.I.E.L.D. CAN OPERATE IN THE OPEN AGAIN.
SO, IT'S BUSINESS-AS-USUAL AGAIN ALREADY? STARK IS GOOD.
I WOULDN'T SAY AS USUAL... S.H.I.E.L.D.'S CREDIBILITY IS DAMAGED.
ALL OUR OPS ON U.S. SOIL ARE GOING UNDER A MICROSCOPE... FOR NOW.
WHICH MEANS, WHAT?
THAT SINCE YOU'RE NOW FRONT PAGE NEWS, YOU AND I WON'T BE SEEING AS MUCH OF EACH OTHER.
OH...
OKAY.
DO YOU REMEMBER IT ALL? OUR TIME TOGETHER, WHEN I WAS YOUNG?

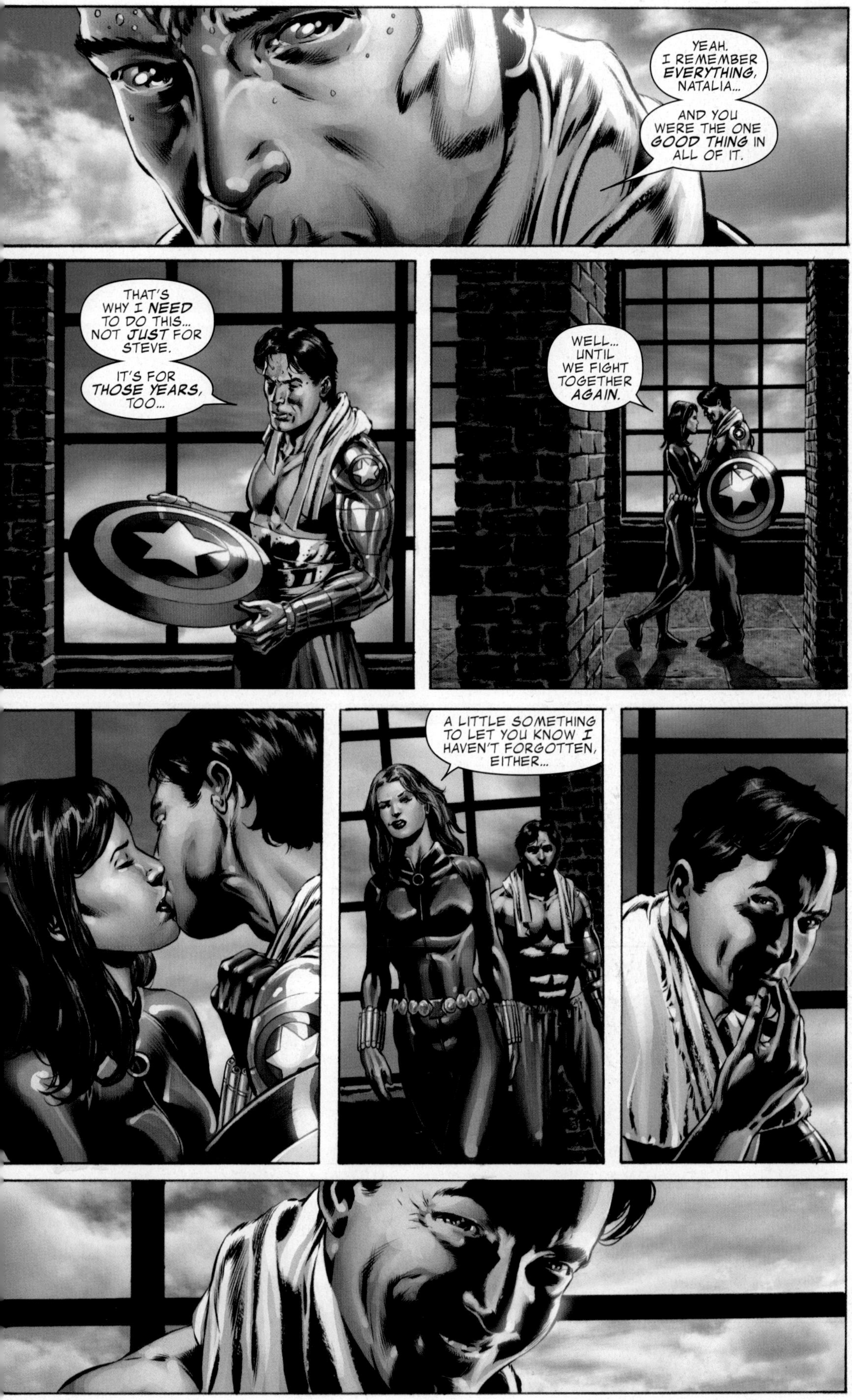
YEAH. I REMEMBER EVERYTHING, NATALIA...
AND YOU WERE THE ONE GOOD THING IN ALL OF IT.
THAT'S WHY I NEED TO DO THIS... NOT JUST FOR STEVE.
IT'S FOR THOSE YEARS, TOO...
WELL... UNTIL WE FIGHT TOGETHER AGAIN.
A LITTLE SOMETHING TO LET YOU KNOW I HAVEN'T FORGOTTEN, EITHER...

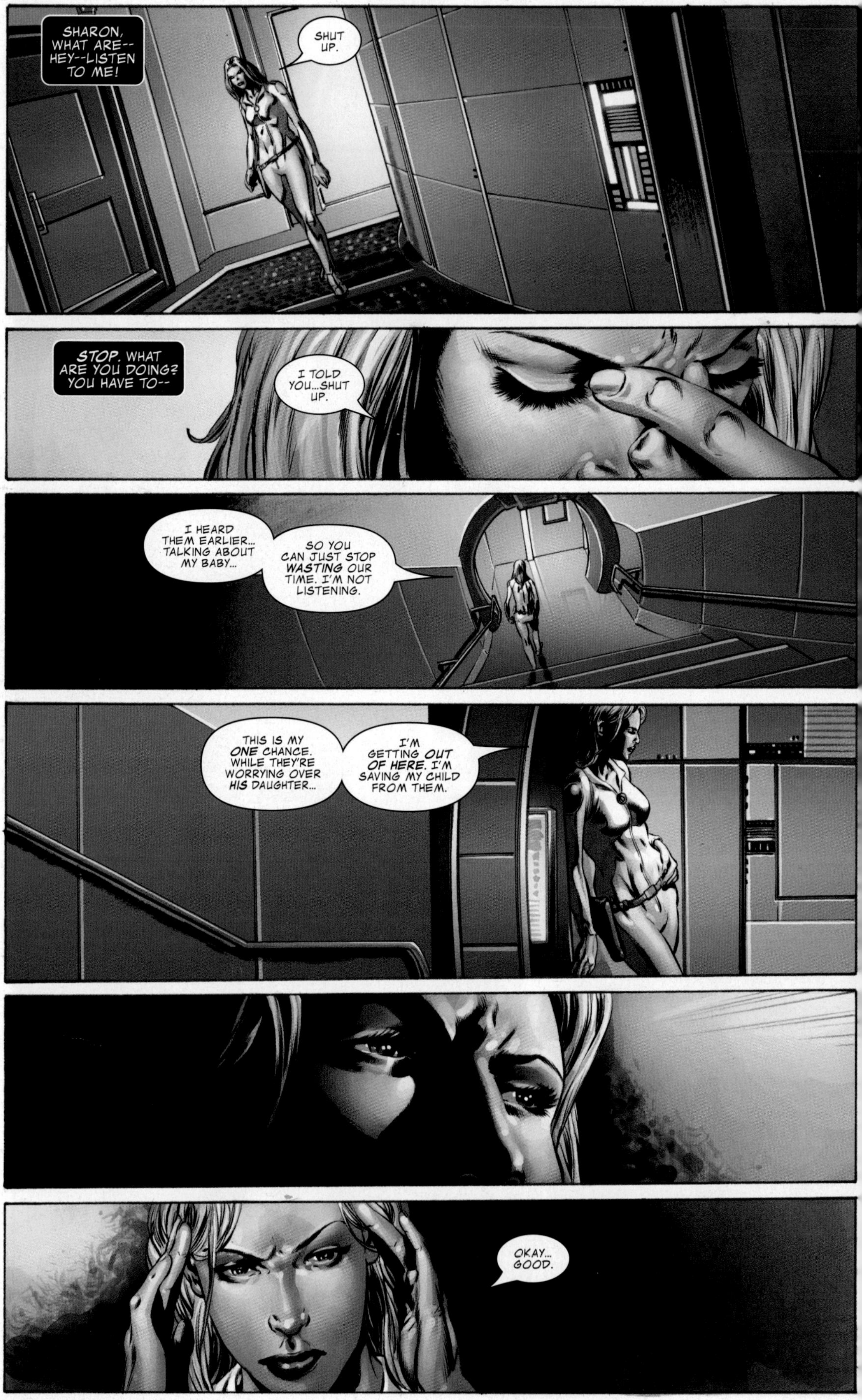
SHARON, WHAT ARE-- HEY--LISTEN TO ME!
SHUT UP.
STOP. WHAT ARE YOU DOING? YOU HAVE TO--
I TOLD YOU...SHUT UP.
I HEARD THEM EARLIER... TALKING ABOUT MY BABY...
SO YOU CAN JUST STOP WASTING OUR TIME. I'M NOT LISTENING.
THIS IS MY ONE CHANCE. WHILE THEY'RE WORRYING OVER HIS DAUGHTER...
I'M GETTING OUT OF HERE. I'M SAVING MY CHILD FROM THEM.
OKAY... GOOD.

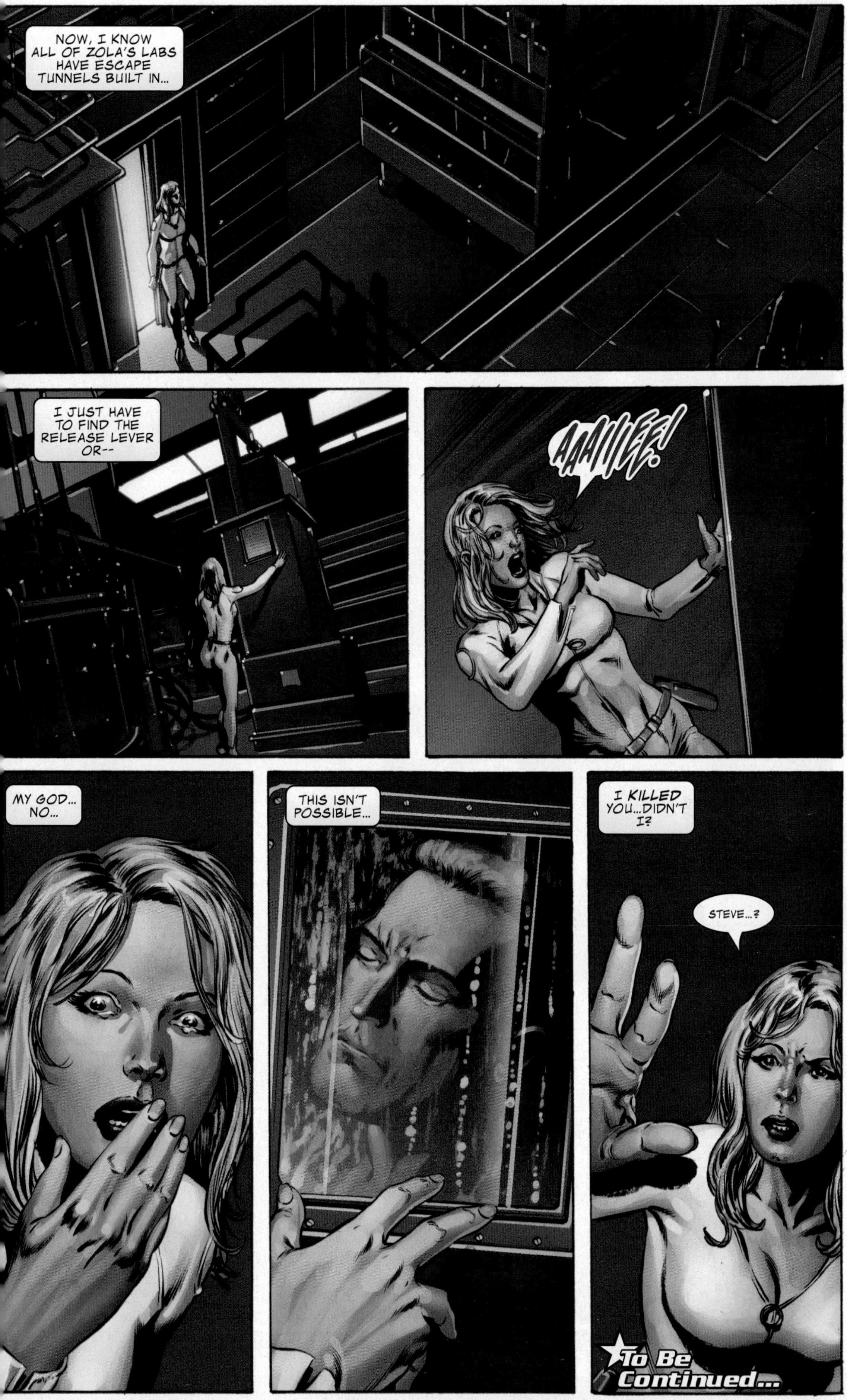
NOW, I KNOW ALL OF ZOLA'S LABS HAVE ESCAPE TUNNELS BUILT IN...
I JUST HAVE TO FIND THE RELEASE LEVER OR--
AAAIIIEE!
MY GOD... NO...
THIS ISN'T POSSIBLE...
I KILLED YOU...DIDN'T I?
STEVE...?
To Be Continued...

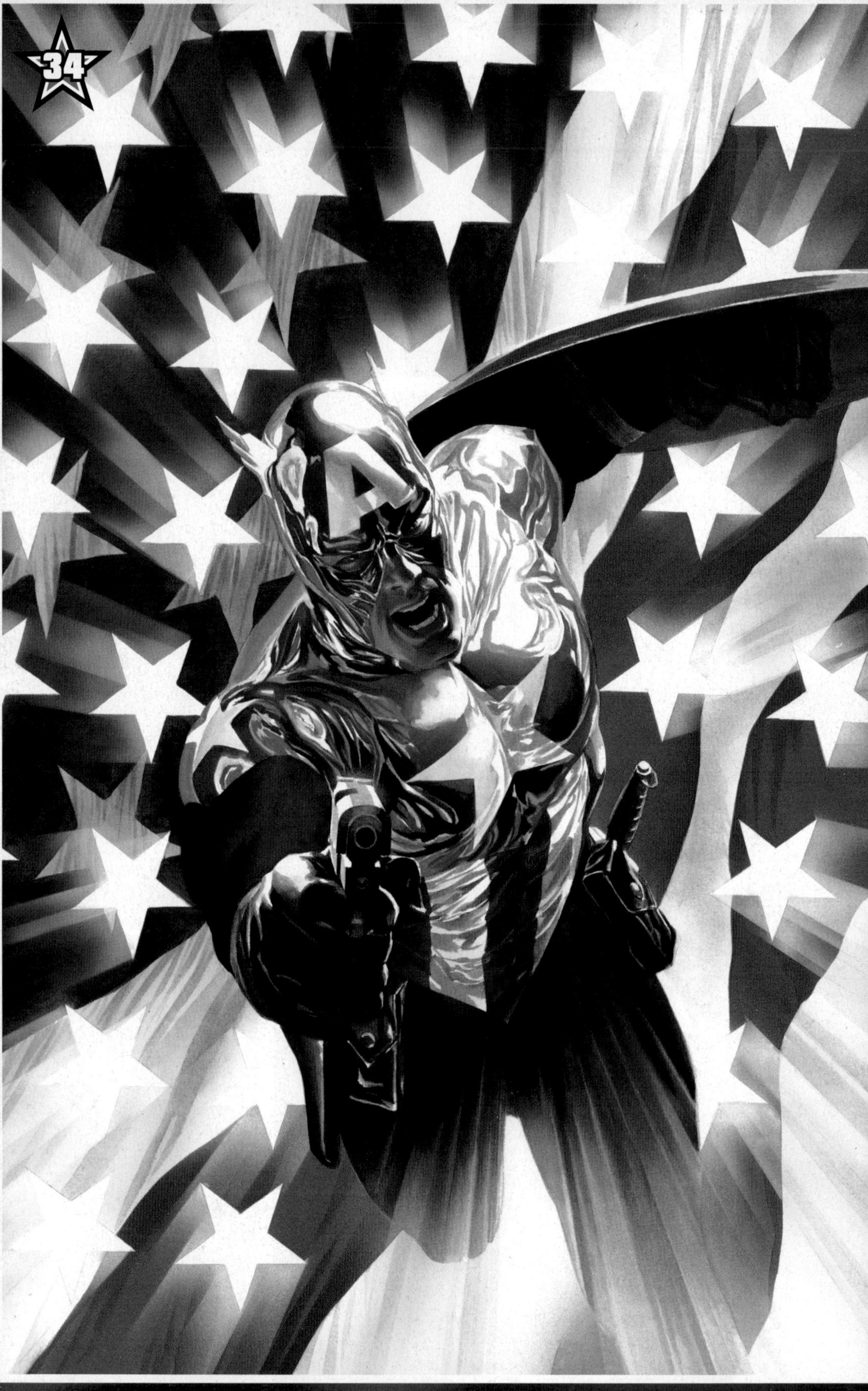
34

VARIANT BY ALEX ROSS

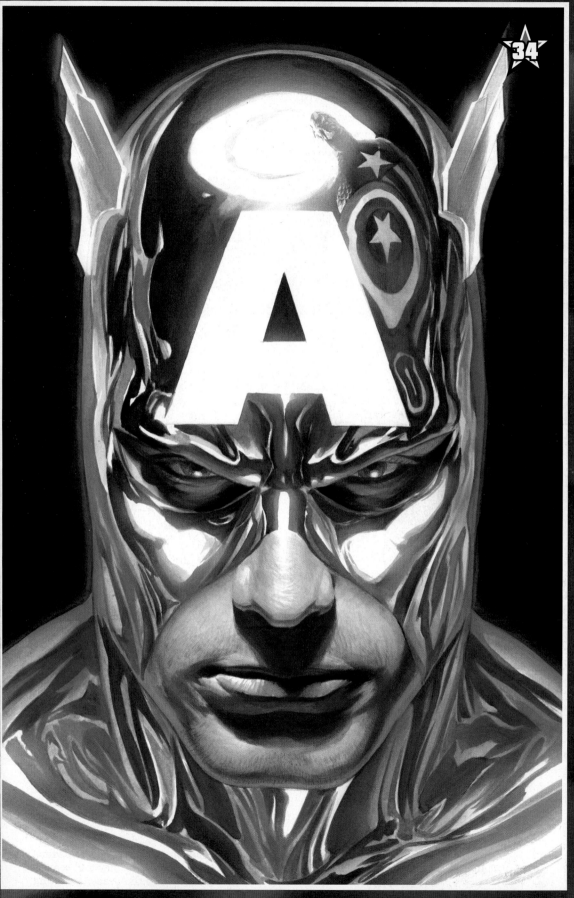

34

DYNAMIC FORCES VARIANT BY ALEX ROSS

CAPTAIN AMERICA #34 SCRIPT

Script By Ed Brubaker ★ Art By Steve Epting & Butch Guice

The Death of Captain America – Act Two

The Burden of Dreams – Part Four

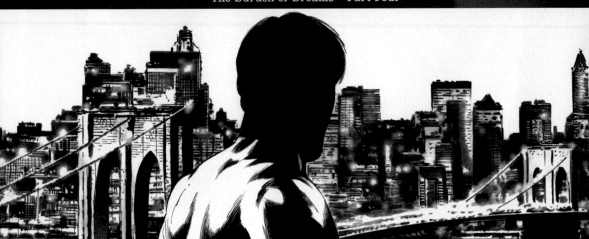

Previously text and title will go on the page before the story starts this month.

PAGE ONE

1—Full tier. Night time. Close on Bucky, standing on a rooftop, looking out at the NY city skyline and the Brooklyn bridge. He's on the roof of Steve's building, but we don't know that yet, and we can't see anything below his shoulders.

NARR: It can all fall apart so quickly that we don't even realize it... How fragile this country -- this society -- really is.
NARR: People grow complacent or look the other way, while the things that hold us together erode or are sold off.

2—The next 8 panels are all TV screens and the news. This is a shot of a female reporter at the desk, with a graphic behind her of the stock market with an arrow jagging down down down. Maybe the words DOW JONES somewhere, too.

NARR: And then it all comes crashing down...
TV: Shocking increases in worldwide oil prices in the wake of energy giant Kronas corporation's loss of CEO Aleksander Lukin...
TV(linked): ...Have led to another disastrous day on Wall Street, with the Dow plunging to its lowest levels in thirty years.

3—Then the woman is gone, and the pic is replaced with an image of a mean looking Russian with red hair, who looks about 55 or so. Under his pic it reads: NEW KRONAS CEO VLAD MOROVIN

TV: New Kronas CEO, Vladmir Morovin has yet to make a public statement on their move to more than double the price per barrel...

4—Now the woman is back, and the image behind her is a classic US suburban home with a big red X over it.

TV: ...Or on the decision of another arm of Kronas, Peggy Day finance, which has announced it will foreclose on thousands of mortgages around the US.
TV: Our analyst Matthew Fritchmann has the reaction to this move...

5—Now the woman is replaced with an older man who looks like a geek in a suit. Think Paul Krugman, but taller and thinner.

TV: Well Toni, until there's some official explanation for Kronas' actions the past two days... all I can say is, new CEO Morovin must hate the American people...

PAGE TWO

1—Same, basically, as this guy talks. Behind him, the image changes to read: MORTGAGE CRISIS 2008

TV: While some of the homes being foreclosed on were part of the sub-prime lending scandal of earlier this year...
TV: ...Most are simply homes of hard-working Americans who failed to read the fine print.

2—Now the image is replaced with a shot of hundreds of protesters in the streets in NYC, carrying signs and some throwing Molotovs, and police in riot gear facing them.

TV: And as we already saw last night, they're taking to the streets in protest.
TV: One thing is for sure, the US economy is very suddenly on the brink, and for once, its citizens are noticing.

3—And now the shot changes to some other protest and cops image, from a more dramatic angle. Really show people angry and scared, and cops trying to keep the peace, arresting people, whatever works.

TV: And in fact, last night's protests in New York, Chicago, and Washington D.C. have resulted in hundreds of arrests...

4—And now the woman is back, and that last image fills the screen behind her, with the words: ECONOMY IN CRISIS over it.

TV: ...With police warning of escalation and possible rioting if something is not done.

5—Another full tier. And we're back with Bucky on the roof of Steve's old building in Brooklyn. Now we pull back for a wider shot, as he turns to look back over his shoulder, where Black Widow is standing near a small SHIELD airship (something big enough for maybe six people inside) that has its side door slid open. And now we see that Bucky is holding Cap's shield, and that he's wearing a plain dark body suit (the black and dark dark blue under-part of his new uniform). He looks a little concerned and not sure of himself, frowning a little. She raises one brow at him, smiling a little. She's got old feelings for him.
WIDOW: You ready to go, James?
BUCKY: As much as I'll ever be, I guess.

PAGE THREE
1—As they get into the airship, Widow takes a seat behind the controls and Bucky looks at her, frowning a little.

BUCKY: But I can't help noticing that even though I told Stark I wouldn't answer to him...
BUCKY: ...The first time I'm needed, it's you that shows up, Natalia.
WIDOW: I'm not giving you any orders.

2—She smiles back over her shoulder at him, raising one brow a little.

WIDOW: I'm just here to give you a ride...And some help.

3—Bucky sets the shield into some kind of safe clipped area along the inner wall of the airship, about the same height as his head or shoulders, so it won't bounce around in flight. He looks at Natasha as he does this.

BUCKY: Not to keep an eye on me for S.H.I.E.L.D.?

4—The airship flies now, towards Manhattan, the lights of the city before them.

WIDOW(from ship): S.H.I.E.L.D. has no record of your existence.
WIDOW(from ship/linked): Not anymore.

5—Widow at the controls, as Bucky sort of stands and leans over the seat next to her, not sitting down.

WIDOW: Director Stark's deal with you was personal.

WIDOW: He can't be seen to publicly advocate an unregistered hero.

PAGE FOUR
1—He smiles at her.

BUCKY: But here you are... an Avenger.
BUCKY: How's he going to answer that if it gets out?
2—She makes a face, like, well, who can say?
WIDOW: Ah, well... I'm the Black Widow...
WIDOW: I live among shades of grey.

3—Then she glances at him, and he scowls a bit.

WIDOW: Now, are you planning to finish suiting-up or are you having second thoughts?
BUCKY: Hell, I'm way past second thoughts... but there's no turning back.
WIDOW: No. There never is.

4—Closer on the Widow, piloting the ship.

WIDOW: But I was surprised to see you designing a new suit with Tony.

5—Bucky is picking up the blue slightly metallic part of his new costume now, and looking down at the stars and stripes. Serious.

BUCKY: I could never wear Steve's uniform.
BUCKY: I'm not him and I won't pretend I am.

6—She glances back at him, as he starts to pull that part of the suit over his head.

WIDOW: Yet you're trying to fulfill his last wishes. Strange.
BUCKY: Just 'cause I'm not him doesn't mean I can't honor his memory.

PAGE FIVE
1—Now the shoulders and front are in place, but the cowl is still hanging back like a hood that's not pulled up yet. Bucky frowns.

BUCKY: And Stark was right...
BUCKY: I would never have let anyone else do this.

2—She smiles at him.
WIDOW: Yes, I remember.
WIDOW: And I hope you've been practicing with that shield since you stole it from me.

3—Now we get a good look at him standing there, and we see the gun on his hip, as she looks at him. He's holding the shield on his left arm now, too.
WIDOW: But that gun on your hip tells me... maybe not.
BUCKY: Don't worry. I can handle the shield...
BUCKY: My arm makes me one of the few who could, probably.

4—She looks away, to steer around the skyscrapers, etc.

WIDOW: So, why the weaponry, then?

5—He stands right behind her, the star on his chest near her eye level. She nods.

BUCKY: I've always carried weapons. And now that I've painted a red, white and blue target on myself...
BUCKY: I'm guessing I'm gonna need them more than ever.
WIDOW: Good point.

PAGE SIX

1—Full tier. The ship flies high over a street in Manhattan, and we can see throngs of protesters below, being held back by the police.

BUCKY(from ship):
Damn... Look at that. They're out in force again tonight.
BUCKY(from ship/linked): The Red Skull's really making a mess of things.

2—Bucky sits next to her in the passenger seat now, his cowl still hanging behind his head, not on.

BUCKY: I hope Stark is telling his higher-ups who they're really dealing with...
WIDOW: Let's let Tony worry about the politicians.
WIDOW: You and I have more immediate concerns.

3—He looks at her, brows raised. She gives a little smile, mocking, as she punches something on the dashboard.
BUCKY: Oh god... I hope you don't expect me to address protesters...
WIDOW: No, lucky for you. Look at this...

4—Now we're looking over his shoulder at a satellite shot of a NYC street, with AIM guys pouring out of a ship, in full costume. Another ship is landing near it. This screen we're looking at is on the dashboard, of course.

WIDOW(off): We received a tip that A.I.M. and R.A.I.D. were going after Wall Street's gold reserves...
WIDOW(off): ...While the police are tied-up with crowd control.

5—Bucky scowls at her, and she nods, looking out the front window.

BUCKY: So the Skull wants to hit the economy from all sides... until he's watching our cities burn...
WIDOW: Apparently.

6—He silently pulls on the cowl.

7—And then he's Captain America, not Bucky, and he's all business.

CAP: All right then. Let's go stop him.

PAGE SEVEN

1—Down at the scene of the crime. Wall Street, big buildings, including a bank. An AIM leader is yelling back at several other guys in AIM and RAID outfits. He's holding a machine gun and gesturing toward one of the ships, that has its back bay door open, and we maybe can see some machinery inside.

AIM GUY: Our clock is ticking, people!
AIM GUY: You two, get those Turbo-walkers down here -- stat!

2—Closer on the AIM guy, gesturing towards a wall near the bank building. Behind him, we can see two of the robot-things that Cap, Falcon and Iron Man fought in issue 13, with AIM guys inside, controlling them. They're walking toward the bank.

AIM GUY: Once we breach that wall, we have about two minutes until everything in a uniform or a mask gets here!
AIM GUY: And I want us long gone by then!

3—The AIM guy continues to yell at his men, and a RAID guy who is not far from him, looks at something off-panel, tilting his head.
AIM GUY: Remember, the Red Skull rewards only those who —
RAID GUY (cutting him off): Hey, what's —

4—And – BANG – Cap's shield hits the RAID guy right in the head, sending him reeling.

SFX: BLAANG

PAGE EIGHT

1—And the AIM agents watch the shield rebound up and back the way it came, as the guy hits the ground, KOed.

2—And the shield arcs down.

3—BIG PANEL (most of the page) – The New Cap, left arm raised, is catching the shield in a cool pose as he runs right toward them. The Black Widow is a ways behind him, bounding off a parked car, following him into the fray.
CAP: Sorry. I guess we're early.
CAP: No evil Nazi rewards for you.

PAGE NINE

1—The AIM leader stands there as Cap rushes at him, sneering a little.

AIM GUY: Who the hell-- ?

2—And then Cap decks him (right-hand blow) as the other AIM and RAID guys react, drawing weapons, etc.
SFX: KRAK

3—A RAID guy stands by the two Turbo-walker bot things and yells, as they both start shooting.

RAID GUY: Take them!
RAID GUY: Turbo-walkers – open fire!
SFX: CHUDD CHUDD CHUDD

4—Cap barely manages to get his shield up in time to block the blast, which ricochets upwards.

CAP: Uhn!
NARR: This isn't my usual kind of fight.

PAGE TEN

1—Cap rolls with the blow and dodges another blast, doing a backflip hand-plant, and yelling to the Black Widow, who is kicking an AIM guy in the background and grabbing his gun at the same time.

CAP: Widow – Cover me!
CAP: We gotta take those things down!
NARR: Not since the war, at least.

2—Closer on her as she opens fire with the sci-fi machine gun and yells back.

WIDOW: Stop talking and just do it!
SFX: BLAM BLAM BLAM

3—An AIM guy yells at one of the Turbo-walkers as it fires. Cap is running away from them, at an angle.

AIM GUY: Shoot him, damn you!
SFX: CHUDD CHUDD

4—Cap leaps over a parked car as the blast wrecks it and shatters all the windows out.

SFX: KRSSHHH
NARR: Charging right in... Steve was always better at that.
5—He pivots off a parking sign pole and swings around to kick a RAID guy in the head.

SFX: WHUDD
NARR: Of course, Steve was about three times stronger and faster than me, too.

PAGE ELEVEN

1—Cap keeps moving, as the Turbo-walker keeps firing at him, ripping through the street and through cars. The RAID and AIM guys are under fire from Widow, too.

NARR: But it's not like I haven't fought whole hordes of bad guys in my day.

2—Cap kicks an AIM guy into another, barely dodging a blast.

NARR: I'm just more used to doing it covertly and taking out specific targets.
NARR: Tactical hits designed to do the most harm with the least effort.

3—Cap leaps over the falling AIM guy while reaching into his utility belt. The Turbo-walker is tracking him, blasting.

NARR: And using the enemy's strengths against them.

4—The Turbo-walker blasts at Cap, but it misses, and the AIM guy near it yells, seeing what Cap is doing.

NARR: But those methods still work.
AIM GUY: NOOO!
SFX: CHUDDD

5—As the blast hits the other Turbo-walker instead, and shreds part of it, knocking it backwards, off its feet. The guy inside it screams.

NARR: They just need a little adapting.
SFX: KKRIPPP
DRIVER: Yaaaiii!

PAGE TWELVE

1—Now Cap is diving right at the legs of the other Turbo-walker, a metallic disk in his hand, about the size of a hockey puck, as the AIM guy opens fire at him. He's got his shield up, though, deflecting the bullets.

NARR: The shield helps a lot. It slows them down.

AIM GUY: Yaaaahhh!
SFX: BLAM BLAM BLAM

2—Cap's hand sticks the metallic disk to one of the legs of the Turbo-walker.
SFX: shhnnk

3—And he keeps moving, slamming into a RAID soldier, shield-first, sending him sprawling.

NARR: Puts a scare in them, because they know who's supposed to carry it...
SFX: SMAKK

4—And the Turbo-walker's leg blows up where he planted the disc.

SFX: KA-WHOOM

5—And it topples on it's side, as the AIM and RAID soldiers look on, in horror.
NARR: ...But they still have no idea who the hell I am.

PAGE THIRTEEN
1—The Helicarrier in the night sky above DC. If we can see crowds of protesters on the streets and look up from that to the Helicarrier, that'd be great, if you want to just show the carrier, that's great, too.

LOCATION CAPS: The S.H.I.E.L.D. Helicarrier
TEXT: Currently hovering above Washington D.C.
NO POINTER: Mr. Secretary, I don't care what reports you've seen...

2—Inside, on a command deck, Tony Stark, in shirt and tie, is arguing with some politician in a suit, someone very conservative-looking, and angry. It's some under-Secretary of some White House dept. In the background, there are big screens with satellite and news-feeds, etc, and a few S.H.I.E.L.D. agents in uniform monitoring them and working at stations. The hustle and bustle of S.H.I.E.L.D. in a crisis, basically.

TONY: ... I have reliable intel that the body found in that plane crash was not Aleksander Lukin.
TONY: I've been telling you people this for days, but it seems no one will hear me.
SECRETARY: Don't take a tone with me, Director Stark.

3—The Secretary sneers at Stark.

SECRETARY: This country is in the midst of a major crisis...

SECRETARY: So your unfounded allegations about dead men are going to have to wait until it's resolved.

4—Tony gestures at a screen in the background that has a freeze-frame of the new Kronas CEO and some schematics analyzing it, running boxes of stats, etc. Tony looks frustrated, the Sec. looks confused, and irritated.

TONY: It won't be resolved unless you listen. Aleksander Lukin is not dead.
TONY: And it's likely that Vladmir Morovin doesn't really exist.
SECRETARY: What does that even mean?

5—Tony puts a finger to the man's chest, scowling.

TONY: That this entire crisis is an orchestrated attack on the U.S. by the Kronas Corporation...
TONY: Because they're really being run by the Red Skull.

PAGE FOURTEEN
1—In a huge underground lab somewhere, the Skull stands near Arnim Zola, who is working on some crazy Kirby-science machines. The face on Zola's screen is scowling.

LOCATION CAPS: Somewhere in upstate New York...
SKULL: What news from your field squads in the city? Have they secured the gold reserves?
ZOLA: They are not my squadrons, herr Skull... I did not train them.
SKULL: I hope that isn't some form of passing blame for failure, Zola.

2—Zola glances back at the Skull, still irritated.
ZOLA: They have not reported in... This is all I know for now.
ZOLA: Forgive me if I have other more pressing matters at hand.

3—Then he turns back to his work, as the Skull rubs his own chin, thinking.

ZOLA: But you wanted the chamber ready, did you not?
ZOLA: And the schematics for Faustus' contraption upgraded?
SKULL: Yes... so I did.

4—The Skull glances around the lab, thinking, smiling a bit. Maybe he makes a fist or grasps one hand in front of himself dramatically, as he's wont to do at times.
SKULL: It matters little, in any case... We've already knocked them to their knees.
SKULL: I merely want to keep them there until we strike the killing blow.

5—Then the Skull walks out through sliding doors, and Zola begins to follow him. The hallways outside the lab look sci-fi-esque.

SKULL: And it's nearly time for Faustus to activate his <u>first wave</u>... You should come watch this <u>with me</u>, Zola.
SKULL: I think that you'll appreciate the <u>irony</u> of it.
ZOLA: I am certain of <u>that</u>, Herr Skull.

PAGE FIFTEEN
1—Back with Cap and the Widow, in their brawl against the last of the AIM and RAID goons. There's about six of them left, and Widow is dodging some blaster rifle fire, bounding off a wall in the background, while in the foreground, the new Cap is slamming a fist into a RAID guy, KOing him.

NARR: Have to admit, it feels weird... to be wearing the flag.
NARR: To be carrying Steve's shield.

2—Then he spins to dodge some blaster fire, and kicks another one in the head.

NARR: Fighting, <u>that</u> feels natural.

3—He deflects some fire with his shield and glances back to see Widow kicking her attacker in the face, knocking out some teeth.

NARR: But fighting for the bigger cause?
NARR: It's been so long since I had one of those.

4—Three guys, two AIM guys and a RAID guy all open fire at Cap, desperate, trying to move back, toward their escape ship.

NARR: It does remind me of the war, though.
AIM GUY: <u>Hold him off!</u>
AIM GUY: <u>Keep him back!</u>

PAGE SIXTEEN
1—He does a cool hand vault to dodge the blaster fire and throws the shield.

NARR: Steve isn't leading the way up the battlefield...
NARR: Yet I can almost feel him here.

2—The shield misses them all, though, going over their heads by about a foot or two, and hitting the wall behind them.

NARR: But he's guiding me now... instead of haunting me.

3—And then it rebounds wildly, upwards. Give it space to show this, like it's a huge mistake he's just made, this thing is going up like a badly rebounding basketball or something.

NARR: I <u>can't</u> be him.
4—The Widow looks up at it from where she's crouched, making a face, like, uh oh. Wincing a little.

WIDOW: <u>Oooh</u>.

5—Pull back to show the three guys he threw it at all looking up, watching it soar -- the RAID guy starting to smile. Steve, it's a complicated shot, but all this should seem like it's happening at once, the rebound, Widow looking, and the bad guys looking up, all distracted.

NARR: No one <u>ever</u> could.
RAID GUY: <u>Captain America</u>, hunh?
AIM GUY: Yeah, <u>right</u>...

PAGE SEVENTEEN
1—But Cap is already holding his pistol and firing it three times, a hard look on his face.

NARR: But I can try to make him proud...
SFX: BLAM BLAM BLAM

2—And – His bullets hit each of them in the knee, and they scream, reaching for their legs as they fall.

AIM GUY: Aahh!
RAID GUY: Uhhggh!
AIM GUY: $#@@%%!

3—Cap bends his right arm at the elbow now, the gun pointing up, smoke trailing out of the barrel, and he smiles, just a little.

Behind him, we see the shield arcing down to the ground about ten or twenty feet up the wartorn street, and hitting the last guy shooting at Black Widow. It slams him right in the back of the head, knocking him forward, off his feet.

CAP: Actually... I did that <u>on purpose</u>.
SFX(shield hitting guy): Bnnk
NARR: ...In my own way.

PAGE EIGHTEEN
1—The Widow stands next to him, and he gives her a gruff smile as he puts his shield on his back.

WIDOW: Nicely done.
CAP: You weren't trying <u>too hard</u> to help, I notice.
WIDOW: Hey, this was meant to be <u>your</u> show... Not mine.

2—Then he looks around. She's touching something on the underside on her wrist blaster, standing over the KOed bad guys.

CAP: So, what now?
WIDOW: I'm calling in a clean-up crew now, so we can get back in the air...

3—Closer on her, as her hair whips in the dusty breeze of the night air.

WIDOW: There's chaos all over this city, and in D.C. and Chicago, too... And it's likely to spread.
WIDOW: Who knows where we'll be needed next?

4—Cap scowls. He wants to go right for the Skull's throat.

CAP: Damn it... We're two steps behind when we should be tracking him down.
CAP: This is what he wants us to be doing.

5—She shakes her head at him.
WIDOW: No, the Red Skull wanted another wave of economic fear to rip through the country... we just stopped that.
WIDOW: And we'll keep at it.

6—Then she starts to walk away, back toward their airship in the distance. He stands, looking at the remnants of the fight they just waged, thinking, hands on hips.

WIDOW: That's what Captain America does, remember?
CAP: Yeah, I guess it is.
WIDOW: Now let's get moving, before you get your picture on the news.

PAGE NINETEEN
1—Back in the Helicarrier command deck, the Secretary looks like he's in denial, and Tony gestures at the screens all around them.

SECRETARY: That... That can't be true. That's an outrageous allegation.
TONY: Look around you, Secretary.

2—Following Tony's gesture, we see a few screens showing protesters marching in city streets, with police in riot gear.

TONY: We've got near-riot conditions in four major metropolises tonight.
TONY: The stock market is hanging by a thread...

3—Full tier. A screen shot of the white house, with a huge mob with signs that read stuff like: GOP RIPPED US OFF! And: SAVE OUR HOMES, NOT YOUR BONUSES! Real basic stuff. A line of uniformed S.H.I.E.L.D. agents stands before the wall and metal wrought fence, holding rifles like soldiers or riot cops. In the background, we see the White House, lit up at night.

TONY(off): I've even got S.H.I.E.L.D. agents keeping a mob in check outside the White House.

4—Now Tony looks serious.
TONY: If someone hated us... If someone wanted to really cripple this country...
TONY: Isn't this what the first steps would look like?

5—The Secretary fumbles for words, in denial still.

SECRETARY: No... Kronas is just... they're playing hardball.
SECRETARY: Trying to raise first quarter profits or...
TONY: How much have they donated to you and your friends?

PAGE TWENTY
1—Then he looks up at Tony, suddenly pissed and insulted.

SECRETARY: What?! How dare you --

2—Tony just gives him a hard stare, though.

TONY: I know how corporations and politics work, Mr. Secretary.

3—An agent approaches Tony, with an urgent look, and Tony barely glances at him. The Secretary is watching this, still pissed at Tony.

AGENT: Director Stark.
TONY: Not now.
AGENT: It's important, sir.

4—The agent hands Tony an electronic hand-held clipboard-type device.

AGENT: We just got a fix on our missing agents. Their GPS tags all just went live.
TONY: What? Where?
AGENT: They're in D.C. sir...

5—Full tier. And now we're down in the crowd before the White House gates again, and we see the mob yelling, and throwing tin cans at the S.H.I.E.L.D. agents. But there are three agents who look almost robotic here, too. These are our bad guys.

VOICE-OVER BOX: "...in the crowd-control unit."
PROTESTER: Go back to Germany, you fascists!
PROTESTER: You people sold us out! Sold our country!

PAGE TWENTY ONE
1—Back in the helicarrier command deck, Tony is standing over a work station, pushing some buttons and yelling into a mic. The secretary is behind him, looking concerned. The other agents are all working their stations, and all the screens fill with scenes of the mob outside the White House.

TONY: All Washington ground units, this is Director Stark!
TONY: We have rogue agents in the field!
SECRETARY: What's going on, Stark?!

2—In a dimly lit office, we see Dr. Faustus speaking into a sophisticated walkie-talkie of some kind. A man in a suit stands behind him, facing away, looking out the windows, holding the curtains back. We can see some DC landmarks outside the window. This is a Senator's office, and this Senator is one of Faustus people who we'll meet next issue.

FAUSTUS: All right, boys... It's time...

3—Back with the S.H.I.E.L.D. agents at the front of the mob. The three agents all look at each other.

RADIO(from agent's ear): ...Show them what the good doctor's training is for.
AGENT 1: It's time.

AGENT 2: It's time.
AGENT 3: It's time.

4—Just at the edge of the crowd, we see a young girl reporter with dark curly hair and glasses, holding her mic, and gesturing to her cameramen to climb onto the roof of their van. The van reads: WDCN-News on the side. The crowd is in the background, and the evil S.H.I.E.L.D. agents will be in view once this guy starts filming. He's climbing up to the roof, with his video camera on his shoulder.
REPORTER: No... move it. Get up on the roof. We want an extreme angle.
CAMERAMAN: Okay, Molly... Just get into position.

PAGE TWENTY TWO
1—Back with Tony, as he is getting frantic, still talking into the mic at the workstation. The secretary is moving closer to him, yelling.

TONY: You're to subdue these agents, by any means necessary!
SECRETARY: Director Stark! I demand to know what is happening!

2—And suddenly these three S.H.I.E.L.D. agents raise their guns and open fire into the mob, killing several of the crowd. It's a complete shock to the crowd.

SFX: BLAM BLAM BLAM BLAM BLAM BLAM BLAM

3—They keep firing into the crowd and the crowd starts reacting — screaming, running away, some of them dying — getting hit in the head or chest, and blood exploding out. It's a horror show, and the agents are like robots almost, no expression. If we can see it in the background, the cameraman is standing on the roof of the van, with his camera raised. But that's not that important, really.

FROM CROWD: Aaaiiieee!
FROM CROWD: NOOOO!
SFX: BLAM BLAM BLAM BLAM BLAM

4—Back with Tony, move in closer on him. His eyes go wide, and he looks stunned. The Secretary is right up on him, yelling in her ear, practically.

SECRETARY: Director Stark!
TONY(small): no...

TO BE CONTINUED...

PRELIMINARY CAPTAIN AMERICA DESIGNS

By Alex Ross

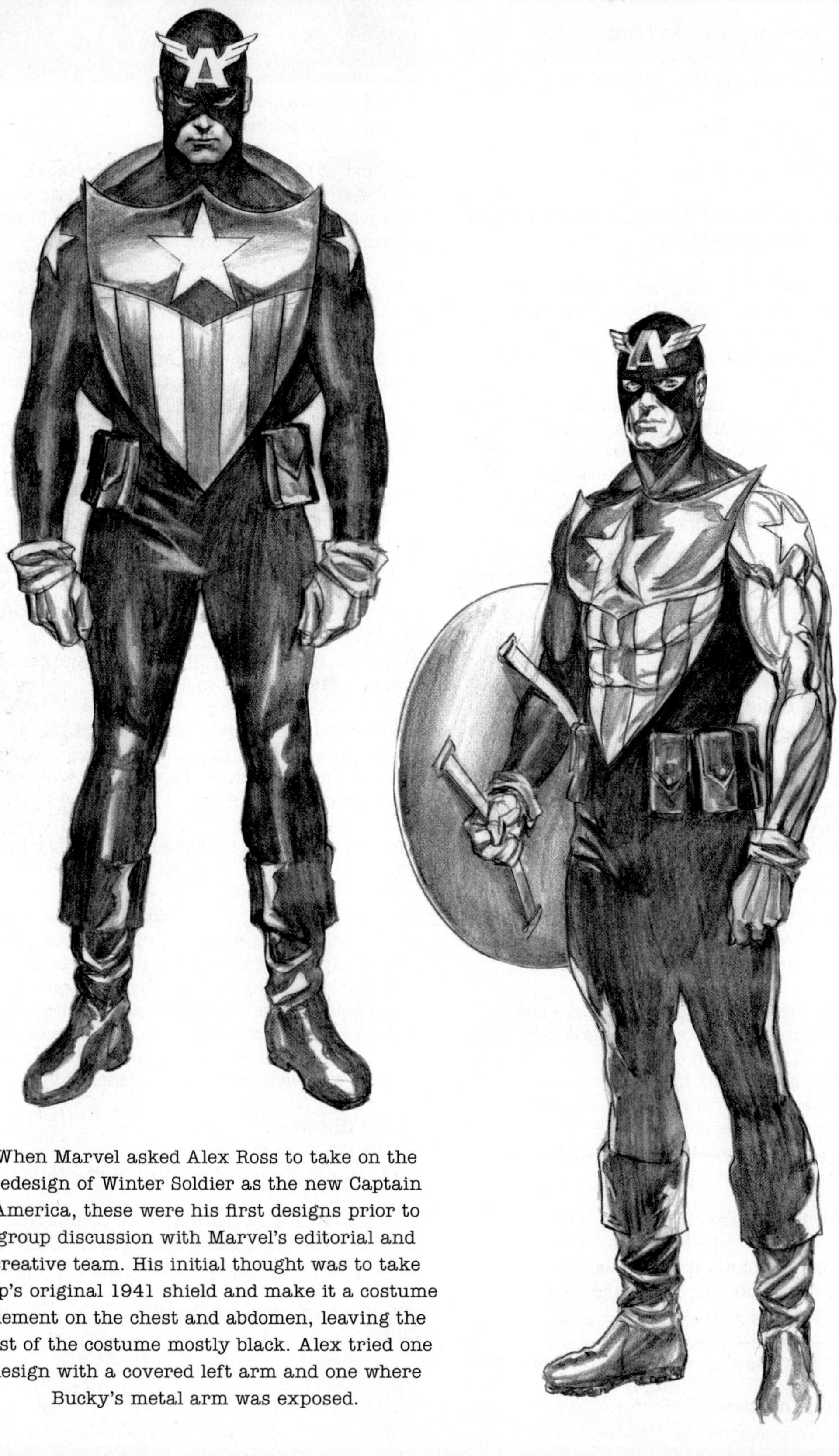

When Marvel asked Alex Ross to take on the redesign of Winter Soldier as the new Captain America, these were his first designs prior to group discussion with Marvel's editorial and creative team. His initial thought was to take Cap's original 1941 shield and make it a costume element on the chest and abdomen, leaving the rest of the costume mostly black. Alex tried one design with a covered left arm and one where Bucky's metal arm was exposed.

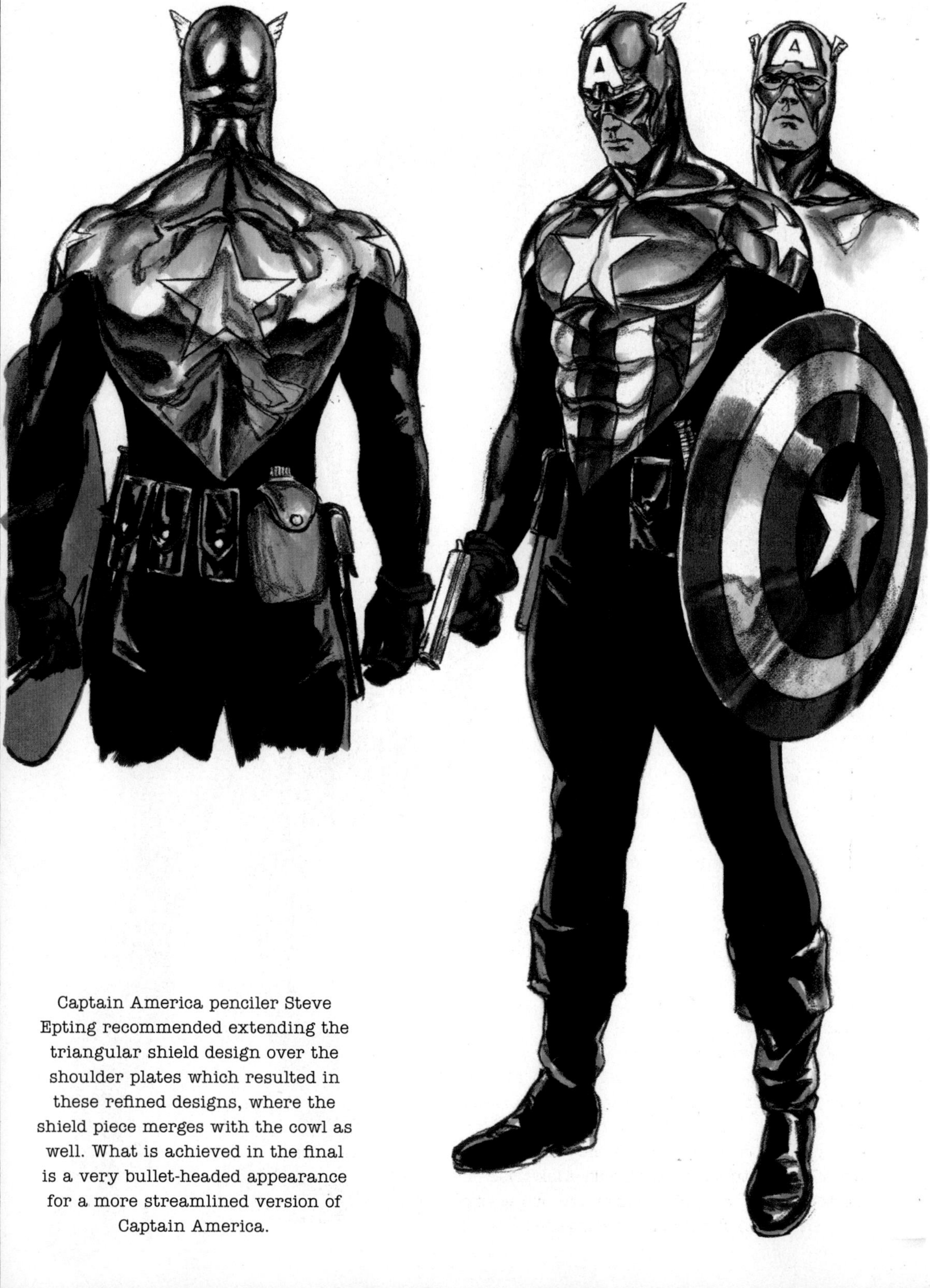

Captain America penciler Steve Epting recommended extending the triangular shield design over the shoulder plates which resulted in these refined designs, where the shield piece merges with the cowl as well. What is achieved in the final is a very bullet-headed appearance for a more streamlined version of Captain America.

FINAL CAPTAIN AMERICA DESIGN

By Alex Ross

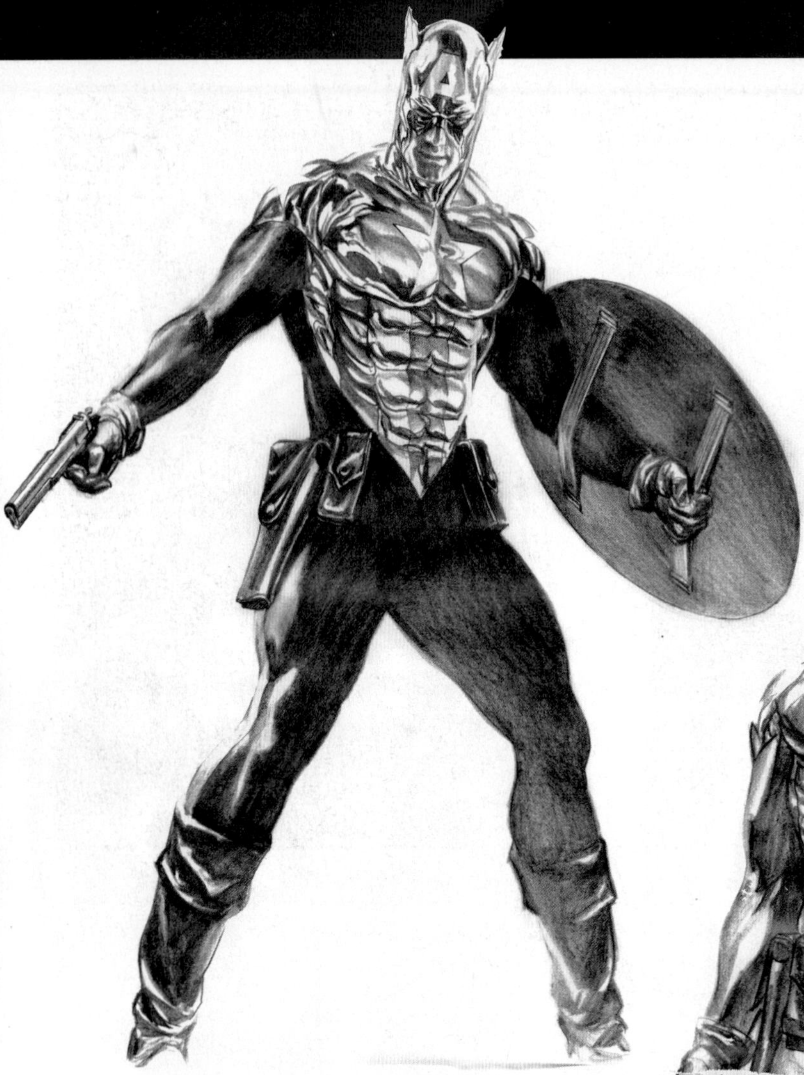

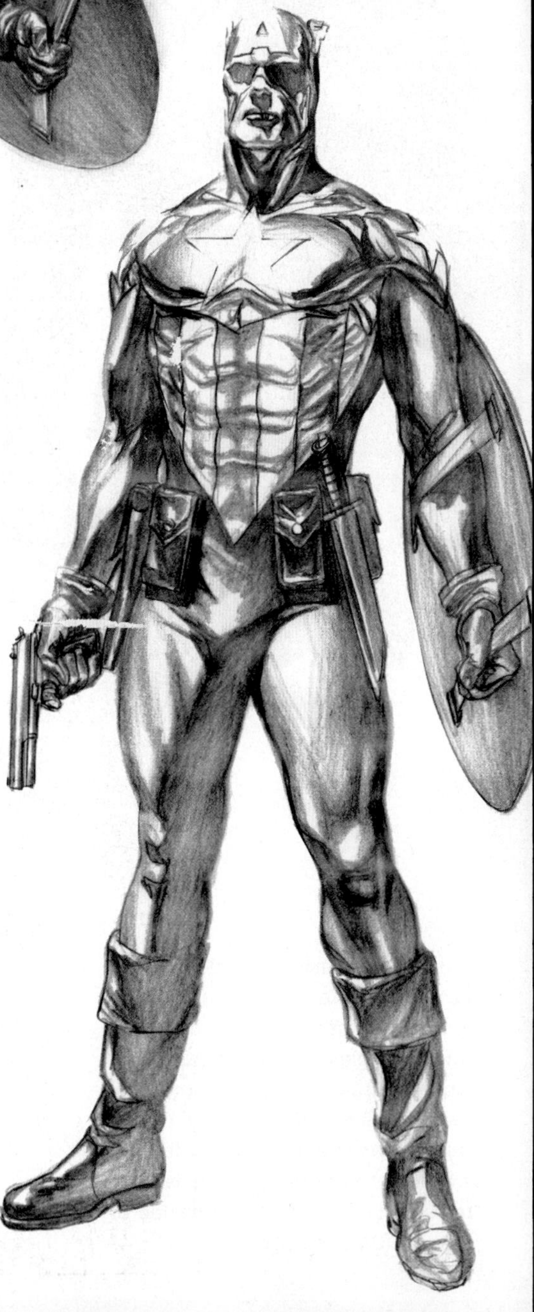

Final pencil studies for presentation of the new costume design.

CAPTAIN AMERICA #34
COVER ROUGHS
By Alex Ross and Steve Epting

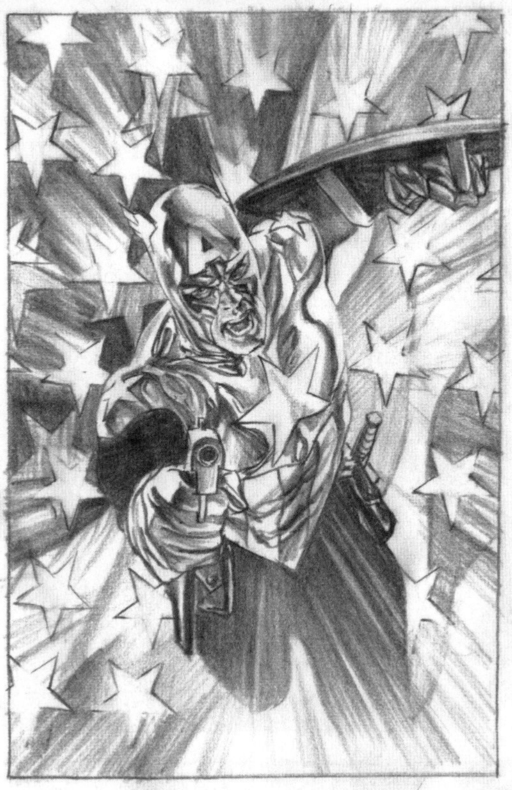

MARVEL COVER

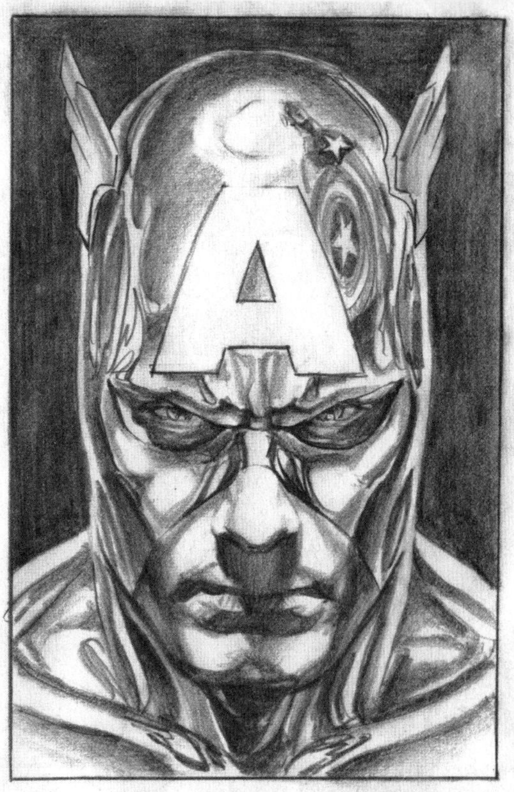

DYNAMITE VARIANT COVER

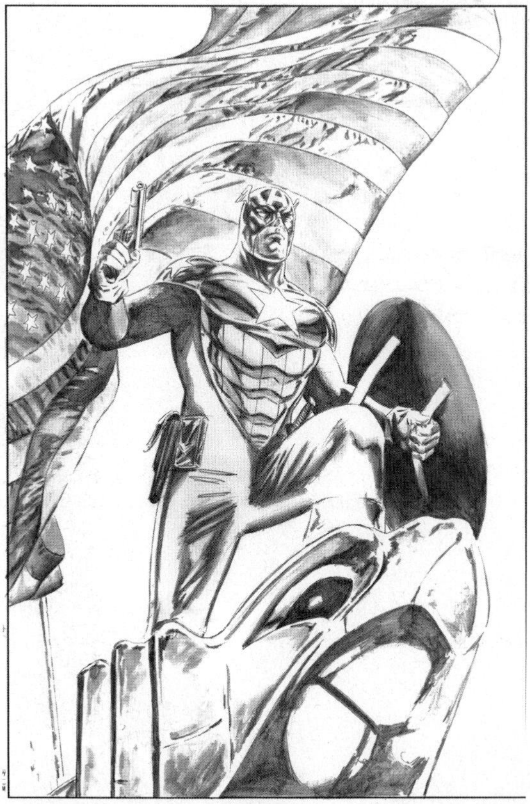

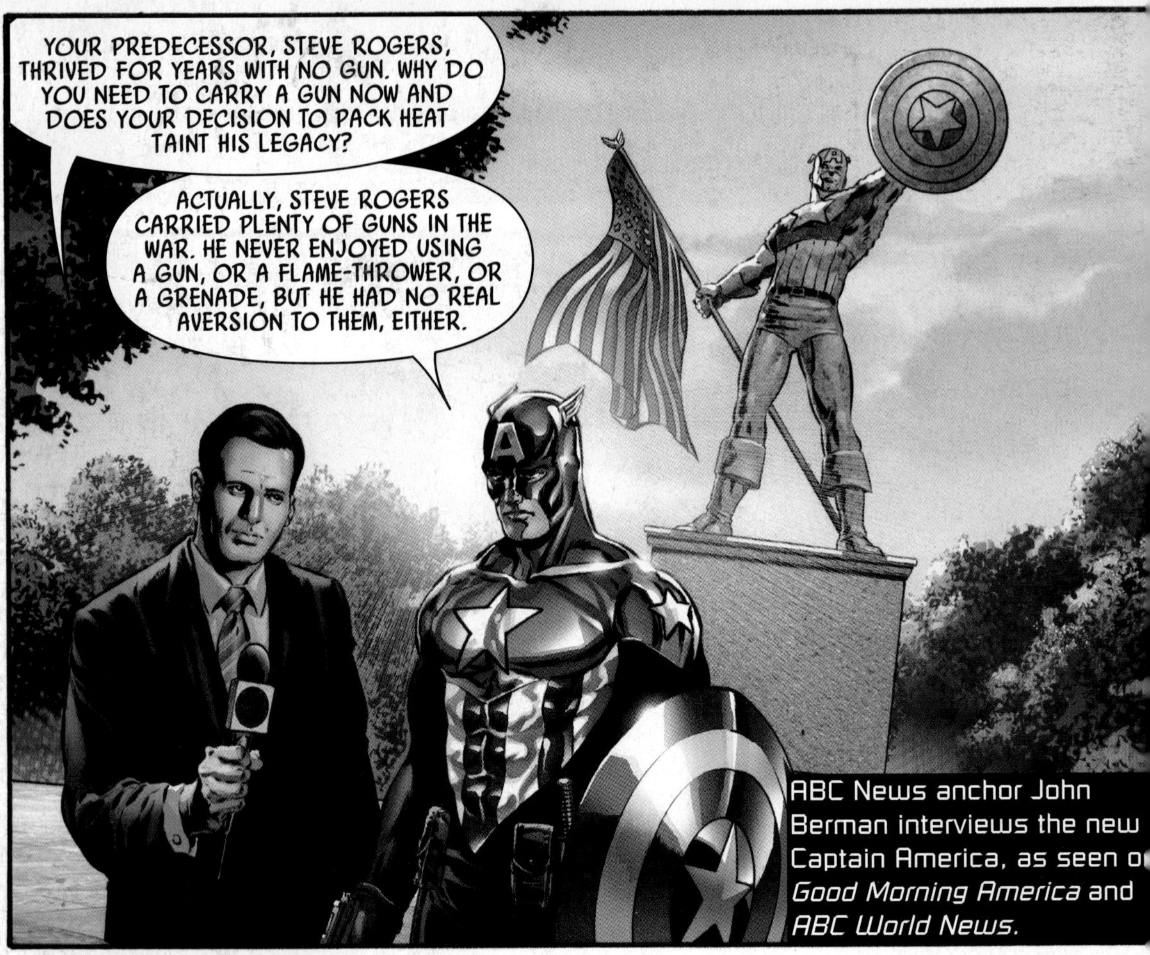
YOUR PREDECESSOR, STEVE ROGERS, THRIVED FOR YEARS WITH NO GUN. WHY DO YOU NEED TO CARRY A GUN NOW AND DOES YOUR DECISION TO PACK HEAT TAINT HIS LEGACY?
ACTUALLY, STEVE ROGERS CARRIED PLENTY OF GUNS IN THE WAR. HE NEVER ENJOYED USING A GUN, OR A FLAME-THROWER, OR A GRENADE, BUT HE HAD NO REAL AVERSION TO THEM, EITHER.
ABC News anchor John Berman interviews the new Captain America, as seen o *Good Morning America* and *ABC World News.*

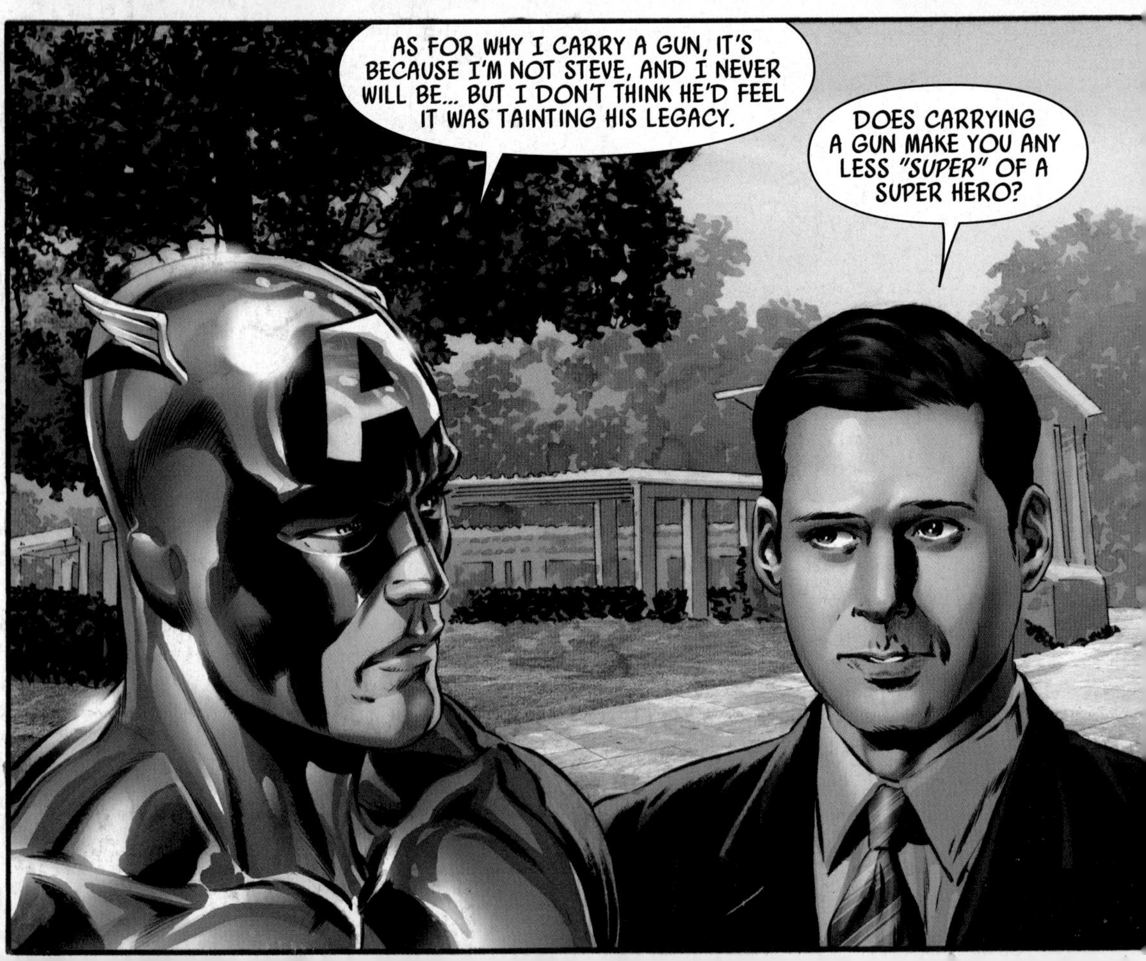
AS FOR WHY I CARRY A GUN, IT'S BECAUSE I'M NOT STEVE, AND I NEVER WILL BE... BUT I DON'T THINK HE'D FEEL IT WAS TAINTING HIS LEGACY.
DOES CARRYING A GUN MAKE YOU ANY LESS *"SUPER"* OF A SUPER HERO?

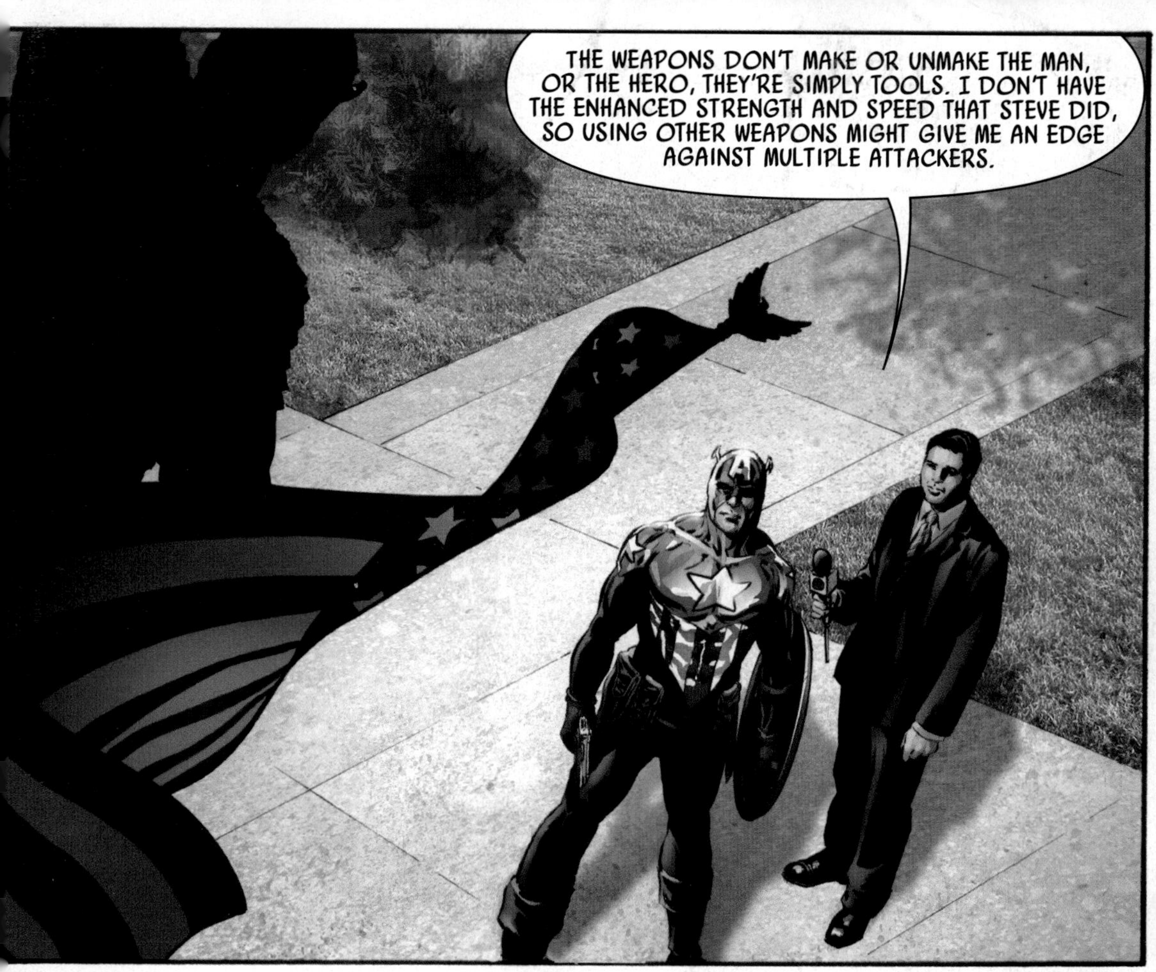
THE WEAPONS DON'T MAKE OR UNMAKE THE MAN, OR THE HERO, THEY'RE SIMPLY TOOLS. I DON'T HAVE THE ENHANCED STRENGTH AND SPEED THAT STEVE DID, SO USING OTHER WEAPONS MIGHT GIVE ME AN EDGE AGAINST MULTIPLE ATTACKERS.

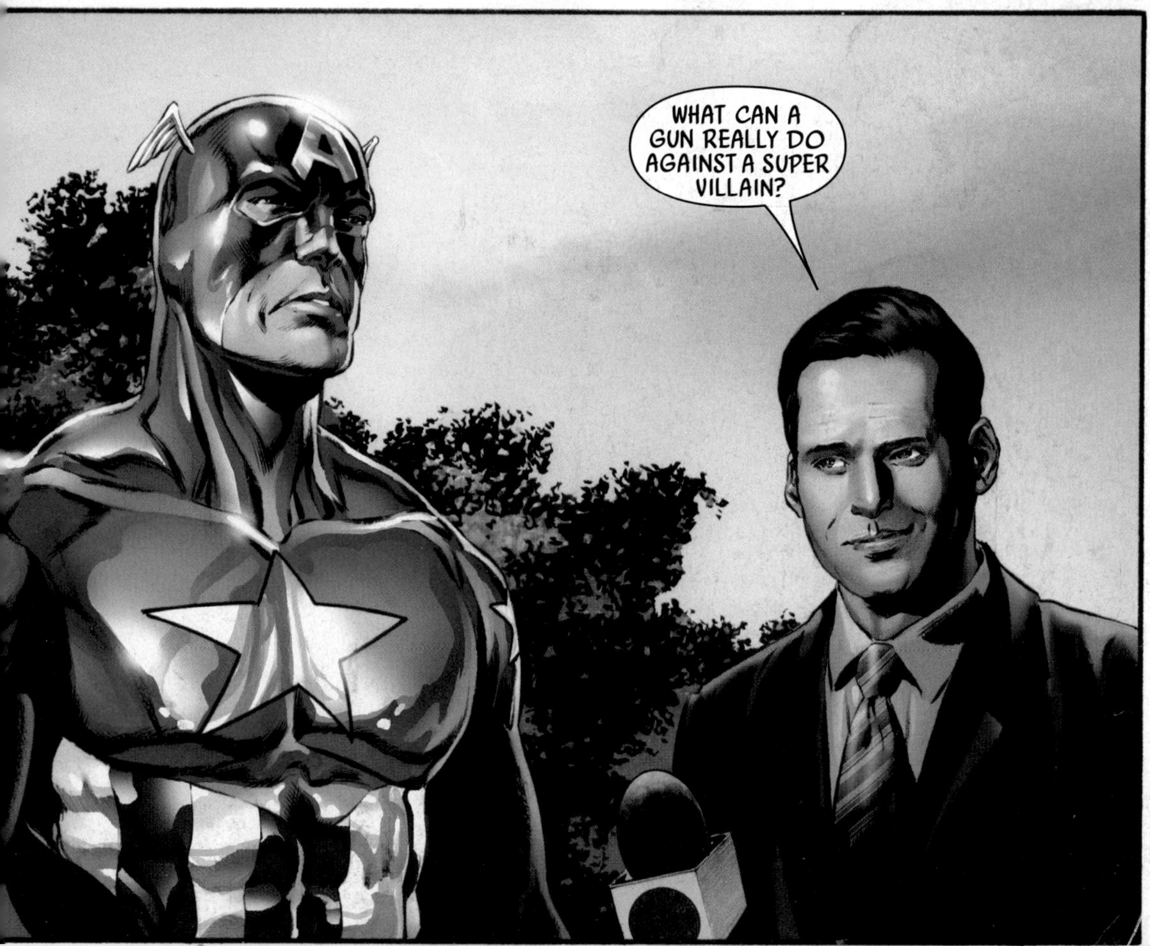
WHAT CAN A GUN REALLY DO AGAINST A SUPER VILLAIN?

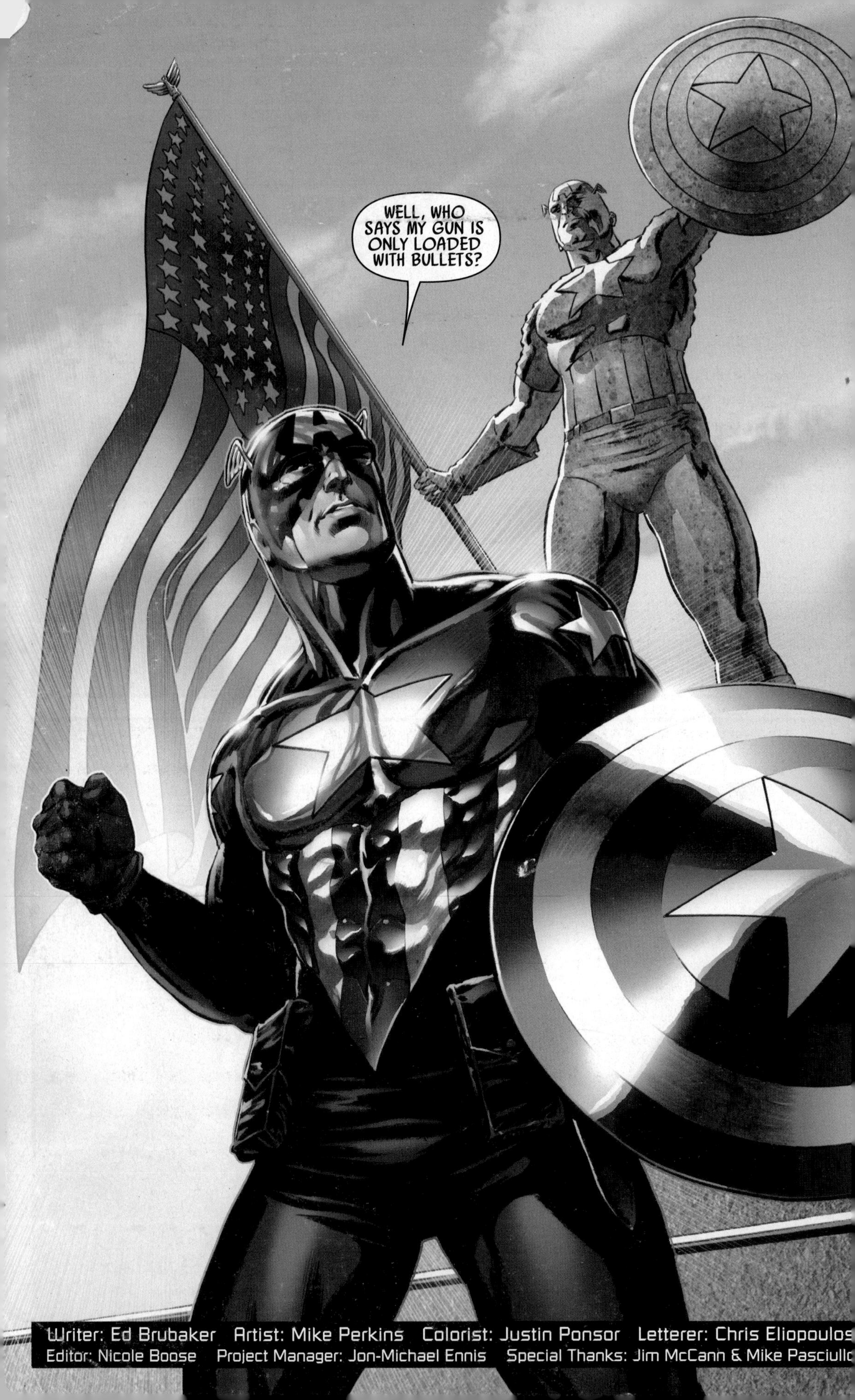
WELL, WHO SAYS MY GUN IS ONLY LOADED WITH BULLETS?

Writer: Ed Brubaker Artist: Mike Perkins Colorist: Justin Ponsor Letterer: Chris Eliopoulos
Editor: Nicole Boose Project Manager: Jon-Michael Ennis Special Thanks: Jim McCann & Mike Pasciullo